Second Edition

PREALGEBRA

Ben Mayo

CONTENTS

CHAPTER 3: An Introduction To Algebra............................ 209

PREFACE

A Note to Instructors

This textbook is intended to create a bridge between arithmetic and beginning algebra. Whenever possible, the problems in this book come from real world situations, such as a visit to the neighborhood grocery store, or looking through a file folder containing bills that need to be paid. It also offers several ways of doing the same types of problems with full explanations, as well as examples for each method, because not all students respond to the same techniques. By introducing different ways to solve a problem, students that struggle with traditional methods can gain confidence and acquire a sense of accomplishment. This confidence, in turn, can help them to overcome the challenges caused by using traditional methods.

Some of the areas where several different methods are introduced include:

- Changing regular numbers into percents and back again by the use of unit conversion factors, changing a percent sign into division by one hundred, or by moving the decimal point two places and adding or removing a percent sign.

- Solving percent problems by using proportions or by using the "percent equation" method.

- Converting within the metric system using unit conversion factors or by moving the decimal point a certain number of places in the correct direction.

The highlights of this book include the following:

- Chapter 1 will teach students how to find the best buy on an item, how to solve problems involving proportions, how to work comfortably in the metric system, and how to convert back and forth between the metric and the American measuring systems.

- Chapter 2 will teach students how to calculate percents involving such topics as sales tax, commission, discount rate, percent of increase, and percent of decrease. They will also learn that problems from all these different topics can be solved using the same techniques.

- Chapter 3 will teach students how to write and solve algebraic equations. They will also be given extensive practice in developing the vocabulary necessary to translate story problems into algebraic equations.

- Chapter 4 will teach students to graph by finding and plotting points. They will also be taught to solve formulas, including putting equations in slope-intercept form.

Students will be challenged continuously with fractions, decimals, and geometry problems throughout much of this book. However, all the exercises in this book are designed to be completed without the need for a calculator.

Acknowledgements

The author would like to thank the following people for their expertise in the areas of encouragement, grammar, inspiration, patience, proofreading, punctuation, and technical support:

- Fellow instructors Dodie Forrest, Mike Jenck, Doug Lewis, Fred Maiocco, and Carolyn McCallum at Yakima Valley Community College, as well as Jessica, Sean, and Sue Mayo.

- Special thanks to Jessica Mayo for the cartoon drawings (without them, my bad jokes wouldn't be the same).

This book is dedicated to Ibrahim Ayyoub (Abe), teacher, mentor, colleague, and friend. Thanks so much for your inspiration and encouragement. It made me want to strive to be a teacher to others the way that you were a teacher to me, always patient and always humble.

A Note to Students

This book was written with you in mind. The idea is to introduce you to the more challenging topics on a basic level so that when you encounter them later they will be less intimidating. Fractions, decimals, and story problems are integrated into the first three chapters, which cover the topics of ratios & proportions, percents, and basic algebra. Chapter 4 focuses primarily on graphing, but does include problems with fractions and decimals as well.

Unlike some textbooks that only work out a few examples of the easier problems and none of the more difficult ones, this book has an abundance of illustrations on several different levels. In addition, the examples show all the little in-between steps that are often left out. If you choose to read the explanations and the examples, you will find it a great help in gaining understanding of these topics. I hope your journey through this book will be an enjoyable one.

CHAPTER 1
RATIOS, PROPORTIONS, & MEASUREMENTS

Section 1: Ratios and Rates

Ratio
Rate
Unit Rate
Unit Price

Section 2: Proportions

Applications
Geometric Applications

Section 3: Measurements (American units)

Length
Perimeter and Circumference
Area
Surface Area
Volume
Weight
Time

Section 4: Measurements (Metric units)

Length
Method 1 (Using unit conversion factors)
Weight
Volume
Area (Measured in square units)
Volume (Measured in cubic units)
Method 2 (Moving the decimal point)

Section 5: Metric-American Conversions

Length
Weight
Volume
Temperature

RATIOS, PROPORTIONS, & MEASUREMENTS

Section 1: Ratios and Rates

A recent series of movies involved pirates in the Caribbean Sea. One of the scenes required blowing up a pirate ship. To reduce the expense of shooting the scene, a model of the ship was built. The model was 1/16 the size of the real ship. To say it another way, the real ship was 16 times the size of the model. In any event, the **ratio** of the size of the model to the size of the real ship was 1 to 16. If, for example, a part of the model was 1 foot long, the corresponding part on the real ship was 16 feet long.

<u>Ratio:</u> **A ratio is a comparison written as the quotient of two numbers, or as the quotient of two quantities with the same units.**

The ratio of 1 to 16 can also be written as a fraction $\left(\dfrac{1}{16} \right)$, or as two numbers separated by a colon (1:16). Other examples of a ratio are: 6 cats to 5 cats, $\dfrac{1}{4}$, and 17:3.

<u>Example 1:</u> Write the ratio 4 to 18 as a fraction in lowest terms.

Solution: 4 to 18 becomes $\dfrac{4}{18}$ which can be reduced by dividing both the numerator and the denominator by 2. $\dfrac{4}{18}$ becomes $\dfrac{4 \div 2}{18 \div 2}$ which then becomes $\dfrac{2}{9}$. Therefore, **the ratio is $\dfrac{2}{9}$.**

Now try problem 9 from exercise set 1.1.

Note: When writing a ratio as a fraction the first number is on the top, or in the numerator of the fraction and the second number is on the bottom, or in the denominator of the fraction.

<u>Example 2:</u> Write the ratio 18 : 4 as a fraction in lowest terms.

Solution: 18 : 4 becomes $\dfrac{18}{4}$ which can be reduced by dividing both the numerator and the denominator by 2. $\dfrac{18}{4}$ becomes $\dfrac{18 \div 2}{4 \div 2}$ which then becomes $\dfrac{9}{2}$. Therefore, **the ratio is $\dfrac{9}{2}$.**

Note: In its simplified form, a ratio should be expressed as a quotient of two whole numbers. Consequently, a ratio that is an improper fraction should not be converted into a mixed number.

Example 3: If a box is 2 feet long and 6 inches wide, what is the ratio of the length to the width of the box, written as a fraction in lowest terms?

Solution: To write the information as a ratio the units must be the same. Since 1 foot is equal to 12 inches then 2 feet would equal 24 inches. Using this information, the length becomes 24 inches. Now the ratio can be written as a fraction $\dfrac{24\ inches}{6\ inches}$. Reducing out the

common unit of inches the ratio becomes $\dfrac{24\ inches}{6\ inches}$ or $\dfrac{24}{6}$. The fraction still needs to be

reduced. This can be accomplished as follows. $\dfrac{24}{6}$ becomes $\dfrac{24 \div 6}{6 \div 6}$ which then becomes

$\dfrac{4}{1}$. Therefore, **the ratio of the length of the box to the width of the box is $\dfrac{4}{1}$.**

Now try problem 27 from exercise set 1.1.

Note: **Any units in a ratio should be reduced out and therefore removed in the final form.**

While a ratio compares two numbers or two quantities with the same units, many comparisons that are made do not have the same units. This type of comparison is called a **rate**.

Rate: **A rate is a comparison written as the quotient of two quantities with different units.**

Example 4: Write the following rate as a fraction in lowest terms. 600 miles in 14 hours.

Solution: 600 miles in 14 hours becomes $\dfrac{600\ miles}{14\ hours}$. The fraction needs to be reduced.

This can be accomplished as follows. $\dfrac{600\ miles}{14\ hours}$ becomes $\dfrac{600\ miles \div 2}{14\ hours \div 2}$ which then

becomes $\dfrac{300\ miles}{7\ hours}$. Therefore, **the rate is $\dfrac{300\ miles}{7\ hours}$.**

Now try problem 29 from exercise set 1.1.

Note: **In its simplified form, a rate should be expressed as a quotient of two whole numbers with different units. These different units cannot be reduced out of the fraction.**

Example 5: The rain fell at a rate of 7.3 inches in 0.5 hour. Express this rate as a fraction in lowest terms.

Solution: 7.3 inches in 0.5 hour becomes $\dfrac{7.3\ inches}{0.5\ hour}$. The fraction needs to be

expressed with a whole number in the numerator as well as in the denominator. This

can be accomplished as follows. $\dfrac{7.3\ inches}{0.5\ hour}$ becomes $\dfrac{7.3\ inches \cdot 10}{0.5\ hour \cdot 10}$ which then

becomes $\dfrac{73\ inches}{5\ hours}$. Since this fraction cannot be reduced, **the rate is $\dfrac{73\ inches}{5\ hours}$.**

Another important form of comparison is called a **unit rate**.

Unit rate: A unit rate is a rate in which the denominator is a single unit.

Consequently, this means that the numerator may no longer be a whole number. Examples of a unit rate are: 3.6 miles per gallon, $87\frac{1}{2}$ frogs per week, $16 per day, and 10 slices per pizza.

Example 6: A man earns $46 in 8 hours. What is his hourly rate of pay?

Solution: $46 in 8 hours becomes $\dfrac{\$46}{8\ hours}$. The denominator needs to be a single unit.

This can be accomplished as follows. $\dfrac{\$46}{8\ hours}$ becomes $\dfrac{\$46 \div 8}{8\ hours \div 8}$.

Using long division $8)\overline{\$46.00}^{\ \$5.75}$. Therefore, **his hourly rate of pay is** $\dfrac{\$5.75}{1\ hour}$.

Now try problem 39 from exercise set 1.1.

Example 7: A car traveled 282 miles on 9.4 gallons of gas. What was the car's fuel efficiency in miles per gallon?

Solution: 282 miles on 9.4 gallons of gas becomes $\dfrac{282\ miles}{9.4\ gallons}$.

The denominator needs to be a single unit. This can be accomplished as follows.

$\dfrac{282\ miles}{9.4\ gallons}$ becomes $\dfrac{282\ miles \div 9.4}{9.4\ gallons \div 9.4}$. Using long division $9.4)\overline{282}$

becomes $94)\overline{2{,}820}^{\ 30}$. Therefore, **the car's fuel efficiency was** $\dfrac{30\ miles}{1\ gallon}$.

Example 8: A car traveled 282 miles in 5 hours. What was the car's average rate of speed during this time?

Solution: 282 miles in 5 hours becomes $\dfrac{282\ miles}{5\ hours}$. The denominator needs to be a single unit.

This can be accomplished as follows. $\dfrac{282\ miles}{5\ hours}$ becomes $\dfrac{282\ miles \div 5}{5\ hours \div 5}$. Using

long division $5)\overline{282.0}^{\ 56.4}$. Therefore, **the car's average rate of speed was** $\dfrac{56.4\ miles}{1\ hour}$.

Finally, a unit rate that involves a certain amount of money per one unit of measure is called a **unit price**.

Unit price: A unit price is a rate in which the numerator contains an amount of money and the denominator contains a single unit of some type of item.

Example 9: A 64 fluid ounce bottle of apple-grape juice sells for $1.67. What is the unit price per fluid ounce of the apple-grape juice? Round your answer to the nearest tenth of a cent.

Solution: $1.67 for 64 fluid ounces becomes $\dfrac{\$1.67}{64 \; fl \; oz}$. Since the unit price needs to be to the nearest tenth of a cent we will change $1.67 into 167¢. **By using units of cents rather than dollars, it will be easier to determine where the tenth of a cent column is during the long division process.** Now the fraction becomes $\dfrac{167¢}{64 \; fl \; oz}$. The denominator needs to be a single unit. This can be accomplished as follows. $\dfrac{167¢}{64 \; fl \; oz}$ becomes $\dfrac{167¢ \div 64}{64 \; fl \; oz \div 64}$.

Using long division, go two places past the decimal point to the hundredths place.

$$64\overline{)167.00¢}^{\;2.60¢}$$

Now rounding to the nearest tenth, **the unit price becomes $\dfrac{\textbf{2.6¢}}{\textbf{1 fl oz}}$**.

Now try problem 75 from exercise set 1.1.

Example 10: A 24-ounce box of corn flakes sells for $1.80. A 40-ounce box of corn flakes sells for $2.92. Which is the better buy?

Solution: By finding the unit price of each item it will be easy to determine which is the better buy. $1.80 for 24 ounces becomes $\dfrac{\$1.80}{24 \; ounces}$. The denominator needs to be a single unit.

This can be accomplished as follows. $\dfrac{\$1.80}{24 \; ounces}$ becomes $\dfrac{\$1.80 \div 24}{24 \; ounces \div 24}$.

Using long division $24\overline{)\$1.800}^{\;\$0.075}$. Therefore the unit price is $\dfrac{\textbf{\$0.075}}{\textbf{1 ounce}}$.

$2.92 for 40 ounces becomes $\dfrac{\$2.92}{40 \; ounces}$. The denominator needs to be 1.

This can be accomplished as follows. $\dfrac{\$2.92}{40 \; ounces}$ becomes $\dfrac{\$2.92 \div 40}{40 \; ounces \div 40}$.

Using long division $40\overline{)\$2.920}^{\;\$0.073}$. Therefore the unit price is $\dfrac{\textbf{\$0.073}}{\textbf{1 ounce}}$.

Since $\dfrac{\$0.073}{1 \; ounce}$ is less cents per ounce than $\dfrac{\$0.075}{1 \; ounce}$, **the 40-ounce box is the better buy.**

Now try problem 81 from exercise set 1.1.

Section 1 exercises. Identify each of the following as a ratio, rate, unit rate, or unit price.

1.   300 miles in 7 days

2.   450 pages per hour

3.   34 inches to 3 yards

4. $0.07 per ounce

5.   50 copies per minute

6.   70 hotdogs in 48 minutes

7. $2.99 per gallon

8.   15 days to 3 weeks

Write each ratio as a fraction in lowest terms.

9.   6 to 14

10.   13 to 26

11.   1.9 : 2.4

12.   1.2 : 0.7

13.   6.2 to 4.8

14.   7.4 to 3.8

15.   3 to 20.1

16.   7 to 35.7

17. $1.25 to $0.75

18.   1.5 miles to 3.6 miles

19.   5 sharks to 12 sharks

20.   2 cats to 7 cats

21. $2\frac{1}{4}$ to $3\frac{3}{4}$

22. $5\frac{1}{3}$ to $4\frac{2}{3}$

23. $\frac{1}{5}$ to 0.6

24. $\frac{3}{4}$ to 0.25

25. $\frac{4}{5}$ to $2\frac{2}{5}$

26. $\frac{2}{7}$ to $3\frac{3}{7}$

27.   2 weeks to 4 days

28.   2 feet to 8 inches

Write each rate as a fraction in lowest terms.

29.   8 cups every 10 minutes

30.   500 gallons every 8 hours

31. $50 for 15 dolls

32. $80 for 32 roses

33.   6 bags of gumdrops on 4 dozen cupcakes

34.   3 bags of fertilizer on 12 flowerbeds

Write each rate as a fraction in lowest terms.

35.   2.5 inches of snow in 3 hours   **36.**   4.8 feet of water in 6 days

37. $25 per $6\frac{1}{2}$ dozen   **38.** $6 per $8\frac{1}{4}$ teaspoons

Write each expression as a unit rate.

39.   80 kids from 32 families   **40.**   36 families in 15 houses

41.   30 houses in 2 city blocks   **42.**   48 city blocks in 3 miles

43.   15 countries in 4 weeks   **44.**   18 cities in 8 days

45.   174 miles in 3 hours   **46.**   112 miles on 4 gallons

47.   350 bales from 8 acres   **48.**   228 boxes from 16 trees

Write each expression as a unit price.

49. $78 for 5 video games   **50.** $87.50 for 7 CDs

51. $22 for 8 yards of fabric   **52.** $75 for 12 feet of pipe

53.   25 ounces sell for 60 cents   **54.**   8 gallons sell for $23.60

55. $59.20 for 8 hours   **56.** $850 for 4 nights lodging

57. $4.90 for 14 candy bars   **58.** $9 for 12 hotdogs

Based on Janet's monthly budget, answer questions 59-62:

Janet's Monthly Budget

Item	Cost
Food	$400
Housing	$800
Transportation	$150
Entertainment	$70
Miscellaneous	$300
Gas	$120
Phone	$25
Electricity	$35
Utilities	$100

59.   What is the ratio of food cost to transportation cost?

60.   What is the ratio of phone cost to electricity cost?

61.   What is the ratio of gas cost to utilities cost?

62.   What is the ratio of miscellaneous cost to housing cost?

63.   The price of gas went from $2.50 to $3.00 per gallon. Find the ratio of the increase in price to the original price.

64.   The price of milk went from $3.00 to $2.50 per gallon. Find the ratio of the decrease in price to the original price.

65.   On a recent shopping trip Joan purchased 14 blouses while visiting 4 clothing stores. Write this rate as a fraction in lowest terms.

66.   Bill caught a total of 26 trout in 6 days on a fishing trip. Write this rate as a fraction in lowest terms.

67.   Sean read 350 pages of a book for his English class in 2 weeks. What was his reading rate expressed in pages per day?

68.   Jessica has 300 anytime minutes on her cell phone each month. Assuming that there are 30 days in a month, what is her rate expressed as anytime minutes per day?

69.   David typed 595 words in 7 minutes while working on a history report. What was his typing rate in words per hour?

70.   Patrick stuffed 56 envelopes for mailing in 8 minutes while doing a secretarial job. What was his stuffing rate in envelopes per hour?

71.   Lisa ran 7 miles in 56 minutes during a marathon workout. What was her running rate in miles per minute? What was her running rate in minutes per mile?

72.   Mary washed 5 windows in 20 minutes while earning money for college. What was her window-washing rate in windows per minute? What was her window-washing rate in minutes per window?

Find the unit price for each of the following. Round answers to the nearest tenth of a cent.

73.   A 6 oz can of tuna for 89¢

74.   A 16 oz package of frozen corn for 83¢

75.   A 14 oz bottle of ketchup for $1.79

76.   4 steel wool pads for $1.49

77.   A 10½ oz can of cream of celery soup for $0.84

78.   A 10¾ oz can of tomato soup for $0.66

79.   3.31 lb of chicken drumsticks for $5.26 (Round to the nearest cent)

80.   4.96 lb of hamburger for $12.35 (Round to the nearest cent)

For problems 81-90:

a)   Find the unit price of each item, rounding answers to the nearest tenth of a cent.

b)   Determine the best buy by comparing the results.

81.   Toasted Oat Cereal

   10 oz for $2.28

   15 oz for $2.69

   20 oz for $3.99

82.   Sugar

   5 lb for $2.69

   10 lb for $3.78

   25 lb for $10.99

83.   Picante Sauce

   10 oz for $2.00

   24 oz for $3.89

   64 oz for $6.45

84.   Flour

   5 lb for $2.69

   10 lb for $4.15

   25 lb for $8.99

85. Frozen Apple Juice

12 fl oz for $1.89

16 fl oz for $2.79

86. Name Brand Corn Flakes

12 oz for $2.32

18 oz for $4.15

87. Frozen Orange Juice

12 fl oz for $0.95

16 fl oz on sale 4/$5

88. Pain Reliever

24 tablets for $4.49

50 tablets for $8.78

89. Ice Cream

2 qt for $2.65

5 qt for $6.99

90. Oatmeal

18 oz for $2.49

42 oz for $4.35

91. If a car travels 358 miles in 7.3 hours, what is its average rate of speed to the nearest tenth of a mile per hour?

92. If a truck travels 643 miles in 11.6 hours, what is its average rate of speed to the nearest tenth of a mile per hour?

93. If it takes 3.4 minutes to fill a 16-gallon gas tank, what is the rate of flow of gasoline to the nearest tenth of a gallon per minute?

94. If it takes 5.6 minutes to empty a 50-gallon bathtub, what is the rate of flow of water to the nearest tenth of a gallon per minute?

Writing:

95. Which is the best buy, a 12 pack of 12 fl oz cans of cola for $3.00 or a 6 pack of 24 fl oz bottles of the same cola for $2.69? Why might you decide to purchase the one that isn't the best buy?

96. What difference, if any, is there between a unit rate and a unit price?

RATIOS, PROPORTIONS, & MEASUREMENTS

Section 2: Proportions

A popular television program that focuses on home improvement typically has 7.5 minutes of commercials during the one-hour program. That is to say, the rate of commercials per program is 7.5 minutes per hour or $\dfrac{7.5\ minutes}{1\ hour}$. Recently, during a 2-hour special of this program there were 15 minutes of commercials, or the rate was $\dfrac{15\ minutes}{2\ hours}$. These rates are in fact equal and could be written as follows: $\dfrac{7.5\ minutes}{1\ hour} = \dfrac{15\ minutes}{2\ hours}$ An equation of this type that has two rates set equal to each other is called a **proportion**.

Proportion: A proportion states that two ratios, or two rates, are equal.

Examples of proportions are as follows: $\dfrac{3}{7} = \dfrac{9}{21}$; $\dfrac{5\ sharks}{12\ kittens} = \dfrac{20\ sharks}{48\ kittens}$; $\dfrac{\$8}{1\ hour} = \dfrac{\$40}{5\ hours}$

The way to read a proportion like $\dfrac{3}{7} = \dfrac{9}{21}$ is to say 3 is to 7 as 9 is to 21.

The terms of the proportion are numbered as follows:

First term $\longrightarrow$ $\boxed{\dfrac{3}{7} = \dfrac{9}{21}}$ $\longleftarrow$ Third term

Second term $\longrightarrow$ $\quad\quad\quad\quad$ $\longleftarrow$ Fourth term

The first and fourth terms of a proportion are called the **extremes**, while the second and third terms of a proportion are called the **means**.

In the proportion $\dfrac{4}{9} = \dfrac{12}{27}$, 4 and 27 are the extremes, while 9 and 12 are the means. Note the fact that $4(27) = 108$ and $9(12) = 108$. In the proportion $\dfrac{10}{4} = \dfrac{50}{20}$, 10 and 20 are the extremes, while 4 and 50 are the means. Note the fact that $10(20) = 200$ and $4(50) = 200$. These examples illustrate the following:

Fundamental Property of Proportions: In any proportion, the product of the extremes is equal to the product of the means.

In symbolic form, it looks like this:

If $\dfrac{a}{b} = \dfrac{c}{d}$ then $ad = bc$ with the following restrictions: $b \neq 0$ and $d \neq 0$

since dividing by zero is undefined.

We can use the fundamental property of proportions to determine whether an equation is a proportion.

Example 1: Determine whether the following equation is a proportion. $\dfrac{8}{13} = \dfrac{32}{52}$

Solution: The product of the extremes is $8(52) = 416$. The product of the means is $13(32) = 416$. Since the product of the extremes equals the product of the means, **the equation is a proportion.**

Now try problem 9 from exercise set 1.2.

Note: The product of the extremes and the product of the means are also called cross products.

Example 2: Determine whether the following equation is a proportion. $\dfrac{7}{11} = \dfrac{15}{22}$

Solution: The product of the extremes is $7(22) = 154$. The product of the means is $11(15) = 165$. Since the cross products are not equal, **the equation is not a proportion.** That is, $\dfrac{7}{11} \neq \dfrac{15}{22}$.

Now try problem 11 from exercise set 1.2.

We can also use the fundamental property of proportions to solve proportions. If we know three of the four terms in the proportion, we can solve the proportion in order to find the missing term.

Example 3: What number is to 10 as 6 is to 15?

Solution: Since "what number" is the unknown in the problem, we use a letter called a **variable** to represent this unknown. Though any letter would suffice, most often the letter "x" is used to represent an unknown quantity. The proportion now becomes

$\dfrac{x}{10} = \dfrac{6}{15}$.   Finding the cross products and setting them equal to each other gives us

$(x)(15) = 10(6)$ or

$15x = 60$.   To "solve" this equation for the unknown, or "x," we must get "x" by itself or "isolate" the variable. To accomplish this we divide both sides of the equation by 15 (that is, by the **coefficient** of the variable) to isolate x.

$\dfrac{15x}{15} = \dfrac{60}{15}$ Reducing both sides we get

$\dfrac{\cancel{15}x}{\cancel{15}} = \dfrac{\overset{4}{\cancel{60}}}{\underset{1}{\cancel{15}}}$.   That is, $x = 4$.

In other words, **4** is to 10 as 6 is to 15, or $\dfrac{4}{10} = \dfrac{6}{15}$. We can verify this by the fact that the cross products are equal. That is, $4(15) = 60$ and $10(6) = 60$.

As in example 3 on the previous page, sometimes solving an equation requires removing a coefficient in order to isolate the variable. To do this we use what is called **The Multiplication Property of Equality**.

THE MULTIPLICATION PROPERTY OF EQUALITY:

When a, b, and c are real numbers with $c \neq 0$, the following is true:

$$\text{If} \quad a = b \quad \text{then} \quad a \cdot c = b \cdot c.$$

If the same non-zero quantity is multiplied by both sides of an equation, the new equation is equivalent to the old equation. That is, both equations have the same solution.

Example 4: Solve: $3x = 12$

Solution:

$3x = 12$ — To remove the coefficient of x, which is 3, from the left side of the equation, use the multiplication property of equality. Do this by multiplying both sides of the equation by the reciprocal of 3, which is $\frac{1}{3}$.

$\frac{1}{3} \cdot 3x = \frac{1}{3} \cdot 12$ — Simplify both sides of the equation.

$x = 4$ — To verify the solution, substitute it back into the original equation in place of the variable.

$3x = 12$ — becomes

$3(4) \overset{?}{=} 12$ — which further simplifies to

$12 \overset{\checkmark}{=} 12$. — The statement is true, therefore the solution is correct.

Because division can be rewritten in terms of multiplication (dividing by a number is equivalent to multiplying by its reciprocal) we can use the multiplication property of equality to justify the following.

When a, b, and c are real numbers with $c \neq 0$, the following is true:

$$\text{If} \quad a = b \quad \text{then} \quad \frac{a}{c} = \frac{b}{c}.$$

In other words, if both sides of an equation are divided by the same non-zero number, the new equation is equivalent to the old equation. That is, both equations have the same solution.

Example 5: Solve: $6x = 18$

Solution:	
$6x = 18$	To remove the coefficient of x, which is 6, from the left side of the equation, use the multiplication property of equality. Do this by dividing both sides of the equation by 6.
$\dfrac{6x}{6} = \dfrac{18}{6}$	Simplify both sides of the equation.
$x = 3$	To verify the solution, substitute it back into the original equation in place of the variable.
$6x = 18$	becomes
$6(3) \overset{?}{=} 18$	which further simplifies to
$18 \overset{\checkmark}{=} 18.$	The statement is true, therefore the solution is correct.

From here on, we will use the multiplication property of equality to justify dividing both sides of an equation by the same non-zero number in order to solve the equation.

<u>Example 6:</u> Solve for the variable in the proportion $\dfrac{x}{15} = \dfrac{10}{30}$.

Solution:

$\dfrac{x}{15} = \dfrac{10}{30}$ Finding the cross products gives us

$30x = 15(10)$.   We divide both sides of the equation by 30 to isolate x.

$\dfrac{30x}{30} = \dfrac{15(10)}{30}$ Reducing both sides we get

$\dfrac{\cancel{30}x}{\cancel{30}} = \dfrac{15(1\cancel{0})}{3\cancel{0}}$.   Since $15 \div 3 = 5$, then $x = \mathbf{5}$.

To check the solution, 5 is substituted in the place of x in the original proportion.

$\dfrac{5}{15} = \dfrac{10}{30}$ Verify that the cross products are equal.

$5(30) = 150$ and $15(10) = 150$, so the solution is correct.

Now try problem 21 from exercise set 1.2.

Note: Even though multiplication is commutative, when a number and a variable are being multiplied together it is customary to put the number in front of the variable, as in the case of "30x," as opposed to "x30". This number is called a coefficient. In this particular case it would be called the coefficient of the variable "x". The coefficient of a variable tells how much of that variable we have.

<u>Example 7:</u> Solve for the variable in the proportion $\dfrac{3.6}{5.2} = \dfrac{9}{x}$.

Solution:

$\dfrac{3.6}{5.2} = \dfrac{9}{x}$ Finding the cross products gives us

$3.6x = 5.2(9)$.   We divide both sides of the equation by 3.6 to isolate x.

$\dfrac{3.6x}{3.6} = \dfrac{5.2(9)}{3.6}$ Reducing the left side we get

$\dfrac{\cancel{3.6}x}{\cancel{3.6}} = \dfrac{5.2(9)}{3.6}$. $5.2(9) = 46.8$

Using long division $3.6\overline{)46.8}$ becomes $36\overline{)468}^{\,13}$ then, $x = \mathbf{13}$.

To check the solution, 13 is substituted in the place of x in the original proportion.

$\dfrac{3.6}{5.2} = \dfrac{9}{13}$ Verify that the cross products are equal.

$3.6(13) = 46.8$ and $5.2(9) = 46.8$, so the solution is correct.

<u>Example 8:</u> Solve for the variable in the proportion $\dfrac{\frac{2}{3}}{4} = \dfrac{5}{x}$.

Solution:

$\dfrac{\frac{2}{3}}{4} = \dfrac{5}{x}$ Finding the cross products gives us

$\dfrac{2}{3}x = 4(5)$.   We divide both sides of the equation by $\dfrac{2}{3}$ to isolate x.

$\dfrac{\frac{2}{3}x}{\frac{2}{3}} = \dfrac{4(5)}{\frac{2}{3}}$ Reducing the left side we get

$\dfrac{\frac{2}{3}x}{\frac{2}{3}} = \dfrac{4(5)}{\frac{2}{3}}$.   On the right side $\dfrac{4(5)}{\frac{2}{3}} = 4(5) \div \dfrac{2}{3}$, but **dividing by a fraction is like**

multiplying by its reciprocal, therefore $4(5) \div \dfrac{2}{3}$ becomes $4(5)\left(\dfrac{3}{2}\right)$ or just 30. So, $x = 30$.

Now, consider another approach to this problem. Go back to the step where we divide both

sides of the equation by $\dfrac{2}{3}$ to isolate x. This time, instead of dividing by this fraction we

start out by multiplying both sides of the equation by its reciprocal $\left(\dfrac{3}{2}\right)$. This makes

simplifying much easier.

$\dfrac{2}{3}x = 4(5)$ becomes $\left(\dfrac{3}{2}\right)\dfrac{2}{3}x = \left(\dfrac{3}{2}\right)4(5)$ which reduces to $\left(\dfrac{\cancel{3}}{\cancel{2}}\right)\dfrac{\cancel{2}}{\cancel{3}}x = \left(\dfrac{3}{2}\right)4(5)$ or $x = 30$.

To check the solution, 30 is substituted in the place of x in the original proportion.

$\dfrac{\frac{2}{3}}{4} = \dfrac{5}{30}$ Verify that the cross products are equal.

$\dfrac{2}{3}(30) = 20$ and $4(5) = 20$, so the solution is correct.

Now try problem 31 from exercise set 1.2.

As a general rule, if the coefficient of a variable is a fraction, it is easiest to multiply both sides of the equation by the reciprocal of the coefficient of the variable in order to isolate the variable.

The previous examples lead to the following steps for solving a proportion.

<u>**STEP 1:**</u> **Set the cross products equal to each other.**

<u>**STEP 2:**</u> **Isolate the variable.**

<u>**STEP 3:**</u> **Simplify the answer if possible.**

<u>**STEP 4:**</u> **Check your work.**

Example 9: Solve for the variable in the proportion $\dfrac{x}{12} = \dfrac{5}{-6}$.

Solution:

$$\frac{x}{12} = \frac{5}{-6}$$

<u>**STEP 1:**</u> **Set the cross products equal to each other.**

Finding the cross products gives us

$-6x = 12(5)$.

<u>**STEP 2:**</u> **Isolate the variable.**

We divide both sides of the equation by -6 to isolate x.

$\dfrac{-6x}{-6} = \dfrac{12(5)}{-6}$ Reducing the left side we get

$\dfrac{\cancel{-6}x}{\cancel{-6}} = \dfrac{12(5)}{-6}$.

<u>**STEP 3:**</u> **Simplify the answer if possible.**

Reducing the right side we get

$x = \dfrac{\overset{2}{\cancel{12}}(5)}{\underset{-1}{\cancel{-6}}}$.   Since $2(5) = 10$ and $10 \div (-1) = -10$, then $x = -10$.

<u>**STEP 4:**</u> **Check your work.**

To check the solution, -10 is substituted in the place of x in the original proportion.

$\dfrac{-10}{12} = \dfrac{5}{-6}$ Verify that the cross products are equal.

$-10(-6) = 60$ and $12(5) = 60$, so the solution is correct.

Now try problem 23 from exercise set 1.2.

Example 10: Solve for the variable in the proportion $\dfrac{\frac{3}{4}}{7} = \dfrac{9}{x}$.

Solution:

$$\dfrac{\frac{3}{4}}{7} = \dfrac{9}{x}$$

STEP 1: Set the cross products equal to each other.

Finding the cross products gives us

$$\frac{3}{4}x = 7(9).$$

STEP 2: Isolate the variable.

Since the coefficient of the variable is a fraction, in order to isolate x, we multiply both sides of the equation by the reciprocal of $\dfrac{3}{4}$, which is $\dfrac{4}{3}$.

$$\left(\frac{4}{3}\right)\frac{3}{4}x = \left(\frac{4}{3}\right)7(9) \qquad \text{Reducing the left side we get}$$

$$\left(\frac{\cancel{4}}{\cancel{3}}\right)\frac{\cancel{3}}{\cancel{4}}x = \left(\frac{4}{3}\right)7(9).$$

STEP 3: Simplify the answer if possible.

Reducing the right side we get

$$x = \left(\frac{4}{\cancel{3}}\right)7(\cancel{9}^{3}). \qquad \text{Since } (4)(7)(3) = 84 \text{, then } \boldsymbol{x = 84.}$$
$$\phantom{x = \left(\frac{4}{}\right)}1$$

STEP 4: Check your work.

To check the solution, 84 is substituted in the place of x in the original proportion.

$$\dfrac{\frac{3}{4}}{7} = \dfrac{9}{84} \qquad \text{Verify that the cross products are equal.}$$

$$\frac{3}{4}(84) = 63 \text{ and } 7(9) = 63 \text{, so the solution is correct.}$$

Applications: Proportions can be used to solve a variety of problems in the real world. In these situations we typically know three of the four terms of a proportion and we must solve for the missing term. The challenging part is to put all the terms in the correct place in the proportion statement. A good way to do this is to make sure that the rate on the left side of the equal sign has the same units as the rate on the right side of the equal sign.

<u>Example 11:</u> A cyclist rides 21 miles in 3 hours. If he continues at the same rate, how long will it take him to travel 35 miles?

Solution:

$$\frac{21 \; miles}{3 \; hours} = \frac{35 \; miles}{x}$$ Finding the cross products gives us

$$21x = 3(35).$$ We divide both sides of the equation by 21 to isolate x.

$$\frac{21x}{21} = \frac{3(35)}{21}$$ Reducing both sides we get

$$\frac{\cancel{21}x}{\cancel{21}} = \frac{\overset{1}{\cancel{3}}(35)}{\underset{7}{\cancel{21}}}.$$ Since $35 \div 7 = 5$, then $x = 5$ hours. That is, **it will take 5 hours for him to travel 35 miles**.

To check the solution, 5 hours is substituted in the place of x in the original proportion.

$$\frac{21 \; miles}{3 \; hours} = \frac{35 \; miles}{5 \; hours}$$ Verify that the cross products are equal.

$21(5) = 105$ and $3(35) = 105$, so the solution is correct.

Now try problem 49 from exercise set 1.2.

Note: The rate on both sides of the equal sign is miles/hours.

There are other ways that this proportion could be set up correctly. They are as follows:

$$\frac{3 \; hours}{21 \; miles} = \frac{5 \; hours}{35 \; miles}, \qquad \frac{21 \; miles}{35 \; miles} = \frac{3 \; hours}{5 \; hours}, \text{ and } \qquad \frac{35 \; miles}{21 \; miles} = \frac{5 \; hours}{3 \; hours}$$

Notice that in each case the cross products are equal.

In the case of $\dfrac{3 \; hours}{21 \; miles} = \dfrac{5 \; hours}{35 \; miles}$, both sides of the equal sign have the same rate, hours/miles.

In the case of $\dfrac{21 \; miles}{35 \; miles} = \dfrac{3 \; hours}{5 \; hours}$ and $\dfrac{35 \; miles}{21 \; miles} = \dfrac{5 \; hours}{3 \; hours}$, the units can be reduced out,

producing equivalent ratios. That is, $\dfrac{21 \; miles}{35 \; miles} = \dfrac{3 \; hours}{5 \; hours}$ becomes $\dfrac{21 \; \cancel{miles}}{35 \; \cancel{miles}} = \dfrac{3 \; \cancel{hours}}{5 \; \cancel{hours}}$ and

$\dfrac{35 \; miles}{21 \; miles} = \dfrac{5 \; hours}{3 \; hours}$ becomes $\dfrac{35 \; \cancel{miles}}{21 \; \cancel{miles}} = \dfrac{5 \; \cancel{hours}}{3 \; \cancel{hours}}$.

Recall from page 11: A proportion states that two ratios, or two rates, are equal.

<u>Example 12:</u> If orange juice costs \$5 for 3 cans, how much will 12 cans of orange juice cost?

Solution:

$$\frac{\$5}{3\ cans} = \frac{x}{12\ cans} \qquad \text{Finding the cross products gives us}$$

$$5(12) = 3x\ . \qquad \text{We divide both sides of the equation by 3 to isolate } x.$$

$$\frac{5(12)}{3} = \frac{3x}{3} \qquad \text{Reducing both sides we get}$$

$$\frac{5(\cancel{12})^{4}}{\cancel{3}} = \frac{\cancel{3}x}{\cancel{3}}\ . \qquad \text{Since } 5(4) = 20, \text{ then } x = \$20. \text{ That is, } \textbf{it will}$$
$$\qquad\qquad\qquad\qquad \textbf{cost \$20 for 12 cans of orange juice.}$$

To check the solution, \$20 is substituted in the place of x in the original proportion.

$$\frac{\$5}{3\ cans} = \frac{\$20}{12\ cans} \qquad \text{Verify that the cross products are equal.}$$

$5(12) = 60$ and $3(20) = 60$, so the solution is correct.

Now try problem 53 from exercise set 1.2.

Note: The original proportion also could have been set up as follows:

$$\frac{3\ cans}{\$5} = \frac{12\ cans}{x}\ , \qquad \frac{\$5}{x} = \frac{3\ cans}{12\ cans}, \qquad \text{and} \qquad \frac{x}{\$5} = \frac{12\ cans}{3\ cans}$$

Here are some <u>incorrect</u> ways of setting up this proportion.

$$\frac{\$5}{3\ cans} = \frac{12\ cans}{x} \qquad \textbf{The rate on both sides of the equal sign is not the same.}$$

$$\frac{\$5}{x} = \frac{12\ cans}{3\ cans} \qquad \textbf{Even though the units could be reduced out of the problem, the resulting ratios would be such that "}x\textbf{" would have to be smaller than \$5. This can't be correct since "}x\textbf{" represents the price of 12 cans.}$$

<u>Example 13:</u> A cookie recipe calls for $1\frac{1}{2}$ cups of flour for every $\frac{3}{4}$ cup of sugar. How many cups of sugar are needed if $2\frac{1}{2}$ cups of flour are used?

Solution:

$$\frac{1\frac{1}{2} \text{ cups of flour}}{\frac{3}{4} \text{ cup of sugar}} = \frac{2\frac{1}{2} \text{ cups of flour}}{x}$$ Finding the cross products gives us

$$1\frac{1}{2}x = \frac{3}{4}\left(2\frac{1}{2}\right).$$ Change the mixed numbers into improper fractions in order to simplify the problem.

$$\frac{3}{2}x = \frac{3}{4}\left(\frac{5}{2}\right)$$ We multiply both sides of the equation by the reciprocal of $\frac{3}{2}$ which is $\frac{2}{3}$, in order to isolate x.

$$\left(\frac{2}{3}\right)\frac{3}{2}x = \left(\frac{2}{3}\right)\frac{3}{4}\left(\frac{5}{2}\right)$$ Reducing both sides we get

$$\left(\frac{\cancel{2}}{\cancel{3}}\right)\frac{\cancel{3}}{\cancel{2}}x = \left(\frac{\cancel{2}}{\cancel{3}}\right)\frac{\cancel{3}}{4}\left(\frac{5}{\cancel{2}}\right).$$ Then, $x = \frac{5}{4}$ cups of sugar. However, in cooking we express cups of sugar as a mixed number, rather than an improper fraction. Therefore, $x = 1\frac{1}{4}$ cups of sugar. That is, **the recipe will need $1\frac{1}{4}$ cups of sugar**.

To check the solution, $1\frac{1}{4}$ cups of sugar is substituted in the place of x in the original proportion.

$$\frac{1\frac{1}{2} \text{ cups of flour}}{\frac{3}{4} \text{ cup of sugar}} = \frac{2\frac{1}{2} \text{ cups of flour}}{1\frac{1}{4} \text{ cups of sugar}}$$ Verify that the cross products are equal.

Again we change the mixed numbers into improper fractions in order to simplify the problem.

$$\frac{3}{2}\left(\frac{5}{4}\right) = \frac{15}{8} \text{ and } \frac{3}{4}\left(\frac{5}{2}\right) = \frac{15}{8}, \text{ so the solution is correct.}$$

Now try problem 61 from exercise set 1.2.

Example 14: The scale on a map indicates that 1 inch on the map corresponds to an actual distance of 25 miles. If two cities are approximately 2.5 inches apart on the map, then what is the actual distance between them?

Solution:

$$\frac{1\ inch}{25\ miles} = \frac{2.5\ inches}{x}$$ Finding the cross products gives us

$$1x = 25(2.5).$$

Since the coefficient of x is already a 1, all we need to do is simplify the answer.

Since $25(2.5) = 62.5$, $x = 62.5$ miles.

That is, **the actual distance between the two cities is approximately 62.5 miles.**

To check the solution, 62.5 miles is substituted in the place of x in the original proportion.

$$\frac{1\ inch}{25\ miles} = \frac{2.5\ inches}{62.5\ miles}$$ Verify that the cross products are equal.

$1(62.5) = 62.5$ and $25(2.5) = 62.5$, so the solution is correct.

Now try problem 63 from exercise set 1.2.

Note: We use the word "approximately" in example 12 because it would be difficult to produce an exact measurement on a map.

Example 15: If 3 out of 5 people like chocolate ice cream, in a crowd of 75 people, how many would you expect to like chocolate ice cream?

Solution:

$$\frac{3\ like\ choc.\ ice\ cream}{5\ people} = \frac{x}{75\ people}$$ Finding the cross products gives us

$$3(75) = 5x\ .$$ We divide both sides of the equation by 5 to isolate x.

$$\frac{3(75)}{5} = \frac{5x}{5}$$ Reducing both sides we get

$$\frac{3(\overset{15}{\cancel{75}})}{\cancel{5}} = \frac{\cancel{5}x}{\cancel{5}}\ .$$ Since $3(15) = 45$, then $x = 45$.

That is, **you would expect 45 people to like chocolate ice cream.**

To check the solution, 45 is substituted in the place of x in the original proportion.

$$\frac{3\ like\ choc.\ ice\ cream}{5\ people} = \frac{45\ like\ choc.\ ice\ cream}{75\ people}$$ Verify that the cross products are equal.

$3(75) = 225$ and $5(45) = 225$, so the solution is correct.

<u>Geometric Applications:</u>   Proportions involving similar triangles.

Suppose we took a piece of paper and drew a triangle on it that had sides of 3 units, 4 units and 5 units in length. It would look something like this:

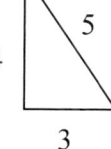

Now suppose we put this drawing of a triangle in a photocopying machine and we enlarged it to twice its original size. Then it would look something like this:

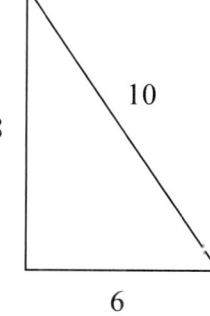

Notice that even though the new triangle isn't the same size as the original triangle, it is the same shape. If two triangles have the same shape (but not necessarily the same size) they are called **similar triangles**. It should also be noted that corresponding angles of similar triangles have the same measure.

Similar triangles are useful mathematically, in that the ratios of the lengths of corresponding sides are equal.

The corresponding sides of these two triangles are as follows: The side of the large triangle that is 6 units long corresponds to the side of the small triangle that is 3 units long. The side of the large triangle that is 8 units long corresponds to the side of the small triangle that is 4 units long. The side of the large triangle that is 10 units long corresponds to the side of the small triangle that is 5 units long.

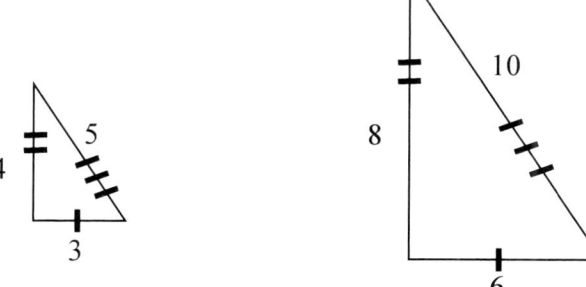

Notice that the ratios of corresponding sides are, in fact, equal. That is, starting with the large triangle and moving to the small triangle we get the following: $\dfrac{6}{3} = \dfrac{8}{4} = \dfrac{10}{5}$ Starting with the small triangle and moving to the large triangle we get: $\dfrac{3}{6} = \dfrac{4}{8} = \dfrac{5}{10}$ There are other sets of ratios having to do with similar triangles that are equal. For instance, the ratio of the shortest side of the small triangle to the longest side of the small triangle is equal to the ratio of the shortest side of the large triangle to the longest side of the large triangle. In other words, $\dfrac{3}{5} = \dfrac{6}{10}$.

<u>Example 16:</u> Find the length of x in the small triangle. Assume that the triangles are similar.

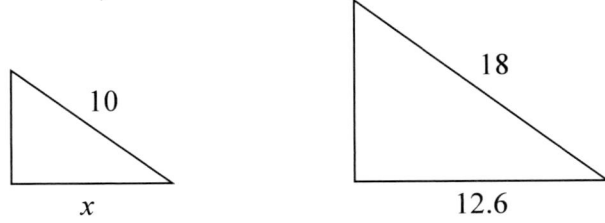

Solution: The side of the small triangle that is 10 corresponds to the side of the large triangle that is 18 and the side of the small triangle that is x corresponds to the side of the large triangle that is 12.6. This leads to the following proportion:

$\dfrac{10}{18} = \dfrac{x}{12.6}$ Finding the cross products gives us

$10(12.6) = 18x$.   We divide both sides of the equation by 18 to isolate x.

$\dfrac{10(12.6)}{18} = \dfrac{18x}{18}$ Reducing the right side we get

$\dfrac{10(12.6)}{18} = \dfrac{\cancel{18}x}{\cancel{18}}$.   Since $10(12.6) = 126$ and $126 \div 18 = 7$, then $x = 7$.
          That is, **the length of x is** 7.

To check the solution, 7 is substituted in the place of x in the original proportion.

$\dfrac{10}{18} = \dfrac{7}{12.6}$ Verify that the cross products are equal.

$10(12.6) = 126$ and $18(7) = 126$, so the solution is correct.

Now try problem 73 from exercise set 1.2.

<u>Example 17</u>: Find the length of y in the large triangle. Assume that the triangles are similar.

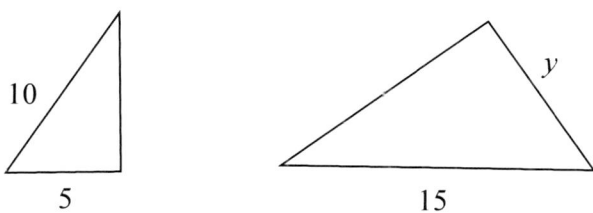

Solution: The large triangle has been rotated counter clockwise compared to the small triangle. This makes the identification of corresponding sides a bit tricky. The side of the small triangle that is 5 is the shortest side, so it corresponds to the side of the large triangle that is y, since it is also the shortest side. Therefore, the side of the small triangle that is 10 is the longest side, so it corresponds to the side of the large triangle that is 15 since it is also the longest side. This leads to the following proportion:

$$\frac{5}{y} = \frac{10}{15}$$ Finding the cross products gives us

$5(15) = 10y.$ We divide both sides of the equation by 10 to isolate y.

$$\frac{5(15)}{10} = \frac{10y}{10}$$ Reducing both sides we get

$$\frac{\overset{1}{\cancel{5}}(15)}{\underset{2}{\cancel{10}}} = \frac{\cancel{10}y}{\cancel{10}}.$$ Since $15 \div 2 = 7.5$, then $y = 7.5$.
      That is, **the length of y is 7.5.**

To check the solution, 7.5 is substituted in the place of y in the original proportion.

$$\frac{5}{7.5} = \frac{10}{15}$$ Verify that the cross products are equal.

$5(15) = 75$ and $7.5(10) = 75$, so the solution is correct.

<u>Example 18:</u> Find the height of a flagpole that casts a 48-foot shadow, if at the same time a 6-foot pole casts a 9-foot shadow.

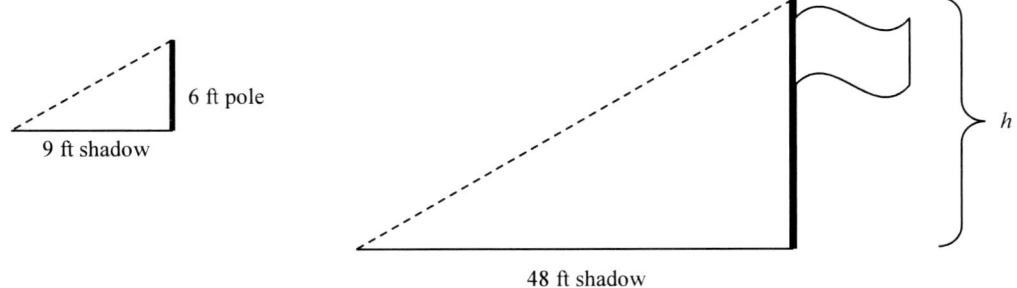

Solution: The triangles shown are similar, so this leads to the following proportion:

$$\frac{9 \text{ ft shadow}}{48 \text{ ft shadow}} = \frac{6 \text{ ft pole}}{h}$$ Finding the cross products gives us

$9h = 48(6)$.   We divide both sides of the equation by 9 to isolate h.

$$\frac{9h}{9} = \frac{48(6)}{9}$$ Reducing both sides we get

$$\frac{\cancel{9}h}{\cancel{9}} = \frac{48(\cancel{6})^2}{\cancel{9}_3} \quad \text{or} \quad h = \frac{48(2)}{3}.$$ Reducing the right side further we get

$$h = \frac{\overset{16}{\cancel{48}}(2)}{\cancel{3}_1}.$$ Since $16(2) = 32$, then $h = 32$. That is, **the height of the flagpole is 32 feet.**

To check the solution, 32 is substituted in the place of h in the original proportion.

$$\frac{9 \text{ ft shadow}}{48 \text{ ft shadow}} = \frac{6 \text{ ft pole}}{32 \text{ ft pole}}$$ Verify that the cross products are equal.

$9(32) = 288$ and $48(6) = 288$, so the solution is correct.

Now try problem 79 from exercise set 1.2.

Note: The original proportion in example 16 could have been set up correctly several other ways. One of them is as follows:

$$\frac{6 \text{ ft pole}}{9 \text{ ft shadow}} = \frac{h}{48 \text{ ft shadow}}$$

<u>Example 19:</u> If a 20-foot flagpole casts a 40-foot shadow, how long of a shadow would be cast by a 6-foot tall man by the name of Doubt? Now suppose that a man by the name of Guilty is standing 13 feet away from the man named Doubt. What can we conclude about Mr. Guilty?

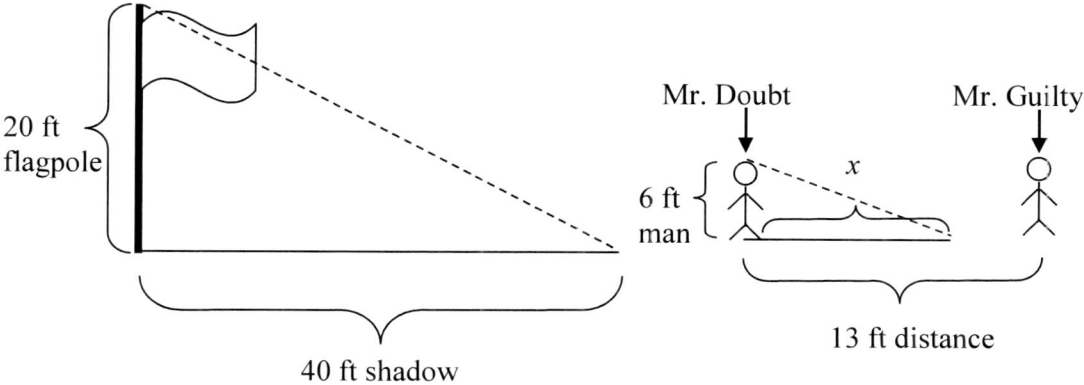

20 ft flagpole

40 ft shadow

Mr. Doubt   Mr. Guilty

6 ft man

x

13 ft distance

Solution: The triangles shown are similar, so this leads to the following proportion:

$$\frac{20 \; ft \; pole}{40 \; ft \; shadow} = \frac{6 \; ft \; man}{x}$$
Finding the cross products gives us

$$20x = 40(6).$$
We divide both sides of the equation by 20 to isolate x.

$$\frac{20x}{20} = \frac{40(6)}{20}$$
Reducing both sides we get

$$\frac{\cancel{20}x}{\cancel{20}} = \frac{\overset{2}{\cancel{40}}(6)}{\underset{1}{\cancel{20}}} \quad \text{or} \quad x = 2(6).$$
Since $2(6) = 12$, then $x = 12$. That is, **the length of Mr. Doubt's shadow is 12 feet.**

Now what can we conclude about Mr. Guilty? Since Mr. Doubt's shadow is 12 feet long and Mr. Guilty is standing 13 feet away, not only is he guilty, but he is **guilty beyond a shadow of a doubt!!**

Section 2 exercises. For each of the following proportions, identify which quantities are the extremes and which quantities are the means.

1. $\dfrac{3}{25} = \dfrac{12}{100}$

2. $\dfrac{5}{19} = \dfrac{20}{76}$

3. $\dfrac{6.2}{9.3} = \dfrac{12}{18}$

4. $\dfrac{35}{60} = \dfrac{4.2}{7.2}$

5. $\dfrac{\frac{4}{7}}{\frac{6}{5}} = \dfrac{10}{21}$

6. $\dfrac{12}{35} = \dfrac{\frac{2}{7}}{\frac{5}{6}}$

7. $\dfrac{6\ possums}{9\ skunks} = \dfrac{12\ possums}{18\ skunks}$

8. $\dfrac{11\ chipmunks}{4\ squirrels} = \dfrac{77\ chipmunks}{28\ squirrels}$

Determine whether the following equations are proportions.

9. $\dfrac{4}{19} = \dfrac{12}{57}$

10. $\dfrac{85}{60} = \dfrac{34}{24}$

11. $\dfrac{38}{17} = \dfrac{68}{37}$

12. $\dfrac{52}{93} = \dfrac{44}{85}$

13. $\dfrac{1.24}{3.6} = \dfrac{2.46}{7.2}$

14. $\dfrac{8.6}{1.42} = \dfrac{4.3}{0.71}$

15. $\dfrac{\frac{3}{5}}{8} = \dfrac{\frac{3}{4}}{10}$

16. $\dfrac{\frac{5}{8}}{6} = \dfrac{\frac{13}{16}}{9}$

17. $\dfrac{4\frac{1}{5}}{3} = \dfrac{4}{2\frac{6}{7}}$

18. $\dfrac{3\frac{3}{4}}{4} = \dfrac{5}{5\frac{1}{3}}$

19. $\dfrac{2\frac{1}{5}}{8.96} = \dfrac{1\frac{3}{8}}{5.6}$

20. $\dfrac{5\frac{1}{2}}{13.4} = \dfrac{3\frac{1}{8}}{7.4}$

Solve for the variable in the following proportions.

21. $\dfrac{7}{18} = \dfrac{35}{x}$

22. $\dfrac{9}{17} = \dfrac{54}{x}$

23. $\dfrac{7}{-2.4} = \dfrac{x}{-6}$

24. $\dfrac{7.6}{-19} = \dfrac{x}{-7}$

25. $\dfrac{x}{1\frac{1}{2}} = \dfrac{1.7}{\frac{5}{6}}$

26. $\dfrac{x}{1\frac{1}{3}} = \dfrac{0.7}{\frac{4}{9}}$

27. $\dfrac{-3}{x} = \dfrac{21}{98}$

28. $\dfrac{6}{x} = \dfrac{48}{-88}$

29. $\dfrac{x}{6.3} = \dfrac{2.08}{7.2}$

30. $\dfrac{x}{4.8} = \dfrac{2.1}{1.5}$

31. $\dfrac{2\frac{4}{5}}{1\frac{1}{3}} = \dfrac{3\frac{1}{2}}{x}$

32. $\dfrac{5\frac{2}{3}}{\frac{4}{5}} = \dfrac{\frac{1}{12}}{x}$

33. $\dfrac{9}{4} = \dfrac{x}{5}$

34. $\dfrac{8}{5} = \dfrac{x}{7}$

35. $\dfrac{-4.2}{3.5} = \dfrac{3.6}{x}$

36. $\dfrac{5.4}{-4.5} = \dfrac{7.2}{x}$

37. $\dfrac{\frac{5}{4}}{x} = \dfrac{0.75}{\frac{3}{8}}$

38. $\dfrac{3}{x} = \dfrac{0.24}{\frac{12}{5}}$

39. $\dfrac{x}{28} = \dfrac{7}{36}$

40. $\dfrac{x}{27} = \dfrac{9}{33}$

41. $\dfrac{2.8}{x} = \dfrac{1.6}{2.1}$

42. $\dfrac{3.5}{x} = \dfrac{8}{5.2}$

43. $\dfrac{-\frac{2}{5}}{3\frac{1}{2}} = \dfrac{x}{1\frac{1}{4}}$

44. $\dfrac{\frac{7}{8}}{-\frac{3}{5}} = \dfrac{x}{\frac{2}{5}}$

List three other ways that each of the following proportions could be correctly written.

45. $\dfrac{170\ miles}{5\ hours} = \dfrac{x}{12\ hours}$

46. $\dfrac{35\ dogs}{7\ kennels} = \dfrac{x}{16\ kennels}$

47. $\dfrac{9\ weeks}{515\ customers} = \dfrac{45\ weeks}{x}$

48. $\dfrac{49\ pizzas}{5\ hours} = \dfrac{168\ pizzas}{x}$

Application Problems: Translate each of the following word problems into a proportion. Then, solve the proportion in order to answer the question.

49. Ben goes to the grocery store at a rate of 3 times a week. How many times would he be expected to go to the grocery store in 16 weeks?

50. Sue goes to the fabric store at a rate of twice a month. How many times would she be expected to go to the fabric store in 8 months?

51.   A tile store charges $243 to install 54 square feet of tile. Assuming they charge the same rate per square foot regardless of the amount of tile installed, how much would they charge to install 100 square feet of tile? What is the unit price for installation per square foot of tile?

52.   A carpet store charges $238 to install 56 square yards of carpet. Assuming they charge the same rate per square yard regardless of the amount of carpet installed, how much would they charge to install 100 square yards of carpet? What is the unit price for installation per square yard of carpet?

53.   Calvin's Concrete Company supplied a contractor with 14 cubic yards of concrete at a cost of $1,211. Assuming they charge the same rate per cubic yard regardless of the amount of concrete supplied, what would they charge for 24 cubic yards of concrete?

54.   Gwen's Gravel Company supplied a homeowner with 42 cubic yards of gravel for his driveway at a cost of $546. Assuming they charge the same rate per cubic yard regardless of the amount of gravel supplied, what would they charge for 58 cubic yards of gravel?

55.   Wanda's Well Drilling charges $30 a foot to drill a well. Assuming they charge the same rate per foot regardless of the depth of the well drilled, how deep of a well could be drilled for $2,370?

56.   Ralph's Residential Roofing charges $2 a square foot for installation to roof a building. Assuming they charge the same rate per square foot regardless of the size of the roof, how many square feet of roofing could be installed for $654?

57.   If a 32-gram serving of breakfast cereal contains 1.5 grams of fat, then how many grams of fat are in a box containing 416 grams of the same breakfast cereal?

58.   If a 26-gram serving of breakfast cereal contains 1.5 grams of fat, then how many grams of fat are in a box containing 416 grams of the same breakfast cereal?

59.   If a 30-acre alfalfa field produces 180 tons of hay, how many acres would a field need to be in order to produce 288 tons of hay?

60.   If a 20-acre field produces 1,200 bushels of dry land wheat, how many acres would a field need to be in order to produce 3,120 bushels of dry land wheat?

61. A recipe for lemon tea cookies calls for $1\frac{3}{4}$ cups of flour for every $\frac{3}{4}$ cup of sugar. How many cups of sugar are needed if $2\frac{1}{3}$ cups of flour are used?

62. A recipe for snickerdoodles calls for $3\frac{3}{4}$ cups of flour for every 2 cups of sugar. How many cups of sugar are needed if $2\frac{1}{2}$ cups of flour are used?

63. The scale on a map indicates that 1 centimeter on the map corresponds to an actual distance of 30 kilometers. If two cities are approximately 2.3 centimeters apart on the map, then what is the actual distance between them?

64. The scale on a map indicates that 1 inch on the map corresponds to an actual distance of 25 miles. If two cities are approximately 3.5 inches apart on the map, then what is the actual distance between them?

65. If an exercise enthusiast can do 75 pushups in 6 minutes, how long would it take her to do 325 pushups if she continued at the same rate?

66. If a gymnast can do 18 jumping jacks in 20 seconds, how long would it take for him to do 45 jumping jacks if he continued at the same rate?

67. If 8 young apple trees can produce 288 boxes of apples, then how many young apple trees would it take to produce 432 boxes of apples if they produce at the same rate?

68. If 8 mature pear trees can produce 300 boxes of pears, then how many mature pear trees would it take to produce 525 boxes of pears if they produce at the same rate?

69. Red and blue ceramic tiles are laid according to a pattern such that for every 17 red tiles used, 8 blue tiles are used. If a total of 375 tiles are used, how many of them are blue?

70. Green and white ceramic tiles are laid according to a pattern such that for every 13 green tiles used, 7 white tiles are used. If a total of 380 tiles are used, how many of them are white?

71. The ratio of the number of female students compared to the number of male students that attend Yakima Valley College is 13 to 7.

    a) What fraction of the students that attend Y.V.C. are male?

    b) What fraction of the students that attend Y.V.C. are female?

    c) If 6,000 students attend Y.V.C., how many are male? If necessary, round your answer to the nearest whole student.

72. The ratio of the number of right-handed students compared to the number of left-handed students that attend Yakima Valley College is 15 to 2.

    a) What fraction of the students that attend Y.V.C. are left-handed?

    b) What fraction of the students that attend Y.V.C. are right-handed?

    c) If 6,000 students attend Y.V.C., how many are left-handed? If necessary, round your answer to the nearest whole student.

Find the unknown lengths for each pair of similar triangles.

73.

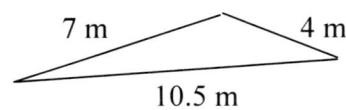

74.

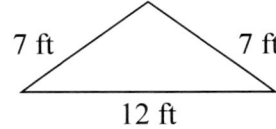

75.

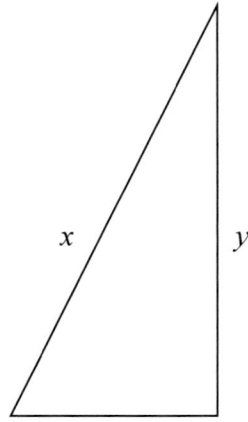
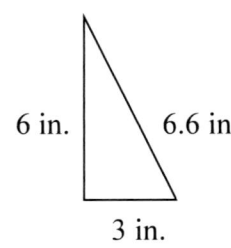

76.

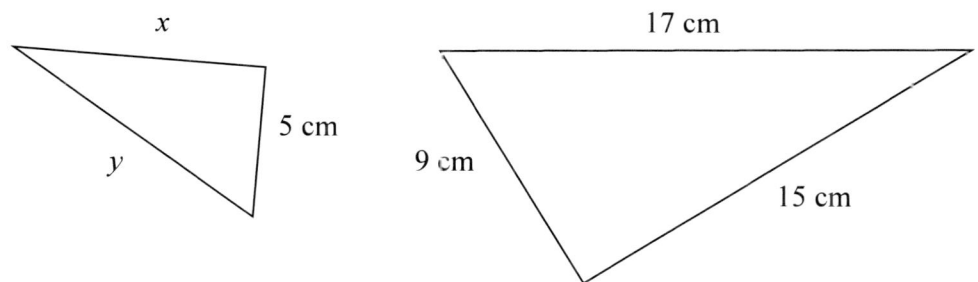

Find the perimeter of each triangle. Assume the triangles are similar. The perimeter of a triangle is found by adding the lengths of all three sides of the triangle.

77.

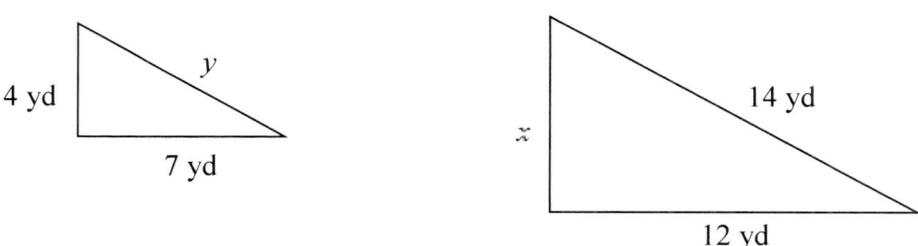

78.

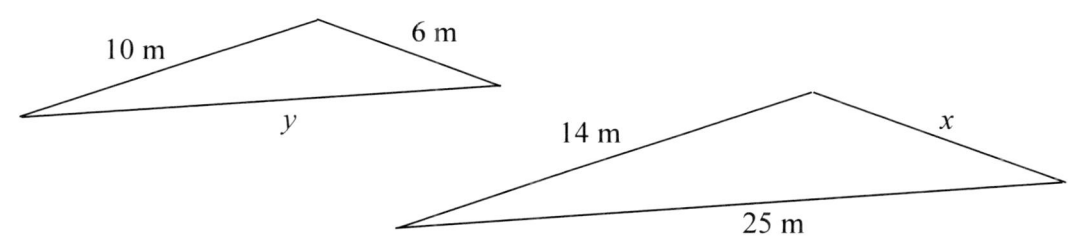

79. If a 15-foot tree casts a 40-foot shadow, how tall is a tree that casts a 64-foot shadow?

80. If a 28-foot tree casts a 40-foot shadow, how tall is a tree that casts a 90-foot shadow?

81. If a 10-meter flagpole casts a shadow that is 26 meters long, how long is the shadow cast by a tree that is 16 meters high?

82. If a 50-meter tower casts a shadow that is 120 meters long, how long is the shadow cast by a telephone pole that is 18 meters high?

83.   Suppose you are standing such that a 20-foot tree is directly between you and the sun. If you are standing 40 feet away from the tree and the tree casts a 50-foot shadow, how tall could you be and still be completely in the shadow of the tree?

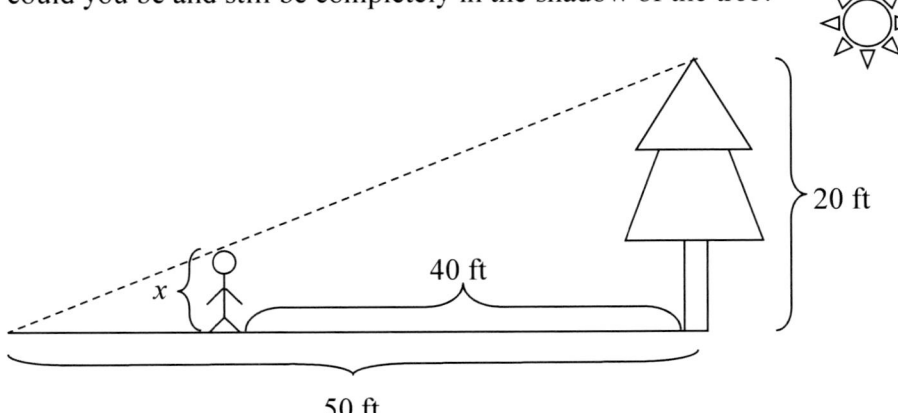

84.   Suppose you are standing such that a 24-foot tree is directly between you and the sun. If you are standing 32.5 feet away from the tree and the tree casts a 40-foot shadow, how tall could you be and still be completely in the shadow of the tree?

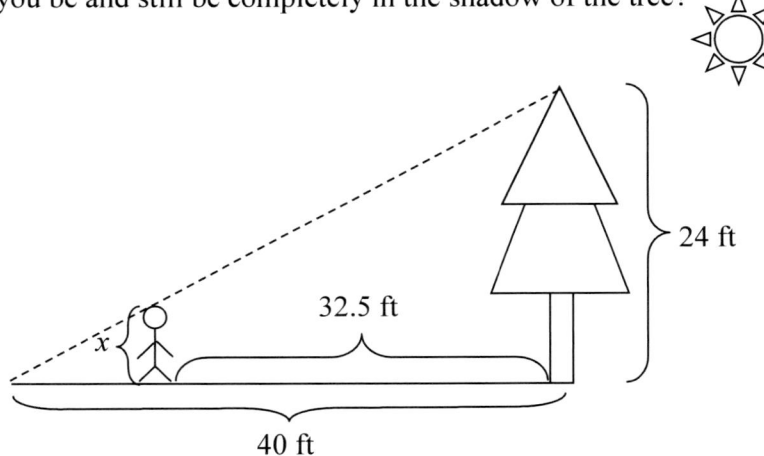

85.   Suppose you are standing such that a 20-foot tree is directly between you and the sun. If you are 6 feet tall and the tree casts a 50-foot shadow, how far away from the tree can you stand and still be completely in the shadow of the tree?

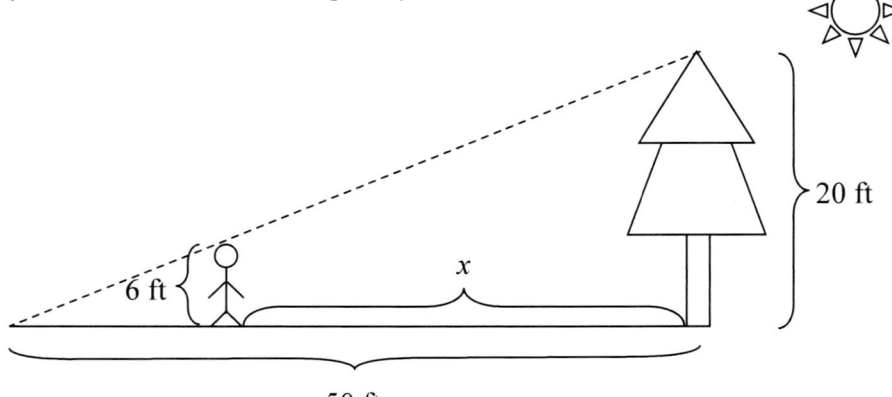

86.   Suppose you are standing such that a 24-foot tree is directly between you and the sun. If you are 4.8 feet tall and the tree casts a 40-foot shadow, how far away from the tree can you stand and still be completely in the shadow of the tree?

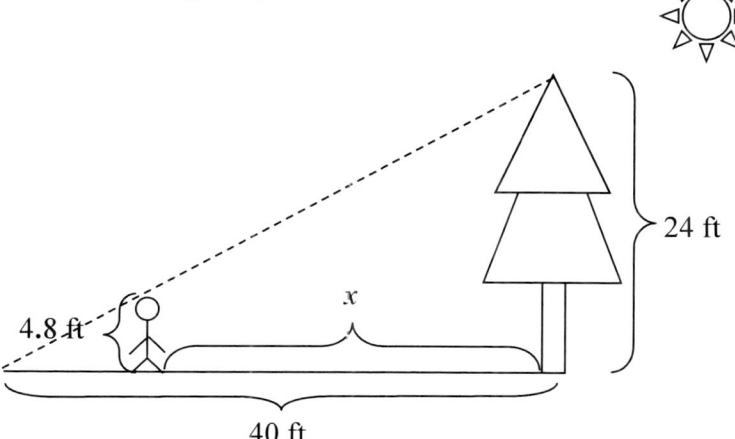

Writing:

87.   If it takes a man 5 minutes to run 1 mile, then in 50 minutes he should be able to run 10 miles. What assumption is being made in this scenario? Is it a reasonable assumption to make? Why or why not?

88.   If it takes a woman 4 minutes to ride a bicycle 1 mile, then in 40 minutes she should be able to ride a bicycle 10 miles. What assumption is being made in this scenario? Is it a reasonable assumption to make? Why or why not?

89.   In a survey, 6 out of 10 people like to eat their eggs scrambled. At this rate, of the 50 customers at Barney's Breakfast Bar, how many ordered scrambled eggs this morning? Can you think of a reason why 30 might not be a good answer?

RATIOS, PROPORTIONS, & MEASUREMENTS

Section 3: Measurements (American Units)

If you live in the United States, every day you are surrounded by measurements that are part of the American (or English) system. You might drive 10 **miles** to work and then walk 50 **feet** from your car to your office. After putting in an 8-**hour** day at work, perhaps you **inch** your way through busy traffic to a local grocery store where you buy a **gallon** of milk or a **pound** of butter or a **quart** of orange juice. In any event, your life is bombarded with measurements. In this section we will look at how these measurements relate to each other and how to convert from one unit of measurement to another.

Length: First, we will consider units of length. American units of length work together in the following ways:

AMERICAN UNITS OF LENGTH

12 inches (in.) = 1 foot (ft)   3 feet (ft) = 1 yard (yd)   5,280 feet (ft) = 1 mile (mi)

In order to change from one kind of unit to another, let's say from feet to inches, we will use a process called converting units. To carry out this process, we will use what are known as **unit conversion factors**.

Unit conversion factors are based on the fact that if you multiply a quantity by the number 1, the value of the original quantity doesn't change. For instance, 7(1) = 7. How you go about writing the "1" is what becomes most important.

$\frac{12}{12} = 1$, $\frac{6,423}{6,423} = 1$, and $\frac{1\,dead\,skunk}{1\,dead\,skunk} = 1$ In fact, any quantity divided by itself is equal to 1.

(Except $\frac{0}{0}$, and we'll leave that for calculus students to deal with.)

$\frac{7+6}{13} = 1$. Even though 7 + 6 doesn't look like 13, because 7 + 6 = 13, $\frac{7+6}{13} = 1$. More

examples are 12 inches = 1 foot, so $\frac{12\,inches}{1\,foot} = 1$ and $\frac{1\,foot}{12\,inches} = 1$. Fractions like

$\frac{12\,inches}{1\,foot}$ and $\frac{1\,foot}{12\,inches}$ are called unit conversion factors. When we wish to change one unit

into another, such as to change feet into inches, a unit conversion factor is multiplied by the original unit. In the process, this original unit is converted into a new unit contained within the unit conversion factor.

<u>Example 1</u>: Convert 7 feet to inches.

Solution: Multiply 7 feet by the unit conversion factor $\dfrac{12\ inches}{1\ foot}$.

$\left(\dfrac{7\ feet}{1}\right)\left(\dfrac{12\ inches}{1\ foot}\right)$ Reducing out the units of feet or foot we get

$\left(\dfrac{7\ \cancel{feet}}{1}\right)\left(\dfrac{12\ inches}{1\ \cancel{foot}}\right)$.   Then, since 7(12) = 84, the answer is **84 inches**.

Now try problem 1 from exercise set 1.3.

Note: If the unit we are trying to eliminate is in the <u>numerator</u> of the original quantity, then that same unit must be in the <u>denominator</u> of the unit conversion factor in order for the "like" units to reduce out properly. If, however, the unit conversion factor is written in such a way that the "like" units are on the same line as in the original quantity then the units don't reduce out properly.

CORRECT	**INCORRECT**
$\left(\dfrac{7\ \cancel{feet}}{1}\right)\left(\dfrac{12\ inches}{1\ \cancel{foot}}\right)$	$\left(\dfrac{7\ feet}{1}\right)\left(\dfrac{1\ foot}{12\ inches}\right)$
CORRECT	**INCORRECT**
$\left(\dfrac{48\ \cancel{inches}}{1}\right)\left(\dfrac{1\ foot}{12\ \cancel{inches}}\right)$	$\left(\dfrac{48\ inches}{1}\right)\left(\dfrac{12\ inches}{1\ foot}\right)$

As in example 1, sometimes it is necessary to multiply a quantity by the number 1 or by a unit conversion factor that is equivalent to 1. To justify this process, we use what is called **<u>The Identity Property of Multiplication.</u>**

THE IDENTITY PROPERTY OF MULTIPLICATION:

For any real number a,

$a \cdot 1 = a$ and $1 \cdot a = a$.

If 1 is multiplied by any real number a, the product is a.

Note: The number 1 is called the <u>multiplicative identity</u>.

Example 2: Convert 4 yards to inches.

Solution: We were not provided with information to go directly from yards to inches. So, we need to determine a "road map". We can go from yards to feet and then from feet to inches. Now we can solve this problem by multiplying together several unit conversion factors.

$$\left(\frac{4\ yards}{1}\right)\left(\frac{3\ feet}{1\ yard}\right)\left(\frac{12\ inches}{1\ foot}\right)$$

Reducing out units common to the numerator and the denominator we get

$$\left(\frac{4\ \cancel{yards}}{1}\right)\left(\frac{3\ \cancel{feet}}{1\ \cancel{yard}}\right)\left(\frac{12\ inches}{1\ \cancel{foot}}\right).$$

Then, since $4(3)(12)=144,$ the answer is **144 inches**.

Now try problem 17 from exercise set 1.3.

Example 3: A board that is 4 feet long is cut into two pieces. If one of the pieces is 1 foot 4 inches long, then how long is the other piece?

Solution: We need to subtract 1 foot 4 inches from 4 feet. To accomplish this we will take 1 foot from the 4 feet and turn it into 12 inches. So, 4 feet becomes 3 feet 12 inches. This gives us the following subtraction problem.

> 3 feet 12 inches
> −1 foot 4 inches
> _____
> 2 feet   8 inches

Consequently, **the other piece is 2 feet 8 inches long**.

Now try problem 173 from exercise set 1.3.

Perimeter and circumference: One of the things that length is used for is to measure the distance around an object. In the case of a **rectangle**, a **square**, or a **triangle** this distance is called the **perimeter**. In the case of a **circle** this distance is called the **circumference**.

A **rectangle** is a four-sided figure with sides that meet in such a way as to form right or 90° angles. These sides are said to be perpendicular to each other. Opposite sides of a rectangle are parallel and are of the same length.

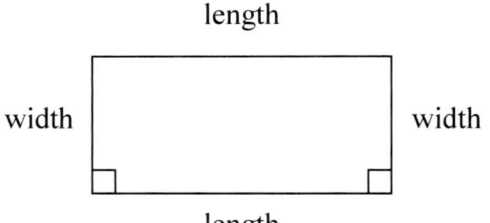

Each of the longer sides of a rectangle are called the length (*L*), and each of the shorter sides are called the width (*W*).

Note: The little squares in each corner of this rectangle indicate that the sides meet at right angles, implying that the drawing is in fact a rectangle.

Since the perimeter (*P*) of a rectangle has 2 equal lengths and 2 equal widths,

---

FORMULA FOR THE PERIMETER OF A RECTANGLE:

$$P = 2L + 2W$$

<u>Example 4</u>: Find the perimeter of the following rectangle.

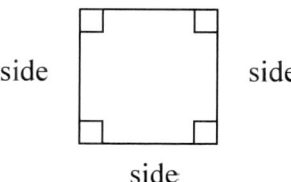

8 ft

4 ft   4 ft

8 ft

Solution: The length is 8 ft and the width is 4 ft. Using the formula for the perimeter of a rectangle, $P = 2L + 2W$ gives us

$P = 2(8 \text{ ft}) + 2(4 \text{ ft})$ which simplified further becomes

$P = 16 \text{ ft} + 8 \text{ ft}$ and finally

$P = 24 \text{ ft}.$

Consequently, **the perimeter of the rectangle is 24 feet.**

A **square** is a rectangle with all four sides the same length.

side

side   side

side

Since the perimeter (P) of a square has 4 sides (s) of equal length,

FORMULA FOR THE PERIMETER OF A SQUARE:

$$P = 4s$$

<u>Example 5</u>: Find the perimeter of the following square.

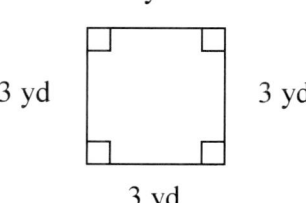

3 yd

3 yd   3 yd

3 yd

Solution: The length of each side is 3 yd. Using the formula for the perimeter of a square,

$P = 4s$ gives us

$P = 4(3 \text{ yd})$ which simplified becomes

$P = 12 \text{ yd}.$

Consequently, **the perimeter of the square is 12 yards.**

A **triangle** is a three-sided figure. These sides may or may not be equal in length. Below are some examples of triangles.

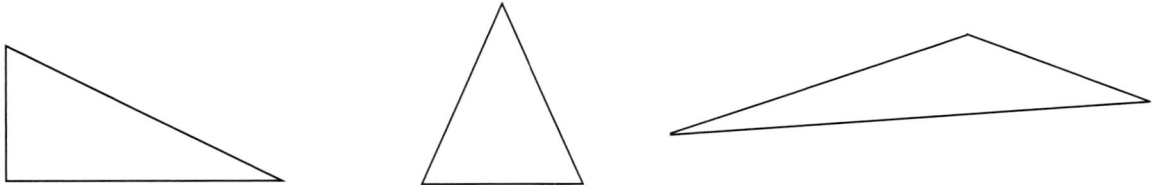

Because there are so many types of triangles, the easiest way to generalize a formula for the perimeter (*P*) of a triangle is simply to add together the lengths of all three sides.

FORMULA FOR THE PERIMETER OF A TRIANGLE:

P = **THE SUM OF ALL THREE SIDES OF THE TRIANGLE**

Example 6: Find the perimeter of the following triangle.

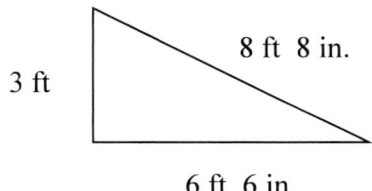

Solution: The lengths of the three sides are 3 ft, 6 ft 6 in. and 8 ft 8 in. respectively. Using the formula for the perimeter of a triangle,

P = THE SUM OF ALL THREE SIDES OF A TRIANGLE   gives us

P = 3 ft + 6 ft 6 in. + 8 ft 8 in.

Adding like units we get the following: 3 ft
                                          6 ft   6 in.
                                    +   8 ft   8 in.
                              P = 17 ft 14 in.

Using the fact that 12 in. equals 1 ft,   14 in. becomes 1 ft 2 in.

Now we get the following: 17 ft
                            +   1 ft 2 in.
                     P =   18 ft 2 in.

Consequently, **the perimeter of the triangle is 18 feet 2 inches**.

A **circle** is the set of all points in a plane that are the same distance from a point called the **center** of the circle. This distance from the center to a point on the circle is called the **radius** of the circle. A line segment that passes through the center of a circle and extends to two points on the circle is called the **diameter** of the circle. The length of the diameter of a circle is 2 times the length of its radius.

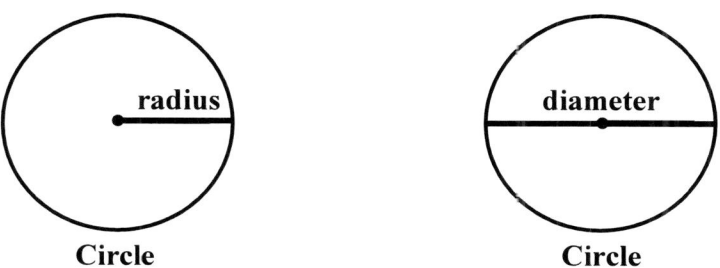

Circle   Circle

While the distance around a rectangle or a square is called the perimeter, the distance around a circle is called the **circumference**. When the circumference of a circle is divided by its diameter, no matter what size the circle is, the result always comes out to be the same ratio. This ratio is a number that is slightly larger than three. This number is known in the mathematics world as π **(pi)**. π is an irrational number. This means that π can't be written exactly as a fraction or a decimal number. The best we can do is to approximate it. For the purpose of calculations, use the symbol π in answers that are to be exact. We will use the fact that π ≈ 3.14 for answers that are to be approximations. The symbol ≈ means "**is approximately equal to**." This all leads to the following formula.

FORMULA FOR THE CIRCUMFERENCE OF A CIRCLE:

$$C = \pi d$$

where *C* is the circumference and *d* is the length of the diameter.

Using the fact that the diameter of a circle is twice as long as the radius, we can replace *d* in the formula with **2r** to get another version of this formula.

ALTERNATIVE FORMULA FOR THE CIRCUMFERENCE OF A CIRCLE:

$$C = 2\pi r$$

where *C* is the circumference and *r* is the length of the radius.

<u>Example 7:</u> Find the circumference of the following circle. Give both the exact answer and an approximation using the fact that $\pi \approx 3.14$.

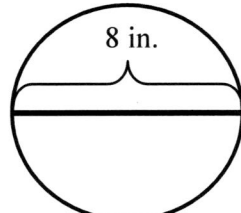

Solution: Since the diameter of the circle is 8 in., using the formula for the circumference of a circle,

$C = \pi d$ gives us

$C = \pi (8 \text{ in.})$ or $C = 8\pi$ in.   So,

the exact circumference of the circle is 8π inches.

Using the fact that $\pi \approx 3.14$,

$C \approx (8)(3.14)$ in.   Since $(8)(3.14)$ in. $= 25.12$ in., then

$C \approx 25.12$ in.   Consequently,

the approximate circumference of the circle is 25.12 inches.

<u>Example 8:</u> Find the circumference of the following circle. Give both the exact answer and an approximation using the fact that $\pi \approx 3.14$.

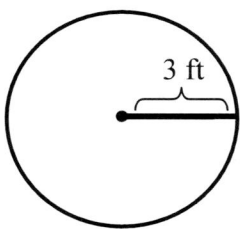

Solution: Since the radius of the circle is 3 ft, using the alternative formula for the circumference of a circle,

$C = 2\pi r$ gives us

$C = 2\pi (3 \text{ ft})$ or $C = 6\pi$ ft.   So,

the exact circumference of the circle is 6π feet.

Using the fact that $\pi \approx 3.14$,

$C \approx (6)(3.14)$ ft.   Since $(6)(3.14)$ ft $= 18.84$ ft, then

$C \approx 18.84$ ft.   Consequently,

the approximate circumference of the circle is 18.84 feet.

Note: We could have used the original formula for the circumference of a circle and just multiplied the length of the radius by two before inserting the number into the formula.

Area: Next, we will consider units of area. American units of area work together in the following ways:

AMERICAN UNITS OF AREA

$144 \text{ in.}^2 = 1 \text{ ft}^2$ $9 \text{ ft}^2 = 1 \text{ yd}^2$ $43{,}560 \text{ ft}^2 = 1 \text{ acre}$ $640 \text{ acres} = 1 \text{ mi}^2$

Note: Area is frequently measured in two-dimensional units such as square feet or square inches. Also note that an expression written as 144 in.^2 is read "one hundred and forty four square inches," not "one hundred and forty four inches squared."

Example 9: Convert 2 ft^2 to square inches.

Solution: Multiply 2 ft^2 by the unit conversion factor $\dfrac{144 \text{ in.}^2}{1 \text{ ft}^2}$.

$\left(\dfrac{2 \text{ ft}^2}{1} \right) \left(\dfrac{144 \text{ in.}^2}{1 \text{ ft}^2} \right)$ Reducing out the units of square feet we get

$\left(\dfrac{2 \cancel{\text{ft}^2}}{1} \right) \left(\dfrac{144 \text{ in.}^2}{1 \cancel{\text{ft}^2}} \right)$.   Then, since $2(144) = 288$, the answer is **288**
        square inches or 288 in.^2 .

Now try problem 29 from exercise set 1.3.

Example 10: Convert 4.5 mi^2 to acres.

Solution: Multiply 4.5 mi^2 by the unit conversion factor $\dfrac{640 \text{ acres}}{1 \text{ mi}^2}$.

$4.5 \text{ mi}^2 \left(\dfrac{640 \text{ acres}}{1 \text{ mi}^2} \right)$ Reducing out the units of square miles we get

$4.5 \cancel{\text{mi}^2} \left(\dfrac{640 \text{ acres}}{1 \cancel{\text{mi}^2}} \right)$.   Then, since $4.5(640) = 2{,}880$, the answer is
        2,880 acres.

Now try problem 41 from exercise set 1.3.

Rectangles, squares, triangles and circles all have area. We will now look at formulas for calculating area for each of these figures. "*A*" stands for area and as before, "*L*" stands for length while "*W*" stands for width.

FORMULA FOR THE AREA OF A RECTANGLE:

$$A = LW$$

<u>Example 11</u>: Find the area of the following rectangle.

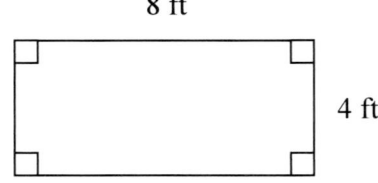

8 ft

4 ft

Solution: The length is 8 ft and the width is 4 ft. Using the formula for the area of a rectangle,

$A = LW$ gives us

$A = (8\ \text{ft})(4\ \text{ft})$ which simplified further becomes

$A = 32\ \text{ft}^2$.   Consequently, **the area of the rectangle is 32 square feet or 32 ft^2.**

*Now try problem 181 from exercise set 1.3. (Find the area.) See example 4 for the perimeter.

In the formula for the area of a square "*A*" stands for area and "*s*" stands for the length of the side of a square. (Remember that it doesn't matter which side is used because with a square all four sides are the same length.)

FORMULA FOR THE AREA OF A SQUARE:

$$A = s \cdot s \ \text{ or } \ A = s^2$$

<u>Example 12</u>: Find the area of the following square.

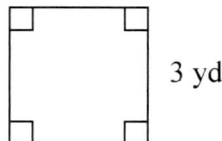

3 yd

Solution: The length of each side is 3 yd. Using the formula for the area of a square,

$A = s^2$ gives us

$A = (3\ \text{yd})^2$ which simplified becomes

$A = 9\ \text{yd}^2$.   Consequently, **the area of the square is 9 square yards or 9 yd^2.**

*Now try problem 183 from exercise set 1.3. (Find the area.) See example 5 for the perimeter.

In the formula for the area of a triangle "*A*" stands for area, "*b*" stands for the **base** of the triangle and "*h*" stands for the **height** of the triangle. The base and the height of the triangle are always perpendicular to each other. Likewise, if a triangle has two sides that are perpendicular to each other, then these sides are considered to be the base and the height as in the following triangle:

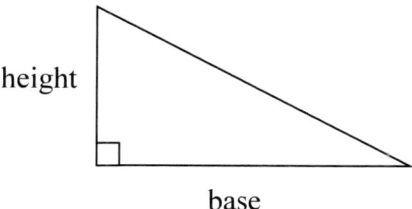

In the case where no two sides of the triangle are perpendicular to each other, one of the sides becomes the base and a line drawn perpendicular to the base that extends from the base to the highest point of the triangle becomes the height. (This line is also called the **altitude** of the triangle.) Below is such a triangle:

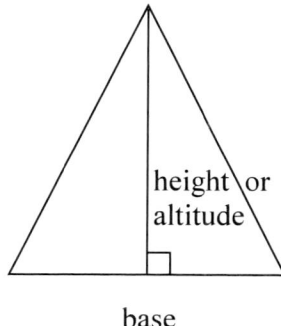

FORMULA FOR THE AREA OF A TRIANGLE:

$$A = \tfrac{1}{2}bh$$

<u>Example 13:</u> Find the area of the following triangle.

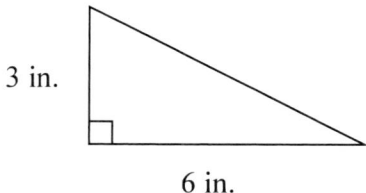

Solution: The base is 6 in. and the height is 3 in. Using the formula for the area of a triangle,

$A = \tfrac{1}{2}bh$ gives us

$A = \dfrac{1}{2}(6 \text{ in.})(3 \text{ in.}).$ Reducing we get

$A = \dfrac{1}{\cancel{2}}(\overset{3}{\cancel{6}}\text{ in.})(3 \text{ in.}).$ Simplifying further we get

$A = 9 \text{ in.}^2.$ Consequently, **the area of the triangle is 9 square inches or 9 in.**^{2}.

Now try problem 185 from exercise set 1.3. (Find the area.) See example 6 for the perimeter.

In the formula for the area of a circle "*A*" stands for area, and "*r*" stands for the length of the radius of the circle.

> **FORMULA FOR THE AREA OF A CIRCLE:**
>
> $$A = \pi r^2$$

<u>Example 14:</u> Find the area of the following circle. Give both the exact answer and an approximation using the fact that $\pi \approx 3.14$.

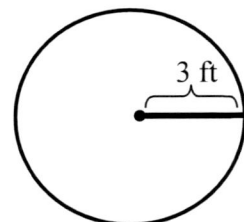
3 ft

Solution: Since the radius of the circle is 3 ft, using the formula for the area of a circle,

$$A = \pi r^2 \qquad \text{gives us}$$

$A = \pi (3 \text{ ft})^2$ or $A = 9\pi \text{ ft}^2$. So,

the exact area of the circle is 9π square feet or $9\pi \text{ ft}^2$.

Using the fact that $\pi \approx 3.14$,

$A \approx (9)(3.14) \text{ ft}^2$.   Since $(9)(3.14) \text{ ft}^2 = 28.26 \text{ ft}^2$, then

$A \approx 28.26 \text{ ft}^2$.   Consequently,

the approximate area of the circle is 28.26 square feet or 28.26 ft^2.

*Now try problem
 199 from exercise set 1.3. (Find the area.) See example 8 for the circumference.

<u>Example 15:</u> Find the area of the following circle. Give both the exact answer and an approximation using the fact that $\pi \approx 3.14$.

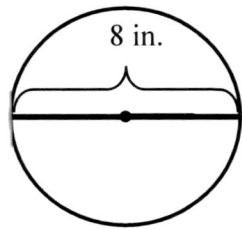
8 in.

Solution: Since the radius of the circle is one half of the diameter and the diameter is 8 in., then the radius is 4 in. Using the formula for the area of a circle,

$$A = \pi r^2 \qquad \text{gives us}$$

$A = \pi (4 \text{ in.})^2$ or $A = 16\pi \text{ in.}^2$ So,

the exact area of the circle is 16π square inches or $16\pi \text{ in.}^2$.

Using the fact that $\pi \approx 3.14$,

$A \approx (16)(3.14) \text{ in.}^2$.   Since $(16)(3.14) \text{ in.}^2 = 50.24 \text{ in.}^2$ then,

$A \approx 50.24 \text{ in.}^2$.   Consequently,

the approximate area of the circle is 50.24 square inches or 50.24 in.^2.

*Now try problem
 197 from exercise set 1.3. (Find the area.) See example 7 for the circumference.

Surface Area: When determining the area of a three-dimensional object such as a box, we refer to total area taken up by all sides or surfaces as the surface area. In this chapter, we will focus on the surface area of **rectangular solids (box-like shapes)** and **cubes**.

A rectangular solid is a three-dimensional object such as a box or a block of wood. All six of its sides or faces as they are referred to are rectangles.

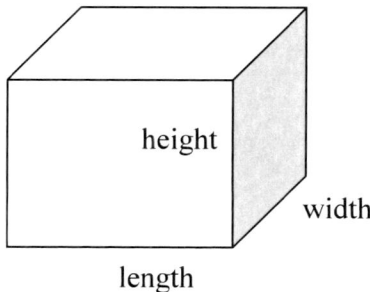

We determine the surface area of a rectangular solid by finding the sum of the areas of all six of its faces. Below is a diagram to illustrate what a rectangular solid looks like when all six of its faces are exposed at the same time.

Note that in the above diagram, the back and the front each have the same area consisting of length times height or *LH.* In a similar fashion, the top and the bottom each have the same area consisting of length times width or *LW.* Finally, each end has the same area, height times width or *HW.* This leads to the following formula:

FORMULA FOR THE SURFACE AREA OF A RECTANGULAR SOLID:

Surface Area or SA = 2LW + 2LH + 2WH

Example 16: Find the surface area of the following rectangular solid in square inches.

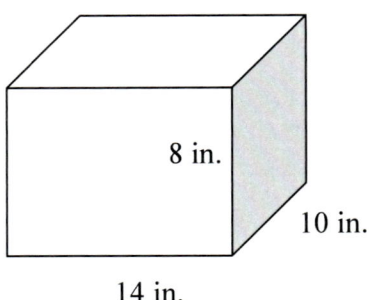

8 in.

10 in.

14 in.

Solution: The length is 14 in., the width is 10 in. and the height is 8 in. Using the formula for the surface area of a rectangular solid,

$SA = 2LW + 2LH + 2WH$ gives us

$SA = 2(14 \text{ in.})(10 \text{ in.}) + 2(14 \text{ in.})(8 \text{ in.}) + 2(10 \text{ in.})(8 \text{ in.})$.

Following order of operations we get

$SA = 280 \text{ in.}^2 + 224 \text{ in.}^2 + 160 \text{ in.}^2$ which simplified further becomes

$SA = 664 \text{ in.}^2$.

Consequently, **the surface area of the rectangular solid is 664 square inches or 664 in.^2**.

A cube is a rectangular solid that has six sides, all of which are squares.

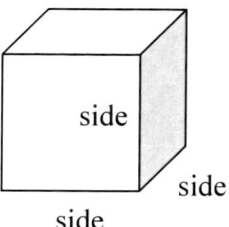

We determine the surface area of a cube by finding the sum of the areas of all six of its sides. Since with a cube, each side is a square with an area of s^2, the formula for the surface area of a cube is as follows.

FORMULA FOR THE SURFACE AREA OF A CUBE:

$$SA = 6s^2$$

<u>Example 17:</u> Find the surface area of the following cube in square feet.

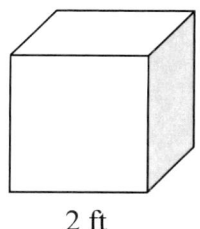

2 ft

Solution: The length of each side is 2 ft. Using the formula for the surface area of a cube,

$SA = 6s^2$ gives us

$SA = 6(2 \text{ ft})^2$.   Following order of operations we get

$SA = 6(4 \text{ ft}^2)$ which simplified further becomes

$SA = 24 \text{ ft}^2$.   Consequently, **the surface area of the cube is 24 square feet or 24 ft^2.**

Volume: After area we will look at units of volume. American units of volume work together in the following ways:

**AMERICAN UNITS OF VOLUME
MEASURED IN CUBIC UNITS**

$1,728 \text{ in.}^3 = 1 \text{ ft}^3$ $27 \text{ ft}^3 = 1 \text{ yd}^3$

Note: Volume is frequently measured in three-dimensional units such as cubic feet or cubic inches. Also note that an expression written as 27 ft^3 is read "twenty seven cubic feet," not "twenty seven feet cubed."

Example 18: Convert 2 yd^3 to cubic feet.

Solution: Multiply 2 yd^3 by the unit conversion factor $\dfrac{27 \ ft^3}{1 \ yd^3}$.

$\left(\dfrac{2 \ yd^3}{1}\right)\left(\dfrac{27 \ ft^3}{1 \ yd^3}\right)$ Reducing out the units of cubic yards we get

$\left(\dfrac{2 \ \cancel{yd^3}}{1}\right)\left(\dfrac{27 \ ft^3}{1 \ \cancel{yd^3}}\right)$.   Since $(2)(27 \text{ ft}^3) = 54 \text{ ft}^3$, the answer is
         54 cubic feet or 54 ft^3 .

Now try problem 51 from exercise set 1.3.

Example 19: Convert 3.5 ft^3 to cubic inches.

Solution: Multiply 3.5 ft^3 by the unit conversion factor $\dfrac{1,728 \ in.^3}{1 \ ft^3}$.

$\left(\dfrac{3.5 \ ft^3}{1}\right)\left(\dfrac{1,728 \ in.^3}{1 \ ft^3}\right)$ Reducing out the units of cubic yards we get

$\left(\dfrac{3.5 \ \cancel{ft^3}}{1}\right)\left(\dfrac{1,728 \ in.^3}{1 \ \cancel{ft^3}}\right)$.   Since $(3.5)(1,728 \text{ in.}^3) = 6,048$, the answer is
         6,048 cubic inches or 6,048 in.^{3} .

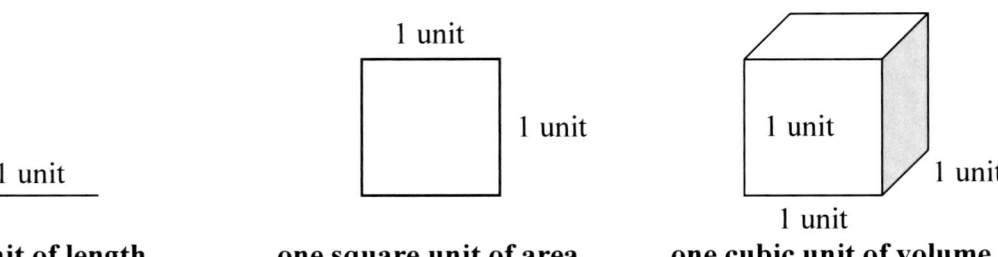

1 unit

1 unit   1 unit

1 unit

1 unit

1 unit

one unit of length   **one square unit of area**   **one cubic unit of volume**

Though there are many different solid shapes of which the volume can be calculated, in this chapter, we will limit our study to **rectangular solids (box-like shapes)** and **cubes**.

As previously mentioned, a rectangular solid is a three-dimensional object such as a box or a block of wood. All of its sides are rectangles and its volume measures the space it encloses.

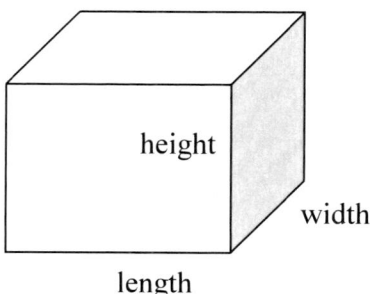

In the formula for the volume of a rectangular solid, "V" stands for volume, "H" stands for height, "W" stands for width and "L" stands for length.

FORMULA FOR THE VOLUME OF A RECTANGULAR SOLID:

$$V = LWH$$

Example 20: Find the volume of the following box in cubic inches.

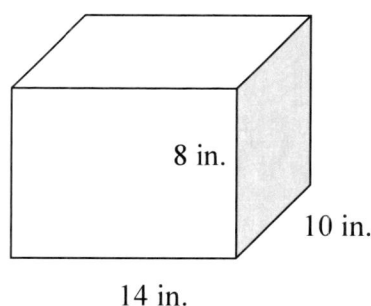

Solution: The length is 14 in., the width is 10 in. and the height is 8 in. Using the formula for the volume of a rectangular solid,

$V = LWH$ gives us

$V = (14 \text{ in.})(10 \text{ in.})(8 \text{ in.})$ which simplified further becomes

$V = 1,120 \text{ in.}^3$.

Consequently, **the volume of the box is 1,120 cubic inches or 1,120 in.^{3}**.

Now try problem 201 from exercise set 1.3. (Find the volume.) See example 16 for the surface area.

As previously mentioned, a cube is a rectangular solid that has six sides, all of which are squares.

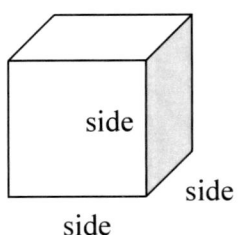

side

side

side

In the formula for the volume of a cube "V" stands for volume and "s" stands for the length of the side of a cube. (Remember that it doesn't matter which side is used because with a cube all sides are the same length.)

FORMULA FOR THE VOLUME OF A CUBE:

$$V = s^3$$

<u>Example 21:</u> Find the volume of the following cube in cubic feet.

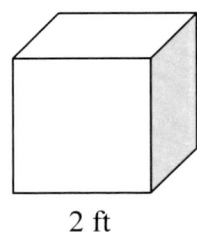

2 ft

Solution: The length of each side is 2 ft. Using the formula for the volume of a cube,

$V = s^3$ gives us

$V = $ (2 ft)(2 ft)(2 ft)   which simplified further becomes

$V = $ 8 ft^3 .

Consequently, **the volume of the cube is 8 cubic feet or 8 ft^3** .

Now try problem 203 from exercise set 1.3. (Find the volume.) See example 17 for the surface area.

While some units of volume are measured in cubic units, others are not. Here are some of those other units.

OTHER AMERICAN UNITS OF VOLUME

1 cup (c) = 8 fluid ounces (fl oz)   1 pint (pt) = 2 cups (c)

1 quart (qt) = 2 pints (pt)   1 gallon (gal) = 4 quarts (qt)

Note: Sometimes the word "capacity" is used to describe units of measure like quarts, pints, cups, etc.

<u>Example 22:</u> Convert $3\frac{1}{2}$ gallons to quarts.

Solution: Multiply $3\frac{1}{2}$ gallons by the unit conversion factor $\frac{4\ quarts}{1\ gallon}$.

$\left(\dfrac{3\frac{1}{2}\ gallons}{1}\right)\left(\dfrac{4\ quarts}{1\ gallon}\right)$ Changing $3\frac{1}{2}$ into $\frac{7}{2}$ we get

$\left(\dfrac{7\ gallons}{2}\right)\left(\dfrac{4\ quarts}{1\ gallon}\right)$.   Reducing out the units of gallons or gallon we get

$\left(\dfrac{7\ \cancel{gallons}}{2}\right)\left(\dfrac{4\ quarts}{1\ \cancel{gallon}}\right)$.   Reducing further we get

$\dfrac{7}{\cancel{2}_{1}}\left(\dfrac{\overset{2}{\cancel{4}}\ quarts}{1}\right)$.   Then, since 7(2 quarts) = 14 quarts, the answer is **14 quarts**.

Now try problem 67 from exercise set 1.3.

<u>Example 23:</u> Convert 44 fluid ounces to pints.

Solution: We can solve this problem by multiplying together several unit conversion factors.

$\left(\dfrac{44\ fl\ oz}{1}\right)\left(\dfrac{1\ cup}{8\ fl\ oz}\right)\left(\dfrac{1\ pint}{2\ cups}\right)$ Reducing out units common to the numerator and the denominator we get

$\left(\dfrac{44\ \cancel{fl\ oz}}{1}\right)\left(\dfrac{1\ \cancel{cup}}{8\ \cancel{fl\ oz}}\right)\left(\dfrac{1\ pint}{2\ \cancel{cups}}\right)$.   Reducing further we get

$\left(\dfrac{\overset{11}{\cancel{44}}}{1}\right)\left(\dfrac{1}{\cancel{8}_{2}}\right)\left(\dfrac{1\ pint}{2}\right)$.   Then, since $\dfrac{11}{(2)(2)} = \dfrac{11}{4}$ and using long division,

$4\overline{)11.00}$ with quotient 2.75, the answer is **2.75 pints**.

Now try problem 73 from exercise set 1.3.

Weight: Still to be considered are units of weight. American units of weight work together in the following ways:

AMERICAN UNITS OF WEIGHT

16 ounces (oz) = 1 pound (lb)

2,000 pounds (lb) = 1 ton (T)

Example 24: Convert 17 pounds to ounces.

Solution: Multiply 17 pounds by the unit conversion factor $\dfrac{16\ oz}{1\ lb}$.

$\left(\dfrac{17\ lb}{1}\right)\left(\dfrac{16\ oz}{1\ lb}\right)$ Reducing out the units of pounds we get

$\left(\dfrac{17\ \cancel{lb}}{1}\right)\left(\dfrac{16\ oz}{1\ \cancel{lb}}\right)$.   Then, since 17(16 oz) = 272 oz, the answer is **272 ounces**.

Now try problem 95 from exercise set 1.3.

Note: Be careful not to confuse ounces with fluid ounces. While an ounce is a unit of weight, a fluid ounce is a unit of volume.

Time: Finally, we come to units of time. American units of time are the same as units of time in other countries. Though, as we will see in the next section, units of time are about the only units that seem to be universal.

UNITS OF TIME

1 minute (min) = 60 seconds (sec)	1 hour (hr) = 60 minutes (min)
1 day = 24 hours (hr)	1 week (wk) = 7 days
1 year (yr) = 12 months	1 year (yr) = 365 days

Example 25: Convert 4 hours to minutes.

Solution: Multiply 4 hours by the unit conversion factor $\dfrac{60\ min}{1\ hr}$.

$\left(\dfrac{4\ hr}{1}\right)\left(\dfrac{60\ min}{1\ hr}\right)$ Reducing out the units of hours we get

$\left(\dfrac{4\ \cancel{hr}}{1}\right)\left(\dfrac{60\ min}{1\ \cancel{hr}}\right)$.   Then, since 4(60 min) = 240 min, the answer is **240 minutes**.

Now try problem 113 from exercise set 1.3.

Example 26: Convert 5 hours to seconds.

Solution: We can solve this problem by multiplying together several unit conversion factors.

$$\left(\frac{5\ hr}{1}\right)\left(\frac{60\ min}{1\ hr}\right)\left(\frac{60\ sec}{1\ min}\right)$$ Reducing out units common to the numerator and the denominator we get

$$\left(\frac{5\ \cancel{hr}}{1}\right)\left(\frac{60\ \cancel{min}}{1\ \cancel{hr}}\right)\left(\frac{60\ sec}{1\ \cancel{min}}\right).$$ Then, since $5(60)(60\ sec) = 18{,}000$ sec, the answer is **18,000 seconds**.

Now try problem 127 from exercise set 1.3.

Example 27: Convert $5 per pound to cents per ounce.

Solution: We can solve this problem by multiplying together several unit conversion factors.

$$\left(\frac{\$5}{1\ lb}\right)\left(\frac{100¢}{\$1}\right)\left(\frac{1\ lb}{16\ oz}\right)$$ Reducing out units common to the numerator and the denominator we get

$$\left(\frac{\cancel{\$}5}{1\ \cancel{lb}}\right)\left(\frac{100¢}{\cancel{\$}1}\right)\left(\frac{1\ \cancel{lb}}{16\ oz}\right).$$ Then, since $(5)(100) = 500$ and using long division,

$$16\overline{)500.00}^{\ 31.25}$$, the answer is **31.25 cents per ounce**.

Example 28: Convert 15 miles per hour to feet per second.

Solution: We can solve this problem by multiplying together several unit conversion factors.

$$\left(\frac{15\ miles}{1\ hr}\right)\left(\frac{5{,}280\ ft}{1\ mile}\right)\left(\frac{1\ hr}{60\ min}\right)\left(\frac{1\ min}{60\ sec}\right)$$ Reducing out units common to the numerator and the denominator we get

$$\left(\frac{15\ \cancel{miles}}{1\ \cancel{hr}}\right)\left(\frac{5{,}280\ ft}{1\ \cancel{mile}}\right)\left(\frac{1\ \cancel{hr}}{60\ \cancel{min}}\right)\left(\frac{1\ \cancel{min}}{60\ sec}\right).$$ Then, since $(15)(5{,}280) = 79{,}200$ and $(60)(60) = 3{,}600$

using long division, $3{,}600\overline{)79{,}200}^{\ 22}$, the answer is **22 feet per second**.

Now try problem 145 from exercise set 1.3.

Note: In the last two examples above, we needed to change units in both the numerator and the denominator of the original fraction. As before, if the unit we are trying to eliminate is in the <u>numerator</u> of the original quantity, then that same unit must be in the <u>denominator</u> of the unit conversion factor in order for the "like" units to reduce out properly. If, however, the unit we are trying to eliminate is in the <u>denominator</u> of the original quantity, then that same unit must be in the <u>numerator</u> of the unit conversion factor in order for the "like" units to reduce out properly.

<u>Section 3 exercises.</u> Make the following conversions in the American system using the appropriate unit conversion factors.

1.   3.5 ft to inches

2.   7.5 ft to inches

3.   45 in. to feet

4.   51 in. to feet

5. $7\frac{2}{3}$ ft to inches

6. $5\frac{1}{4}$ ft to inches

7.   48 in. to feet

8.   60 in. to feet

9. $4\frac{1}{2}$ yd to feet

10. $5\frac{1}{2}$ yd to feet

11.   47 ft to yards

12.   58 ft to yards

13.   3 mi to feet

14.   4 mi to feet

15.   9,240 ft to miles

16.   11,880 ft to miles

17.   3.6 yd to inches

18.   4.8 yd to inches

19.   126 in. to yards

20.   162 in. to yards

21.   2 mi to yards

22.   5 mi to yards

23.   7,920 yd to miles

24.   5,720 yd to miles

25. $\frac{1}{2}$ mi to inches

26. $\frac{1}{4}$ mi to inches

27.   126,720 in. to miles

28.   190,080 in. to miles

29. $3\,\text{ft}^2$ to square inches

30. $4\,\text{ft}^2$ to square inches

31.   828 in.^{2} to square feet   **32.**   504 in.^{2} to square feet

33.   6.2 yd^2 to square feet   **34.**   7.8 yd^2 to square feet

35.   25 ft^2 to square yards   **36.**   34 ft^2 to square yards

37. $2\frac{1}{2}$ yd^2 to square inches   **38.** $3\frac{1}{2}$ yd^2 to square inches

39.   5,508 in.^{2} to square yards   **40.**   7,452 in.^{2} to square yards

41.   5.2 mi^2 to acres   **42.**   4.6 mi^2 to acres

43.   1,664 acres to square miles   **44.**   1,152 acres to square miles

45.   1.1 acres to square yards   **46.**   2.1 acres to square yards

47.   3 acres to square feet   **48.**   5 acres to square feet

49.   3 ft^3 to cubic inches   **50.**   4 ft^3 to cubic inches

51.   6 yd^3 to cubic feet   **52.**   5 yd^3 to cubic feet

53.   81 ft^3 to cubic yards   **54.**   135 ft^3 to cubic yards

55. $7\frac{2}{3}$ c to fluid ounces   **56.** $4\frac{1}{3}$ c to fluid ounces

57.   24 fl oz to cups   **58.**   40 fl oz to cups

59.   5 pt to cups   **60.**   7 pt to cups

61.   15 c to pints

62.   25 c to pints

63. $4\frac{7}{8}$ qt to pints

64. $3\frac{3}{8}$ qt to pints

65.   6 pt to quarts

66.   10 pt to quarts

67. $1\frac{1}{2}$ gal to quarts

68. $5\frac{1}{2}$ gal to quarts

69.   15 qt to gallons

70.   25 qt to gallons

71. $2\frac{1}{2}$ pt to fl oz

72. $4\frac{1}{2}$ pt to fl oz

73.   40 fl oz to pints

74.   72 fl oz to pints

75.   2.5 qt to cups

76.   3.5 qt to cups

77.   22 c to quarts

78.   18 c to quarts

79.   2 gal to pints

80.   3 gal to pints

81.   42 pt to gallons

82.   20 pt to gallons

83.   3 qt to fluid ounces

84.   2 qt to fluid ounces

85.   100 fl oz to quarts

86.   120 fl oz to quarts

87. $4\frac{1}{8}$ gal to cups

88. $3\frac{5}{8}$ gal to cups

89.   40 c to gallons

90.   52 c to gallons

91.   3 gal to fluid ounces

92.   2 gal to fluid ounces

93.   192 fl oz to gallons

94.   288 fl oz to gallons

95. $3\dfrac{1}{3}$ lb to ounces

96. $5\dfrac{2}{3}$ lb to ounces

97.   4.8 lb to ounces

98.   6.4 lb to ounces

99.   42 oz to pounds

100.   54 oz to pounds

101.   1.7 T to pounds

102.   0.8 T to pounds

103.   4,500 lb to tons

104.   6,800 lb to tons

105.   2 T to ounces

106.   4 T to ounces

107.   56,000 oz to tons

108.   38,400 oz to tons

109.   15 min to seconds

110.   20 min to seconds

111.   480 sec to minutes

112.   240 sec to minutes

113.   2.4 hr to minutes

114.   3.6 hr to minutes

115.   200 min to hours

116.   400 min to hours

117.   3 days to hours

118.   7 days to hours

119.   30 hr to days

120.   40 hr to days

121.   6 wk to days

122.   4 wk to days

123. $4\dfrac{1}{2}$ yr to months

124. $2\dfrac{1}{4}$ yr to months

125.   17 months to years

126.   19 months to years

127. $3\frac{1}{2}$ hr to seconds

128. $2\frac{1}{3}$ hr to seconds

129.   4,680 sec to hours

130.   10,440 sec to hours

131. $\frac{1}{2}$ day to minutes

132. $1\frac{1}{2}$ days to minutes

133.   2,520 min to days

134.   3,168 min to days

135. $3\frac{1}{4}$ wk to hours

136. $5\frac{1}{3}$ wk to hours

137.   1 day to seconds

138.   2 days to seconds

139.   103,680 sec to days

140.   155,520 sec to days

141.   2 wk to minutes

142.   3 wk to minutes

143.   0.5 wk to seconds

144.   2.5 wk to seconds

145.   Convert 60 miles per hour to feet per second.

146.   Convert 30 miles per hour to feet per second.

147.   Convert 66 feet per second to miles per hour.

148.   Convert 22 feet per second to miles per hour.

149.   Which is a faster rate of speed, 70 miles per hour or 100 feet per second?

150.   Which is a faster rate of speed, 28 miles per hour or 42 feet per second?

151.   Convert 32 pounds per square inch to tons per square foot.

152.   Convert 65 pounds per square inch to tons per square foot.

153.   Convert 1 ton per square foot to pounds per square inch.

154.   Convert 2 tons per square foot to pounds per square inch.

155.   Which is a greater amount of pressure, 30 pounds per square inch or 2 tons per square foot?

156.   Which is the greater amount of pressure, 40 pounds per square inch or 3 tons per square foot?

157.   Convert 30 miles per gallon to feet per pint.

158.   Convert 26 miles per gallon to feet per pint.

159.   Convert 18 inches per cup to yards per quart.

160.   Convert 45 inches per cup to yards per quart.

161.   Which represents more distance per volume, 45 feet per quart or 8 yards per pint?

162.   Which represents more distance per volume, 21 feet per quart or 3 yards per pint?

163.   Which is a better buy, $\frac{1}{2}$ gallon of ice cream for $2.65 or 5 quarts of ice cream for $6.99?

164.   Which is a better buy, $\frac{1}{2}$ gallon of orange sherbet for $2.39 or 3 quarts of orange sherbet for $3.49?

165.   Which is a better buy, 64 ounces of ketchup for $4.39 or a 2-pack of ketchup totaling 6 pounds 5 ounces for $6.99?

166.   Which is a better buy, 72 ounces of mayonnaise for $5.69 or a 2-pack of mayonnaise totaling 7 pounds 8 ounces for $8.99?

167.   Which is a better buy, 5 pounds of coffee for $12.50 or 3 ounces of the same coffee for 49¢?

168.   Which is a better buy, 8 pounds of jellybeans for $19.12 or 5 ounces of the same jelly beans for 79¢?

169.   At the track meet on Saturday, Tom participated in the long jump event. His three jumps were 21 feet 8 inches, 19 feet 6 inches, and 20 feet 7 inches. What is the total distance of his three jumps?

170.   At the track meet on Saturday, Mark participated in the high jump event. His three jumps were 6 feet 10 inches, 7 feet 5 inches, and 6 feet 11 inches. What is the total height of his three jumps?

171.   A set of triplets had the following birth weights. Tammy weighed 3 pounds 7 ounces, Tracy weighed 4 pounds 5 ounces, and Teresa weighed 3 pounds 8 ounces. What was their total birth weight?

172.   Jake purchased three different kinds of meat at the local deli. He bought 1 pound 6 ounces of ham, 2 pounds 4 ounces of turkey, and 1 pound 7 ounces of roast beef. What was the total weight of his meat order?

173.   2 pieces are cut from a board that is 10 feet in length. The first piece is 1 foot 8 inches long and the second piece is 1 foot 6 inches long. What is the length of the remaining piece of board?

174.   2 pieces are cut from a chain that is 8 feet in length. The first piece is 3 feet 7 inches long and the second piece is 2 feet 9 inches long. What is the length of the remaining piece of chain?

175.   Ben buys a gallon of vanilla ice cream and eats 1 quart and 1 pint of it. Then his daughter Jessica eats 1 pint and 1 cup of it. Finally his son Sean eats 1 quart and 1 cup of it. How many 1-cup servings are left for his wife Sue to eat?

176.   Anthony buys a gallon of milk at the store. If he drinks 1 quart for breakfast, then 1 pint for lunch and finally 1 quart and 1 cup for dinner, how many cups of milk should still be left in the container?

177.   How many 6 fluid ounce servings are in $2\frac{1}{4}$ gallons of apple juice?

178.   How many 8 fluid ounce servings are in $3\frac{1}{2}$ gallons of orange juice?

179.   If each member of a family of 4 were to drink the entire contents of a 6 fluid ounce juice box per day during lunch, what would be the total amount of juice drunk from juice boxes by the family in 1 week? Give the answer in gallons.

180.   If each member of a family of 5 were to drink 3 cups of tea per day, what would be the total amount of tea drunk by the family in 1 week? Give the answer in gallons.

Find the perimeter and area of each figure.

181.

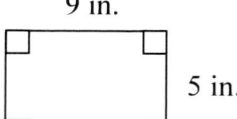

9 in.

5 in.

182.

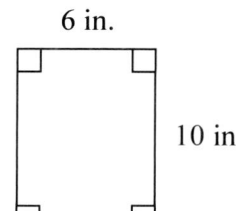

6 in.

10 in.

183.

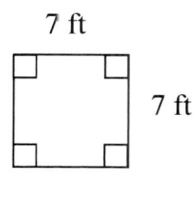

7 ft

7 ft

184.

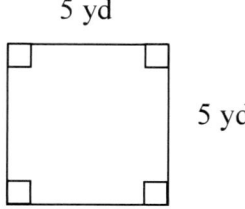

5 yd

5 yd

185.

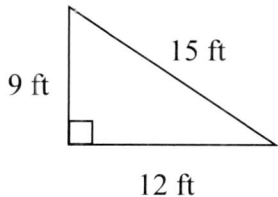

15 ft

9 ft

12 ft

186.

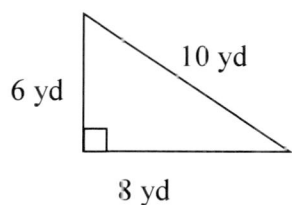

10 yd

6 yd

8 yd

187.

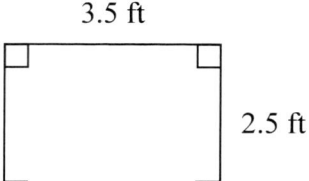

3.5 ft

2.5 ft

188.

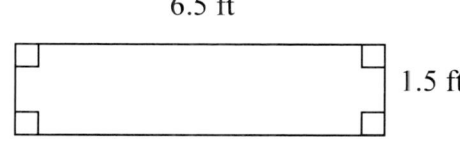

6.5 ft

1.5 ft

189.

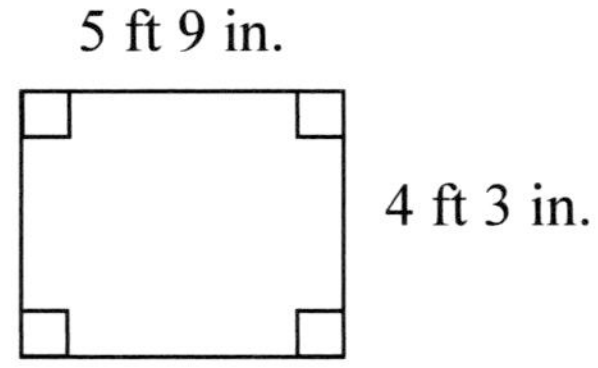

5 ft 9 in.

4 ft 3 in.

190.

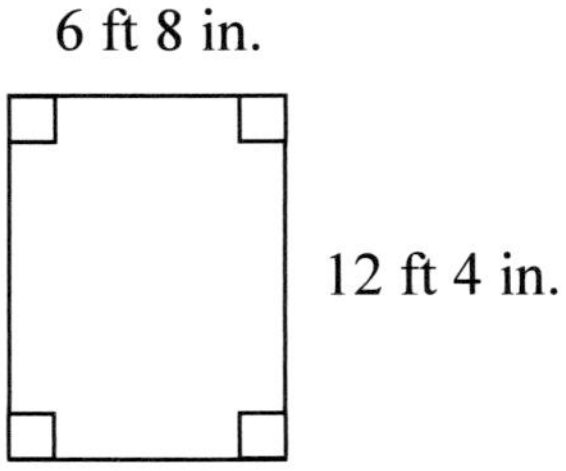

6 ft 8 in.

12 ft 4 in.

191.

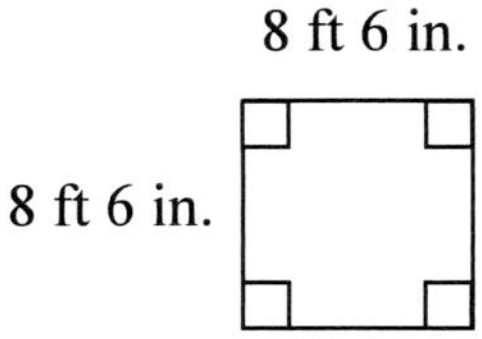

8 ft 6 in.

8 ft 6 in.

192.

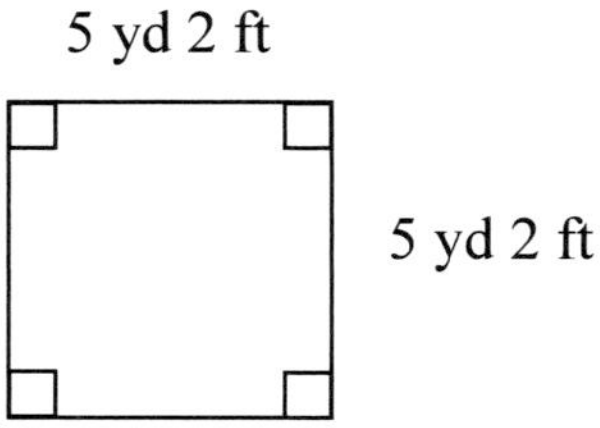

5 yd 2 ft

5 yd 2 ft

193.

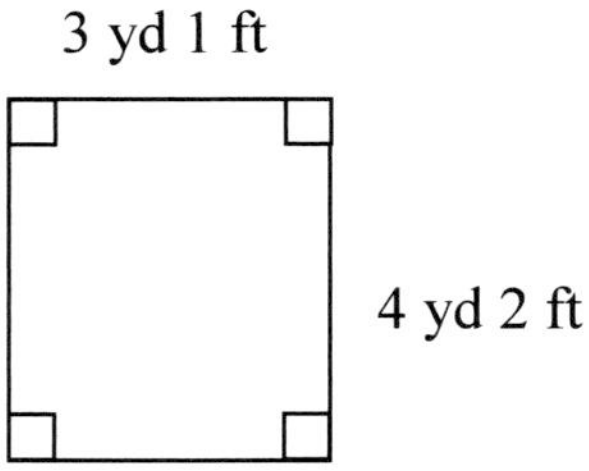

3 yd 1 ft

4 yd 2 ft

194.

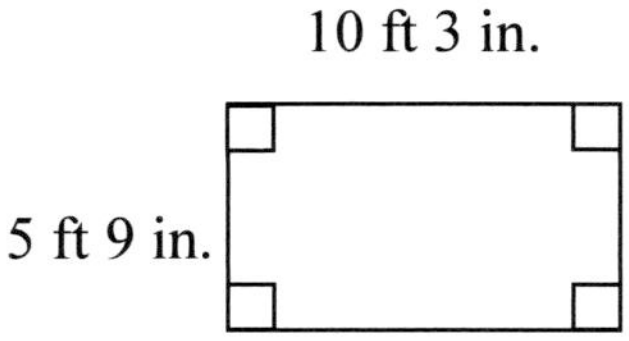

10 ft 3 in.

5 ft 9 in.

195.

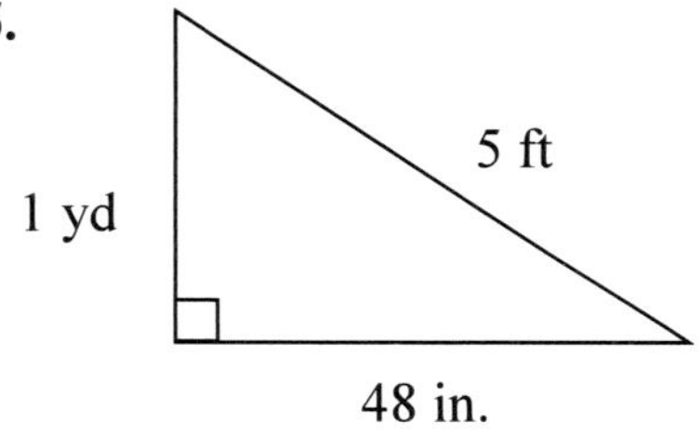

5 ft

1 yd

48 in.

196.

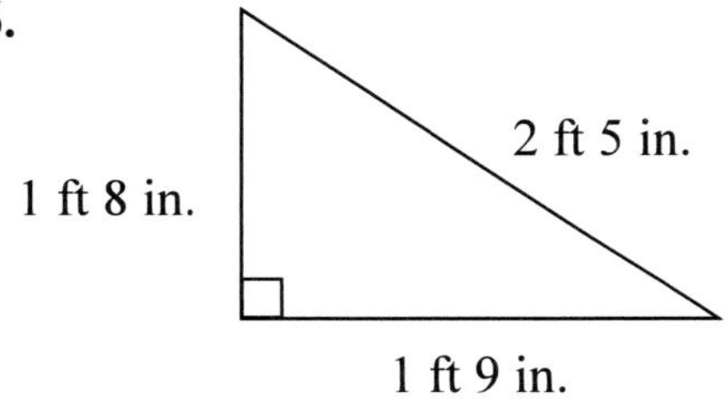

2 ft 5 in.

1 ft 8 in.

1 ft 9 in.

Find the circumference and area of each circle. Give the exact answers and the approximations using the fact that $\pi \approx 3.14$.

197.

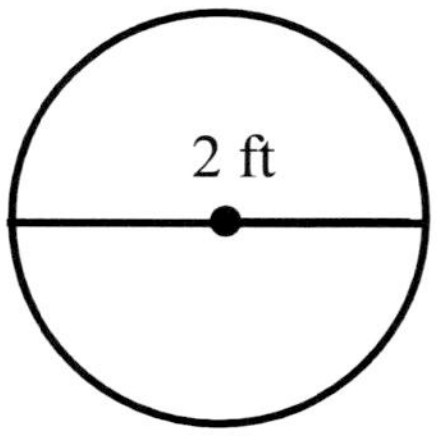

2 ft

198.

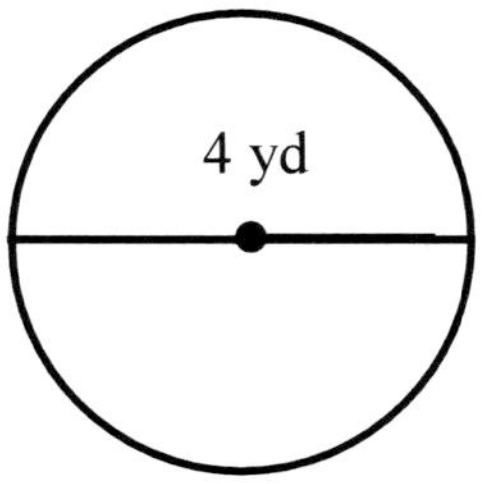

4 yd

199.

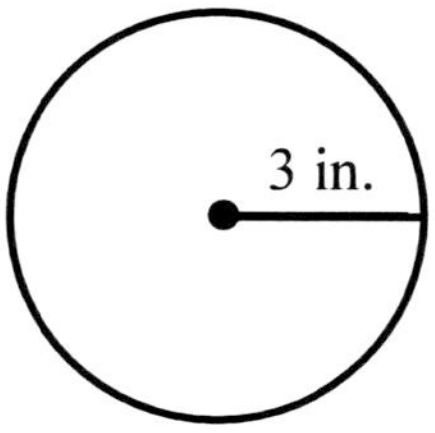

3 in.

200.

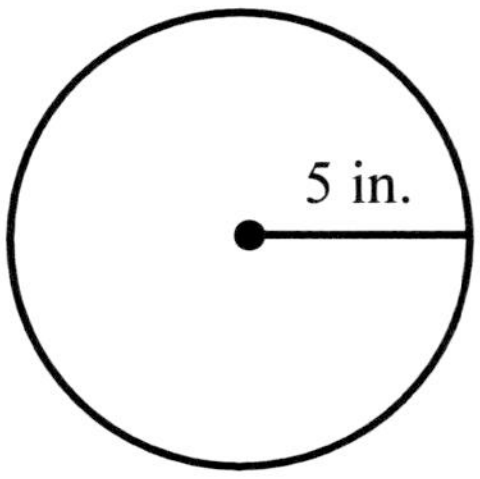

5 in.

Find the surface area and volume of each figure.

201.

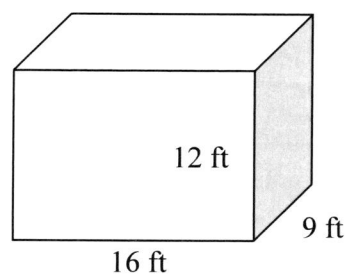

12 ft
16 ft
9 ft

202.

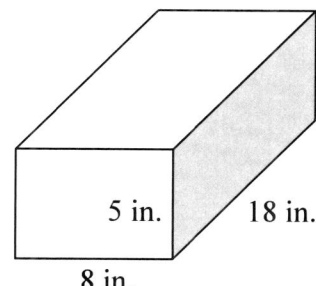

5 in.   18 in.
8 in.

203.

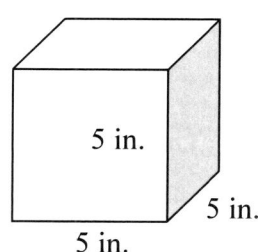

5 in.
5 in.
5 in.

204.

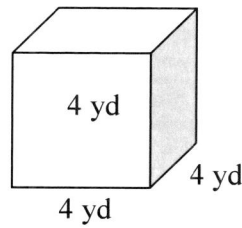

4 yd
4 yd
4 yd

205.

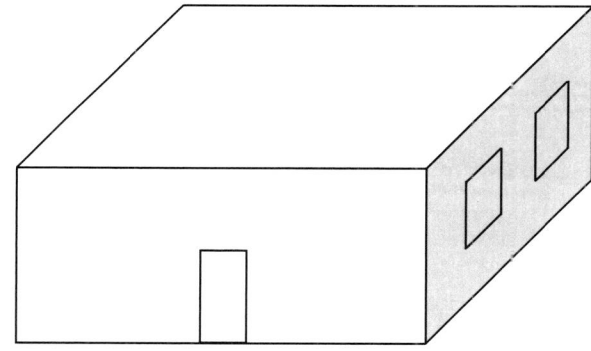

An interior designer is redecorating a room that is 22 feet long by 16 feet wide by 8 feet high. At one end of the room is a door that is 6 feet 6 inches high and 4 feet wide. One of the walls contains 2 windows, each of which is 2 feet wide by 2 feet 6 inches high.

a)   How much will it cost to carpet the floor if the carpet sells for $18.00 a square yard?

b)   How much will it cost to wallpaper all four walls if wallpaper costs $0.75 per square foot? (Hint: It's generally considered a bad idea to cover a door or windows with wallpaper.)

c)   How much will it cost to paint the ceiling using paint that sells for $25 per gallon if a quart of paint will cover 88 square feet?

d)   What will be the cost of the entire project?

206.

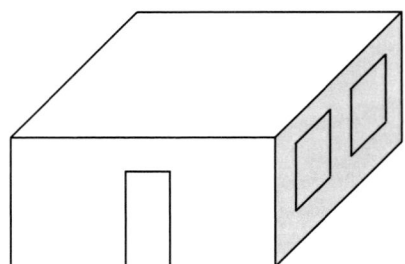

An interior designer is redecorating a room that is 24 feet long by 14 feet wide by 8 feet high. At one end of the room is a door that is 6 feet 6 inches high and 4 feet wide. One of the walls contains 2 windows, each of which is 2 feet wide by 3 feet 6 inches high.

a) How much will it cost to carpet the floor if the carpet sells for $15.00 a square yard?

b) How much will it cost to wallpaper all four walls if wallpaper costs $0.75 per square foot? (Hint: It's generally considered a bad idea to cover a door or windows with wallpaper.)

c) How much will it cost to paint the ceiling using paint that sells for $28 per gallon if a quart of paint will cover 42 square feet?

d) What will be the cost of the entire project?

207. Pete's Pizza Parlor sells pizzas with diameters of 14 inches, 16 inches and 18 inches. Assuming that all pizzas at Pete's are the same thickness and have the same amount of toppings per square inch:

a) Which is the best buy for the money, the 14-inch pizza for $7.49, the 16-inch pizza for $9.49 or the 18-inch pizza for $12.49? (Use the fact that $\pi \approx 3.14$ to make your calculations.)

b) Which pizza is the most expensive per square inch? (Use the fact that $\pi \approx 3.14$ to make your calculations.)

208. Polly's Pizzeria sells pizzas with diameters of 14 inches, 16 inches and 18 inches. Assuming that all pizzas at Polly's are the same thickness and have the same amount of toppings per square inch:

a) Which is the best buy for the money, the 14-inch pizza for $11.99, the 16-inch pizza for $15.89 or the 18-inch pizza for $17.14? (Use the fact that $\pi \approx 3.14$ to make your calculations.)

b) Which pizza is the most expensive per square inch? (Use the fact that $\pi \approx 3.14$ to make your calculations.)

209. What is the approximate area of a circle enclosed by a piece of rope 37.68 inches long? (Use the fact that $\pi \approx 3.14$ to make your calculations.)

210. What is the width of a rectangle that has an area of 27 ft^2 and a length of 6 feet?

RATIOS, PROPORTIONS, & MEASUREMENTS

Section 4: Measurements (Metric Units)

The American system of measurement is based on the system used by the British. Most of the rest of the world, however, uses what is known as the **metric system**. This system was developed many years ago in France. Unlike the American or British systems, the metric system bases everything on the number 10.

In the metric system, the basic unit of <u>**length**</u> is called a **meter (m)**. A meter is slightly longer than 1 yard, or about 39 inches in length. All units of length in the metric system are based on the meter. Prefixes are used in combination with the word meter to name the different units of length.

The prefix **kilo (k)** means 1,000, so a **kilometer (km)** is 1,000 meters.

The prefix **hecto (h)** means 100, so a **hectometer (hm)** is 100 meters.

The prefix **deka (da)** means 10, so a **dekameter (dam)** is 10 meters.

The prefix **deci (d)** means $\frac{1}{10}$ or 0.1, so a **decimeter (dm)** is $\frac{1}{10}$ meter or 0.1 meter.

The prefix **centi (c)** means $\frac{1}{100}$ or 0.01, so a **centimeter (cm)** is $\frac{1}{100}$ or 0.01 meter.

The prefix **milli (m)** means $\frac{1}{1,000}$ or 0.001, so a **millimeter (mm)** is $\frac{1}{1,000}$ or 0.001 meter.

Metric units of length work together in the following ways:

METRIC UNITS OF LENGTH		
1 kilometer (km) = 1,000 meters	therefore,	1 meter = $\frac{1}{1,000}$ kilometer
1 hectometer (hm) = 100 meters	therefore,	1 meter = $\frac{1}{100}$ hectometer
1 dekameter (dam) = 10 meters	therefore,	1 meter = $\frac{1}{10}$ dekameter
1 decimeter (dm) = $\frac{1}{10}$ meter	therefore,	1 meter = 10 decimeters
1 centimeter (cm) = $\frac{1}{100}$ meter	therefore,	1 meter = 100 centimeters
1 millimeter (mm) = $\frac{1}{1,000}$ meter	therefore,	1 meter = 1,000 millimeters

Note: The abbreviation for deka is "da" while the abbreviation for deci is "d." The abbreviation for milli is "m" and the abbreviation for meter is also "m." This is not a problem however, because a metric prefix will not be by itself as a unit. In other words, 12 m will always mean 12 meters and 12mm will always mean 12 millimeters.

Because everything in the metric system is based on the number 10, converting units in the metric system is much easier than in the American system. There are **TWO METHODS** of converting units that will be discussed in this section.

METHOD 1 (Using unit conversion factors)

As was discussed previously in the section on American units of measure, unit conversion factors can be used to change one metric unit of length or distance into another. Since all the different metric units of measure are compared to meters in the chart above, it is easiest to use unit conversion factors that involve meters.

Example 1: Convert 15 hectometers to centimeters.

Solution: To convert from hectometers to centimeters we will use two unit conversion factors. First, we will use the fact that 1 hectometer = 100 meters. Second, we will use the fact that 1 meter = 100 centimeters. Now we can solve this problem by multiplying together several unit conversion factors.

$$\left(\frac{15\ hm}{1}\right)\left(\frac{100\ m}{1\ hm}\right)\left(\frac{100\ cm}{1\ m}\right)$$

$$\left(\frac{15\ hm}{1}\right)\left(\frac{100\ m}{1\ hm}\right)\left(\frac{100\ cm}{1\ m}\right).$$ Since <u>multiplying a number by 100 results in</u>

<u>moving the decimal point of the number two places to the right</u>, and since the 15 is being multiplied by 2 factors of 100, the decimal point ends up being moved a total of 4 places to the right and the resulting product is **150,000 centimeters**.

Now try problem 25 from exercise set 1.4.

Example 2: Convert 2,500 decimeters to kilometers.

Solution: To convert from decimeters to kilometers we will use two unit conversion factors. First we will use the fact that 1 meter = 10 decimeters. Second we will use the fact that 1 kilometer = 1,000 meters. Now we can solve this problem by multiplying together several unit conversion factors.

$$\left(\frac{2,500\ dm}{1}\right)\left(\frac{1\ m}{10\ dm}\right)\left(\frac{1\ km}{1,000\ m}\right)$$

$$\left(\frac{2,500\ dm}{1}\right)\left(\frac{1\ m}{10\ dm}\right)\left(\frac{1\ km}{1,000\ m}\right).$$ Reducing further we get

$$\left(\frac{2,500\ dm}{1}\right)\left(\frac{1\ m}{10\ dm}\right)\left(\frac{1\ km}{1,000\ m}\right).$$ Since <u>dividing a number by 100 results in moving the</u>

<u>decimal point of the number two places to the left</u>, the resulting quotient is **0.25 kilometers**.

Now try problem 27 from exercise set 1.4.

In the metric system the basic unit of **mass** is called a **gram (g)**. Most often we refer to the weight of an object rather than its mass. The difference is that the mass of an object remains constant because it is based on the amount of matter it contains. Weight, on the other hand, is affected by the Earth's gravity. If a person (such as an astronaut) travels away from the Earth, his or her weight changes because of a decrease in the Earth's gravitational pull on them. Their mass however, remains constant. Because most of us remain fairly close to the Earth, we will use the terms weight and mass interchangeably. A gram is much smaller than an American ounce. There are about 28.35 grams in an ounce. All units of weight in the metric system are based on the gram. Prefixes are used in combination with the word gram to name the different units of weight. Conveniently, they are the same prefixes used for length.

Metric units of weight work together in the following ways:

METRIC UNITS OF WEIGHT

1 kilogram (kg) = 1,000 grams	therefore,	1 gram = $\frac{1}{1,000}$ kilogram
1 hectogram (hg) = 100 grams	therefore,	1 gram = $\frac{1}{100}$ hectogram
1 dekagram (dag) = 10 grams	therefore,	1 gram = $\frac{1}{10}$ dekagram
1 decigram (dg) = $\frac{1}{10}$ gram	therefore,	1 gram = 10 decigrams
1 centigram (cg) = $\frac{1}{100}$ gram	therefore,	1 gram = 100 centigrams
1 milligram (mg) = $\frac{1}{1,000}$ gram	therefore,	1 gram = 1,000 milligrams

---

Example 3: Convert 8.7 dekagrams to milligrams.

Solution: To convert from dekagrams to milligrams we will use two unit conversion factors. First, we will use the fact that 1 dekagram = 10 grams. Second, we will use the fact that 1 gram = 1,000 milligrams. Now we can solve this problem by multiplying together several unit conversion factors.

$$\left(\frac{8.7 \; dag}{1}\right)\left(\frac{10 \; g}{1 \; dag}\right)\left(\frac{1,000 \; mg}{1 \; g}\right)$$

$$\left(\frac{8.7 \; \cancel{dag}}{1}\right)\left(\frac{10 \; \cancel{g}}{1 \; \cancel{dag}}\right)\left(\frac{1,000 \; mg}{1 \; \cancel{g}}\right).$$ Since multiplying a number by 10 results in

moving the decimal point of the number one place to the right, and since multiplying a number by 1,000 results in moving the decimal point of the number three places to the right, the decimal point ends up being moved a total of 4 places to the right and the resulting product is **87,000 milligrams**.

In the metric system the basic unit of **volume** is called a **liter (L)**. A liter is related to metric length in that a cube measuring 10 cm on each side holds exactly 1 liter. 1 liter is a little more than a quart. Units of volume in the metric system are based on the liter or on units of length expressed in three dimensions, such as cubic centimeters. Prefixes are used in combination with the word liter to name the different units of volume. Conveniently, they are the same prefixes used for length and weight.

Metric units of volume work together in the following ways:

METRIC UNITS OF VOLUME

1 kiloliter (kL) = 1,000 liters   therefore,   1 liter = $\frac{1}{1,000}$ kiloliter

1 hectoliter (hL) = 100 liters   therefore,   1 liter = $\frac{1}{100}$ hectoliter

1 dekaliter (daL) = 10 liters   therefore,   1 liter = $\frac{1}{10}$ dekaliter

1 deciliter (dL) = $\frac{1}{10}$ liter   therefore,   1 liter = 10 deciliters

1 centiliter (cL) = $\frac{1}{100}$ liter   therefore,   1 liter = 100 centiliters

1 milliliter (mL) = $\frac{1}{1,000}$ liter   therefore,   1 liter = 1,000 milliliters

---

Note: A capital L is used to abbreviate liter so as not to confuse it with the number 1.

Example 4: Convert 2.5 liters to centiliters.

Solution: To convert from liters to centiliters we will use the fact that 1 liter = 100 centiliters.

$$\left(\frac{2.5\ L}{1}\right)\left(\frac{100\ cL}{1\ L}\right)$$

$$\left(\frac{2.5\ \cancel{L}}{1}\right)\left(\frac{100\ cL}{1\ \cancel{L}}\right).$$ Since multiplying a number by 100 results in

moving the decimal point of the number two place to the right, the resulting product is **250 centiliters**.

Now try problem 7 from exercise set 1.4.

Note: Sometimes the word "capacity" is used instead of volume, to describe units of measure like kiloliters, liters, milliliters, etc.

Example 5: How many 200-milliliter servings are in 2 liters of apple juice?

Solution: To determine the number of servings we must divide 2 liters by 200 milliliters. To do this, first we must have both quantities in the same units. So, we will convert 2 liters to milliliters using the fact that 1 liter = 1,000 milliliters.

$$\left(\frac{2\,L}{1}\right)\left(\frac{1,000\,mL}{1\,L}\right)$$

$$\left(\frac{2\,\cancel{L}}{1}\right)\left(\frac{1,000\,mL}{1\,\cancel{L}}\right).$$ Since <u>multiplying a number by 1,000 results in</u>

<u>moving the decimal point of the number three place to the right</u>, the resulting product is **2,000 milliliters**.

Now we can divide 2,000 milliliters by 200 milliliters. Using long division, $200\overline{)2,000}$ with quotient 10. So, **the number of 200-milliliter servings of apple juice is 10**.

Now try problem 105 from exercise set 1.4.

As with American units of area, metric units of area also come in square units. These work together in the following ways:

METRIC UNITS OF AREA MEASURED IN SQUARE UNITS

$$1\,cm^2 = 100\,mm^2 \qquad 1\,dm^2 = 100\,cm^2 \qquad 1\,m^2 = 100\,dm^2$$

$$1\,are\,(a) = 100\,m^2 \qquad 1\,hectare\,(ha) = 100\,a$$

Example 6: How many square meters are in 2.4 hectares?

Solution: To convert from hectares to square meters we will use two unit conversion factors. First, we will use the fact that 1 hectare = 100 ares. Second, we will use the fact that 1 are = 100 square meters. Now we can solve this problem by multiplying together several unit conversion factors.

$$\left(\frac{2.4\,ha}{1}\right)\left(\frac{100\,a}{1\,ha}\right)\left(\frac{100\,m^2}{1\,a}\right)$$

$$\left(\frac{2.4\,\cancel{ha}}{1}\right)\left(\frac{100\,\cancel{a}}{1\,\cancel{ha}}\right)\left(\frac{100\,m^2}{1\,\cancel{a}}\right).$$ Since <u>multiplying a number by 100 results in</u>

<u>moving the decimal point of the number two places to the right</u>, and since the 2.4 is being multiplied by 2 factors of 100, the decimal point ends up being moved a total of 4 places to the right and the resulting product is **24,000 square meters or 24,000 m²**.

Now try problem 37 from exercise set 1.4.

As with American units of volume, metric units of volume also come in cubic units. These work together in the following ways:

METRIC UNITS OF VOLUME MEASURED IN CUBIC UNITS

$$1 \text{ cm}^3 = 1,000 \text{ mm}^3 \qquad 1 \text{ dm}^3 = 1,000 \text{ cm}^3 \qquad 1 \text{ m}^3 = 1,000 \text{ dm}^3$$

Example 7: How many cubic centimeters are in 4 cubic meters?

Solution: To convert from cubic meters to cubic centimeters we will use two unit conversion factors. First, we will use the fact that 1 cubic meter = 1,000 cubic decimeters. Second, we will use the fact that 1 cubic decimeter = 1,000 cubic centimeters. Now we can solve this problem by multiplying together several unit conversion factors.

$$\left(\frac{4 \ m^3}{1} \right)\left(\frac{1,000 \ dm^3}{1 \ m^3} \right)\left(\frac{1,000 \ cm^3}{1 \ dm^3} \right)$$

$$\left(\frac{4 \ \cancel{m^3}}{1} \right)\left(\frac{1,000 \ \cancel{dm^3}}{1 \ \cancel{m^3}} \right)\left(\frac{1,000 \ cm^3}{1 \ \cancel{dm^3}} \right). \qquad \text{Since \underline{multiplying a number by 1,000 results in}}$$

\underline{moving the decimal point of the number three places to the right}, and since the 4 is being multiplied by 2 factors of 1,000, the decimal point ends up being moved a total of 6 places to the right and the resulting product is **4,000,000 cubic centimeters or 4,000,000 cm^3**.

Now try problem 41 from exercise set 1.4.

Note: In the metric system, units of length, units of weight and units of volume are interrelated in the following ways. 1 cubic centimeter (cc) of water weighs 1 gram and 1 cubic centimeter (cc) of volume is equal to 1 milliliter of volume.

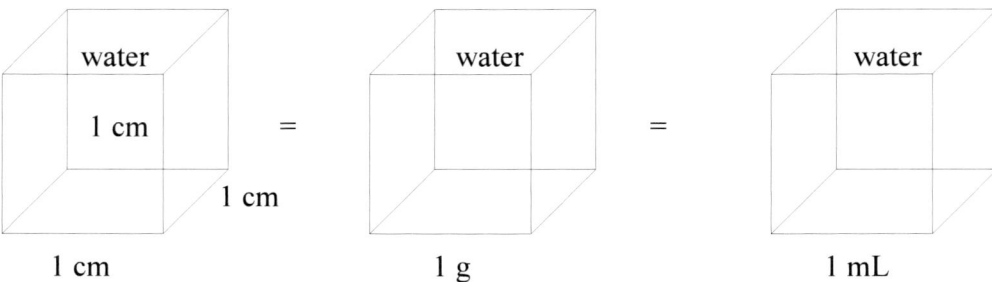

Note: Based on the above information we get the following. 1cc = 1 mL.

METHOD 2 (Moving the decimal point)

Because everything in the metric system is based on the number 10, unit conversions can be made within the metric system just by moving the decimal point. We can determine the appropriate number of places to move the decimal point by using the following chart:

km hm dam m dm cm mm

Example 8: Convert 35 hectometers to decimeters.

Solution: To convert from one unit to another, move the decimal point the same number of places and in the same direction as you move on the chart. For instance, to go from hm to dm on the chart, you move 3 places to the right.

km   hm   dam   m   dm   cm   mm
      1   2   3

Likewise, to convert 35 hm to dm, you move the decimal point 3 places to the right.

35 hm or 35. 0 0 0 hm becomes **35,000 dm.**
        1 2 3

Now try problem 59 from exercise set 1.4.

Example 9: Convert 842 millimeters to kilometers.

Solution: To go from mm to km on the chart, you move 6 places to the left.

km   hm   dam   m   dm   cm   mm
 6   5   4   3   2   1

Likewise, to convert 842 mm to km, you move the decimal point 6 places to the left.

842 mm or 0 0 0 0 8 4 2. mm becomes **0.000842 km.**
      6 5 4 3 2 1

Now try problem 71 from exercise set 1.4.

Note: Remember that a whole number has an implied decimal point to the right of the last digit, that is, the digit in the "ones" column. For example, 12 is the same as 12. whether the decimal point is written out or not.

The idea of moving the decimal point can be used on units involving liters and grams as well.

<u>Example 10:</u> Convert 46.8 dekaliters to milliliters.

Solution: To go from daL to mL on the chart, you move 4 places to the right.

     kL   hL   daL   L   dL   cL   mL

              1   2   3   4

Likewise, to convert 46.8 daL to mL, you move the decimal point 4 places to the right.

46.8 daL or 46. 8 0 0 0 daL becomes **468,000 mL**.

            1 2 3 4

Now try problem 57 from exercise set 1.4.

<u>Example 11:</u> Convert 50,000 centiliters to liters.

Solution: To go from cL to L on the chart, you move 2 places to the left.

     kL   hL   daL   L   dL   cL   mL

                       2   1

Likewise, to convert 50,000 cL to L, you move the decimal point 2 places to the left.

50,000 cL or 50, 0 0 0 cL becomes **500 L**.

            2 1

<u>Example 12:</u> Convert 17.34 kilograms to grams.

Solution: To go from kg to g on the chart, you move 3 places to the right.

     kg   hg   dag   g   dg   cg   mg

              1   2   3

Likewise, to convert 17.34 kg to g, you move the decimal point 3 places to the right.

17.34 kg or 17. 3 4 0 kg becomes **17,340 g**.

            1 2 3

Now try problem 73 from exercise set 1.4.

Section 4 exercises. Make the following conversions in the metric system using the appropriate unit conversion factors (Method 1).

1.   42 dm to centimeters

2.   63 km to hectometers

3.   65.7 daL to deciliters

4.   23.4 hL to liters

5.   0.098 kg to grams

6.   0.086 cg to dekagrams

7.   4,780 m to dekameters

8.   5,780 dam to hectometers

9.   0.3 hL to kiloliters

10.   0.8 mL to centiliters

11.   16 kg to dekagrams

12.   45 g to centigrams

13.   12,300 mm to meters

14.   34,500 hm to decimeters

15.   8.906 kL to centiliters

16.   7.084 hL to milliliters

17.   2.6 cg to milligrams

18.   8.3 g to decigrams

19.   34.65 m to hectometers

20.   23.68 dm to dekameters

21.   3.14 kL to deciliters

22.   2.71 mL to dekaliters

23.   486 dg to milligrams

24.   597 dag to kilograms

25.   0.007 dam to centimeters

26.   0.006 m to millimeters

27.   40.404 mL to hectoliters

28.   58.585 cL to kiloliters

29.   5,713 hg to dekagrams

30.   2,340 dag to grams

31.   1 cm to meters

32.   10 mm to decimeters

33.   28 cL to hectoliters

34.   54 cL to deciliters

35.   75,000 mm^2 to dm^2 **36.**   4.37 m^2 to cm^2

37.   0.36 a to dm^2 **38.**   25,650 m^2 to ha

39.   600,000 mm^3 to dm^3 **40.**   55,000 cm^3 to m^3

41.   0.0056 m^3 to cm^3 **42.**   1.74 dm^3 to mm^3

On problems 43 and 44 use the fact that 1 metric ton (t) = 1,000 kilograms.

43.   2.6 t to kilograms   **44.**   45,000 kg to metric tons

Make the following conversions in the metric system by moving the decimal point (Method 2).

45.   2 kL to hectoliters   **46.**   9 dL to centiliters

47.   74 hm to meters   **48.**   83 dam to decimeters

49.   4.05 cg to dekagrams   **50.**   6.02 kg to grams

51.   5,692 daL to hectoliters   **52.**   1,100 L to dekaliters

53.   0.0045 mm to centimeters   **54.**   0.0061 hm to kilometers

55.   764,892 g to centigrams   **56.**   168,487 kg to dekagrams

57.   354 hL to deciliters   **58.**   630 mL to liters

59.   31 hm to millimeters   **60.**   64 km to centimeters

61.   296 g to decigrams   **62.**   549 cg to milligrams

63.   69.273 dL to dekaliters   **64.**   37.369 L to hectoliters

65.   2,360 mm to dekameters   **66.**   1,265 km to decimeters

67. 29 dag to kilograms

68. 52 dg to milligrams

69. 77.7 L to milliliters

70. 88.4 daL to centiliters

71. 510 cm to kilometers

72. 590 mm to hectometers

73. 123 dag to grams

74. 511 hg to dekagrams

75. 942.6 mL to deciliters

76. 846.3 cL to liters

77. 7,915.9 cm to decimeters

78. 7,546.3 cm to hectometers

79. 5 hg to centigrams

80. 8 kg to milligrams

81. 35.87 mL to kiloliters

82. 20.43 dL to liters

83. 9,652 m to kilometers

84. 1,112 dm to hectometers

85. 4.39 dg to kilograms

86. 6.28 dag to milligrams

On problems 87-90 use the fact that 1 cubic centimeter (cc) = 1 milliliter.

87. 50 mL to cubic centimeters

88. 125 mL to cubic centimeters

89. 12,000 cc to liters

90. 8,500 cc to liters

Application Problems: Solve each of the following problems using either method.

91. A bottle of pain reliever contains 500 tablets weighing 200 mg each. What is the total weight of the tablets in kilograms?

92. A bottle of pain reliever contains 400 tablets weighing 220 mg each. What is the total weight of the tablets in kilograms?

93. If a box containing 34 graham crackers weighs 0.459 kg, how many grams does 1 graham cracker weigh?

94. If a box containing 1 dozen cookies weighs 0.216 kg, how many grams does 1 cookie weigh?

95.   A can of diced tomatoes contains 380 mg of sodium. How many grams of sodium is this?

96.   A can of tuna contains 18 g of protein. How many milligrams of protein is this?

97.   A can of enchilada sauce contains $4\frac{1}{2}$ servings. If one serving contains 270 mg of sodium, how many grams of sodium are in the entire can?

98.   A can of tomato soup contains 2.5 servings. If one serving contains 740 mg of sodium, how many grams of sodium are in an entire can?

99.   A bottle of nasal spray has a net fill weight of 5.1 g. If the bottle contains 60 sprays, what is the weight of each spray in milligrams?

100.   A bottle of nasal spray has a net fill weight of 10 g. If the bottle contains 40 sprays, what is the weight of each spray in milligrams?

101.   A bottle of saline nasal spray contains 45 mL of solution. How many liters of solution is this?

102.   A bottle of contact lens conditioning solution contains 120 mL of solution. How many liters of solution is this?

103.   If a rope 3 m long is cut into 25 equal pieces, how many centimeters long is each piece?

104.   If a cord 4 m long is cut into 50 equal pieces, how many centimeters long is each piece?

105.   How many 20 dL servings are in a 2-liter bottle of root beer?

106.   How many liters of water are in a 750-milliliter bottle?

107.   How many hectares are contained within a square piece of land that has a side of 1 hectometer?

108.   How many hectares are contained within a square piece of land that has a side of 50 meters?

Find the perimeter and area of each figure.

109.

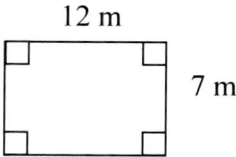

12 m

7 m

110.

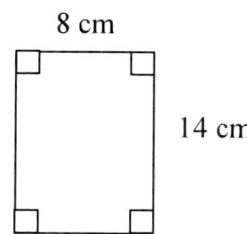

8 cm

14 cm

111.

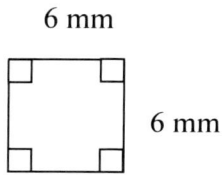

6 mm

6 mm

112.

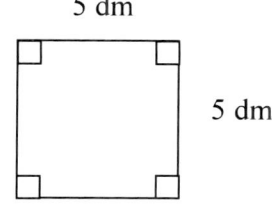

5 dm

5 dm

113.

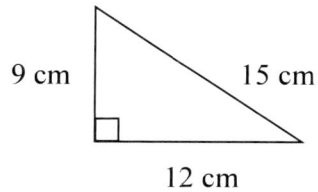

9 cm

15 cm

12 cm

114.

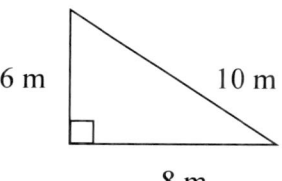

6 m

10 m

8 m

115.

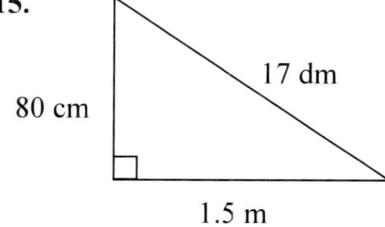

17 dm

80 cm

1.5 m

116.

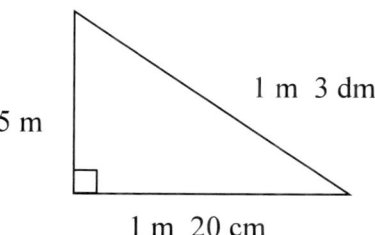

1 m 3 dm

0.5 m

1 m 20 cm

Find the circumference and area of each circle. Give the exact answers and the approximations using the fact that $\pi \approx 3.14$.

117.

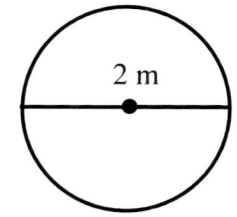

2 m

118.

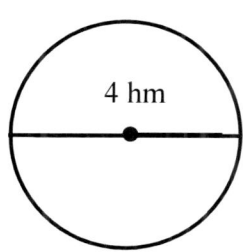

4 hm

119.   **120.**

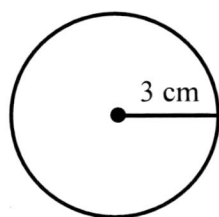   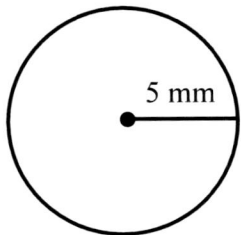

Find the surface area in units of square meters and the volume in units of cubic centimeters for each figure.

121.   **122.**

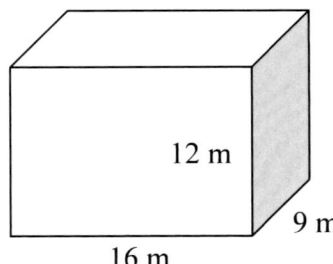   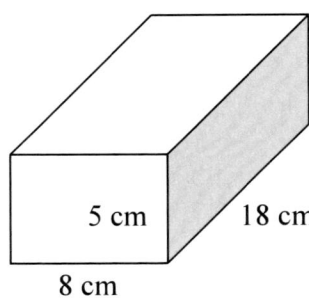

123.   **124.**

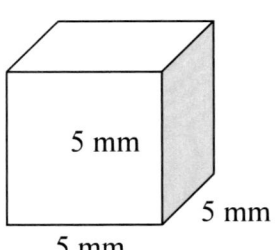   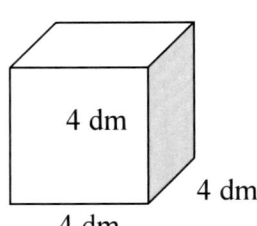

Writing:

125.   Describe how to make a chart like the one on the top of page 73 that could be used to convert from one square unit in the metric system to another. Explain how moves on the chart would correspond to moves of the decimal point and why this is so.

126.   Describe how to make a chart like the one on the top of page 73 that could be used to convert from one cubic unit in the metric system to another. Explain how moves on the chart would correspond to moves of the decimal point and why this is so.

RATIOS, PROPORTIONS, & MEASUREMENTS

Section 5: Metric-American Conversions

Until the United States switches to using the metric system entirely, it will be necessary to convert back and forth between the two systems. While some information is easy to use, such as 1 inch = 2.54 centimeters, other information is more cumbersome, such as 1 mile = 1.609344 kilometers. Because of this, we will round information between the two systems to the nearest hundredth or the nearest thousandth when appropriate. Also, when we use unit conversion factors between the two systems, we will round final answers to the nearest hundredth. To go back and forth between units of length we will use the following information:

LENGTH	
American to Metric	Metric to American
1 mi ≈ 1.61 km	1 km ≈ 0.62 mi
1 yd ≈ 0.91 m	1 m ≈ 1.09 yd
1 ft ≈ 0.30 m	1 m ≈ 3.28 ft
1 in. = 2.54 cm	1 cm ≈ 0.39 in.

Note: Recall that the symbol ≈ means, "is approximately equal to."

Example 1: Convert 3 miles to kilometers.

Solution: Since converting from miles to kilometers is going from American units to metric units, we will use the fact that $1 \text{ mi} \approx 1.61 \text{ km}$.

$\left(\dfrac{3 \, mi}{1}\right)\left(\dfrac{1.61 \, km}{1 \, mi}\right)$ Reducing out units common to the numerator and the denominator we get

$\left(\dfrac{3 \, \cancel{mi}}{1}\right)\left(\dfrac{1.61 \, km}{1 \, \cancel{mi}}\right)$.   Then, 3(1.61 km) ≈ 4.83 km. In this case, rounding the final answer to the nearest hundredth isn't necessary.

Thus, we get the following:

3 miles ≈ 4.83 km

Now try problem 49 from exercise set 1.5.

Note: We could use the fact that $1 \text{ km} \approx 0.62 \text{ mi}$ to set up the problem like this,

$\left(\dfrac{3 \, mi}{1}\right)\left(\dfrac{1 \, km}{0.62 \, mi}\right)$. **Then, however, we would have to divide 3 by 0.62 instead of multiplying 3 by 1.61. Generally it is easier to multiply than divide. Be sure to pay special attention to whether we are converting from American to metric or from metric to American, and then use the chart accordingly.**

Example 2: Convert 7 feet to centimeters.

Solution: Since converting from feet to centimeters is going from American units to metric units, we will use information on the left side of the "LENGTH" chart. However, we can't get directly from feet to centimeters with this chart. We must either go from feet to meters and then from meters to centimeters or from feet to inches and then from inches to centimeters. We will explore both options. First, we will go from feet to meters and then from meters to centimeters.

$$\left(\frac{7\,ft}{1}\right)\left(\frac{0.30\,m}{1\,ft}\right)\left(\frac{100\,cm}{1\,m}\right)$$ Reducing out units common to the numerator and the denominator we get

$$\left(\frac{7\,ft}{1}\right)\left(\frac{0.30\,m}{1\,ft}\right)\left(\frac{100\,cm}{1\,m}\right).$$ Then, $7(0.30) \approx 2.1$.

Next, since <u>multiplying a number by 100 results in moving the decimal point of the number two places to the right</u>, $2.1(100\,cm) \approx 210\,cm$. In this case, rounding the final answer to the nearest hundredth isn't necessary. Thus, we get the following:

7 feet $\approx$ 210 centimeters

Now let's do the same conversion but this time go from feet to inches and then from inches to centimeters.

$$\left(\frac{7\,ft}{1}\right)\left(\frac{12\,in.}{1\,ft}\right)\left(\frac{2.54\,cm}{1\,in.}\right)$$ Reducing out units common to the numerator and the denominator we get

$$\left(\frac{7\,ft}{1}\right)\left(\frac{12\,in.}{1\,ft}\right)\left(\frac{2.54\,cm}{1\,in.}\right).$$ Then $7(12) = 84$. Next, $84(2.54\,cm) \approx 213.36$ cm.

Again, rounding the final answer to the nearest hundredth isn't necessary.
Thus, we get the following:

7 feet $\approx$ 213.36 centimeters

Make note of a couple of things. First, the answers were slightly different. This is because the information we used had been rounded. Both answers are considered correct, depending on which way you try to solve the problem. Secondly, it was easier to do the problem the first way rather than the second way. This is because it is easier to work in the metric system than in the American system. As a rule of thumb, when converting to the metric system, get to the metric system as soon as possible and when converting from the metric system stay in the metric system as long as possible.

Now try problem 63 from exercise set 1.5.

Example 3: Convert 4 meters to feet.

Solution: Since converting from meters to feet is going from metric units to American units, we will use the fact that $1 \, m \approx 3.28 \, ft$.

$\left(\dfrac{4 \, m}{1} \right) \left(\dfrac{3.28 \, ft}{1 \, m} \right)$ Reducing out units common to the numerator and the denominator we get

$\left(\dfrac{4 \, \cancel{m}}{1} \right) \left(\dfrac{3.28 \, ft}{1 \, \cancel{m}} \right)$.   Then, $4(3.28 \, ft) \approx 13.12 \, ft$. Rounding the final answer to the nearest hundredth isn't necessary.

Thus, we get the following:

4 meters $\approx$ 13.12 feet

Now try problem 51 from exercise set 1.5.

Example 4: Convert 6 kilometers to feet.

Solution: Since converting from kilometers to feet is going from metric units to American units, we will use information on the right side of the "LENGTH" chart. However, we can't get directly from feet to centimeters with this chart. We must either go from kilometers to meters and then from meters to feet or from kilometers to miles and then from miles to feet. The first choice is the best because it involves only one conversion involving the American system.

$\left(\dfrac{5 \, km}{1} \right) \left(\dfrac{1{,}000 \, m}{1 \, km} \right) \left(\dfrac{3.28 \, ft}{1 \, m} \right)$ Reducing out units common to the numerator and the denominator we get

$\left(\dfrac{5 \, \cancel{km}}{1} \right) \left(\dfrac{1{,}000 \, \cancel{m}}{1 \, \cancel{km}} \right) \left(\dfrac{3.28 \, ft}{1 \, \cancel{m}} \right)$.   Then, $6(3.28 \, ft) \approx 19.68 \, ft$.

Next, since <u>multiplying a number by 1,000 results in moving the decimal point of the number three places to the right</u>, $(19.68 \, ft)(1{,}000) \approx 19{,}680 \, ft$. In this case, rounding the final answer to the nearest hundredth isn't necessary.

Thus, we get the following:

6 kilometers $\approx$ 19,680 feet

Now try problem 57 from exercise set 1.5.

To go back and forth between units of weight we will use the following information:

<table>
<tr><td colspan="2" align="center">**WEIGHT**</td></tr>
<tr><td align="center">American to Metric</td><td align="center">Metric to American</td></tr>
<tr><td align="center">1 lb ≈ 0.454 kg</td><td align="center">1 kg ≈ 2.20 lb</td></tr>
<tr><td align="center">1 oz ≈ 28.35 g</td><td align="center">1 g ≈ 0.035 oz</td></tr>
</table>

Example 5: Convert 12.4 grams to ounces.

Solution: Since converting from grams to ounces is going from metric units to American units, we will use the fact that $1 \text{ g} \approx 0.035 \text{ oz}$.

$$\left(\frac{12.4 \ g}{1}\right)\left(\frac{0.035 \ oz}{1 \ g}\right)$$ Reducing out units common to the numerator and the denominator we get

$$\left(\frac{12.4 \ \cancel{g}}{1}\right)\left(\frac{0.035 \ oz}{1 \ \cancel{g}}\right).$$ Then, $12.4(0.035 \text{ oz}) \approx 0.434 \text{ oz}$. Rounding the final answer to the nearest hundredth, we get the following: **12.4 grams ≈ 0.43 ounces**

Now try problem 67 from exercise set 1.5.

Example 6: Convert 5 pounds to grams.

Solution: Since converting from pounds to grams is going from American units to metric units, we will use the left side of the "WEIGHT" chart. However, we can't get directly from pounds to grams with this chart. We must either go from pounds to ounces and then from ounces to grams or from pounds to kilograms and then from kilograms to grams. The second choice is the best because it involves only one conversion involving the American system.

$$\left(\frac{5 \ lb}{1}\right)\left(\frac{0.454 \ kg}{1 \ lb}\right)\left(\frac{1{,}000 \ g}{1 \ kg}\right)$$ Reducing out units common to the numerator and the denominator we get

$$\left(\frac{5 \ \cancel{lb}}{1}\right)\left(\frac{0.454 \ \cancel{kg}}{1 \ \cancel{lb}}\right)\left(\frac{1{,}000 \ g}{1 \ \cancel{kg}}\right).$$ Then, $5(0.454) \approx 2.27$. Next, since <u>multiplying a number by 1,000 results in moving the decimal point of the number three places to the right,</u>

$$(2.27)(1{,}000 \text{ g}) \approx 2{,}270 \text{ g}.$$

In this case, rounding the final answer to the nearest hundredth isn't necessary. Thus, we get the following: **5 pounds ≈ 2,270 grams**

Now try problem 71 from exercise set 1.5.

To go back and forth between units of volume we will use the following information:

VOLUME	
American to Metric	Metric to American
1 gal ≈ 3.785 L	1 L ≈ 0.264 gal
1 qt ≈ 0.946 L	1 L ≈ 1.06 qt
1 pt ≈ 0.473 L	1 L ≈ 2.1 pt
1 fl oz ≈ 0.030 L	1 L ≈ 33.8 fl oz

Example 7: Convert 3 quarts to centiliters.

Solution: Since converting from quarts to centiliters is going from American units to metric units, we will use the left side of the "VOLUME" chart. However, we can't get directly from quarts to centiliters with this chart. We will go from quarts to liters and then from liters to centiliters.

$$\left(\frac{3\,qt}{1}\right)\left(\frac{0.946\,L}{1\,qt}\right)\left(\frac{100\,cL}{1\,L}\right)$$ Reducing out units common to the numerator and the denominator we get

$$\left(\frac{3\,qt}{1}\right)\left(\frac{0.946\,L}{1\,qt}\right)\left(\frac{100\,cL}{1\,L}\right).$$ Then, $3(0.946) \approx 2.838$. Next, since <u>multiplying a number by 100 results in moving the decimal point of the number two places to the right</u>, $(2.838)(100\,cL) \approx 283.8\,cL$.

In this case, rounding the final answer to the nearest hundredth isn't necessary. Thus, we get the following: **3 quarts ≈ 283.8 centimeters**

Now try problem 77 from exercise set 1.5.

Example 8: How many 8-ounce servings of fruit punch can be made from 4 liters of fruit punch?

Solution: In order to determine the number of 8-ounce servings in 4 liters, we will need to divide 4 liters by 8 ounces. To do this we must get the same units for both quantities. We can either change ounces into liters or change liters into ounces. We will change ounces into liters. Since converting from ounces to liters is going from American units to metric units, we will use the fact that $1\,fl\,oz \approx 0.030\,L$.

$$\left(\frac{8\,fl\,oz}{1}\right)\left(\frac{0.030\,L}{1\,fl\,oz}\right)$$ Reducing out units common to the numerator and the denominator we get

$$\left(\frac{8\,fl\,oz}{1}\right)\left(\frac{0.030\,L}{1\,fl\,oz}\right).$$ Then, $8(0.030\,L) \approx 0.24\,L$. Using long division $0.24\,L\overline{)4\,L}$

becomes $24\,L\overline{)400\,L}$ with $16.\overline{6}$. Rounding the final answer to the nearest hundredth, we get the following: **The number of 8-ounce servings of fruit punch in 4 liters of fruit punch is approximately 16.67.**

Now try problem 101 from exercise set 1.5.

Our final topic of discussion for this section is temperature. The American system uses the **Fahrenheit** scale to measure temperature. On the Fahrenheit scale, water boils at 212 degrees and freezes at 32 degrees. When writing a temperature using the Fahrenheit scale, we follow the number with a degree symbol and a capital F. Thus, 40 degrees Fahrenheit is written 40°F.

The metric system uses the **Celsius** scale to measure temperature. On the Celsius scale, water boils at 100 degrees and freezes at 0 degrees. When writing a temperature using the Celsius scale, we follow the number with a degree symbol and a capital C. Thus 12 degrees Celsius is written 12°C.

This gives us the following equivalencies: 212°F = 100°C and 32°F = 0°C. From this information, using math that is a bit beyond the scope of this course, we arrive at the following formulas that are used to convert back and forth between temperatures in the two systems.

TEMPERATURE

Fahrenheit to Celsius   Celsius to Fahrenheit

$$C = \frac{5(F-32)}{9}$$ $$F = \frac{9}{5}C + 32$$

F is the temperature in degrees Fahrenheit
and C is the temperature in degrees Celsius.

Note: Converting temperatures between the two systems is exact, so we don't need to round the final answers.

Example 9: Convert 65°F to Celsius.

Solution: To convert from Fahrenheit to Celsius we use the formula on the left side of the "TEMPERATURE" chart.

$C = \dfrac{5(F-32)}{9}$ Since 65°F is our starting temperature,
65 is substituted in the place of F in the formula.

$C = \dfrac{5\big((65)-32\big)}{9}$ Following order of operations,
simplify the numerator of the fraction.

First, subtract inside the parentheses: $65-32=33$

$C = \dfrac{5(33)}{9}$ Then multiply: $5(33)=165$

$C = \dfrac{165}{9}$ Now, divide the numerator of the fraction by the denominator.

$9\overline{)165.0}$ = $18.\overline{3}$ Thus, we get the following:

65 degrees Fahrenheit equals 18.$\overline{3}$ degrees Celsius or 65°F equals 18.$\overline{3}$°C.

Now try problem 89 from exercise set 1.5.

Example 10: Convert 78°C to Fahrenheit.

Solution: To convert from Celsius to Fahrenheit we use the formula on the right side of the "TEMPERATURE" chart.

$$F = \frac{9}{5}C + 32$$

Since 78°C is our starting temperature, 78 is substituted in the place of C in the formula.

$$F = \frac{9(78)}{5} + 32$$

Multiply: 9(78) = 702

$$F = \frac{702}{5} + 32$$

Then, divide the numerator of the fraction by the denominator.

$$\begin{array}{r} 140.4 \\ 5)\overline{702.0} \end{array}$$

$$F = 140.4 + 32$$

Now add: 140.4 + 32 = 172.4

Thus, we get the following:

78 degrees Celsius equals 172.4 degrees Fahrenheit or 78°C equals 172.4°F.

Now try problem 91 from exercise set 1.5.

Section 5 exercises.

For each of the following problems, choose which one is the greater distance.

1.   A yard or a meter?   **2.**   A meter or a foot?

3.   An inch or a centimeter?   **4.**   A kilometer or a mile?

For each of the following problems, choose which one is the greater weight.

5.   A pound or a kilogram?   **6.**   A gram or an ounce?

For each of the following problems, choose which one is the greater volume.

7.   A cup or a milliliter?   **8.**   A pint or a milliliter

9.   A pint or a liter?   **10.**   A liter or a quart?

11.   A gallon or a liter?   **12.**   A gallon or a kiloliter?

For each of the following problems, choose which temperature is most appropriate for the given scenario.

13.   A cold winter's day: 25°F or 25°C?

14.   A hot summer's day: 35°F or 35°C

15.   Baking brownies in an oven: 350°C or 350°F

16.   Chilling water in a refrigerator: 2°C or 2°F

17.   Heating water for hot chocolate: 60°F or 60°C

18.   Water in a swimming pool: 76°F or 76°C

For each of the following problems, choose the measurement that best approximates the given distance.

19.	The length of a pencil:	18 mm	18 cm	180 cm
20.	The length of a credit card:	8.5 mm	8.5 cm	85 cm
21.	The diameter of a basketball:	220 mm	2.2 cm	220 cm
22.	The diameter of a baseball:	67 cm	6.7 mm	67 mm
23.	The length of a baseball bat:	7.2 cm	72 cm	7.2 m
24.	The length of a skateboard:	720 mm	720 cm	72 mm
25.	The height of a doorway:	200 mm	20 cm	2 m
26.	The height of a refrigerator:	170 mm	1.7 cm	1.7 m
27.	The width of your little finger:	1.5 mm	15 mm	15 cm
28.	The width of a pencil:	80 cm	8 cm	8 mm

For each of the following problems, choose the measurement that best approximates the given weight.

29.	The weight of a can of oranges:	300 mg	300 g	300 kg
30.	The weight of a can of beans:	450 mg	450 g	450 kg
31.	The weight of an aspirin tablet:	500 mg	500 g	5 kg
32.	The weight of a penny:	2.5 mg	2.5 g	2.5 kg

33.   The weight of a train engine: 64,000 mg   6,400 g   640,000 kg

34.   The weight of a dump truck: 3,100 mg   3,100 g   3,100 kg

For each of the following problems, choose the measurement that best approximates the given volume.

35.   The volume of a car's gas tank: 700 mL   70 L   7 kL

36.   The volume of water in a bathtub: 150 L   150 kL   150 mL

37.   The volume of a can of soda: 35 mL   350 mL   3,500 mL

38.   The volume of a quart of milk: 95 mL   95 L   0.95 L

39.   The volume of water in a raindrop: 0.03 mL   3 mL   0.3 L

40.   The volume of a dose of cough medicine: 5 mL   50 mL   500 mL

For each of the following problems, choose the measurement that best approximates the given temperature.

41.   The temperature of a snowman: − 5°C   5°C   50°C

42.   The temperature of hot bath water: − 5°C   5°C   50°C

43.   The temperature for baking a cake: 350°C   180°C   100°C

44.   The temperature of boiling water: 0°C   100°C   212°C

45.   The temperature of a boy with a mild fever: 99°C   38°C   42°C

46.   The temperature inside of a freezer: −18°C   0°C   18°C

Make the following approximate conversions from the American system to the metric system or from the metric system to the American system. Round answers to the nearest hundredth, if necessary.

47.   4 m to yards

48.   4 yd to meters

49.   5.5 mi to kilometers

50.   5.5 km to miles

51.   17 m to feet

52.   17 ft to meters

53.   26 in. to centimeters

54.   26 cm to inches

55.   2.3 mi to meters

56.   2,300 m to miles

57.   150 cm to yards

58.   1.5 yd to centimeters

59.   4,500 ft to kilometers

60.   4.5 km to feet

61.   4.6 m to inches

62.   46 in. to meters

63.   2 ft to centimeters

64.   40 cm to feet

65.   6 lb to kilograms

66.   6 kg to pounds

67.   120 g to ounces

68.   12 oz to grams

69.   50 oz to kilograms

70.   5 kg to ounces

71.   2.7 lb to grams

72.   2,700 g to pounds

73.   3 gal to liters

74.   30 L to gallons

75.   7 L to quarts

76.   7 qt to liters

77.   6 pt to liters

78.   6 L to pints

79.   12 L to fluid ounces   80.   400 fl oz to liters

81.   2 gal to milliliters   82.   20,000 mL to gallons

83.   42 dL to quarts   84.   4.2 qt to deciliters

85.   60 pt to dekaliters   86.   6 dekaliters to pints

87.   8 hL to fluid ounces   88.   8,000 fl oz to hectoliters

89.   78°F to Celsius   90.   65°C to Fahrenheit

91.   46.2°C to Fahrenheit   92.   18.4°F to Celsius

93.   −16°F to Celsius   94.   −26°C to Fahrenheit

95.   −8.4°C to Fahrenheit   96.   −4.8°F to Celsius

Application Problems: Solve each of the following problems. Round answers to the nearest hundredth, if necessary.

97.   Many cameras use 35 mm film. Convert 35 millimeters to inches.

98.   A typical extra-large pizza is 16 inches in diameter. What is the diameter in centimeters?

99.   Convert 55 miles per hour to kilometers per hour.

100.   Convert 120 kilometers per hour to miles per hour.

101.   A party punch recipe calls for 6 quarts of lemon-lime soda. How many 2-liter bottles of lemon-lime soda must be purchased to have enough for the punch?

102.   A recipe calls for 3 cups of oil. How many milliliters of oil is this?

103.   Which is a better buy, 9 ounces of cookies for $2.00 or 300 grams of the same kind of cookies for $2.29?

104.   Which is a better buy, 5 pounds of cheese for $12.99 or 3 kilograms of the same kind of cheese for $16.99?

105.   Convert 60 miles per hour to meters per second.

106.   Convert 60 kilometers per hour to feet per second.

107.   A runner ran 1 mile in 4 minutes and 48 seconds. A second runner ran 1,600 meters in 4 minutes and 50 seconds. Who ran at the fastest rate?

108.   A carpentry job calls for the use of a ¼ inch drill bit. However, the carpenter's drill bits are a metric set. The set contains 6.30 mm, 6.35 mm, and 6.40 mm sized bits. Which one is closest to the size she needs?

109.   If a car gets 25 miles per gallon of gasoline, how many kilometers per liter of gasoline would it get?

110.   If a truck gets 12 kilometers per liter of gasoline, how many miles per gallon of gasoline would it get?

111.   Use the fact that 1 milliliter of water weighs 1 gram to determine the weight of a gallon of water in pounds.

112.   Use the fact that 1 milliliter of water weighs 1 gram to determine the weight of a fluid ounce of water in ounces.

113.   Convert the following saying to the American system. 28.35 grams of prevention is worth 0.454 kilograms of cure.

114.   Convert the following saying to the American system. Give them 2.54 centimeters and they'll take 1.61 kilometers.

115.   Convert the following slogan to the American system. I'd like a 0.1135 kilogrammer with cheese.

116.   Convert the following song lyrics to the American system. Ya take 14,528 kilograms and what do you get? Another day older and deeper in debt.

For the following figures, give the perimeter in centimeters and the area in square inches. Round answers to the nearest hundredth, if necessary.

117.

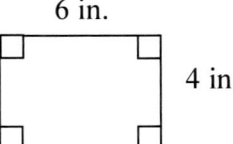

6 in.

4 in.

118.

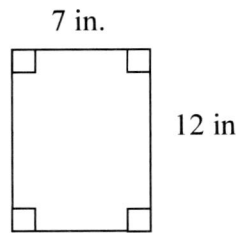

7 in.

12 in.

119.

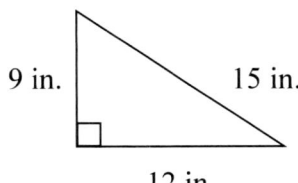

9 in.   15 in.

12 in.

120.

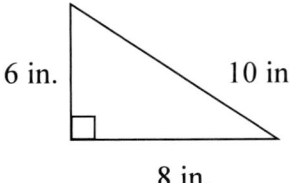

6 in.   10 in.

8 in.

For the following circles, approximate the circumference in meters and the area in square feet. Use the fact that $\pi \approx 3.14$. Round answers to the nearest hundredth, if necessary.

121.

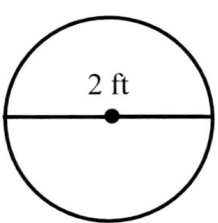

2 ft

122.

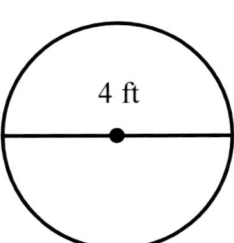

4 ft

Writing:

123.   The instructions on a pizza box say "bake at 400 degrees for 20 minutes." Do you think these instructions are in Fahrenheit or Celsius? Explain your reasoning.

124.   Your friend calls and says to come over and go swimming because it's 35 degrees in the shade. Do you think your friend means Fahrenheit or Celsius? Explain your reasoning.

RATIOS, PROPORTIONS, & MEASUREMENTS

Chapter Review

Section 1: Ratios and Rates

Review Exercises: Write each ratio as a fraction in lowest terms.

1.   0.3 to $\frac{1}{3}$

2. $\frac{3}{7}$ to $1\frac{2}{7}$

3.   4 inches to 3 feet

Write each rate as a fraction in lowest terms.

4.   6.5 inches of rain in 3 days

5.   \$3 per $2\frac{1}{4}$ cups

Write each expression as a unit rate.

6.   17 dogs in 5 kennels

7.   9 states in 4 days

8.   Paul shredded 78 confidential documents in 6 minutes while working as an undercover spy. What was his shredding rate in documents per hour?

9.   Joyce painted 5 window frames in 4 hours while earning money for college. What was her painting rate in window frames per hour? What was her painting rate in hours per window frame?

10.   If it takes 12.3 minutes to empty a 75-gallon bathtub, what is the rate of flow of water to the nearest tenth of a gallon per minute?

Write the expression as a unit price.

11.   7 quarts sell for \$23.59

12.

a)   Find the unit price of each item, rounding answers to the nearest tenth of a cent.

b)   Determine the best buy by comparing the results.

Rice:

5 lb for $2.99

10 lb for $5.29

25 lb for $13.39

Section 2: Proportions

Review Exercises: For the following proportion, identify which quantities are the extremes and which quantities are the means.

13. $\dfrac{\frac{3}{5}}{1.5} = \dfrac{1\frac{2}{5}}{3.5}$

Determine whether the following equations are proportions.

14. $\dfrac{7.2}{3.6} = \dfrac{2.46}{1.24}$ **15.** $\dfrac{4\frac{1}{5}}{4} = \dfrac{3}{2\frac{6}{7}}$

Solve for the variable in the following proportions.

16. $\dfrac{x}{1\frac{1}{3}} = \dfrac{3\frac{1}{2}}{2\frac{4}{5}}$ **17.** $\dfrac{4.2}{3.6} = \dfrac{-3.5}{x}$

List three other ways that the following proportion could be correctly written.

18. $\dfrac{13\ gallons}{7\ hours} = \dfrac{x}{12\ hours}$

Application Problems: Translate each of the following word problems into a proportion. Then, solve the proportion in order to answer the question.

19.   Calvin's Concrete Company supplied a contractor with 8 cubic yards of concrete at a cost of $692. Assuming they charge the same rate per cubic yard regardless of the amount of concrete supplied, what would they charge for 22 cubic yards of concrete?

20.   If a 28-gram serving of breakfast cereal contains 1.6 grams of fat, then how many grams of fat are in a box containing 350 grams of the same breakfast cereal?

21.   A recipe for sugar cookies calls for $1\frac{3}{4}$ cups of flour for every $1\frac{1}{2}$ cups of sugar. How many cups of sugar are needed if $2\frac{1}{3}$ cups of flour are used?

22.   The scale on a map indicates that 1 inch on the map corresponds to an actual distance of 35 miles. If two cities are approximately 3.2 inches apart on the map, then what is the actual distance between them?

Find the unknown lengths for the pair of similar triangles.

23.

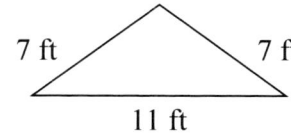   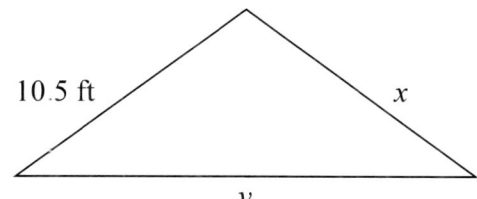

24.   If a 63-foot tree casts a 90-foot shadow, how tall is a tree that casts a 40-foot shadow?

25.   Suppose you are standing such that a 30-foot tree is directly between you and the sun. If you are standing 40 feet away from the tree and the tree casts a 50-foot shadow, how tall could you be and still be completely in the shadow of the tree?

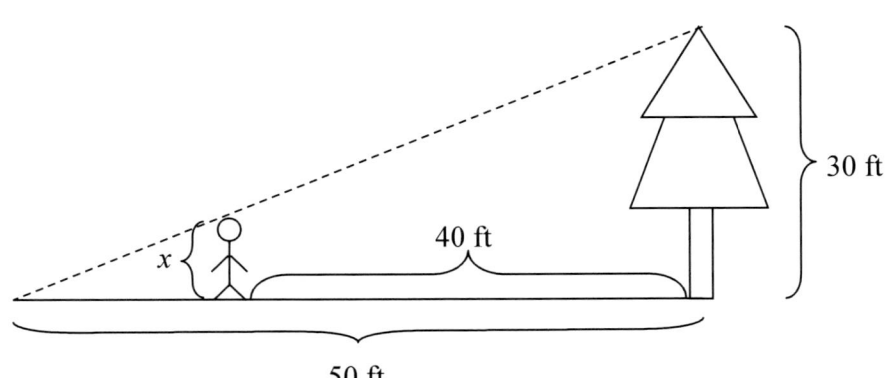

Section 3: Measurements (American Units)

Review Exercises: Make the following conversions in the American system using the appropriate unit conversion factors.

26.   117 in. to yards

27. $3\frac{1}{4}$ yd^2 to square inches

28.   1.6 acres to square yards

29.   1.5 gal to fluid ounces

30.   66 oz to pounds

31. $2\frac{1}{2}$ hr to seconds

32.   Convert 15 miles per hour to feet per second.

33.   Which is a better buy, 5 pounds of coffee for $17.50 or 1 ounce of the same coffee for 19¢?

34.   2 pieces are cut from a board that is 12 feet in length. The first piece is 2 feet 9 inches long and the second piece is 3 feet 5 inches long. What is the length of the remaining piece of board?

35.   How many 8 fluid ounce servings are in $3\dfrac{1}{4}$ gallons of orange juice?

Find the perimeter and area of each figure.

36.

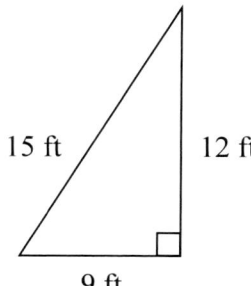

37.

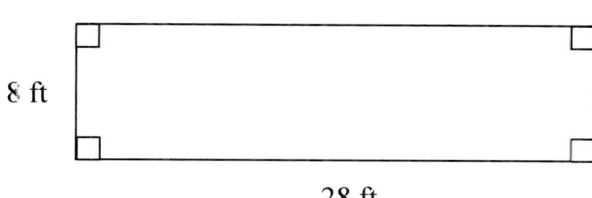

Find the surface area and volume of each figure.

38.

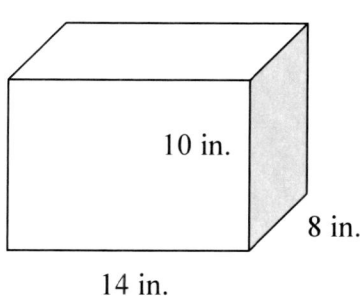

39.

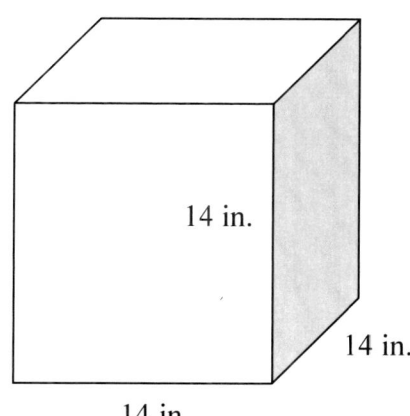

40.   What is the length of a rectangle that has an area of $27\,\text{ft}^2$ and a width of 4 feet?

Section 4: Measurements (Metric Units)

Review Exercises: Make the following conversions in the metric system using the appropriate unit conversion factors (Method 1).

41.   47 km to hectometers

42.   9.403 kL to centiliters

43.   6.7 g to decigrams

44.   3.76 mL to dekaliters

Use the fact that 1 metric ton (t) = 1,000 kilograms

45.   5.3 t to kilograms

Make the following conversions in the metric system by moving the decimal point (Method 2).

46.   0.00023 mm to centimeters

47.   2,651 km to decimeters

48.   92 dag to kilograms

49.   40.32 dL to liters

Make the following conversion in the metric system using the appropriate unit conversion factors.

50.   9,300 cc to liters

Application Problems: Solve each of the following problems.

51.   A can of enchilada sauce contains $7\frac{1}{2}$ servings. If one serving contains 240 mg of sodium, how many grams of sodium are in the entire can?

52.   A bottle of nasal spray has a net fill weight of 12 g. If the bottle contains 40 sprays, what is the weight of each spray in milligrams?

53.   How many hectares are contained within a square piece of land that has a side of 500 meters?

Find the circumference and area of the circle. Give the exact answers and the approximations using the fact that $\pi \approx 3.14$.

54.

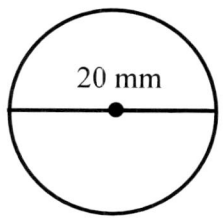

20 mm

Section 5: Metric-American Conversions

Review Exercises: Make the following approximate conversions from the American system to the metric system or from the metric system to the American system. Round answers to the nearest hundredth, if necessary.

55. 3.2 mi to meters   **56.** 50 cm to feet

57. 4 kg to ounces   **58.** 3.7 lb to grams

59. 3 gal to milliliters   **60.** 5 dekaliters to pints

Make the following temperature conversions from the American system to the metric system or from the metric system to the American system.

61. 16.8°F to Celsius   **62.** -7.3°C to Fahrenheit

Application Problems: Solve each of the following problems. Round answers to the nearest hundredth, if necessary.

63. Which is a better buy, 5 pounds of coffee for $18.99 or 3 kilograms of the same kind of coffee for $23.99?

64. If your car gets 20 miles per gallon of gasoline, how many kilometers per liter of gasoline would it get?

RATIOS, PROPORTIONS, & MEASUREMENTS

Chapter Test

Write each ratio as a fraction in lowest terms.

1.   0.6 to $\dfrac{1}{3}$

2.   12 days to 3 weeks

Write the rate as a fraction in lowest terms.

3.   4.5 inches of snow in 3 hours

Write as a unit rate.

4.   If it takes 9.4 minutes to empty a 60-gallon bathtub, what is the rate of flow of water to the nearest tenth of a gallon per minute?

Solve for the variable in the following proportions.

5. $\dfrac{x}{-\frac{2}{5}} = \dfrac{1\frac{1}{4}}{3\frac{1}{2}}$

6. $\dfrac{5.4}{7.2} = \dfrac{-4.5}{x}$

Application Problems: Translate each of the following word problems into a proportion. Then, solve the proportion in order to answer the question.

7.   A recipe for biscuits calls for $1\dfrac{3}{4}$ cups of flour for every $\dfrac{1}{2}$ tablespoon of baking soda. How many tablespoons of baking soda are needed if $2\dfrac{1}{3}$ cups of flour are used?

8.   The scale on a map indicates that 1 centimeter on the map corresponds to an actual distance of 14 kilometers. If two cities are approximately 4.7 centimeters apart on the map, then what is the actual distance between them?

Find the unknown lengths for the pair of similar triangles.

9.

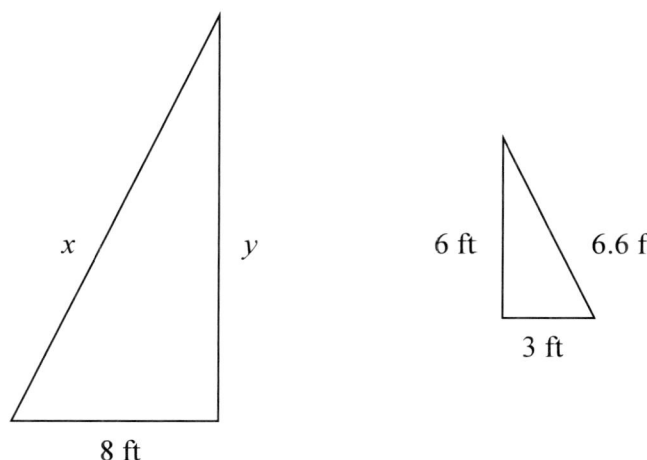

Make the following conversions in the American system using the appropriate unit conversion factors.

10.   207 in. to yards

11. $2\dfrac{3}{4}$ ft^2 to square inches

12.   1.25 gal to fluid ounces

Application Problems: Solve each of the following problems.

13.   3 pieces are cut from a board that is 18 feet in length. The first piece is 4 feet 7 inches long. The second piece is 3 feet 6 inches long. And, the third piece is twice as long as the first piece. What is the length of the remaining piece of board?

14.   How many $\dfrac{1}{2}$ cup servings are in $2\dfrac{1}{4}$ gallons of cranberry juice?

Find the perimeter and area of the figure.

Find the circumference and area of the circle. Give the exact answers and the approximations using the fact that $\pi \approx 3.14$.

15.

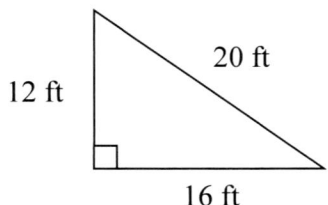

16.

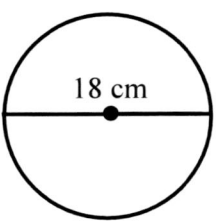

Find the surface area and volume of the figure.

17.

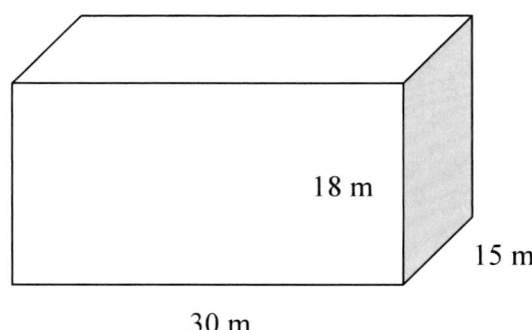

Make the following conversions in the metric system using the appropriate unit conversion factors (Method 1).

18.   0.867 kL to centiliters

19.   458 g to decigrams

20.   720 cc to liters

Make the following conversions in the metric system by moving the decimal point (Method 2).

21.   0.0056 dag to kilograms

22.   356.8 dL to liters

Application Problems: Solve each of the following problems.

23.   A can of tomato sauce contains $5\frac{1}{2}$ servings. If one serving contains 380 mg of sodium, how many grams of sodium are in the entire can?

24.   A bottle of nasal spray has a net fill weight of 18 g. If the bottle contains 40 sprays, what is the weight of each spray in milligrams?

Make the following approximate conversions from the American system to the metric system or from the metric system to the American system. Round answers to the nearest hundredth, if necessary.

25.   7,000 g to ounces

26.   3.5 daL to pints

Make the following temperature conversions from the American system to the metric system or from the metric system to the American system.

27. $-28.6°F$ to Celsius

28.   37°C to Fahrenheit

Application Problems: Solve each of the following problems. Round answers to the nearest hundredth, if necessary.

29.   Which is a better buy, 3 gallons of milk for $5.97 or 10 liters of the same brand of milk for $5.39?

30.   If a motorcycle gets 30 kilometers per liter of gasoline, how many miles per gallon of gasoline would it get?

CHAPTER 2

PERCENTS

Section 1: Fractions, Decimals, and Percents

Method 1 (Using unit conversion factors)
Method 2 (Using the fact that percent means "per 100")
Method 3 (Shortcut involving moving the decimal place)

Section 2: Solving Percent Problems Using Equations

Method 1 (The percent equation)
Method 2 (Using a proportion)

Section 3: Applications of Percents

Method 1 (The percent equation)
Method 2 (Using a proportion)

Section 4: Interest

Simple Interest
Compound Interest

PERCENTS

Section 1: Fractions, Decimals and Percents

Fractions, decimals and percents are different ways of expressing the same information. Depending on the situation, one form may be considered more appropriate than another. For instance, we might say that a baseball player has a .335 batting average instead of saying that he gets a hit 33.5% of the time. We also might say that items are on sale for 20% off instead of saying they are on sale for 1/5 off. A television commercial states that 4 out of 5 dentists surveyed recommend sugarless gum for their patients who chew gum. Could the advertisers have felt that 4 out of 5 sounded more impressive to the television audience than just saying 80%?

There is a need to have information expressed in different forms. This leads us to a discussion of **THREE METHODS** used to change the form between percents and equivalent fractions or decimals.

METHOD 1 (Using unit conversion factors)

The process of changing a quantity from a percent to a fraction or decimal form, or from a fraction or decimal form to a percent includes 2 steps.

Step 1: **CONVERT**   Step 2: **CLEAN UP**

CONVERT is the author's terminology for the use of unit conversion factors.

$1 = 100\%$ From this equation we get the following unit conversion factors:

$\left(\dfrac{1}{100\%}\right)$ which is equal to 1,   and $\left(\dfrac{100\%}{1}\right)$ which also equals 1.

CLEAN UP is the author's terminology for simplifying or reducing.

Example 1: Change 70% into a decimal number.

Step 1: **CONVERT**   70% needs to become a decimal number.
We must get rid of the percent sign, so the setup is as follows:

$$70\%\left(\dfrac{1}{100\%}\right) \ = \ 70\%\left(\dfrac{1}{100\%}\right)$$

Step 2: **CLEAN UP** $70\left(\dfrac{1}{100}\right) \ = \ \dfrac{70}{100} \ = \ \dfrac{70}{100} \ = \ \dfrac{7}{10} \ = \ 0.7$

Now try problem 55 from exercise set 2.1. (using method 1)

<u>Example 2:</u> Rewrite 4.3 in percent form.

Step 1: **CONVERT**   4.3 needs to become a percent. We must include a percent sign, so the setup is as follows: $4.3\left(\dfrac{100\%}{1}\right)$

Step 2: **CLEAN UP** $4.3\left(\dfrac{100\%}{1}\right)$ $=$ $4.3\,(100\%)$ $=$ **430%**

Now try problem 5 from exercise set 2.1. (using method 1)

<u>Example 3:</u> Change 65% into a proper fraction or a mixed number.

Step 1: **CONVERT**   65% needs to become a proper fraction or mixed number. We must get rid of the percent sign, so the setup is as follows:

$65\%\left(\dfrac{1}{100\%}\right)$ $=$ $65\%\left(\dfrac{1}{100\%}\right)$

Step 2: **CLEAN UP** $65\left(\dfrac{1}{100}\right)$ $=$ $\dfrac{65}{100}$ $=$ $\dfrac{13\cdot 5}{20\cdot 5}$ $=$ $\dfrac{13\cdot\cancel{5}}{20\cdot\cancel{5}}$ $=$ $\dfrac{\mathbf{13}}{\mathbf{20}}$

Now try problem 69 from exercise set 2.1. (using method 1)

Note: 65% does not convert to a mixed number. For a percent to become a mixed number, the percent would have to be larger than 100%.

<u>Example 4:</u> Express $4\dfrac{2}{3}$ as a percent.

Step 1: **CONVERT** $4\dfrac{2}{3}$ needs to become a percent.

We must include a percent sign, so the setup is as follows: $4\dfrac{2}{3}\left(\dfrac{100\%}{1}\right)$

Step 2: **CLEAN UP** $4\dfrac{2}{3}\left(\dfrac{100\%}{1}\right)$ $=$ $\dfrac{14}{3}\left(\dfrac{100\%}{1}\right)$ $=$ $\dfrac{1{,}400}{3}\%$ $=$ $\mathbf{466\dfrac{2}{3}\%}$

Now try problem 31 from exercise set 2.1. (using method 1)

Note: Even though $\dfrac{1{,}400}{3}\%$ and $466\dfrac{2}{3}\%$ are equivalent, it is customary to write a percent using a mixed number as opposed to an improper fraction.

Example 5: Rewrite 118% as an improper fraction.

Step 1: **CONVERT**   118% needs to become an improper fraction. We must get rid of the percent sign, so the setup is as follows:

$$118\% \left(\frac{1}{100\%} \right) \;=\; 118\% \left(\frac{1}{100\%} \right)$$

Step 2: **CLEAN UP** $118 \left(\dfrac{1}{100} \right) \;=\; \dfrac{118}{100} \;=\; \dfrac{59 \cdot 2}{50 \cdot 2} \;=\; \dfrac{59 \cdot \cancel{2}}{50 \cdot \cancel{2}} \;=\; \dfrac{59}{50}$

Now try problem 65 from exercise set 2.1. (using method 1)

Note: Unless told to do otherwise, always reduce a fraction to lowest terms.

Example 6: Change 157% into a proper fraction or a mixed number.

Step 1: **CONVERT**   157% needs to become a proper fraction or mixed number. We must get rid of the percent sign, so the setup is as follows:

$$157\% \left(\frac{1}{100\%} \right) \;=\; 157\% \left(\frac{1}{100\%} \right)$$

Step 2: **CLEAN UP** $157 \left(\dfrac{1}{100} \right) \;=\; \dfrac{157}{100} \;=\; 1\dfrac{57}{100}$

Note: 157% could not be converted to a proper fraction. For a percent to become a proper fraction, it would have to be smaller than 100%.

Example 7: Express $15\dfrac{1}{7}\%$ as a decimal number.

Step 1: **CONVERT** $15\dfrac{1}{7}\%$ needs to become a decimal number.

We must get rid of the percent sign, so the setup is as follows:

$$15\frac{1}{7}\% \left(\frac{1}{100\%} \right) \;=\; 15\frac{1}{7}\% \left(\frac{1}{100\%} \right)$$

Step 2: **CLEAN UP** $15\dfrac{1}{7} \left(\dfrac{1}{100} \right) \;=\; \dfrac{106}{7} \left(\dfrac{1}{100} \right) \;=\; \dfrac{106}{700} \;=\; 0.15\overline{142857}$

Now try problem 59 from exercise set 2.1. (using method 1)

Sometimes decimal answers aren't nice!

<u>Example 8:</u> Change $6\frac{2}{7}\%$ into a proper fraction or a mixed number.

Step 1: **CONVERT** $6\frac{2}{7}\%$ needs to become a proper fraction or mixed

number. We must get rid of the percent sign, so the setup is as follows:

$$6\frac{2}{7}\%\left(\frac{1}{100\%}\right) \;=\; 6\frac{2}{7}\cancel{\%}\left(\frac{1}{100\cancel{\%}}\right)$$

Step 2: **CLEAN UP** $6\frac{2}{7}\left(\frac{1}{100}\right) = \frac{44}{7}\left(\frac{1}{100}\right) = \frac{44}{700} = \frac{11\cdot4}{175\cdot4} = \frac{11\cdot\cancel{4}}{175\cdot\cancel{4}} = \frac{\mathbf{11}}{\mathbf{175}}$

Now try problem 71 from exercise set 2.1. (using method 1)

<u>Example 9:</u> Rewrite 6.8% as a fraction.

Step 1: **CONVERT**   6.8% needs to become a fraction.
We must get rid of the percent sign, so the setup is as follows:

$$6.8\%\left(\frac{1}{100\%}\right) \;=\; 6.8\cancel{\%}\left(\frac{1}{100\cancel{\%}}\right)$$

Step 2: **CLEAN UP**

$$6.8\left(\frac{1}{100}\right) \;=\; \frac{6.8}{100} \;=\; \frac{6.8}{100}\left(\frac{10}{10}\right) \;=\; \frac{68}{1,000} \;=\; \frac{17\cdot4}{250\cdot4} \;=\; \frac{17\cdot\cancel{4}}{250\cdot\cancel{4}} \;=\; \frac{\mathbf{17}}{\mathbf{250}}$$

Now try problem 67 from exercise set 2.1. (using method 1)

<u>Example 10:</u> Express $\frac{2}{9}$ as a percent. Round to the nearest hundredth.

Step 1: **CONVERT** $\frac{2}{9}$ needs to become a percent.

We must include a percent sign, so the setup is as follows: $\frac{2}{9}\left(\frac{100\%}{1}\right)$

Step 2: **CLEAN UP** $\frac{2}{9}\left(\frac{100\%}{1}\right) \;=\; \frac{200}{9}\% \;=\; 22.\overline{2}\%$

But, if rounded to the nearest hundredth, the answer is **22.22%**.

Now try problem 77 from exercise set 2.1. (using method 1)

Example 11: Mike cut a pizza into 8 equal pieces. Ben ate 3 of the pieces. What percent of the pizza did Ben eat?

Solution: Ben ate 3 out of 8 pieces or $\frac{3}{8}$ of the pizza. So $\frac{3}{8}$ must be changed into a percent.

Step 1: **CONVERT** $\frac{3}{8}$ needs to become a percent.

We must include a percent sign, so the setup is as follows: $\frac{3}{8}\left(\frac{100\%}{1}\right)$

Step 2: **CLEAN UP** $\frac{3}{8}\left(\frac{100\%}{1}\right)$ $=$ $\frac{300}{8}\%$ $=$ $37\frac{1}{2}\%$

Ben ate $37\frac{1}{2}\%$ of the pizza.

Now try problem 101 from exercise set 2.1. (using method 1)

Note: The answer could also be written as 37.5%.

Example 12: Carolyn has 4 horses, 3 dogs, and 9 cats. What percent of her animals are cats?

Solution: 9 out of 16 animals or $\frac{9}{16}$ are cats. So $\frac{9}{16}$ must be changed into a percent.

Step 1: **CONVERT** $\frac{9}{16}$ needs to become a percent.

We must include a percent sign, so the setup is as follows: $\frac{9}{16}\left(\frac{100\%}{1}\right)$

Step 2: **CLEAN UP**

$\frac{9}{16}\left(\frac{100\%}{1}\right)$ $=$ $\frac{9}{4\cdot4}\left(\frac{25\cdot4}{1}\%\right)$ $=$ $\frac{9}{4\cdot\cancel{4}}\left(\frac{25\cdot\cancel{4}}{1}\%\right)$ $=$ $\frac{9}{4}\left(\frac{25}{1}\%\right)$ $=$ $\frac{225}{4}\%$ $=$ $56\frac{1}{4}\%$

$56\frac{1}{4}\%$ of Carolyn's animals are cats.

Now try problem 109 from exercise set 2.1. (using method 1)

Note: The answer could also be written as 56.25%.

METHOD 2   (Using the fact that percent means "per 100")

Percent means "per 100". In fact, if you take the 1 and the two 0's in 100 and you rearrange them you get the percent sign %. <u>Cent</u> is a root word meaning 100, like a <u>cent</u>ury is 100 years.

The process of changing a quantity from a percent to a fraction/decimal, or from a fraction/decimal to a percent includes 2 steps.

Step 1: **CONVERT**   Step 2:   **CLEAN UP**

<u>The converting process</u> uses the fact that percent means "per 100"

and the fact that 1 = 100%.

<u>The clean up process</u> involves simplifying or reducing.

<u>Example 13</u>: Change 30% into a decimal number.

Step 1: **CONVERT**   30% needs to become a decimal number. We must get rid of the percent sign, so the setup is as follows:

$$30\% \;\; = \;\; 30 \text{ per } 100 \;\; = \;\; \frac{30}{100}$$

Step 2: **CLEAN UP** $\dfrac{30}{100} \;\; = \;\; \dfrac{3\cancel{0}}{10\cancel{0}} \;\; = \;\; \dfrac{3}{10} \;\; = \;\; \mathbf{0.3}$

Now try problem 57 from exercise set 2.1. (using method 2)

<u>Example 14</u>: Rewrite 6.2 in percent form.

Step 1: **CONVERT**   6.2 needs to become a percent. We must include a percent sign, so the setup is as follows:

6.2 (100%)

Step 2: **CLEAN UP**   6.2 (100%)   =   **620%**

Now try problem 9 from exercise set 2.1. (using method 2)

<u>Example 15:</u> Change 85% into a proper fraction or a mixed number.

Step 1: **CONVERT**   85% needs to become a proper fraction or mixed number. We must get rid of the percent sign, so the setup is as follows:

$$85\% \;=\; 85 \text{ per } 100 \;=\; \frac{85}{100}$$

Step 2: **CLEAN UP** $\dfrac{85}{100} \;=\; \dfrac{17 \cdot 5}{20 \cdot 5} \;=\; \dfrac{17 \cdot \cancel{5}}{20 \cdot \cancel{5}} \;=\; \dfrac{17}{20}$

Now try problem 69 from exercise set 2.1. (using method 2)

Note: 85% does not convert to a mixed number. For a percent to become a mixed number, the percent would have to be larger than 100%.

<u>Example 16:</u> Express $5\dfrac{2}{7}$ as a percent.

Step 1: **CONVERT** $5\dfrac{2}{7}$ needs to become a percent.

We must include a percent sign, so the setup is as follows: $5\dfrac{2}{7}\,(100\%)$

Step 2: **CLEAN UP**

$$5\frac{2}{7}\,(100\%) \;=\; \frac{37}{7}\,(100\%) \;=\; \frac{3{,}700}{7}\% \;=\; 528\frac{4}{7}\%$$

Now try problem 37 from exercise set 2.1. (using method 2)

Note: Even though $\dfrac{3{,}700}{7}\%$ and $528\dfrac{4}{7}\%$ are equivalent, it is customary to write a percent using a mixed number as opposed to an improper fraction.

<u>Example 17:</u> Rewrite 145% as an improper fraction.

Step 1: **CONVERT**   145% needs to become an improper fraction. We must get rid of the percent sign, so the setup is as follows:

$$145\% \;=\; 145 \text{ per } 100 \;=\; \frac{145}{100}$$

Step 2: **CLEAN UP** $\dfrac{145}{100} \;=\; \dfrac{29 \cdot 5}{20 \cdot 5} \;=\; \dfrac{29 \cdot \cancel{5}}{20 \cdot \cancel{5}} \;=\; \dfrac{29}{20}$

Now try problem 65 from exercise set 2.1. (using method 2)

Note: Unless told to do otherwise, always reduce a fraction to lowest terms.

Example 18: Change 263% into a proper fraction or a mixed number.

Step 1: **CONVERT**   263% needs to become a proper fraction or mixed number. We must get rid of the percent sign, so the setup is as follows:

$$263\% \;=\; 263 \text{ per } 100 \;=\; \frac{263}{100}$$

Step 2: **CLEAN UP** $\dfrac{263}{100} \;=\; 2\dfrac{63}{100}$

Note: 263% could not be converted to a proper fraction. For a percent to become a proper fraction it would have to be smaller than 100%.

Example 19: Express $18\dfrac{3}{7}\%$ as a decimal number.

Step 1: **CONVERT** $18\dfrac{3}{7}\%$ needs to become a decimal number.

We must get rid of the percent sign, so the setup is as follows:

$$18\tfrac{3}{7}\% \;=\; 18\tfrac{3}{7} \text{ per } 100 \;=\; \frac{18\tfrac{3}{7}}{100}$$

Step 2: **CLEAN UP**

$$\frac{18\tfrac{3}{7}}{100} \;=\; \frac{\tfrac{129}{7}}{100} \;=\; \frac{129}{7} \div 100 \;=\; \frac{129}{7}\left(\frac{1}{100}\right) \;=\; \frac{129}{700} \;=\; \mathbf{0.18\overline{428571}}$$

Now try problem 59 from exercise set 2.1. (using method 2)

Decimal answers aren't always nice!

Example 20: Change $9\frac{4}{7}\%$ into a proper fraction or a mixed number.

Step 1: **CONVERT** $9\frac{4}{7}\%$ needs to become a proper fraction or mixed number.

We must get rid of the percent sign, so the setup is as follows:

$$9\frac{4}{7}\% \quad = \quad 9\frac{4}{7} \text{ per } 100 \quad = \quad \frac{9\frac{4}{7}}{100}$$

Step 2: **CLEAN UP** $\dfrac{9\frac{4}{7}}{100} \quad = \quad \dfrac{\frac{67}{7}}{100} \quad = \quad \dfrac{67}{7} \div 100 \quad = \quad \dfrac{67}{7}\left(\dfrac{1}{100}\right) \quad = \quad \mathbf{\dfrac{67}{700}}$

Now try problem 71 from exercise set 2.1. (using method 2)

Example 21: Rewrite 7.2% as a fraction.

Step 1: **CONVERT**   7.2% needs to become a fraction.
We must get rid of the percent sign, so the setup is as follows:

$$7.2\% \quad = \quad 7.2 \text{ per } 100 \quad = \quad \frac{7.2}{100}$$

Step 2: **CLEAN UP** $\dfrac{7.2}{100} \quad = \quad \dfrac{7.2}{100}\left(\dfrac{10}{10}\right) \quad = \quad \dfrac{72}{1{,}000} \quad = \quad \dfrac{9 \cdot 8}{125 \cdot 8} \quad = \quad \dfrac{9 \cdot \cancel{8}}{125 \cdot \cancel{8}} \quad = \quad \mathbf{\dfrac{9}{125}}$

Now try problem 67 from exercise set 2.1. (using method 2)

Example 22: Express $\dfrac{4}{9}$ as a percent. Round to the nearest hundredth.

Step 1: **CONVERT** $\dfrac{4}{9}$ needs to become a percent.

We must include a percent sign, so the setup is as follows: $\dfrac{4}{9}(100\%)$

Step 2: **CLEAN UP** $\dfrac{4}{9}(100\%) \quad = \quad \dfrac{400}{9}\% \quad = \quad 44.\overline{4}\%$

But, if rounded to the nearest hundredth the answer is **44.44%**.

Now try problem 77 from exercise set 2.1. (using method 2)

<u>Example 23:</u> In a recent basketball game between Greg and Matt, Greg made 5 out of 8 free throws. What percent of the free throws did Greg make?

Solution: Greg made 5 out of 8 free throws or he was successful $\frac{5}{8}$ of the time.

So, $\frac{5}{8}$ must be changed to a percent.

Step 1: **CONVERT** $\frac{5}{8}$ needs to become a percent.

We must include a percent sign, so the setup is as follows: $\frac{5}{8}(100\%)$

Step 2: **CLEAN UP** $\frac{5}{8}(100\%) \;=\; \frac{500}{8}\% \;=\; 62\frac{1}{2}\%$

Greg made $62\frac{1}{2}\%$ of the free throws.

Now try problem 105 from exercise set 2.1. (using method 2)

Note: The answer could also be written as 62.5%.

<u>Example 24:</u> On a recent fishing trip to Montana, Marty spent 4 days driving there and back, 5 days fishing and 3 days visiting with relatives. What percent of the time did Marty spend fishing?

Solution: 5 out of 12 days were spent fishing. So, $\frac{5}{12}$ must be changed into a percent.

Step 1: **CONVERT** $\frac{5}{12}$ needs to become a percent.

We must include a percent sign, so the setup is as follows: $\frac{5}{12}(100\%)$

Step 2: **CLEAN UP**

$\frac{5}{12}(100\%) \;=\; \frac{5}{3\cdot4}(25\cdot4)\% \;=\; \frac{5}{3\cdot\cancel{4}}(25\cdot\cancel{4})\% \;=\; \frac{5}{3}(25)\% \;=\; \frac{125}{3}\% \;=\; 41\frac{2}{3}\%$

Marty spent $41\frac{2}{3}\%$ of the time fishing.

Now try problem 111 from exercise set 2.1. (using method 2)

Note: The answer could also be written as $41.\overline{6}\%$.

METHOD 3 (Shortcut involving moving the decimal place)

Look at example 1 and example 13 in the previous methods discussed. Notice that when converting a percent to a decimal the following two things happen: the percent sign disappears, and the decimal point moves two places to the left. It is the fact that we divide by 100 in both methods which results in the decimal point being moved two places to the left.

This brings us to the following shortcut:

> ***When converting a percent to a decimal, move the decimal point two places to the left and remove the percent sign.***

Look at example 2 and example 14 in the previous methods discussed. Notice that when converting a decimal to a percent the following two things happen: the percent sign appears, and the decimal point moves two places to the right. It is the fact that we multiply by 100 in both methods that results in the decimal point being moved two places to the right.

This brings us to the following shortcut:

> ***When converting a decimal to a percent, move the decimal point two places to the right and include a percent sign after the number.***

In order to effectively use method 3, the number or percent that is to be changed needs to be in decimal form. So, the 2-step process is reversed.

Step 1: **CLEAN UP**

Step 2: **CONVERT**

The clean up process involves changing the original quantity into decimal form if it isn't already in that form.

The converting process involves moving the decimal point 2 places and removing or including a percent sign depending on which way things are being converted.

As you will see in some of the following examples, when converting involves repeating decimals, things can get a little tricky!

Example 25: Change 43% into a decimal number.

Step 1: **CLEAN UP**   No clean up is necessary.

Step 2: **CONVERT**   43%

Move the decimal point two places to the left and remove the percent sign.

$$43\% = \mathbf{0.43}$$

Now try problem 55 from exercise set 2.1. (using method 3)

Example 26: Change 7.9 into percent form.

Step 1: **CLEAN UP**   No clean up is necessary.

Step 2: **CONVERT**   7.9

Move the decimal point two places to the right and include a percent sign after the number. $7.9 = \mathbf{790\%}$

Now try problem 41 from exercise set 2.1. (using method 3)

Note: Be careful to put the decimal point in the right place. A quick way to check the answer is that since 7.9 is between 7 and 8 then the answer should be between 700% and 800%.

Example 27: Change $5\dfrac{2}{3}$ into a percent.

Step 1: **CLEAN UP** $5\dfrac{2}{3}$ becomes $5.\overline{6}$

Step 2: **CONVERT** $5.\overline{6} = \mathbf{566.\overline{6}\%}$

Now try problem 37 from exercise set 2.1. (using method 3)

Note: Remember $5.\overline{6}$ implies the 6 continues to the right forever. $566\overline{\%}$ is not acceptable. The repeating bar must be to the right of the decimal point.

Example 28: Express $16\dfrac{3}{7}\%$ as a decimal number.

Step 1: **CLEAN UP** $16\dfrac{3}{7}\%$ becomes $16.\overline{428571}\%$

Step 2: **CONVERT** $16.\overline{428571}\% = \mathbf{0.16\overline{428571}}$

Now try problem 71 from exercise set 2.1. (using method 3)

<u>Example 29:</u> Rewrite 0.75% in decimal form.

Step 1: **CLEAN UP**   No clean up is necessary.

Step 2: **CONVERT**   0.75% = **0.0075**

Now try problem 61 from exercise set 2.1. (using method 3)

<u>Example 30:</u> In a recent photo contest 8 out of 12 pictures that Dan entered in the contest won a 1st place ribbon. What percent of the photos won 1st place? Round the answer to the nearest tenth of a percent.

Step 1: **CLEAN UP**   8 out of 12 $= \dfrac{8}{12} = \dfrac{2 \cdot 4}{3 \cdot 4} = \dfrac{2 \cdot \cancel{4}}{3 \cdot \cancel{4}} = \dfrac{2}{3} = 0.\overline{6}$

Step 2: **CONVERT** $0.\overline{6} = 66.\overline{6}\% = 66.7\%$ to the nearest tenth of a percent.

66.7% of Dan's photos won 1st place.

Now try problem 117 from exercise set 2.1. (using method 3)

The following is a list of fractions, decimals and percents that commonly occur. It would be a good idea to memorize the information in this table for future use.

Fraction	Decimal	Percent	Fraction	Decimal	Percent	Fraction	Decimal	Percent
$\dfrac{1}{2}$	0.5	50%	$\dfrac{3}{4}$	0.75	75%	$\dfrac{4}{5}$	0.8	80%
$\dfrac{1}{3}$	$0.\overline{3}$	$33.\overline{3}\%$ or $33\frac{1}{3}\%$	$\dfrac{1}{5}$	0.2	20%	$\dfrac{1}{10}$	0.1	10%
$\dfrac{2}{3}$	$0.\overline{6}$	$66.\overline{6}\%$ or $66\frac{2}{3}\%$	$\dfrac{2}{5}$	0.4	40%	$\dfrac{1}{20}$	0.05	5%
$\dfrac{1}{4}$	0.25	25%	$\dfrac{3}{5}$	0.6	60%	$\dfrac{1}{100}$	0.01	1%

Adding or subtracting percents:

Example 31:

An item is on sale for 15% off the regular price. What percent of the regular price would you have to pay to purchase this item?

Solution: The regular price would be 100% of the regular price. 15% off the regular price would be $100\% - 15\% = 85\%$. So, you would pay 85% of the regular price to purchase this item.

Now try problem 123 from exercise set 2.1.

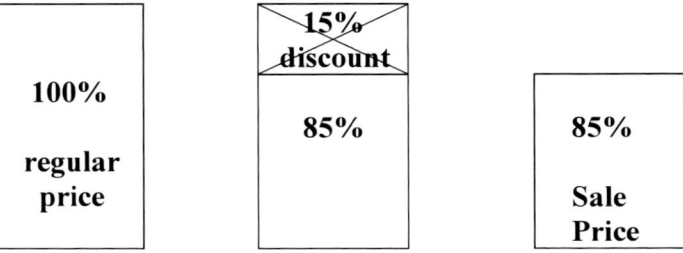

Example 32:

The price of an item at a skate shop is marked up 30% from wholesale cost for retail sale. What percent of the wholesale cost is the retail price?

Solution: The wholesale cost would be 100% of the wholesale cost. A 30% mark up would be $100\% + 30\% = 130\%$. So, you would pay 130% of the wholesale cost if you bought this item at the retail price.

Now try problem 125 from exercise set 2.1.

<u>Section 1 exercises.</u> Change each fraction, mixed number or decimal to a percent. Give exact answers (don't round).

1.   7

2.   5

3. $\dfrac{3}{25}$

4. $\dfrac{7}{25}$

5.   6.2

6.   4.6

7. $\dfrac{23}{100}$

8. $\dfrac{47}{100}$

9.   0.6

10.   0.2

11. $\dfrac{7}{10}$

12. $\dfrac{3}{10}$

13.   43

14.   19

15. $\dfrac{59}{40}$

16. $\dfrac{73}{40}$

17.   10.64

18.   83.52

19. $\dfrac{3}{4}$

20. $\dfrac{9}{4}$

21.   0.00478

22.   0.00652

23. $\dfrac{2}{3}$

24. $\dfrac{5}{3}$

25. $\dfrac{17}{20}$

26. $\dfrac{47}{20}$

27.   0.114

28.   0.98

29. $\dfrac{3}{5}$

30. $\dfrac{7}{5}$

31. $2\dfrac{3}{4}$

32. $2\dfrac{1}{4}$

33. $\dfrac{1}{8}$

34. $\dfrac{7}{8}$

35.   0.417

36.   0.631

37. $4\dfrac{2}{3}$

38. $4\dfrac{1}{3}$

39. $\dfrac{7}{6}$

40. $\dfrac{5}{6}$

41.   9.104

42.   3.056

43. $\dfrac{2}{7}$

44. $\dfrac{4}{7}$

45. $5\dfrac{7}{8}$

46. $5\dfrac{3}{8}$

47. $\dfrac{5}{16}$

48. $\dfrac{7}{16}$

49.   1.0103

50.   2.807

51. $5\dfrac{1}{6}$

Change each percent into a decimal number. Give exact answers (don't round).

52.   39.8%

53.   6.9%

54.   650%

55.   17%

56.   0.043%

57.   1%

58. $7\dfrac{2}{3}\%$

59. $4\dfrac{1}{3}\%$

60.   87.3%

61.   0.314%

62. $0.\overline{2}\%$

63. $0.\overline{4}\%$

Change each percent into a fraction or mixed number. Give exact answers (don't round).

64.   190%

65.   740%

66.   7.5%

67.   6.4%

68.   48%

69.   56%

70. $6\dfrac{3}{7}\%$

71. $8\dfrac{5}{7}\%$

72. $\dfrac{2}{5}\%$

73. $\dfrac{3}{5}\%$

74.   21.3%

75.   43.6%

Change each fraction or mixed number to a percent. Round answers to the nearest hundredth.

76. $5\dfrac{5}{6}$

77. $\dfrac{1}{3}$

78. $\dfrac{2}{3}$

79. $2\dfrac{1}{6}$

80. $3\dfrac{5}{6}$

81. $4\dfrac{2}{7}$

82. $9\dfrac{4}{7}$

83. $2\dfrac{4}{9}$

84. $5\dfrac{7}{9}$

Complete the following table. Give exact answers (don't round).

	Decimal	Fraction	Percent
85.	_____	$\dfrac{9}{10}$	_____
86.	0.001	_____	_____
87.	_____	_____	$\dfrac{3}{4}\%$
88.	_____	$\dfrac{5}{9}$	_____
89.	0.4	_____	_____
90.	_____	_____	$5\dfrac{1}{2}\%$
91.	_____	$\dfrac{3}{5}$	_____
92.	$0.\overline{6}$	_____	_____
93.	_____	_____	155%
94.	_____	$\dfrac{1}{3}$	_____
95.	0.875	_____	_____
96.	_____	_____	20%
97.	_____	$\dfrac{1}{25}$	_____
98.	0.65	_____	_____
99.	_____	_____	$\dfrac{1}{2}\%$

Application problems:

100.   Sue spent her spring vacation doing laundry and working in her garden. During a typical 24-hour day she spent 6 hours doing laundry, 10 hours working in her garden, and 8 hours sleeping. What percent of the time did she spend doing laundry?

101.   Sean spent his spring vacation watching television and playing video games. During a typical 24-hour day he spent 11 hours playing video games, 3 hours watching television, and 10 hours sleeping. What percent of the time did he spend sleeping?

102.   Jessica has a 0.87 success rate when it comes to getting tickets to see a movie. What percent of the time is she successful at getting tickets to see a movie?

103.   a) Sonny owns 10 CDs, 3 of which are rock-and-roll. What percent of Sonny's CDs are rock-and-roll?

   b) Cher owns 15 CDs, 3 of which are rock-and-roll. What percent of Cher's CDs are rock-and roll?

   c) If Sonny and Cher got married and combined their CD collection, what percent of their CDs would be rock-and-roll?

104.   a) Tom owns 4 CDs, 3 of which are classical music. What percent of Tom's CDs are classical music?

   b) Lyn owns 16 CDs, 4 of which are classical music. What percent of Lyn's CDs are classical music?

   c) If Tom and Lyn got married and combined their CD collection, what percent of their CDs would be classical music?

105.   John plays shortstop for the Pumpkin Center Penguins. Last season he got 17 hits in 40 at bats. What percent of his at bats did John get a hit?

106.   Maria plays soccer for the Selah Super Stars. Last season she scored 19 of the team's 40 goals. What percent of the team's goals did Maria score?

107.   In 50 turns at bat Joe got a hit 18 times and struck out the rest of the time. What percent of the time did Joe strike out?

108.   In 20 times at bat Ralph got a hit 7 times and struck out the rest of the time. What percent of the time did Ralph strike out?

Based on Janet's monthly budget:

109.   What percent is budgeted for food?

110.   What percent is budgeted for housing?

111.   What percent is budgeted for miscellaneous?

112.   What percent is budgeted for transportation and utilities?

113.   What percent is budgeted for entertainment?

114.   What percent is budgeted for gas and electricity?

115.   What percent is budgeted for the phone bill?

Janet's Monthly Budget

Item	Cost
Food	$400
Housing	$800
Transportation	$150
Entertainment	$70
Miscellaneous	$300
Gas	$120
Phone	$25
Electricity	$35
Utilities	$100

116.   On a recent math assignment consisting of 30 problems, Alvin had 14 application problems and the rest involved only computation. What percent of the assignment was only computation? Round your answer to the nearest tenth of a percent.

117.   On a multiple-choice test over English vocabulary, Kelly got 17 out of 22 correct. What percent of the test did she miss? Round your answer to the nearest tenth of a percent.

118.   In a recent taste test, 3 out of 5 people surveyed preferred Burpsie Cola to Slurpie Cola. What percent of the people surveyed did not prefer Burpsie Cola?

119.   In a recent survey, 7 out of 8 people chose fluoride toothpaste over tarter control toothpaste. What percent of those surveyed did not choose fluoride toothpaste?

120.   Recently local sales tax went up to 8.2%. Express this amount as a decimal number.

121.   Jerry had a reduction in his income tax rate. He now only has to pay at a rate of 14.3%. Express this amount as a decimal number.

122.   An item is on sale for 20% off the original price. What percent of the original price would you have to pay to purchase this item?

123.   A coat is on sale for 37% off the original price. What percent of the original price would you have to pay to buy the coat?

124.   The wholesale cost of an item is marked up 40% for retail sale. What percent of the wholesale cost is the retail price?

125.   The wholesale cost of an item at a specialty shop is marked up 100% for retail sale. What percent of the wholesale cost is the retail price?

126.   If 24% of a snowman has melted, what percent of the snowman is still left?

127.   A glass that was full of water lost 58% of its contents due to evaporation. What percent of the original contents is left in the glass?

128.   If Judy bought a guitar and paid 8% sales tax on her purchase, what percent of the purchase price of the guitar did she pay as the total bill?

129.   If Steven bought a video game and paid 7% sales tax on his purchase, what percent of the purchase price of the game did he pay as the total bill?

130.   Over the summer Jack sprouted like a beanstalk and grew 15% taller than his original height. What percent of his original height was he at the end of the summer?

Writing:

131.   Describe a quick and easy way to find 10% of a number.

132.   If an item is being clearanced out at 50% off the original price and then it is an additional 50% off the clearance price, is the item free? Why or why not?

133.   Sometimes a coach asks an athlete to give 110% effort in a sport. Is this really possible to do? Explain your answer.

134.   Yogi Berra, a famous former baseball player is quoted as having once said, "Baseball is 90% mental—the other half is physical." Does this quote make sense? Why or why not?

135.   Upon eating an entire pie you might say that you ate 100% of the pie. Could you eat 200% of a single pie? Explain your answer.

136.   If you invested $100 in the stock market and the value of your investment increased later to $300 would you have a profit of 200% on your original investment? Explain your answer.

PERCENTS

Section 2: Solving Percent Problems Using Equations

Fran wants to purchase a book regularly priced at $20. However, the book is currently on sale for 30% off the regular price. If Fran wants to know how much her savings will be, she would need the answer to the following question: **What amount of money is 30% of $20?**

For tax purposes the county assesses the value of a house at 16% of its market value. Chad is looking into buying a house that has an assessed value of $8,371. If Chad wants to know the market value of the house, he needs the answer to the following question: **$8,371 is 16% of how much money?**

Bruce is a great waiter, but not too good at math. Recently, after providing excellent service at a restaurant, he was given a tip of $9 on a $45 meal purchase. If Bruce wants to know how good his tip was, he needs the answer to the following question: **$9 is what percent of $45?**

This leads us to a discussion of **TWO METHODS** used to find answers to these types of questions.

METHOD 1 (The Percent Equation)

Each of the above questions is an example of a percent problem that can be written as an equation, and then solved in order to answer the given question. Each question has three parts. These are, the ***amount***, the ***percent*** and the ***base***. In each case, the ***amount*** is a ***percent*** of the ***base***. Furthermore, the word "**is**" becomes an equal sign and the word "**of**" becomes a multiplication sign.

So,   the *amount*   is   a *percent*   of   the *base*   becomes

$$\boxed{\textbf{\textit{amount = percent} \cdot \textbf{\textit{base}}}}$$

In Fran's scenario: **What amount of money is 30% of $20?** "What amount of money" is the *amount*, "30%" is the *percent* and "$20" is the *base*. Since "what amount of money" is the unknown in the problem, we use a letter called a **variable** to represent this unknown. Though any letter would suffice, most often the letter "x" is used to represent an unknown quantity. Also, we must convert the percent into a fraction or decimal number to be used in the equation.

So, **what amount of money   is   30%   of $20?"**   becomes
              ↓   ↓   ↓   ↓   ↓
    The unknown equals 0.30 (converted from 30%) times $20   or

          x =   0.30($20)

To "solve" this equation for the unknown or "x", we multiply 0.30 by $20 and get $6. So x = $6. This means that $6 is 30% of $20. Fran's savings will be **$6** if she purchases the book on sale.

In Chad's scenario: **$8,371 is 16% of how much money?** "$8,371" is the *amount*, "16%" is the *percent* and "how much money" is the *base*. Since "how much money" is the unknown in the problem, we will use the variable "x" to represent this unknown.

So,   **"$8,371   is   16%   of   how much money?"   becomes**

$\downarrow$ $\downarrow$ $\downarrow$ $\downarrow$ $\downarrow$

$8,371 equals 0.16 (converted from 16%) times the unknown   or

$$\$8{,}371 \;=\; 0.16x$$

To "solve" this equation for the unknown or "x" we must get "x" by itself or "isolate" the variable. If we divide both sides of the equation by 0.16 and then reduce each side we will solve for x.

$$\frac{\$8{,}371}{0.16} = \frac{0.16x}{0.16} \quad \text{becomes} \quad \frac{\$8{,}371}{0.16} = \frac{\cancel{0.16}x}{\cancel{0.16}}. \quad \frac{\$8{,}371}{0.16} = x \quad \text{or} \quad x = \frac{\$8{,}371}{0.16}.$$

Now, by using long division $16{\overline{)\,\$837{,}100.00}}^{\,\$52{,}318.75}$. $x = \$52{,}318.75$ and **$52,318.75** is the market value of the house.

In Bruce's scenario: **$9 is what percent of $45?** "$9" is the *amount*, "what percent" is the *percent* and "$45" is the *base*. Since "what percent" is the unknown in the problem, we will use the variable "x" to represent this unknown.

So,   **"$9   is   what percent   of $45?"   becomes**

$\downarrow$ $\downarrow$ $\downarrow$ $\downarrow$ $\downarrow$

$9 equals the unknown percent times $45   or

$$\$9 \;=\; x\,(\$45)$$

Before actually solving this equation we will rewrite it like this:

$$\$9 \;=\; \$45x$$

The reason for doing this is as follows: when a number and a variable are being multiplied together, it is customary to put the number in front of the variable. This number is called a **coefficient**. In this particular case it would be called the coefficient of the variable "x". The coefficient of a variable tells how much of that variable we have. Now, back to solving the equation.

To "solve" this equation for the unknown or "x" we must get "x" by itself or "isolate" the variable. If we divide both sides of the equation by $45 (that is, by the coefficient of the variable) and then reduce each side we will solve for x.

$$\frac{\$9}{\$45} = \frac{\$45x}{\$45} \quad \text{becomes} \quad \frac{\cancel{\$9}}{\cancel{\$45}} = \frac{\cancel{\$45}x}{\cancel{\$45}}. \quad \frac{9}{45} = x \quad \text{or} \quad x = \frac{9}{45}. \quad \text{Reducing further we get } x = \frac{1}{5}.$$

But wait!! We aren't done yet because $x = \dfrac{1}{5}$ still needs to be converted into a percent. Recall that in the first two scenarios we had to convert percents to decimal or fraction form in order to put them into the equation. When we are looking for a percent using the percent equation method, the number we find is actually a decimal or fraction and must still be converted to a percent at the end of the problem.

Now, let's convert $\dfrac{1}{5}$ into a percent. $\dfrac{1}{5}\left(\dfrac{100\%}{1}\right) = \dfrac{100\%}{5} = 20\%$

Bruce got a **20%** tip.

Example 1:   What number is 85% of 200?

Solution: "What number" is the *amount*, "85%" is the *percent* and "200" is the *base*.

amount $=$ *percent* $\bullet$ *base*

$\quad x \;=\; 85\% \;\bullet\; 200 \qquad$ Converting 85% to 0.85   we get the equation

$\quad x \;=\; 0.85(200).$

Since $0.85(200) = 170,$ $\qquad$ then $x = 170,$ and $\quad$ **170** is 85% of 200.

Now try problem 1 from exercise set 2.2. (using method 1)

Example 2:   175% of 20 is what number?

Solution: "What number" is the *amount*, "175%" is the *percent* and "20" is the *base*.

amount $=$ *percent* $\bullet$ *base*

$\quad x \;=\; 175\% \;\bullet\; 20 \qquad$ Converting 175% to 1.75   we get the equation

$\quad x \;=\; 1.75(20).$

Since $1.75(20) = 35,$ $\qquad$ then $x = 35,$ and $\quad$ **35** is 175% of 20.

Now try problem 11 from exercise set 2.2. (using method 1)

Note: In this example the *amount* is larger than the *base*. This is because the *percent* is greater than 100%. When you find more than 100% of something, the resulting *amount* you get will be larger than the *base* amount you started with.

Example 3:   6 is 0.3% of what number?

Solution: "6" is the *amount*, "0.3%" is the *percent* and "what number" is the *base*.

amount = *percent* • *base*

6 = 0.3% • x Converting 0.3% to 0.003   we get the equation

6 = 0.003x.   We divide both sides of the equation by 0.003 to isolate x.

$\dfrac{6}{0.003} = \dfrac{0.003x}{0.003}$ becomes $\dfrac{6}{0.003} = \dfrac{\cancel{0.003}x}{\cancel{0.003}}$.

Using long division $0.003\overline{)6}$ becomes $3\overline{)6,000}$ ($2{,}000$). $x = 2{,}000$ and

6 is 0.3% of **2,000**.

Now try problem 3 from exercise set 2.2. (using method 1)

Example 4:   800% of what number is 54?

Solution: "54" is the *amount*, "800%" is the *percent* and "what number" is the *base*.

amount = *percent* • *base*

54 = 800% • x Converting 800% to 8   we get the equation

54 = 8x.   We divide both sides of the equation by 8 to isolate x.

$\dfrac{54}{8} = \dfrac{8x}{8}$ becomes $\dfrac{54}{8} = \dfrac{\cancel{8}x}{\cancel{8}}$.

Using long division $8\overline{)54.00}$ (6.75). $x = 6.75$ and   54 is 800% of **6.75**.

Now try problem 7 from exercise set 2.2. (using method 1)

Note: As with example 2, the *amount* is larger than the *base*. Again, this is because the *percent* is greater than 100%.

Example 5: 18 is what percent of 30?

Solution: "18" is the *amount*, "what percent" is the *percent* and "30" is the *base*.

amount = *percent* • *base*

$\quad$ 18 = $\quad$ x • 30 $\qquad$ Rewriting the equation with the coefficient
$\qquad\qquad\qquad\qquad\qquad\qquad$ in front of the variable we get

$\quad$ 18 = 30x. $\qquad$ We divide both sides of the equation by 30 to isolate x.

$\dfrac{18}{30} = \dfrac{30x}{30}$ becomes $\dfrac{18}{30} = \dfrac{\cancel{30}x}{\cancel{30}}$. Reducing further we get $\dfrac{3}{5} = x$ or $x = \dfrac{3}{5}$.

But wait!! Don't forget that we need to convert $\dfrac{3}{5}$ into a percent.

$\dfrac{3}{5} = 0.6$ and $0.6 = 60\%$. $\qquad$ 18 is **60%** of 30.

Now try problem 5 from exercise set 2.2. (using method 1)

Example 6: What percent of 18 is 0.4?

Solution: "0.4" is the *amount*, "what percent" is the *percent* and "18" is the *base*.

amount = *percent* • *base*

$\quad$ 0.4 = $\quad$ x • 18 $\qquad$ Rewriting the equation with the coefficient
$\qquad\qquad\qquad\qquad\qquad\qquad$ in front of the variable we get

$\quad$ 0.4 = 18x. $\qquad$ We divide both sides of the equation by 18 to isolate x.

$\dfrac{0.4}{18} = \dfrac{18x}{18}$ becomes $\dfrac{0.4}{18} = \dfrac{\cancel{18}x}{\cancel{18}}$. $\quad$ Using long division $\quad 18\overline{)0.40}^{\;0.0\overline{2}}$.

$x = 0.0\overline{2}$

But wait!! Don't forget that we need to convert $0.0\overline{2}$ into a percent.

$0.0\overline{2} = 2.\overline{2}\%$ $\qquad$ 0.4 is **2.$\overline{2}$%** of 18.

Now try problem 9 from exercise set 2.2. (using method 1)

Note: $2.\overline{2}\%$ could also be written as $2\dfrac{2}{9}\%$.

<u>Example 7:</u>   What percent of $\dfrac{2}{9}$ is $\dfrac{5}{9}$?

Solution: "$\dfrac{5}{9}$" is the *amount*, "what percent" is the *percent* and "$\dfrac{2}{9}$" is the *base*.

$$amount \;=\; percent \;\bullet\; base \qquad becomes \qquad \dfrac{5}{9} \;=\; x \;\bullet\; \dfrac{2}{9}.$$

Rewriting the equation with the coefficient in front of the variable we get

$\dfrac{5}{9} = \dfrac{2}{9}x$.   We divide both sides of the equation by $\dfrac{2}{9}$ to isolate x.

$\dfrac{\frac{5}{9}}{\frac{2}{9}} = \dfrac{\frac{2}{9}}{\frac{2}{9}}x$ Reducing the right side we get $\dfrac{\frac{5}{9}}{\frac{2}{9}} = \dfrac{\cancel{2}}{\cancel{2}}x$.   On the left side

$\dfrac{\frac{5}{9}}{\frac{2}{9}} = \dfrac{5}{9} \div \dfrac{2}{9}$ but dividing by a fraction is like multiplying by its reciprocal.

$\dfrac{5}{9} \div \dfrac{2}{9}$ becomes $\dfrac{5}{9} \cdot \dfrac{9}{2}$ which reduces to $\dfrac{5}{\cancel{9}} \cdot \dfrac{\cancel{9}}{2}$ or $\dfrac{5}{2} \cdot \dfrac{5}{2} = x$ or $x = \dfrac{5}{2}$.

But wait!! Don't forget that we need to convert $\dfrac{5}{2}$ into a percent.

$\dfrac{5}{2} = \dfrac{5}{2}\left(\dfrac{100\%}{1}\right) = \left(\dfrac{500\%}{2}\right) = 250\%$ \qquad $\dfrac{5}{9}$ is **<u>250%</u>** of $\dfrac{2}{9}$.

Now, consider another approach to this problem. Go back to the step where we divide both sides of the equation by $\dfrac{2}{9}$ to isolate x. This time, instead of dividing by this fraction we start out by multiplying both sides of the equation by its reciprocal $\left(\dfrac{9}{2}\right)$. This makes simplifying much easier.

$\dfrac{5}{9} = \dfrac{2}{9}x$ becomes $\left(\dfrac{9}{2}\right)\dfrac{5}{9} = \left(\dfrac{9}{2}\right)\dfrac{2}{9}x$ which becomes $\left(\dfrac{\cancel{9}}{2}\right)\dfrac{5}{\cancel{9}} = \left(\dfrac{\cancel{9}}{\cancel{2}}\right)\dfrac{\cancel{2}}{\cancel{9}}x$ and once again

$x = \dfrac{5}{2}$, and $\dfrac{5}{2}$ converts into 250%. \qquad $\dfrac{5}{9}$ is **<u>250%</u>** of $\dfrac{2}{9}$.

As a general rule, if the coefficient of a variable is a fraction, it is easiest to multiply both sides of the equation by the reciprocal of the coefficient of the variable in order to isolate the variable.

Now try problem 23 from exercise set 2.2. (using method 1)

Example 8: If it takes a whole jar of peanut butter to make 40 sandwiches, what percent of the jar will it take to make 3 sandwiches?

Solution: The question is as follows: 3 sandwiches are what percent of 40 sandwiches? Or, simply: 3 is what percent of 40? "3" is the *amount*, "what percent" is the *percent* and "40" is the *base*.

amount = percent • base

$$3 \; = \; x \; • \; 40 \qquad$$ Rewriting the equation with the coefficient in front of the variable we get

$$3 \; = \; 40x. \qquad$$ We divide both sides of the equation by 40 to isolate x.

$$\frac{3}{40} = \frac{40x}{40} \quad \text{becomes} \quad \frac{3}{40} = \frac{\cancel{40}x}{\cancel{40}}. \qquad \text{Using long division} \quad 40\overline{)3.000}^{\;0.075}.$$

$x = 0.075$.

But wait!! Don't forget that we need to convert 0.075 into a percent. $0.075 = 7.5\%$

3 is **7.5%** of 40 and **7.5%** of the jar is needed to make 3 peanut butter sandwiches.

---

*Now try problem 43 from exercise set 2.2. (using method 1)

Example 9: Last year Jasmine gave $26 a month to World Vision. This was 9% of her monthly income. How much income did she make last year? Round your answer to the nearest dollar

---

Solution: The question asks, "How much income did she make last year?" But, we are told how much she gives per month. So, first lets calculate how much she gives per year.

$26(12) = $312   Now the question becomes: $312 is 9% of how much yearly income? "$312" is the *amount*, "9%" is the *percent* and "how much yearly income" is the *base*.

amount = percent • base

$$\$312 \; = \; 9\% \; • \; x \qquad$$ Converting 9% to 0.09 we get the equation

$$\$312 \; = \; 0.09x. \qquad$$ We divide both sides of the equation by 0.09 to isolate x.

$$\frac{\$312}{0.09} = \frac{0.09x}{0.09} \quad \text{becomes} \quad \frac{\$312}{0.09} = \frac{\cancel{0.09}x}{\cancel{0.09}}.$$

Using long division $0.09\overline{)\$312}$ becomes $9\overline{)\$31,200.0}^{\;\$3,466.\overline{6}}$. $x = \$3,466.\overline{6}$.

But, don't forget that we are to round to the nearest dollar.

Jasmine made **$3,467** as income last year.

---

*Now try problem 51 from exercise set 2.2. (using method 1)

<u>Example 10:</u> The "Nutrition Facts" on the label of a 64 fluid ounce container of apple juice state that a serving size of 8 fluid ounces contains 280 mg of potassium. According to the label, this is 8% of the "Percent Daily Value" based on a 2,000-calorie diet.

Nutrition Facts	
Serving Size 8 fl. oz. (240mL)	
Servings Per Container: 8	
Amount Per Serving	
Calories 120	
% Daily Value*	
Total Fat 0g	**0** %
Sodium 25mg	**1** %
Potassium 280mg	**8** %
Total Carbohydrate 29g	**10** %
Sugars 26g	
Protein 0g	

a) What amount of potassium is 100% of the "Percent Daily Value" based on a 2,000-calorie diet?

b) How much of this apple juice will a person need to drink to get 100% of the "Percent Daily Value" of potassium?

Solution to part a): There are several quantities in this problem that are important information to the consumer but they won't be used on the percent equation that is to be created. The question is: 280 mg of potassium is 8% of how much potassium? "280 mg" is the *amount*, "8%" is the *percent* and "how much potassium" is the *base*.

$amount$ $=$ $percent$ • $base$

280 mg $=$ 8%   • x Converting 8% to 0.08 we get the equation

280 mg $=$ 0.08x.   We divide both sides of the equation by 0.08 to isolate x.

$$\frac{280\,mg}{0.08} = \frac{0.08x}{0.08} \quad \text{becomes} \quad \frac{280\,mg}{0.08} = \frac{\cancel{0.08}x}{\cancel{0.08}}.$$

Using long division $0.08\overline{)280\,mg}$ becomes $8\overline{)28{,}000\,mg}$ $= 3{,}500\,mg$.

$x = 3{,}500\,mg$ and   280 mg of potassium is 8% of **3,500 mg** of potassium.

Solution to part b): Since an 8 fluid ounce serving contains 8% of the "Percent Daily Value," then 100 fluid ounces would contain 100% of the "Percent Daily Value"! The answer is **100 fluid ounces**.

Now try problem 59 from exercise set 2.2. (using method 1)

<u>Example 11:</u> The fine print on a packet of carrot seeds states, "Expect a 70% germination rate." If Sally plants 60 of these carrot seeds, how many should she expect to germinate?

Solution: The question is as follows: What amount of carrot seeds is 70% of 60 carrot seeds? Or, simply: What is 70% of 60? "What" is the *amount*, "70%" is the *percent* and "60" is the *base*.

amount $=$ *percent* $\bullet$ *base*

$x \;=\; 70\% \;\bullet\; 60$ Converting 70% to 0.7 we get the equation

$x \;=\; 0.7(60).$

Since $0.7(60) \;=\; 42,$ then $x \;=\; 42,$ and   <u>42</u> is 70% of 60.

Sally should expect <u>**42**</u> carrot seeds to germinate.

Now try problem 45 from exercise set 2.2. (using method 1)

METHOD 2 (Using A Proportion)

This method uses the same three parts as the percent equation method, plus an additional 4th part to complete the proportion. Starting with

$amount = percent \bullet base$ then dividing both sides by "*base*" we get

$$\frac{amount}{base} = \frac{percent \bullet base}{base}$$ or $$\frac{amount}{base} = \frac{percent \bullet \cancel{base}}{\cancel{base}}$$ that is, $$\frac{amount}{base} = \frac{percent}{1}$$

Since 1 = 100% as was discussed in section one, by replacing 1 with 100% we get

$$\boxed{\frac{\textbf{\textit{amount}}}{\textbf{\textit{base}}} = \frac{\textbf{\textit{percent}}}{\textbf{100\%}}}$$

Recall that in method 1, using the percent equation, there is always an extra step. This consists of either: 1) converting a given percent into a fraction or decimal number to use in the equation or 2) when solving for an unknown percent, converting the fraction or decimal number found into a percent at the end of the problem. In the proportion method this extra step, converting to or from a percent, is already built into the equation and no extra step is required. Remember that the *amount is* a *percent of* the *base*. That is to say, the word "*is*" relates to the *amount* and the word "*of*" relates to the *base*. Think of the line from the song, "My country t*is of* thee". *Is* comes first (on top) and *of* comes last (on the bottom).

<u>Example 12:</u>   What number is 45% of 300?

Solution: "What number" is the *amount*, "45%" is the *percent* and "300" is the bas*e*.

$$\frac{amount}{base} = \frac{percent}{100\%}$$ becomes

$$\frac{x}{300} = \frac{45\%}{100\%}.$$ Reducing out the percent signs we get

$$\frac{x}{300} = \frac{45\cancel{\%}}{100\cancel{\%}}.$$ Finding the cross products gives us

$100x = 300(45).$ We divide both sides of the equation by 100 to isolate x.

$$\frac{100x}{100} = \frac{300(45)}{100}$$ Reducing both sides we get

$$\frac{\cancel{100}x}{\cancel{100}} = \frac{3\cancel{00}(45)}{1\cancel{00}}.$$ Since 45(3) = 135, then x = 135.

<u>**135**</u> is 45% of 300.

Now try problem 15 from exercise set 2.2. (using method 2)

Example 13:   8.2% of 20 is what number?

Solution: "What number" is the *amount*, "8.2%" is the *percent* and "20" is the *base*.

$\dfrac{amount}{base} = \dfrac{percent}{100\%}$ becomes

$\dfrac{x}{20} = \dfrac{8.2\%}{100\%}$.   Reducing out the percent signs we get

$\dfrac{x}{20} = \dfrac{8.2\%}{100\%}$.   Finding the cross products gives us

$100x = 20(8.2)$.   We divide both sides of the equation by 100 to isolate x.

$\dfrac{100x}{100} = \dfrac{20(8.2)}{100}$ Reducing both sides we get

$\dfrac{\cancel{100}x}{\cancel{100}} = \dfrac{2\cancel{0}(8.2)}{10\cancel{0}}$.   Since $2(8.2) = 16.4$,   and $\dfrac{16.4}{10} = 1.64$,   then $x = 1.64$.

1.64 is 8.2% of 20.

Now try problem 33 from exercise set 2.2. (using method 2)

Example 14:   What number is 170% of 60?

Solution: "What number" is the *amount*, "170%" is the *percent* and "60" is the *base*.

$\dfrac{amount}{base} = \dfrac{percent}{100\%}$ becomes

$\dfrac{x}{60} = \dfrac{170\%}{100\%}$.   Reducing out the percent signs we get

$\dfrac{x}{60} = \dfrac{170\%}{100\%}$.   Finding the cross products gives us

$100x = 60(170)$.   We divide both sides of the equation by 100 to isolate x.

$\dfrac{100x}{100} = \dfrac{60(170)}{100}$ Reducing both sides we get

$\dfrac{\cancel{100}x}{\cancel{100}} = \dfrac{6\cancel{0}(17\cancel{0})}{1\cancel{00}}$.   Since $6(17) = 102$, then $x = 102$.   **102** is 170% of 60.

Now try problem 29 from exercise set 2.2. (using method 2)

Note: In this example the "amount" is larger than the "base". This is because the "percent" is greater than 100%. When you find more than 100% of something, the resulting "amount" you get will be larger than the "base" amount you started with.

Example 15:   0.6% of what number is 12?

Solution: "12" is the *amount*, "0.6%" is the *percent* and "what number" is the *base*.

$\dfrac{amount}{base} = \dfrac{percent}{100\%}$ becomes $\dfrac{12}{x} = \dfrac{0.6\%}{100\%}$.   Reducing out the percent signs we get

$\dfrac{12}{x} = \dfrac{0.6\%}{100\%}$.   Finding the cross products gives us

$12(100) = 0.6x$.   We divide both sides of the equation by 0.6 to isolate x.

$\dfrac{12(100)}{0.6} = \dfrac{0.6x}{0.6}$ Reducing the right side we get

$\dfrac{12(100)}{0.6} = \dfrac{0.6x}{0.6}$.   Since $12(100) = 1{,}200$,   then $x = \dfrac{1{,}200}{0.6}$.

Using long division $6\overline{)12{,}000}$ = $2{,}000$. $x = 2{,}000$ and   12 is 0.6% of **2,000**.

Now try problem 35 from exercise set 2.2. (using method 2)

Example 16:   5.4 is 80% of what number?

Solution: "5.4" is the *amount*, "80%" is the *percent* and "what number" is the *base*.

$\dfrac{amount}{base} = \dfrac{percent}{100\%}$ becomes $\dfrac{5.4}{x} = \dfrac{80\%}{100\%}$.   Reducing out the percent signs we get

$\dfrac{5.4}{x} = \dfrac{80\%}{100\%}$.   Finding the cross products gives us

$5.4(100) = 80x$.   We divide both sides of the equation by 80 to isolate x.

$\dfrac{5.4(100)}{80} = \dfrac{80x}{80}$ Reducing both sides we get

$\dfrac{5.4(100)}{80} = \dfrac{80x}{80}$.   Since $5.4(10) = 54$,   then $x = \dfrac{54}{8}$.

Using long division $8\overline{)54.00}$ = 6.75. $x = 6.75$ and   5.4 is 80% of **6.75**.

Now try problem 17 from exercise set 2.2. (using method 2)

<u>Example 17:</u>   12 is what percent of 40?

Solution: "12" is the *amount*, "what percent" is the *percent* and "40" is the *base*.

$\dfrac{amount}{base} = \dfrac{percent}{100\%}$ becomes

$\dfrac{12}{40} = \dfrac{x}{100\%}$.   Finding the cross products gives us

$40x = 12(100\%)$.   We divide both sides of the equation by 40 to isolate x.

$\dfrac{40x}{40} = \dfrac{12(100\%)}{40}$ Reducing both sides we get

$\dfrac{\cancel{40}x}{\cancel{40}} = \dfrac{12(10\cancel{0}\%)}{4\cancel{0}}$.   Since $12(10\%) = 120\%$, and $\dfrac{120\%}{4} = 30\%$, then $x = 30\%$.

12 is **30%** of 40.

Now try problem 27 from exercise set 2.2. (using method 2)

<u>Example 18:</u>   What percent of 27 is 0.06?

Solution: "0.06" is the *amount*, "what percent" is the *percent* and "27" is the *base*.

$\dfrac{amount}{base} = \dfrac{percent}{100\%}$ becomes

$\dfrac{0.06}{27} = \dfrac{x}{100\%}$.   Finding the cross products gives us

$27x = 0.06(100\%)$.   We divide both sides of the equation by 27 to isolate x.

$\dfrac{27x}{27} = \dfrac{0.06(100\%)}{27}$ Reducing the left side we get

$\dfrac{\cancel{27}x}{\cancel{27}} = \dfrac{0.06(100\%)}{27}$.   Since $0.06(100\%) = 6\%$,

and $\dfrac{6\%}{27} = \dfrac{(2 \cdot 3)}{(9 \cdot 3)}\% = \dfrac{(2 \cdot \cancel{3})}{(9 \cdot \cancel{3})}\% = \dfrac{2}{9}\%$, then $x = \dfrac{2}{9}\%$.   0.6 is $\dfrac{\mathbf{2}}{\mathbf{9}}\%$ of 27.

Now try problem 9 from exercise set 2.2. (using method 2)

<u>Example 19:</u> $\dfrac{2}{3}\%$ of what number is 2?

Solution: "2" is the *amount*, "$\dfrac{2}{3}\%$" is the *percent* and "what number" is the *base*.

$\dfrac{amount}{base}=\dfrac{percent}{100\%}$ becomes $\dfrac{2}{x}=\dfrac{\frac{2}{3}\%}{100\%}$.   Reducing out the percent signs we get

$\dfrac{2}{x}=\dfrac{\frac{2}{3}\cancel{\%}}{100\cancel{\%}}$.   Finding the cross products gives us

$2(100)=\dfrac{2}{3}x$.   We divide both sides of the equation by $\dfrac{2}{3}$ to isolate x.

$\dfrac{2(100)}{\frac{2}{3}}=\dfrac{\frac{2}{3}}{\frac{2}{3}}x$ Reducing the right side we get

$\dfrac{2(100)}{\frac{2}{3}}=\dfrac{\cancel{\frac{2}{3}}}{\cancel{\frac{2}{3}}}x$.   On the left side $\dfrac{2(100)}{\frac{2}{3}}=2(100)\div\dfrac{2}{3}$ but dividing by a fraction

is the same as multiplying by its reciprocal so $2(100)\div\dfrac{2}{3}$ becomes $2(100)\left(\dfrac{3}{2}\right)$, which

reduces to $\cancel{2}(100)\left(\dfrac{3}{\cancel{2}}\right)$ or 300. $x=300$ and finally, 2 is $\dfrac{2}{3}\%$ of **<u>300</u>**.

Now, consider another approach to this problem. Go back to the step where we divide

both sides of the equation by $\dfrac{2}{3}$ to isolate x. This time, instead of dividing by this

fraction we start out by multiplying both sides of the equation by its reciprocal $\left(\dfrac{3}{2}\right)$.

This makes simplifying much easier.

$2(100)=\dfrac{2}{3}x$ becomes $\left(\dfrac{3}{2}\right)(2)(100)=\left(\dfrac{3}{2}\right)\dfrac{2}{3}x$ which reduces to

$\left(\dfrac{3}{\cancel{2}}\right)(\cancel{2})(100)=\left(\dfrac{\cancel{3}}{\cancel{2}}\right)\dfrac{\cancel{2}}{\cancel{3}}x$ or $300=x$. $x=300$ and finally, 2 is $\dfrac{2}{3}\%$ of **<u>300</u>**.

As a general rule, if the coefficient of a variable is a fraction, it is easiest to multiply both sides of the equation by the reciprocal of the coefficient of the variable in order to isolate the variable.

Now try problem 25 from exercise set 2.2. (using method 2)

Example 20: If it takes a whole jar of hot fudge topping to make 25 hot fudge sundaes, what percent of the jar will it take to make 3 hot fudge sundaes?

Solution: The question is as follows: 3 servings of hot fudge topping are what percent of 25 servings of hot fudge topping? Or, simply: 3 is what percent of 25? "3" is the *amount*, "what percent" is the *percent* and "25" is the *base*.

$$\frac{amount}{base} = \frac{percent}{100\%}$$ becomes

$$\frac{3}{25} = \frac{x}{100\%}.$$ Finding the cross products gives us

$$25x = 3(100\%).$$ We divide both sides of the equation by 25 to isolate x.

$$\frac{25x}{25} = \frac{3(100\%)}{25}$$ Reducing the left side we get

$$\frac{\cancel{25}x}{\cancel{25}} = \frac{3(100\%)}{25}.$$ Since $3(100\%) = 300\%$, and $\frac{300\%}{25} = \frac{(300 \div 25)}{(25 \div 25)}\% = 12\%$, then

$x = 12\%$, and 3 is **12%** of 25.   **12%** of the jar is needed to make 3 hot fudge sundaes.

Now try problem 43 from exercise set 2.2. (using method 2)

Example 21: The fine print on a packet of radish seeds states, "Expect an 85% germination rate." If Laura plants 60 of these radish seeds, how many should she expect to germinate?

Solution: The question is as follows: What amount of radish seeds is 85% of 60 radish seeds? Or, simply: What is 85% of 60? "What" is the *amount*, "85%" is the *percent* and "60" is the *base*.

$$\frac{amount}{base} = \frac{percent}{100\%}$$ becomes

$$\frac{x}{60} = \frac{85\%}{100\%}.$$ Reducing out the percent signs we get

$$\frac{x}{60} = \frac{85\cancel{\%}}{100\cancel{\%}}.$$ Finding the cross products gives us

$$100x = 60(85).$$ We divide both sides of the equation by 100 to isolate x.

$$\frac{100x}{100} = \frac{60(85)}{100}$$ Reducing both sides we get

$$\frac{\cancel{100}x}{\cancel{100}} = \frac{6\cancel{0}(85)}{10\cancel{0}}.$$ Since $6(85) = 510$ and $\frac{510}{10}$ reduces further to $\frac{51\cancel{0}}{1\cancel{0}}$ or 51, then $x = 51$.

Laura should expect **51** radish seeds to germinate.

Now try problem 45 from exercise set 2.2. (using method 2)

Example 22: The "Nutrition Facts" on the label of a 64 fluid ounce container of grape juice state that a serving size of 8 fluid ounces contains 42 g of carbohydrates. According to the label, this is 14% of the "Percent Daily Value" based on a 2,000-calorie diet. What amount of carbohydrates is 100% of the "Percent Daily Value" based on a 2,000-calorie diet?

Nutrition Facts

Serving Size: 8 FL. OZ. (240mL)
Servings Per Container: 8

Amount Per Serving	
Calories 170	

	% Daily Value*
Total Fat 0g	0 %
Sodium 20mg	1 %
Total Carb. 42g	14 %
Sugars 40g	
Protein 0g	

Solution: There are several quantities in this problem that are important information to the consumer but they won't be used on the percent equation that is to be created. The question is: 42 g of carbohydrates is 14% of how many carbohydrates? "42 g" is the *amount*, "14%" is the *percent* and "how many carbohydrates" is the *base*.

$$\frac{amount}{base} = \frac{percent}{100\%}$$ becomes

$$\frac{42\,g}{x} = \frac{14\%}{100\%}.$$ Reducing out the percent signs we get

$$\frac{42\,g}{x} = \frac{14\cancel{\%}}{100\cancel{\%}}.$$ Finding the cross products gives us

$$14x = 42\,g(100).$$ We divide both sides of the equation by 14 to isolate x.

$$\frac{14x}{14} = \frac{42\,g(100)}{14}$$ Reducing the left side we get

$$\frac{\cancel{14}x}{\cancel{14}} = \frac{42\,g(100)}{14}.$$ $42\,g(100) = 4{,}200\,g$ So $x = \dfrac{4{,}200\,g}{14}.$

Using long division $14\overline{)4{,}200\,g}$ quotient $300\,g$.

$x = 300\,g$ and 42 g of carbohydrates is 14% of **300 g** of carbohydrates.

Now try problem 59 from exercise set 2.2. (using method 2)

<u>Example 23:</u> Last year Anthony gave $14 a month to a local charity. This was 9% of his monthly income. How much income did he make last year? Round your answer to the nearest dollar.

Solution: The question asks, "How much income did he make last year?" But, we are told how much he gives per month. So, first lets calculate how much he gives per year.

$14(12) = $168   Now the question becomes: $168 is 9% of how much yearly income? "$168" is the *amount*, "9%" is the *percent* and "how much yearly income" is the *base*.

$$\frac{amount}{base} = \frac{percent}{100\%}$$ becomes

$$\frac{\$168}{x} = \frac{9\%}{100\%}.$$ Reducing out the percent signs we get

$$\frac{\$168}{x} = \frac{9\%\!\!\!\diagup}{100\%\!\!\!\diagup}.$$ Finding the cross products gives us

$$9x = \$168(100).$$ We divide both sides of the equation by 9 to isolate x.

$$\frac{9x}{9} = \frac{\$168(100)}{9}$$ Reducing the left side we get

$$\frac{\cancel{9}x}{\cancel{9}} = \frac{\$168(100)}{9}.$$ $$\$168(100) = \$16,800$$ $$x = \frac{\$16,800}{9}$$

Using long division $9\overline{)\$16,800.0}$. $x = \$1,866.\overline{6}$

But, don't forget that we are to round to the nearest dollar.

Anthony made **$1,867** as income last year.

Now try problem 51 from exercise set 2.2. (using method 2)

Calculating Grades: The following problems are designed to help you calculate grades on homework assignments and tests. In each case, the answer will be given to the nearest whole-number percent.

The formula used to calculate grades is as follows:

$$\frac{total\ points\ received}{total\ points\ possible} \bullet \frac{100\%}{1} = percent\ correct$$

Example 24: If a student earns 12.5 points out of 18 points on a homework assignment, what percent did they get correct?

Solution: The total amount of points received is 12.5 and the total amount of points possible is 18.

So, $\dfrac{total\ points\ received}{total\ points\ possible} \bullet \dfrac{100\%}{1} = percent\ correct$

becomes $\dfrac{12.5}{18} \cdot \dfrac{100\%}{1} = \dfrac{1{,}250\%}{18}$.

We are going to round this answer to the nearest whole-number percent. Using long division we will go one place past the decimal point to the tenth place $18\overline{)1{,}250.0\%}$ $^{69.4\%}$

and then round this answer to **69%**.

Now try problem 63 from exercise set 2.2.

Example 25: Carolyn wants to calculate her overall test grade midway through the quarter. On four tests she earned the following scores: 79 out of 85, 37 out of 40, 89 out of 100 and 63 out of 80. Assuming that all points on tests have equal value, what overall percent does Carolyn have on her tests?

Solution: The total amount of points received is $79 + 37 + 89 + 63 = 268$.

The total points possible is $85 + 40 + 100 + 80 = 305$.

So, $\dfrac{total\ points\ received}{total\ points\ possible} \bullet \dfrac{100\%}{1} = percent\ correct$

becomes $\dfrac{268}{305} \cdot \dfrac{100\%}{1} = \dfrac{26{,}800\%}{305}$.

We are going to round this answer to the nearest whole-number percent. Using long division we will go one place past the decimal point to the tenth place $305\overline{)26{,}800.0\%}$ $^{87.8\%}$

and then round this answer to **88%**.

Now try problem 71 from exercise set 2.2.

<u>Section 2 exercises.</u>   Solve each of the following problems.

1.   What number is 56% of 350?

2.   What number is 62% of 400?

3.   8 is 12% of what number?

4.   3 is 9% of what number?

5.   216 is what percent of 540?

6.   72 is what percent of 120?

7.   0.3% of what number is 18?

8.   0.6% of what number is 24?

9.   What percent of 2 is 1.4?

10.   What percent of 13 is 2.6?

11.   0.4% of 17 is what number?

12.   7.2% of 60 is what number?

13.   0.07 is what percent of 3.6?

14.   0.09 is what percent of 3.6?

15.   What number is 8% of 6.4?

16.   What number is 12% of 54.5?

17.   2.95 is 40% of what number?

18.   1.76 is 30% of what number?

19.   70% of $\frac{4}{5}$ is what number?

20.   75% of $\frac{3}{4}$ is what number?

21.   40% of what number is $\frac{1}{3}$?

22.   70% of what number is $\frac{2}{9}$?

23.   What percent of $\frac{5}{7}$ is $\frac{2}{7}$?

24.   What percent of $\frac{4}{9}$ is $\frac{2}{9}$?

25.   12 is $\frac{3}{5}$% of what number?

26.   14 is $\frac{2}{9}$% of what number?

27.   65 is what percent of 165?

28.   34 is what percent of 60?

29.   What number is $2\frac{1}{4}$% of 800?

30.   What number is $6\frac{2}{5}$% of 700?

31.   What percent of 3 is 12?

32.   What percent of 1 is 9?

33.   430% of 50 is what number?

34.   285% of 60 is what number?

35.   320% of what number is 600?

36.   140% of what number is 70?

Application Problems:

37. When playing basketball Miguel makes 70% of his free throws. In a recent game Miguel attempted 30 free throws. How many free throws would you expect him to make?

38. When playing basketball Joseph makes 65% of his free throws. In a recent game Joseph attempted 20 free throws. How many free throws would you expect him to make?

39. On a recent utility bill, the water/sewer/garbage portion of the bill was $93.62. This consisted of 73% of the total bill. To the nearest cent, what was the total amount of the utility bill?

40. On a recent utility bill, the water/sewer/garbage portion of the bill was $112.78. This consisted of 73% of the total bill. To the nearest cent, what was the total amount of the utility bill?

41. Doug plans to plow a field in one day. Before lunch he plows 8 acres, which is 40% of the field. How many acres will he have to plow after lunch in order to finish the field?

42. Tracey plans to disk a field in two days. The first day he disks 15 acres, which is 60% of the field. How many acres will he have to disk on the second day in order to finish the field?

43. If it takes a whole can of tuna to make 8 servings of tuna salad, what percent of the can will it take to make 3 servings of tuna salad?

44. If it takes a whole bottle of barbeque sauce to make 16 pounds of barbequed ribs, what percent of the bottle will it take to make 5 pounds of barbequed ribs?

45. Johnny planted 80 apple seeds with a germination rate of 65%. How many apple seeds should he expect to germinate?

46. Peter planted 75 pumpkin seeds with a germination rate of 72%. How many pumpkin seeds should he expect to germinate?

47. On a recent phone bill, the long distance calls portion of the bill was $12.85. This consisted of 55% of the total bill. To the nearest cent, what was the total amount of the phone bill?

48.   On a recent phone bill, the long distance calls portion of the bill was $16.78. This consisted of 65% of the total bill. To the nearest cent, what was the total amount of the phone bill?

49.   Joe must bale the hay in a 20-acre field before sunup. If Joe completes 12 acres before dinner, what percent of the field must Joe bale after dinner in order to finish the entire field?

50.   Bron wants to harvest the wheat in a 40-acre field in two days. If on the first day Bron harvests 16 acres, what percent of the field must she complete the second day?

51.   Last year Percy gave $120 a month to a local mission. If he made $5,000 last year, what percent of his income did he give to a local mission?

52.   Last year Marguerite gave $160 a month to support public television. If she made $6,000 last year, what percent of her income did she give to support public television?

53.   Medical expenses that exceed 7.5% of a person's income may be used as a tax deduction. If Panyada made $57,400 last year, after what amount of medical expenses would she be able to use the remaining expenses as a tax deduction?

54.   Medical expenses that exceed 7.5% of a person's income may be used as a tax deduction. If Ronda made $63,400 last year, after what amount of medical expenses would she be able to use the remaining expenses as a tax deduction?

55.   Last season in summer league baseball Pedro got a hit 40% of the time. If he had a total of 14 hits, how many "at bats" did Pedro have last season?

56.   Last year playing winter league baseball Joe got a hit 30% of the time. If he had a total of 15 hits, how many "at bats" did Joe have last year?

57.   Mike has to milk all the cows at the dairy once a day. If he milks 42 cows in the morning and the other 28 cows in the evening, what percent of the cows does he milk in the evening?

58.   Minnie has to slop all the pigs in the pigsty once a day. If she slops 18 pigs in the morning and the other 22 pigs in the afternoon, what percent of the pigs does she slop in the afternoon?

59.   The "Nutrition Facts" on the label of a 40-ounce jar of peanut butter state that a serving size of 2 tablespoons contains 150 mg of sodium. According to the label, this is 6% of the "Percent Daily Value" based on a 2,000-calorie diet. What amount of sodium is 100% of the "Percent Daily Value" if based on a 2,000-calorie diet?

Nutrition Facts	
Serving Size 2 Tbsp. (32g)	
Servings Per Container about 35	
Amount Per Serving	
Calories	190
Calories from Fat	130
	% Daily Value*
Total Fat 16g	**25** %
Sodium 150mg	**6** %
Total Carbohydrate 7g	**2** %
Sugars 3g	
Protein 8g	

60.   The "Nutrition Facts" on the label of a 21-ounce box of cereal state that a serving size of 3/4 cup contains 80 mg of potassium. According to the label, this is 2% of the "Percent Daily Value" based on a 2,000-calorie diet. What amount of potassium is 100% of the "Percent Daily Value" if based on a 2,000-calorie diet?

Nutrition Facts	
Serving Size 3/4 cup (32g)	
Servings Per Container about 19	
Amount Per Serving	
Calories	120
Calories from Fat	15
	% Daily Value*
Total Fat 1.5g	**2** %
Potassium 80mg	**2** %
Total Carbohydrate 25g	**8** %
Sugars 9g	
Protein 3g	

61.   Jim told his hired hand Syd to round up 75 cows and then split them into two groups. 24% of the cows were to be put into the barn and the rest were to be left out standing in their field. How many cows were out standing in their field?

62.   Bo told her hired hand Jed to gather eggs from the henhouse. Jed collected 40 eggs and brought them to Bo. Bo inspected them and complained that 15% of them were broken. How many of them were still good eggs?

For the following problems, give each answer to the nearest whole-number percent. (For example, 74% stays 74%, but 76.7% rounds to 77% and 69.2% rounds to 69%.) Then, using your instructors grading scale determine what letter grade that percent would become. See examples 24 and 25 on page 144.

63.   If Gene earned 13 points out of 18 points on a homework assignment, what percent did he get correct?

64.   If Carlos earned 7 points out of 12 points on a homework assignment, what percent did he get correct?

65.   If Maria earned 14 points out of 22 points on a homework assignment, what percent did she get correct?

66.   If Becky earned 9 points out of 16 points on a homework assignment, what percent did she get correct?

67.   Bogden wants to calculate his overall homework grade midway through the quarter. On the nine assignments that were graded he earned the following scores: 13 out of 15, 7 out of 10, 9 out of 12, 17 out of 18, 14 out of 15, 20 out of 22, 12 out of 15, 17 out of 20, and 19 out of 21. Assuming that all points on homework have equal value, what overall percent does Bogden have on his homework?

68.   Koku wants to calculate his overall homework grade midway through the quarter. On the nine assignments that were graded he earned the following scores: 15 out of 18, 19 out of 22, 18 out of 22, 14 out of 15, 10 out of 10, 20 out of 24, 16 out of 20, 13 out of 18, and 7 out of 9. Assuming that all points on homework have equal value, what overall percent does Koku have on his homework?

69.   Abba wants to calculate her overall quiz grade midway through the quarter. On the six quizzes that were graded she earned the following scores: 7 out of 10, 12 out of 15, 6 out of 10, 9 out of 15, 8 out of 10, and 11 out of 15. Assuming that all points on quizzes have equal value, what overall percent does Abba have on her quizzes?

70.   Lydia wants to calculate her overall quiz grade midway through the quarter. On the six quizzes that were graded she earned the following scores: 8 out of 12, 15 out of 16, 7 out of 12, 9 out of 16, 10 out of 12, and 11 out of 16. Assuming that all points on quizzes have equal value, what overall percent does Lydia have on her quizzes?

71.   Carol wants to calculate her overall test grade midway through the quarter. On five tests she earned the following scores: 85 out of 100, 83 out of 90, 48 out of 55, 80 out of 85, and 97 out of 100. Assuming that all points on tests have equal value, what overall percent does Carol have on her tests?

72.   Lyn wants to calculate her overall test grade midway through the quarter. On five tests she earned the following scores: 93 out of 100, 89 out of 90, 47 out of 55, 74 out of 85, and 91 out of 100. Assuming that all points on tests have equal value, what overall percent does Lyn have on her tests?

Mixture problems: Give each answer to the nearest whole-number percent.

73.   **a)**   For breakfast Joe ate the following: Chocolate covered donuts weighing 50 grams, 13 grams of which was fat; sticky donuts weighing 71 grams, 8 grams of which was fat; and a serving of orange juice weighing 71 grams, 0 grams of which was fat. What percent of Joe's breakfast was fat?

b)   For lunch Joe ate the following: Macaroni and cheese weighing 340 grams, 15 grams of which was fat; a hot dog weighing 50 grams, 16 grams of which was fat; barbequed potato chips weighing 28 grams, 10 grams of which was fat; and chocolate pudding weighing 99 grams, 5 grams of which was fat. What percent of Joe's lunch was fat?

c)   For dinner Joe ate the following: Pasta weighing 56 grams, 1 gram of which was fat; tomato sauce weighing 62 grams, 0 grams of which was fat; a Caesar salad weighing 100 grams, 14 grams of which was fat; and salad dressing weighing 32 grams, 6 grams of which was fat. What percent of Joe's dinner was fat?

d)   If all Joe ate was breakfast, lunch, and dinner, what percent of his total food intake for the day was fat?

74.   **a)**   For breakfast Allan ate the following: An English muffin weighing 61 grams, 1 gram of which was fat; a serving of oatmeal weighing 40 grams, 3 grams of which was fat; and a serving of apple juice weighing 71 grams, 0 grams of which was fat. What percent of Allan's breakfast was fat?

b)   For lunch Allan ate the following: A five-cheese pizza weighing 131 grams, 12 grams of which was fat; a piece of garlic bread weighing 51 grams, 6 grams of which was fat; a fruit pie weighing 125 grams, 21 grams of which was fat; and a serving of cola weighing 75 grams, 0 grams of which was fat. What percent of Allan's lunch was fat?

c)   For dinner Allan ate the following: A chicken breast weighing 132 grams, 1 gram of which was fat; a potato weighing 148 grams, 0 grams of which was fat; a serving of canned corn weighing 123 grams, 1 gram of which was fat; and a serving of apple sauce weighing 130 grams, 0 grams of which was fat. What percent of Allan's dinner was fat?

d)   If all Allan ate was breakfast, lunch, and dinner, what percent of his total food intake for the day was fat?

Writing:

75.   When using either the percent equation method or the proportion method as explained in this section, is the *amount* larger or smaller than the *base*? Explain your answer.

76.   A recent newspaper article on investing in the stock market had the following two statements. The first statement said, "Fifty percent return on your money? No problem." The second statement said, "You can increase your returns by fifty percent per year." Do these statements mean the same thing? Which of these statements would you rather have applied to your investment? Why?

77.   How can you easily determine that 47% of 180 is slightly less than 90?

78.   Explain how you would quickly estimate 11% of 180.

79.   If you can increase the price of an item by 100%, can you also decrease the price of an item by 100%? Explain.

80.   If you can increase the price of an item by 150%, can you also decrease the price of an item by 150%? Explain.

PERCENTS

Section 3: Applications of Percents

When we purchase an item at a store, not only is money involved, but so is the concept of percent. If an item has **sales tax** applied to it, then this tax is based on a percent of the cost of the item. This percent is called the **tax rate**. If a salesperson works on **commission**, then they are paid based on a percent of the sales. This percent is called the **commission rate**.

An employee working 30 hours per week is asked to increase the number of hours that she works by 20 percent. Since 20 percent of 30 hours is 6 hours, she would increase her hours to 36 per week. In this situation, 20 percent is the **percent of increase** and 6 hours is the **amount of increase**. Another employee working 50 hours per week asks his boss to decrease the amount of hours that he works by 10 percent. This is obviously so he will have more time to spend on his math homework. Since 10 percent of 50 hours is 5 hours, he would decrease his hours to 45 per week. In this situation, 10 percent is the **percent of decrease** and 5 hours is the **amount of decrease**.

An item that is regularly priced at $30 is on sale for 20% off the regular price. Since 20% of $30 is $6, the **sale price** is $24. The **discount** is $6 and the **discount rate** is 20%.

The concepts that are underlined in the previous paragraphs will be discussed in this section. Applications involving these ideas can be solved using two methods, the percent equation method and the proportion method, introduced in section 2 of this chapter.

METHOD 1 (The Percent Equation)

Sales Tax

Sales tax is usually added to the original cost of an item when it is purchased at a store. The amount of sales tax to be added is determined by finding a percent of the cost of an item. This percent is called the *tax rate*. By starting with the percent equation and changing the names to accommodate the sales tax scenario,

$$amount = percent \cdot base$$

becomes the following formula which is used to calculate sales tax.

$$amount\ of\ sales\ tax = tax\ rate \cdot cost\ of\ item$$

Once the amount of sales tax has been calculated, the total cost of an item can be found by using the following formula:

$$total\ cost = cost\ of\ item + sales\ tax$$

Example 1: A polo shirt is on sale for $15. If the sales tax rate is 8.3%, what is the amount of sales tax? What is the total cost of the shirt?

Solution: "What is the amount of sales tax" is the *amount of sales tax*, "8.3%" is the *tax rate* and "$15" is the *cost of item*.

amount of sales tax = tax rate • cost of item

$$x \quad = \quad 8.3\% \quad \bullet \quad \$15 \qquad \text{Converting 8.3\% to 0.083}$$
$$\text{we get the equation}$$
$$x \quad = \quad 0.083(\$15).$$

Since $0.083(\$15) = \$1.245,$ then $x = \$1.245.$

However, since sales tax can only be paid in whole cents, round this amount to the nearest cent.

Now, the amount of sales tax on $15 becomes **$1.25**. Then using the formula:

total cost = cost of item + sales tax

total cost = $15   + $1.25   which is $16.25.

The total cost of the shirt is **$16.25**.

Now try problem 1 from exercise set 2.3. (using method 1)

Example 2: $4.59 is the price of a movie on videotape. If the sales tax on the movie is $0.35, what is the sales tax rate? Give your answer to the nearest tenth of a percent.

Solution: "$0.35" is the *amount of sales tax*, "what is the sales tax rate" is the *tax rate* and "$4.59" is the *cost of item*.

amount of sales tax = tax rate • cost of item

$$\$0.35 \quad = \quad x \quad \bullet \quad \$4.59 \qquad \text{Rewriting the equation with the coefficient}$$
$$\text{in front of the variable we get}$$
$$\$0.35 \quad = \quad \$4.59x. \qquad \text{Divide both sides of the equation by \$4.59 to isolate } x.$$

$$\frac{\$0.35}{\$4.59} = \frac{\$4.59x}{\$4.59} \quad \text{becomes} \quad \frac{\cancel{\$}0.35}{\cancel{\$}4.59} = \frac{\cancel{\$4.59}x}{\cancel{\$4.59}}.$$

Using long division, go four places past the decimal point to the ten thousandth place.

$$4.59\overline{)0.35} \quad \text{becomes} \quad 459\overline{)35.0000}^{\,0.0762}. \quad \text{Now, rounding to the nearest thousandth,}$$

$x = 0.076$.   **But wait!!** Don't forget to convert 0.076 into a percent.

$0.076 = 7.6\%$ The sales tax rate, to the nearest tenth of a percent, is **7.6%**.

Now try problem 49 from exercise set 2.3. (using method 1)

Note: The thousandth place of a regular number is the tenth place of a percent. This is because we move the decimal point two places to the right when we convert to a percent.

Commission

A person who works on **_commission_** has their salary determined by the dollar amount of the merchandise they sell. They are paid a percent of the amount of sales they make. This percent is called the **_commission rate_**. By starting with the percent equation and changing the names to accommodate the commission scenario,

$$amount \quad = \quad percent \quad \bullet \quad base$$

becomes the following formula which is used to calculate commission.

$$commission = commission\ rate \bullet amount\ of\ sales$$

<u>Example 3:</u> What amount of sales will produce a commission of $42 if the commission rate is 7%?

> Solution: "$42" is the *commission,* "7%" is the *commission rate* and "what amount of sales" is the *amount of sales.*
>
> *commission = commission rate • amount of sales*
>
> $\quad\quad\$42 \quad = \quad\quad 7\% \quad\quad \bullet \quad\quad x$ $\quad$ Converting 7% to 0.07 we get the equation
>
> $\quad\quad\$42 \quad = \quad 0.07x.$ $\quad\quad\quad\quad$ Divide both sides of the equation by 0.07 to isolate x.
>
> $\dfrac{\$42}{0.07} = \dfrac{0.07x}{0.07}$ becomes $\dfrac{\$42}{0.07} = \dfrac{\cancel{0.07}x}{\cancel{0.07}}.$
>
> Using long division $\quad 0.07\overline{)\$42} \quad$ becomes $\quad 7\overline{)\$4{,}200}^{\ \$600}. \quad x = \$600$
>
> and the amount of sales is **$600**.

Now try problem 7 from exercise set 2.3. (using method 1)

<u>Example 4:</u> A salesman works for a base salary of $550 a month plus 6% commission on all the merchandise he sells beyond $8,000. If he sells $9,200 worth of merchandise in one month, what will his total salary be for the month?

> Solution: "Commission" is the *commission,* and "6%" is the *commission rate.* To find the amount of sales that the commission is paid on, we subtract $8,000 from $9,200 to get $1,200. "$1,200" is the *amount of sales.*
>
> *commission = commission rate • amount of sales*
>
> $\quad\quad\quad x \quad = \quad\quad 6\% \quad\quad \bullet \quad\quad \$1{,}200 \quad$ Converting 6% to 0.06 we get the equation
>
> $\quad\quad x \quad = \quad 0.06(\$1{,}200).$
>
> Since $\quad 0.06(\$1{,}200) = \$72, \quad$ then $\quad x = \$72.$
>
> The amount of commission on $1,200 is $72. By adding the $72 commission to his base salary of $550 we get his total salary. His total salary is **$622**.

Now try problem 13 from exercise set 2.3. (using method 1)

Example 5: A woman working on commission makes $48 for selling $700 worth of merchandise. What is her commission rate? Give the answer to the nearest tenth of a percent.

Solution: "$48" is the *commission*, "what is her commission rate" is the *commission rate* and "$700" is the *amount of sales*.

commission = *commission rate* • *amount of sales*

$48 = x • $700   Rewriting the equation with the coefficient in front of the variable we get

$48 = 700x$.   Divide both sides of the equation by $300 to isolate x.

$$\frac{\$48}{\$700} = \frac{\$700x}{\$700} \quad \text{becomes} \quad \frac{\$48}{\$700} = \frac{\cancel{\$700}x}{\cancel{\$700}}.$$

Using long division, go four places past the decimal point to the ten thousandth place.

$$700\overline{)48} \quad \text{becomes} \quad 700\overline{)48.0000}^{\;0.0685}. \quad \text{Now, rounding to the nearest thousandth,}$$

$x = 0.069$.   **But wait!!** Don't forget to convert 0.069 into a percent.

$0.069 = 6.9\%$ The commission rate, to the nearest tenth of a percent, is **6.9%**.

Now try problem 69 from exercise set 2.3. (using method 1)

Note: As was mentioned with example 2, the thousandth place of a regular number is the tenth place of a percent.

Example 6: How many CDs will a salesperson need to sell to make $24.30 in commission if the commission rate is 6% and the CDs sell for $15 apiece?

Solution: "$24.30" is the *commission*, and "6%" is the *commission rate*. However, to get the *amount of sales*, we'll need "how many CDs • $15 a piece."

commission = *commission rate* • *amount of sales*

$24.30 =   6%   • x Converting 6% to 0.06 we get the equation

$24.30 = 0.06$x$.   Divide both sides of the equation by 0.06 to isolate x

$$\frac{\$24.30}{0.06} = \frac{0.06x}{0.06} \quad \text{becomes} \quad \frac{\$24.30}{0.06} = \frac{\cancel{0.06}x}{\cancel{0.06}}.$$

Using long division $0.06\overline{)\$24.30}$ becomes $6\overline{)\$2,430}^{\;\$405}$.   Consequently, $x = \$405$

and the amount of sales is $405. This, however, is not the final answer that we are looking for. The question was "How many CDs?" Take the $405 and divide it by $15 to get the

actual number of CDs. Using long division $\$15\overline{)\$405}^{\;27}$.

The number of CDs that the salesperson will need to sell is **27**.

Now try problem 15 from exercise set 2.3. (using method 1)

Amount of increase

Suppose the ***original amount*** of students in a math class was 30, and the number of students in the class was to increase by 10 percent. Since 10 percent of 30 is 3, then the class would increase by 3 students. The new class size would then be 33 students. The 10 percent is called the ***percent of increase*** and the 3 students are called the ***amount of increase.*** By starting with the percent equation and changing the names to accommodate the amount of increase scenario,

$$amount \quad = \quad percent \quad \bullet \quad base$$

becomes the following formula which is used to calculate amount of increase.

$$amount\ of\ increase\ =\ percent\ of\ increase \bullet original\ amount$$

Example 7: Last week Maria spent $52 on groceries. This week her cousin came to visit, causing her grocery bill to increase by 40%. By how much money did her grocery bill increase this week? What is her total grocery bill for this week?

Solution: "By how much money" is the *amount of increase*, "40%" is the *percent of increase* and "$52" is the *original amount.*

amount of increase = percent of increase • original amount

$$x \quad = \quad 40\% \quad \bullet \quad \$52 \qquad \text{Converting 40\% to 0.4}$$
$$\text{we get the equation}$$

$$x = 0.4(\$52).$$

Since $0.4(\$52) = \$20.80,$ then $x = \$20.80,$ and

the amount of increase is **$20.80**.   Maria's grocery bill increased by **$20.80** this week.

To get her total grocery bill for the week, we add the original amount plus the amount of increase to get the total amount. That is, $\$52 + \$20.80 = \$72.80$. **$72.80** is her total grocery bill for the week.

Now try problem 19 from exercise set 2.3. (using method 1)

<u>Example 8:</u> A rare comic book increased in value 300% over the past 5 years. This was an increase of $90. What was the value of the comic book 5 years ago? What is the value of the comic book now?

Solution: "$90" is the *amount of increase*, "300%" is the *percent of increase* and "what was the value of the comic book 5 years ago" is the *original amount.*

amount of increase = percent of increase • original amount

$90   =   300%   • x Converting 300% to 3 we get the equation

$90   =   3x.   Divide both sides of the equation by 3 to isolate x.

$\dfrac{\$90}{3}=\dfrac{3x}{3}$ becomes $\dfrac{\$90}{3}=\dfrac{\cancel{3}x}{\cancel{3}}$.   Using long division $3\overline{)\$90}$ $\overset{\$30}{}$.

$x = \$30$ and the value of the comic book 5 years ago was **$30**.

To get the value of the comic book now, we add the original amount plus the amount of increase to get the total amount. That is, $\$30 + \$90 = \$120$.   The value of the comic book now is **$120**.

Now try problem 21 from exercise set 2.3. (using method 1)

<u>Example 9:</u> The price of a gallon of gasoline rose from 20¢ to $2.40 over the past 35 years. This represents an increase in price of what percent?

Solution: Since the new "higher" price represents the result of an increase, we must subtract the original price from the new "higher" price to find the amount of increase. **However, first we must get both amounts of money in the same units.** If we convert $2.40 into 240¢, then we won't have to worry about decimal numbers. Since $240¢ - 20¢ = 220¢$, then "220¢" is the *amount of increase.* "What percent" is the *percent of increase* and "20¢" is the *original amount.*

amount of increase = percent of increase • original amount

220¢   = x •   20¢   Rewriting the equation with the coefficient in front of the variable we get

220¢   =   20¢(x).   Divide both sides of the equation by 20¢ to isolate x.

$\dfrac{220¢}{20¢}=\dfrac{20¢(x)}{20¢}$ becomes $\dfrac{22\cancel{0¢}}{2\cancel{0¢}}=\dfrac{\cancel{20¢}(x)}{\cancel{20¢}}$.   Using long division $2\overline{)22}$ $\overset{11}{}$. $x = 11$

But wait!! Don't forget that we need to convert 11 into a percent.

$11 = 1{,}100\%$ Therefore, the increase in price is **1,100%** of the original price.

Now try problem 85 from exercise set 2.3. (using method 1)

Amount of decrease

Suppose the ***original amount*** of students in an English class was 24, and the number of students in the class was to decrease by 25 percent. Since 25 percent of 24 is 6, then the class would decrease by 6 students. The new class size would then be 18 students. The 25 percent is called the ***percent of decrease*** and the 6 students are called the ***amount of decrease***. By starting with the percent equation and changing the names to accommodate the amount of decrease scenario,

$$\textit{amount} \quad = \quad \textit{percent} \quad \bullet \quad \textit{base}$$

becomes the following formula which is used to calculate amount of decrease.

$$\textit{amount of decrease} \ = \ \textit{percent of decrease} \bullet \textit{original amount}$$

Example 10: Barney's Bargain Barn sold 1,200 umbrellas in the month of June. In the month of July they decreased their sales by 60 umbrellas. By what percent did they decrease their monthly sales of umbrellas from June to July?

Solution: "60 umbrellas" is the *amount of decrease*, "by what percent did they decrease their sales" is the *percent of decrease* and "1,200 units" is the *original amount.*

amount of decrease = *percent of decrease* • *original amount*

$$60 \quad = \quad x \quad \bullet \quad 1{,}200 \qquad \text{Rewriting the equation with the coefficient in front of the variable we get}$$

$$60 = 1{,}200x. \qquad \text{Divide both sides of the equation by 1,200 to isolate } x.$$

$$\frac{60}{1{,}200} = \frac{1{,}200x}{1{,}200} \quad \text{becomes} \quad \frac{6\cancel{0}}{1{,}20\cancel{0}} = \frac{\cancel{1{,}200}x}{\cancel{1{,}200}}.$$

Using long division $120\overline{)6.00}^{\,0.05}$. Consequently, $x = 0.05$.

But wait!! Don't forget to convert 0.05 into a percent. $0.05 = 5\%$

The percent of decrease is **5%**.

Now try problem 23 from exercise set 2.3. (using method 1)

<u>Example 11:</u> A baseball player's rookie card decreased in value 75% over the past 15 years. This was a decrease of $60. What was the value of the card 15 years ago? What is the current value of the card?

Solution: "$60" is the *amount of decrease*, "75%" is the *percent of decrease* and "what was the value of the card 15 years ago" is the *original amount*.

amount of decrease = percent of decrease • original amount

$$\$60 \quad = \quad 75\% \quad • \quad x$$

Converting 75% to 0.75 we get the equation

$$\$60 = 0.75x.$$

Divide both sides of the equation by 0.75 to isolate x.

$$\frac{\$60}{0.75} = \frac{0.75x}{0.75} \quad \text{becomes} \quad \frac{\$60}{0.75} = \frac{\cancel{0.75}x}{\cancel{0.75}}.$$

Using long division $0.75\overline{)\$60}$ becomes $75\overline{)\$6,000}$ $\quad\overset{\$80}{}$.

$x = \$80$ and the value of the card 15 years ago was **$80**.

To get the current value of the card, we subtract the amount of decrease from the original amount to get the current amount. That is, $\$80 - \$60 = \$20$. The current value of the card is **$20**.

Now try problem 27 from exercise set 2.3. (using method 1)

<u>Example 12:</u> The price of gold went from $400 a troy ounce down to $385 a troy ounce during the past 2 months. This represents a decrease in price of what percent?

Solution: Since the new "lower" price represents the result of a decrease, we must subtract the new "lower" price from the original price to find the amount of decrease. Since $\$400 - \$385 = \$15$, then "$15" is the *amount of decrease*. "What percent" is the *percent of decrease* and "$400" is the *original amount*.

amount of decrease = percent of decrease • original amount

$$\$15 \quad = \quad x \quad • \quad \$400$$

Rewriting the equation with the coefficient in front of the variable we get

$$\$15 = \$400x.$$

Divide both sides of the equation by $400 to isolate x.

$$\frac{\$15}{\$400} = \frac{\$400x}{\$400} \quad \text{becomes} \quad \frac{\cancel{\$15}}{\cancel{\$400}} = \frac{\cancel{\$400}x}{\cancel{\$400}}.$$

Using long division $400\overline{)15.0000}$ $\quad\overset{0.0375}{}$.   Consequently, $x = 0.0375$.

But wait!! Don't forget to convert 0.0375 into a percent. $0.0375 = 3.75\%$

The decrease in price of a troy ounce of gold is **3.75%** of the original price.

Now try problem 29 from exercise set 2.3. (using method 1)

Discount

When the price of an item is reduced or put on sale, we call this reduction a ***discount***. The percent by which it is discounted is called the ***discount rate***. The new lower price of the item is often called the ***sale price***. By starting with the percent equation and changing the names to accommodate the discount scenario,

$$\textit{amount = percent} \bullet \textit{base}$$

becomes the following formula which is used to calculate the amount of discount.

$$\textit{amount of discount = discount rate} \bullet \textit{original price}$$

Once the amount of discount has been calculated, the sale price of an item can be found by using another formula, which is as follows:

$$\textit{sale price = original price - amount of discount}$$

Example 13: A stereo regularly priced at $150 is on sale for 20% off. What is the amount of the discount? What is the sale price?

Solution: "What is the amount of the discount" is the *amount of discount*, "20%" is the *discount rate* and "$150" is the *original price*.

amount of discount = discount rate • original price

x	=	20%	• $150	Converting 20% to 0.2 we get the equation

$$x = 0.2(\$150).$$

Since $0.2(\$150) = \$30$,   then $x = \$30$,   and

the amount of discount is **$30**.

Now, we subtract the amount of discount from the original price to get the sale price. That is, $\$150 - \$30 = \$120$. The sale price for the stereo is **$120**.

Now try problem 31 from exercise set 2.3. (using method 1)

<u>Example 14:</u> A spindle of 100 blank CDs is discounted $16, which is 80% off of the original price. What is the original price?

Solution: "$16" is the *amount of discount*, "80%" is the *discount rate* and "what is the original price" is the *original price.*

amount of discount = discount rate • original price

$16   =   80%   • x Converting 80% to 0.8
                                we get the equation

              $16 = 0.8$x$.   Divide both sides of the equation by 0.8 to isolate x.

$\dfrac{\$16}{0.8} = \dfrac{0.8x}{0.8}$ becomes $\dfrac{\$16}{0.8} = \dfrac{\cancel{0.8}x}{\cancel{0.8}}$.

Using long division $0.8\overline{)\$16}$ becomes $8\overline{)\$160}^{\;\$20}$.

$x = \$20$ and the original price of the CDs is <u>**$20**</u>.

Now try problem 33 from exercise set 2.3. (using method 1)

<u>Example 15:</u> A waffle iron regularly priced at $15 is on sale for $11.25. What is the discount rate?

Solution: Even though we aren't asked to find the amount of the discount, we have to in order to use the formula to find the discount rate. To find the amount of the discount we subtract the sale price from the original price. $15−$11.25 = $3.75   So, "$3.75" is the *amount of discount*, "what is the discount rate" is the *discount rate* and "$15" is the *original price.*

amount of discount = discount rate • original price

$3.75   = x • $15   Rewriting the equation with
                                the coefficient in front of
                                the variable we get

              $3.75 = 15x$.   Divide both sides of the equation by $15 to isolate x.

$\dfrac{\$3.75}{\$15} = \dfrac{\$15x}{\$15}$ becomes $\dfrac{\cancel{\$3.75}}{\cancel{\$15}} = \dfrac{\cancel{\$15}x}{\cancel{\$15}}$. Using long division $15\overline{)3.75}^{\;0.25}$. $x = 0.25$.

But wait!! Don't forget to convert 0.25 into a percent.   0.25 = 25%

Therefore, the discount rate on the waffle iron is <u>**25%**</u>.

Now try problem 35 from exercise set 2.3. (using method 1)

<u>Example 16:</u> A boom box that regularly costs $100 is on sale for 5% off the regular price. If sales tax is applied to the sale price at a rate of 5%, what is the total cost of the boom box?

The typical mistake that people make is to assume the answer is $100 since you subtract 5% (the discount) and then you add 5% (the tax). However, the 5% discount is 5% of $100 while the 5% tax is on the sale price, which is not $100.

Solution: **First**, find the amount of the discount.

"The amount of the discount" is the *amount of discount*, "5%" is the *discount rate* and "$100" is the *original price*.

amount of discount = discount rate • original price

$$x \quad = \quad 5\% \quad • \quad \$100 \qquad \text{Converting 5\% to 0.05}$$
$$\text{we get the equation}$$

$$x \; = \; 0.05(\$100).$$

Since $0.05(\$100) = \$5$,   then $x = \$5$,   and the amount of the discount is <u>**$5**</u>.

Next, get the sale price.

This is done by subtracting the amount of the discount from the original price. That is, $\$100 - \$5 = \$95$. Therefore, the sale price for the boom box is <u>**$95**</u>.

Then, determine the amount of sales tax on the $95.

"What is the amount of sales tax" is the *amount of sales tax*, "5%" is the *tax rate* and "$95" is the (sale price) *cost of item*.

amount of sales tax = tax rate • cost of item

$$x \; = \quad 5\% \quad • \quad \$95 \qquad \text{Converting 5\% to 0.05}$$
$$\text{we get the equation}$$
$$x \; = \; 0.05(\$95).$$

Since $0.05(\$95) = \$4.75$,   then $x = \$4.75$,   and

the amount of sales tax on $95 is <u>**$4.75**</u>.

Finally, calculate the total cost.

Using the formula:

total cost = cost of item + sales tax

total cost = $95   + $4.75   which is $99.75.

The total cost of the boom box is <u>**$99.75**</u>. I know what you're thinking. All that work and the answer is still almost $100.

Now try problem 53 from exercise set 2.3. (using method 1)

Problems involving adding to or subtracting from 100%.

Example 17: The total cost of a microwave oven is $109.14 including tax. If the tax rate is 7%, what is the original cost of the microwave oven before adding the tax?

Solution: The **wrong** answer is to find 7% of $109.14 and subtract it from the $109.14 to try and get back to the original cost. The tax isn't 7% of the total cost; it's 7% of the unknown lesser amount or original cost. Think of the original cost as 100% and the tax as 7% of the original cost. Then, the total cost is 100% + 7% or 107% of the original cost. This gives the following results: $109.14 is equal to 107% of the original cost. Now, "$109.14" is the *amount*, "107%" is the *percent* and "the original cost" is the *base*.

$amount \ = \ percent \ \bullet \ base$

$\$109.14 \ = \ 107\% \ \bullet \ x$ Converting 107% to 1.07 we get the equation

$\$109.14 \ = \ 1.07x.$ Divide both sides of the equation by 1.07 to isolate x.

$\dfrac{\$109.14}{1.07} = \dfrac{1.07x}{1.07}$ becomes $\dfrac{\$109.14}{1.07} = \dfrac{\cancel{1.07}x}{\cancel{1.07}}$.

Using long division $1.07\overline{)\$109.14}$ becomes $107\overline{)\$10{,}914}$ $\overset{\$102}{}$.

$x = \$102$ and the original cost of the microwave oven is **$102**.

Now try problem 77 from exercise set 2.3. (using method 1)

Example 18: Over the past several years the population of a city has been increasing at a rate of 8% per year. If the population of the city is currently 50,220 people, then what was the city's population a year ago?

Solution: Think of the population a year ago as 100% and the increase as 8% of the population a year ago. Then, the current population is 100% + 8% or 108% of the population a year ago. This gives the following results: 50,220 is equal to 108% of the population a year ago. Now, "50,220" is the *amount*, "108%" is the *percent* and "the city's population a year ago" is the *base*.

$amount \ = \ percent \ \bullet \ base$

$50{,}220 \ = \ 108\% \ \bullet \ x$ Converting 108% to 1.08 we get the equation

$50{,}220 \ = \ 1.08x.$ Divide both sides of the equation by 1.08 to isolate x.

$\dfrac{50{,}220}{1.08} = \dfrac{1.08x}{1.08}$ becomes $\dfrac{50{,}220}{1.08} = \dfrac{\cancel{1.08}x}{\cancel{1.08}}$.

Using long division $1.08\overline{)50{,}220}$ becomes $108\overline{)5{,}022{,}000}$ $\overset{46{,}500}{}$.

$x = 46{,}500$ and the city's population a year ago was **46,500**.

Now try problem 65 from exercise set 2.3. (using method 1)

<u>Example 19:</u> Over the past year, attendance at local movie theaters has decreased by 7%. If the total attendance for this year is 16,275, then what was the attendance at local movie theaters last year?

Solution: Think of the attendance last year as 100% and the decrease as 7% of the attendance last year. Then, the total attendance for this year is 100% − 7% or 93% of the attendance last year. This gives the following results: 16,275 is equal to 93% of the attendance last year. Now, "16,275" is the *amount*, "93%" is the *percent* and "the attendance last year" is the *base*.

$$amount \ = \ percent \ \bullet \ base$$

$$16{,}275 \ = \ 93\% \ \bullet \ x \qquad\qquad \text{Converting 93\% to 0.93}$$
$$\text{we get the equation}$$

$$16{,}275 \ = \ 0.93x. \qquad\qquad \text{Divide both sides of the equation by 0.93 to isolate } x.$$

$$\frac{16{,}275}{0.93} = \frac{0.93x}{0.93} \quad \text{becomes} \quad \frac{16{,}275}{0.93} = \frac{\cancel{0.93}x}{\cancel{0.93}}.$$

Using long division $\quad 0.93)\overline{16{,}275} \quad$ becomes $\quad 93)\overline{1{,}627{,}500}\,.$ $\quad x = 17{,}500$
$$17{,}500$$

and the attendance at local movie theaters last year was **17,500**.

Now try problem 57 from exercise set 2.3. (using method 1)

<u>Example 20:</u> A blanket is on sale for $20.40 and has been discounted 15%. What was the original price of the blanket?

Solution: Think of the original price as 100% and the discount as 15% of the original price. Then, the sale price is 100% − 15% or 85% of the original price. This gives the following results: $20.40 is equal to 85% of the original price. Now, "$20.40" is the *amount*, "85%" is the *percent* and "the original price" is the *base*.

$$amount \ = \ percent \ \bullet \ base$$

$$\$20.40 \ = \ 85\% \ \bullet \ x \qquad\qquad \text{Converting 85\% to 0.85}$$
$$\text{we get the equation}$$

$$\$20.40 \ = \ 0.85x. \qquad\qquad \text{Divide both sides of the equation by 0.85 to isolate } x.$$

$$\frac{\$20.40}{0.85} = \frac{0.85x}{0.85} \quad \text{becomes} \quad \frac{\$20.40}{0.85} = \frac{\cancel{0.85}x}{\cancel{0.85}}.$$

Using long division $\quad 0.85)\overline{\$20.40} \quad$ becomes $\quad 85)\overline{\$2{,}040}\,.$
$$\$24$$

$x = \$24$ and the original price of the blanket was **$24**.

Now try problem 51 from exercise set 2.3. (using method 1)

Problems involving multiple discounts.

Example 21: After Christmas, a toy store had some dolls regularly priced at $8.50 on sale for 30% off the regular price. A few weeks later the dolls that hadn't sold were reduced an additional 60% off the sale price. What was the final selling price of the remaining dolls?

Solution: Think of the regular price as 100% and the discount as 30% of the regular price. Then, the sale price was 100%−30% or 70% of the regular price.
This gives the following results: The sale price was equal to 70% of $8.50
Now, "the sale price" is the *amount*, "70%" is the *percent* and "$8.50" is the *base*.

  amount = *percent* • *base*

    x = 70% • $8.50   Converting 70% to 0.7
                                we get the equation

    x = 0.7($8.50).   Since   0.7($8.50) = $5.95,   then x = $5.95,

and the sale price was **$5.95**.

Next, we need to take an additional 60% off the sale price.
At this point, think of the sale price as 100% and the additional discount as 60% of the sale price.
This gives the following results: The final selling price was 100%−60% or 40% of $5.95.

Now, "the final selling price" is the *amount*, "40%" is the *percent* and "$5.95" is the *base*.

  amount = *percent* • *base*

    x = 40% • $5.95   Converting 40% to 0.4
                                we get the equation

    x = 0.4($5.95).   Since   0.4($5.95) = $2.38,   then x = $2.38,

and the final selling price of the remaining dolls was **$2.38**.

There is a way to streamline this problem. It is as follows:
The final selling price was 40% of the sale price, which was 70% of the regular price. Or as an equation it would look like this. x = (0.4)(0.7)($8.50)   Since (0.4)(0.7) = 0.28 and 0.28($8.50) = $2.38, the final selling price of the remaining dolls would be **$2.38**.

Now try problem 87 from exercise set 2.3. (using method 1)

Note: 40% of 70% of the regular price is the same as 28% of the regular price.

METHOD 2 (Using A Proportion)

Recall that in method 1, using the percent equation, there is always an extra step. This consists of either: 1) converting a given percent into a fraction or decimal number to use in the equation or 2) when solving for an unknown percent, converting the fraction or decimal number found into a percent at the end of the problem. In the proportion method this extra step, converting to or from a percent, is already built into the equation and no extra step is required.

Sales Tax

     Sales tax is usually added to the original cost of an item when it is purchased at a store. The amount of sales tax to be added is determined by finding a percent of the cost of an item. This percent is called the *tax rate*. By starting with a proportion and changing the names to accommodate the sales tax scenario,

$$\frac{amount}{base} = \frac{percent}{100\%}$$

becomes the following formula which is used to calculate sales tax.

$$\frac{amount\ of\ sales\ tax}{cost\ of\ item} = \frac{tax\ rate}{100\%}$$

Once the amount of sales tax has been calculated, the total cost of an item can be found by using another formula, which is as follows:

$$total\ cost\ =\ cost\ of\ item\ +\ sales\ tax$$

<u>Example 22:</u> A sweatshirt is on sale for $23. If the sales tax rate is 7.9%, what is the amount of sales tax? What is the total cost of the sweatshirt?

Solution: "What is the amount of sales tax" is the *amount of sales tax*, "7.9%" is the *tax rate* and "$23" is the *cost of item*.

$$\frac{amount\ of\ sales\ tax}{cost\ of\ item} = \frac{tax\ rate}{100\%}$$ becomes

$$\frac{x}{\$23} = \frac{7.9\%}{100\%}.$$ Reducing out the percent signs we get

$$\frac{x}{\$23} = \frac{7.9\cancel{\%}}{100\cancel{\%}}.$$ Finding the cross products gives us

$$100x = \$23(7.9).$$ We divide both sides of the equation by 100 to isolate *x*.

$$\frac{100x}{100} = \frac{\$23(7.9)}{100}$$ Reducing the left side we get

$$\frac{\cancel{100}x}{\cancel{100}} = \frac{\$23(7.9)}{100}.$$ Since $\$23(7.9) = \$181.70$ and $\frac{\$181.70}{100} = \$1.817,$

then $x = \$1.817.$ **However, since sales tax can only be paid in whole cents, round this amount to the nearest cent.**

Now, the amount of sales tax on $23 becomes is **$1.82**. Then using the formula:

total cost = *cost of item* + *sales tax*

total cost = $23   + $1.82   which is $24.82 .

The total cost of the sweatshirt is **$24.82**.

Now try problem 1 from exercise set 2.3. (using method 2)

I find all this math very taxing on my brain.

Example 23: $4.99 is the price of a used DVD at a local pawnshop. If the sales tax on the DVD is $0.37, what is the sales tax rate? Give your answer to the nearest tenth of a percent.

Solution: "$0.37" is the *amount of sales tax*, "what is the sales tax rate" is the *tax rate* and "$4.99" is the *cost of item*.

$$\frac{amount\ of\ sales\ tax}{cost\ of\ item} = \frac{tax\ rate}{100\%}$$ becomes

$$\frac{\$0.37}{\$4.99} = \frac{x}{100\%}.$$ Reducing out the dollar signs we get

$$\frac{\cancel{\$}0.37}{\cancel{\$}4.99} = \frac{x}{100\%}.$$ Finding the cross products gives us

$$4.99x = 0.37(100\%).$$ We divide both sides of the equation by 4.99 to isolate x.

$$\frac{4.99x}{4.99} = \frac{0.37(100\%)}{4.99}$$ Reducing the left side we get

$$\frac{\cancel{4.99}x}{\cancel{4.99}} = \frac{0.37(100\%)}{4.99}.$$ $0.37(100\%) = 37\%$ **and since we are going to round our final answer to the nearest tenth of a percent, we will use long division to go two places**

past the decimal point to the hundredth place. $4.99\overline{)37\%}$ becomes $499\overline{)3,700.00\%}$ $^{7.41\%}$.

Consequently, $x = 7.41\%$.   Now, rounding to the nearest tenth the tax rate is **7.4%**.

Now try problem 49 from exercise set 2.3. (using method 2)

Example 24: If the sales tax on a box of cereal is $0.23, and the tax rate is 8.4%, then what is the cost of the box of cereal? What is the total cost of the box of cereal including tax?

Solution: "$0.23" is the *amount of sales tax*, "8.4%" is the *tax rate* and "what is the cost of the box of cereal" is the *cost of item*.

$$\frac{amount\ of\ sales\ tax}{cost\ of\ item} = \frac{tax\ rate}{100\%}$$ becomes

$$\frac{\$0.23}{x} = \frac{8.4\%}{100\%}.$$ Reducing out the percent signs we get

$$\frac{\$0.23}{x} = \frac{8.4\cancel{\%}}{100\cancel{\%}}.$$ Finding the cross products gives us

$$8.4x = \$0.23(100).$$ We divide both sides of the equation by 8.4 to isolate x.

$$\frac{8.4x}{8.4} = \frac{\$0.23(100)}{8.4}$$ Reducing the left side we get

$$\frac{\cancel{8.4}x}{\cancel{8.4}} = \frac{\$0.23(100)}{8.4}.$$ Since $\$0.23(100) = \$23$, using long division $8.4\overline{)\$23}$

and rounding to the nearest cent we get $84\overline{)\$230.00}$ $^{\$2.74}$. $x = \$2.74$

and the cost of the cereal is **$2.74**. The total cost of the cereal is $2.74 + $0.23 or **$2.97**.

Now try problem 5 from exercise set 2.3. (using method 2)

Commission

A person that works on ***commission*** has their salary determined by the dollar amount of the merchandise they sell. They are paid a percent of the amount of sales they make. This percent is called the ***commission rate.*** By starting with a proportion and changing the names to accommodate the commission scenario,

$$\frac{amount}{base} = \frac{percent}{100\%}$$

becomes the following formula which is used to calculate commission.

$$\frac{commission}{amount\ of\ sales} = \frac{commission\ rate}{100\%}$$

Example 25: A woman working on commission makes $68 for selling $725 worth of merchandise. What is her commission rate? Give the answer to the nearest tenth of a percent.

Solution: "$68" is the *commission*, "what rate of commission" is the *commission rate* and "$725" is the *amount of sales*.

$$\frac{commission}{amount\ of\ sales} = \frac{commision\ rate}{100\%}$$ becomes

$$\frac{\$68}{\$725} = \frac{x}{100\%}.$$ Reducing out the dollar signs we get

$$\frac{\cancel{\$}68}{\cancel{\$}725} = \frac{x}{100\%}.$$ Finding the cross products gives us

$$725x = 68(100\%).$$ We divide both sides of the equation by 725 to isolate x.

$$\frac{725x}{725} = \frac{68(100\%)}{725}$$ Reducing the left side we get

$$\frac{\cancel{725}x}{\cancel{725}} = \frac{68(100\%)}{725}.$$ $68(100\%) = 6,800\%$ **and since we are going to round**

our final answer to the nearest tenth of a percent, we will use long division to go two

places past the decimal point to the hundredth place. $725\overline{)6,800.00\%}$ gives 9.37%

Consequently, $x = 9.37\%$. Now, rounding to the nearest tenth the commission rate is **9.4%**.

Now try problem 69 from exercise set 2.3. (using method 2)

<u>Example 26:</u> How many cell phones will a salesperson need to sell to make $166.50 in commission if the commission rate is 6% and the cell phones sell for $75 apiece?

Solution: "$166.50" is the *commission*, and "6%" is the *commission rate*. However, to get the *amount of sales,* we'll need "how many cell phones • $75 a piece."

$$\frac{commission}{amount\ of\ sales} = \frac{commision\ rate}{100\%}$$ becomes

$$\frac{\$166.50}{x} = \frac{6\%}{100\%}.$$ Reducing out the percent signs we get

$$\frac{\$166.50}{x} = \frac{6\%}{100\%}.$$ Finding the cross products gives us

$$6x = \$166.50(100).$$ We divide both sides of the equation by 6 to isolate *x.*

$$\frac{6x}{6} = \frac{\$166.50(100)}{6}$$ Reducing the left side we get

$$\frac{6x}{6} = \frac{\$166.50(100)}{6}.$$ Since $166.50(100) = $16,650,

and using long division $6)\overline{\$16,650}$, then $x = \$2,775$, and the amount of sales is **$2,775**.

This, however, is not the final answer that we are looking for. The question was "How many cell phones?" Take the $2,775 and divide it by $75 to get the actual number of cell phones.

Using long division $\$75)\overline{\$2,775}$.

The number of cell phones that a salesperson will need to sell is **37**.

Now try problem 15 from exercise set 2.3. (using method 2)

<u>Example 27:</u> A salesman works for a base salary of $600 a month plus 8% commission on all the merchandise he sells beyond $7,000. If he sells $8,700 worth of merchandise in one month, what will his total salary be for the month?

Solution: "Commission" is the *commission*, and "8%" is the *commission rate*. To find the amount of sales that the commission is paid on, we subtract $7,000 from $8,700 to get $1,700. "$1,700" is the *amount of sales.*

$$\frac{commission}{amount\ of\ sales} = \frac{commision\ rate}{100\%}$$ becomes

$$\frac{x}{\$1,700} = \frac{8\%}{100\%}.$$ Reducing out the percent signs we get

$$\frac{x}{\$1,700} = \frac{8\%}{100\%}.$$ Finding the cross products gives us

$$100x = \$1,700(8).$$ We divide both sides of the equation by 100 to isolate *x.*

$$\frac{100x}{100} = \frac{\$1,700(8)}{100}$$ Reducing both sides we get

$$\frac{100x}{100} = \frac{\$1,700(8)}{100}.$$ Since $17(8) = $136, then $x = $136.

The amount of commission on $1,700 is $136. By adding the $136 commission to his base salary of $600 we get his total salary. His total salary is **$736**.

Amount of increase

Suppose the ***original amount*** of students in a math class is 25, and the number of students in the class is to increase by 20 percent. Since 20 percent of 25 is 5, the class will increase by 5 students. The new class size will be 30 students. The 20 percent is called the ***percent of increase*** and the 5 students are called the ***amount of increase.*** By starting with a proportion and changing the names to accommodate the amount of increase scenario,

$$\frac{amount}{base} = \frac{percent}{100\%}$$

becomes the following formula which is used to calculate amount of increase.

$$\frac{amount\ of\ increase}{original\ amount} = \frac{percent\ of\ increase}{100\%}$$

Example 28: Last month Sam spent $120 on his electric bill. This month his bill increased by 18%. By how much money did his electric bill increase? What is his total electric bill for this month?

Solution: "By how much money" is the *amount of increase*, "18%" is the *percent of increase* and "$120" is the *original amount*.

$\dfrac{amount\ of\ increase}{original\ amount} = \dfrac{percent\ of\ increase}{100\%}$	becomes
$\dfrac{x}{\$120} = \dfrac{18\%}{100\%}$.	Reducing out the percent signs we get
$\dfrac{x}{\$120} = \dfrac{18\cancel{\%}}{100\cancel{\%}}$.	Finding the cross products gives us
$100x = \$120(18)$.	We divide both sides of the equation by 100 to isolate x.
$\dfrac{100x}{100} = \dfrac{\$120(18)}{100}$	Reducing both sides we get
$\dfrac{\cancel{100}x}{\cancel{100}} = \dfrac{\$12\cancel{0}(18)}{1\cancel{0}0}$.	Since $\$12(18) = \$216$, then $x = \dfrac{\$216}{10}$.

Dividing by 10 results in moving the decimal point one place to the left. So, $x = \$21.60$ and Sam's electric bill increased by **$21.60** this month. To get his total electric bill for this month, we add the original amount plus the amount of increase to get the total amount. That is, $\$120 + \$21.60 = \$141.60$. His total electric bill for this month is **$141.60**.

Now try problem 19 from exercise set 2.3. (using method 2)

<u>Example 29:</u> A coin increased in value 500% over the past 10 years. This was an increase of $80. What was the value of the coin 10 years ago? What is the value of the coin now?

Solution: "$80" is the *amount of increase*, "500%" is the *percent of increase* and "what was the value of the coin 10 years ago" is the *original amount*.

$$\frac{amount\ of\ increase}{original\ amount} = \frac{percent\ of\ increase}{100\%}$$ becomes

$$\frac{\$80}{x} = \frac{500\%}{100\%}.$$ Reducing out the percent signs we get

$$\frac{\$80}{x} = \frac{500\cancel{\%}}{100\cancel{\%}}.$$ Finding the cross products gives us

$$500x = \$80(100).$$ We divide both sides of the equation by 500 to isolate *x*.

$$\frac{500x}{500} = \frac{\$80(100)}{500}$$ Reducing both sides we get

$$\frac{\cancel{500}x}{\cancel{500}} = \frac{\$80(1\cancel{00})}{5\cancel{00}}.$$ Using long division $5\overline{)\$80}$ gives $\$16$.   Then $x = \$16$,

and the value of the coin 10 years ago was **$16**. To get the value of the coin now, we add the original amount plus the amount of increase to get the total amount. That is, $\$16 + \$80 = \$96$.   The value of the coin now is **$96**.

Now try problem 21 from exercise set 2.3. (using method 2)

<u>Example 30:</u> The price of a gallon of milk rose from 50¢ to $2.50 over the past 45 years. This represents an increase in price of what percent?

Solution: Since the new "higher" price represents the result of an increase, we must subtract the original price from the new "higher" price to find the amount of increase. **However, first we must get both amounts of money in the same units.** If we convert $2.50 into 250¢ then we won't have to worry about decimal numbers. Since $250¢ - 50¢ = 200¢$, then "200¢" is the *amount of increase*. "What percent" is the *percent of increase* and "50¢" is the *original amount*.

$$\frac{amount\ of\ increase}{original\ amount} = \frac{percent\ of\ increase}{100\%}$$ becomes

$$\frac{200\ \cancel{¢}}{50\ \cancel{¢}} = \frac{x}{100\%}.$$ Reducing out the cent signs we get

$$\frac{200\cancel{¢}}{50\cancel{¢}} = \frac{x}{100\%}.$$ Finding the cross products gives us

$$50x = 200(100\%).$$ We divide both sides of the equation by 50 to isolate *x*.

$$\frac{50x}{50} = \frac{200(100\%)}{50}$$ Reducing both sides we get

$$\frac{\cancel{50}x}{\cancel{50}} = \frac{20\cancel{0}(100\%)}{5\cancel{0}}.$$ Since $20(100\%) = 2,000\%$

and using long division $5\overline{)2,000\%}$ gives 400%, $x = 400\%$ and the percent of increase is **400%**.

Amount of decrease

Suppose the ***original amount*** of students in a biology class was 28, and the number of students in the class was to decrease by 25 percent. Since 25 percent of 28 is 7, the class would decrease by 7 students. The new class size would be 21 students. The 25 percent is called the ***percent of decrease*** and the 7 students are called the ***amount of decrease.*** By starting with a proportion and changing the names to accommodate the amount of decrease scenario,

$$\frac{amount}{base} = \frac{percent}{100\%}$$

becomes the following formula, which is used to calculate amount of decrease.

$$\frac{amount\ of\ decrease}{original\ amount} = \frac{percent\ of\ decrease}{100\%}$$

Example 31: Solomon's Sofa Sales sold 600 sofa sets during the month of September. During the month of October, they decreased their sales by 102 sofa sets. By what percent did they decrease their monthly sales of sofa sets from September to October?

Solution: "102 sofa sets" is the *amount of decrease*, "by what percent did they decrease their sales" is the *percent of decrease* and "600 sofa sets" is the *original amount.*

$\dfrac{amount\ of\ decrease}{original\ amount} = \dfrac{percent\ of\ decrease}{100\%}$ becomes

$\dfrac{102}{600} = \dfrac{x}{100\%}$. Finding the cross products gives us

$600x = 102(100\%)$. We divide both sides of the equation by 600 to isolate x.

$\dfrac{600x}{600} = \dfrac{102(100\%)}{600}$ Reducing both sides we get

$\dfrac{\cancel{600}x}{\cancel{600}} = \dfrac{102(1\cancel{00}\%)}{\cancel{6}\cancel{00}}$. Using long division $6\overline{)102\%}$ with quotient 17%,

$x = 17\%$ and the percent of decrease is **17%**.

*Now try problem 23 from exercise set 2.3. (using method 2)

Example 32: This year the cost of cable television is 18% less per month than it was last year. This is a decrease of $7.20 per month over last year. How much per month was the cost of cable television last year? How much per month is the cost of cable television this year?

Solution: "$7.20" is the *amount of decrease*, "18%" is the *percent of decrease* and "how much per month was the cost of cable television last year" is the *original amount*.

$$\frac{amount\ of\ decrease}{original\ amount} = \frac{percent\ of\ decrease}{100\%} \quad \text{becomes}$$

$$\frac{\$7.20}{x} = \frac{18\%}{100\%}. \qquad \text{Reducing out the percent signs we get}$$

$$\frac{\$7.20}{x} = \frac{18\cancel{\%}}{100\cancel{\%}}. \qquad \text{Finding the cross products gives us}$$

$$18x = \$7.20(100). \qquad \text{We divide both sides of the equation by 18 to isolate } x.$$

$$\frac{18x}{18} = \frac{\$7.20(100)}{18} \qquad \text{Reducing the left side we get}$$

$$\frac{\cancel{18}x}{\cancel{18}} = \frac{\$7.20(100)}{18}. \qquad \text{Since } \$7.20(100) = \$720$$

and using long division $18\overline{)\$720}$, $\ \ x = \$40$ and the cost of cable television last year was **$40** per month. To determine the monthly cost of cable television this year, we subtract the amount of decrease from the original amount to get this year's amount. That is, $\$40 - \$7.20 = \$32.80$. The cost per month of cable television this year is **$32.80**.

Now try problem 79 from exercise set 2.3. (using method 2)

Example 33: The price of milk went from $3.20 a gallon down to $2.72 a gallon over the past month. This represents a decrease in price of what percent?

Solution: Since the new "lower" price represents the result of a decrease, we must subtract the new "lower" price from the original price to find the amount of decrease. Since $\$3.20 - \$2.72 = \$0.48$, then "$0.48" is the *amount of decrease*. "What percent" is the *percent of decrease* and "$3.20" is the *original amount*.

$$\frac{amount\ of\ decrease}{original\ amount} = \frac{percent\ of\ decrease}{100\%} \quad \text{becomes}$$

$$\frac{\$0.48}{\$3.20} = \frac{x}{100\%}. \qquad \text{Reducing out the dollar signs we get}$$

$$\frac{\cancel{\$}0.48}{\cancel{\$}3.20} = \frac{x}{100\%}. \qquad \text{Finding the cross products gives us}$$

$$3.2x = 0.48(100\%). \qquad \text{We divide both sides of the equation by 3.2 to isolate } x.$$

$$\frac{3.2x}{3.2} = \frac{0.48(100\%)}{3.2} \qquad \text{Reducing the left side we get}$$

$$\frac{\cancel{3.2}x}{\cancel{3.2}} = \frac{0.48(100\%)}{3.2}. \qquad \text{Since } 0.48(100\%) = 48\%$$

and using long division $3.2\overline{)48\%}$ becomes $32\overline{)480\%}$, $\ \ x = 15\%$ and the decrease in price of a gallon of milk is **15%** of the original price.

Now try problem 29 from exercise set 2.3. (using method 2)

Discount

When the price of an item is reduced or put on sale, we call this reduction a _**discount.**_ The percent by which it is discounted is called the _**discount rate.**_ The new lower price of the item is often called the _**sale price.**_ By starting with a proportion and changing the names to accommodate the discount scenario,

$$\frac{amount}{base} = \frac{percent}{100\%}$$

becomes the following formula which is used to calculate the amount of discount.

$$\frac{amount\ of\ discount}{original\ price} = \frac{discount\ rate}{100\%}$$

Once the amount of discount has been calculated, the sale price of an item can be found by using another formula, which is as follows:

$$sale\ price\ =\ original\ price\ -\ amount\ of\ discount$$

Example 34: A computer that is last year's model was regularly priced at $1,500. Now it is on sale at 40% off of the regular price. What is the amount of discount? What is the sale price?

Solution: "What is the amount of the discount" is the _amount of discount,_ "40%" is the _discount rate_ and "$1,500" is the _original price._

$$\frac{amount\ of\ discount}{original\ price} = \frac{discount\ rate}{100\%}$$ becomes

$$\frac{x}{\$1,500} = \frac{40\%}{100\%}.$$ Reducing out the percent signs we get

$$\frac{x}{\$1,500} = \frac{40\cancel{\%}}{100\cancel{\%}}.$$ Finding the cross products gives us

$$100x = \$1,500(40).$$ We divide both sides of the equation by 100 to isolate x.

$$\frac{100x}{100} = \frac{\$1,500(40)}{100}$$ Reducing both sides we get

$$\frac{\cancel{100}x}{\cancel{100}} = \frac{\$1,5\cancel{00}(40)}{1\cancel{00}}.$$ Since $15(40) = \$600$, then $x = \$600$,

and the amount of discount is **$600**. Now, we subtract the amount of discount from the original price to get the sale price. That is, $1500 - $600 = $900. The sale price for the computer is **$900**.

Now try problem 47 from exercise set 2.3. (using method 2)

Example 35: A washing machine is discounted $20, which is 5% off of the original price. What is the original price?

Solution: "$20" is the *amount of discount*, "5%" is the *discount rate* and "what is the original price" is the *original price*.

$$\frac{amount\ of\ discount}{original\ price} = \frac{discount\ rate}{100\%}$$ becomes

$$\frac{\$20}{x} = \frac{5\%}{100\%}.$$ Reducing out the percent signs we get

$$\frac{\$20}{x} = \frac{5\cancel{\%}}{100\cancel{\%}}.$$ Finding the cross products gives us

$$5x = \$20(100).$$ We divide both sides of the equation by 5 to isolate x.

$$\frac{5x}{5} = \frac{\$20(100)}{5}$$ Reducing the left side we get

$$\frac{\cancel{5}x}{\cancel{5}} = \frac{\$20(100)}{5}.$$ Since $\$20(100) = \$2,000$

and using long division $5\overline{)\$2,000}^{\$400}$, then $x = \$400$. The original price of the washing machine is **$400**.

Now try problem 33 from exercise set 2.3. (using method 2)

Example 36: A curling iron regularly priced at $16 is on sale for $13.60. What is the discount rate?

Solution: Even though we aren't asked to find the amount of the discount, we have to in order to use the formula to find the discount rate. To find the amount of the discount we subtract the sale price from the original price. $\$16 - \$13.60 = \$2.40$ So, "$2.40" is the *amount of discount*, "what is the discount rate" is the *discount rate* and "$16" is the *original price*.

$$\frac{amount\ of\ discount}{original\ price} = \frac{discount\ rate}{100\%}$$ becomes

$$\frac{\$2.40}{\$16} = \frac{x}{100\%}.$$ Reducing out the dollar sign we get

$$\frac{\cancel{\$}2.40}{\cancel{\$}16} = \frac{x}{100\%}.$$ Finding the cross products gives us

$$16x = 2.40(100\%).$$ We divide both sides of the equation by 16 to isolate x.

$$\frac{16x}{16} = \frac{2.40(100\%)}{16}$$ Reducing the left side we get

$$\frac{\cancel{16}x}{\cancel{16}} = \frac{2.40(100\%)}{16}.$$ Since $2.40(100\%) = 240\%$

and using long division $16\overline{)240\%}^{15\%}$, then $x = 15\%$. The discount rate is **15%**.

Now try problem 35 from exercise set 2.3. (using method 2)

Example 37: A bicycle that regularly costs $100 is on sale for 8% off the regular price. If sales tax is applied to the sale price at a rate of 8%, what is the total cost of the bicycle?

The typical mistake that people make is to assume the answer is $100 since you subtract 8% (the discount) and then you add 8% (the tax). However, the 8% discount is 8% of $100 while the 8% tax is on the sale price, which is not $100.

Solution: **First**, find the amount of the discount. "The amount of the discount" is the *amount of discount*, "8%" is the *discount rate* and "$100" is the *original price*.

$$\frac{amount\ of\ discount}{original\ price} = \frac{discount\ rate}{100\%}$$ becomes

$$\frac{x}{\$100} = \frac{8\%}{100\%}.$$ Reducing out the percent signs we get

$$\frac{x}{\$100} = \frac{8\%}{100\%}.$$ Finding the cross products gives us

$$100x = \$100(8).$$ We divide both sides of the equation by 100 to isolate x.

$$\frac{100x}{100} = \frac{\$100(8)}{100}$$ Reducing both sides we get

$$\frac{100x}{100} = \frac{\$100(8)}{100}.$$ $x = \$8$ and the amount of discount is **$8**.

Next, get the sale price. This is done by subtracting the amount of the discount from the original price. That is, $\$100 - \$8 = \$92$. Therefore, the sale price for the bicycle is **$92**.

Then, determine the amount of sales tax on the $92. "What is the amount of sales tax" is the *amount of sales tax*, "8%" is the *tax rate* and "$92" is the (sale price) *cost of item*.

$$\frac{amount\ of\ sales\ tax}{cost\ of\ item} = \frac{tax\ rate}{100\%}$$ becomes

$$\frac{x}{\$92} = \frac{8\%}{100\%}.$$ Reducing out the percent sign we get

$$\frac{x}{\$92} = \frac{8\%}{100\%}.$$ **Finding the cross products gives us**

$$100x = \$92(8).$$ **We divide both sides of the equation by 100 to isolate x.**

$$\frac{100x}{100} = \frac{\$92(8)}{100}$$ Reducing the left side we get

$$\frac{100x}{100} = \frac{\$92(8)}{100}.$$ Since $\$92(8) = \$736$, then $x = \dfrac{\$736}{100}$.

Dividing by 100 results in moving the decimal point two places to the left. Consequently, $x = \$7.36$ and the amount of sales tax on $92 is **$7.36**.

Finally, calculate the total cost. Using the formula:

total cost = *cost of item* + *sales tax*

total cost = $92   + $7.36   which is $99.36.

The total cost of the bicycle is **$99.36**.

Now try problem 53 from exercise set 2.3. (using method 2)

Problems involving adding to or subtracting from 100%.

Example 38: The total cost of a bed frame is $158.36 including tax. If the tax rate is 7%, what is the original cost of the bed frame before adding the tax?

Solution: The **wrong** answer is to find 7% of $158.36 and subtract it from the $158.36 to try and get back to the original cost. The tax isn't 7% of the total cost; it's 7% of the unknown lesser amount or original cost. Think of the original cost as 100% and the tax as 7% of the original cost. The total cost is 100% + 7% or 107% of the original cost. This gives the following results: $158.36 is equal to 107% of the original cost. Now, "$158.36" is the *amount*, "107%" is the *percent* and "the original cost" is the *base*.

$$\frac{amount}{base} = \frac{percent}{100\%}$$ becomes

$$\frac{\$158.36}{x} = \frac{107\%}{100\%}.$$ Reducing out the percent signs we get

$$\frac{\$158.36}{x} = \frac{107\cancel{\%}}{100\cancel{\%}}.$$ Finding the cross products gives us

$$107x = \$158.36(100).$$ We divide both sides of the equation by 107 to isolate x.

$$\frac{107x}{107} = \frac{\$158.36(100)}{107}$$ Reducing the left side we get

$$\frac{\cancel{107}x}{\cancel{107}} = \frac{\$158.36(100)}{107}.$$ Since $158.36(100) = $15,836 and using long division

$$107\overline{)15{,}836}^{\$148}, \quad \text{then } x = \$148.$$ The original cost of the bed frame is **$148**.

Now try problem 77 from exercise set 2.3. (using method 2)

Example 39: Over the past several years, the population of a town has been increasing at a rate of 6% per year. If the population of the town is currently 477 people, then what was the town's population a year ago?

Solution: Think of the population a year ago as 100% and the increase as 6% of the population a year ago. The current population is 100% + 6% or 106% of the population a year ago. This gives the following results: 477 is equal to 106% of the population a year ago. Now, "477" is the *amount*, "106%" is the *percent* and "the town's population a year ago" is the *base*.

$$\frac{amount}{base} = \frac{percent}{100\%}$$ becomes

$$\frac{477}{x} = \frac{106\%}{100\%}.$$ Reducing out the percent signs we get

$$\frac{477}{x} = \frac{106\cancel{\%}}{100\cancel{\%}}.$$ Finding the cross products gives us

$$106x = 477(100).$$ We divide both sides of the equation by 106 to isolate *x*.

$$\frac{106x}{106} = \frac{477(100)}{106}$$ Reducing the left side we get

$$\frac{\cancel{106}x}{\cancel{106}} = \frac{477(100)}{106}.$$ Since $477(100) = 47,700$ and using long division

$$106\overline{)47{,}700}^{450}, \quad \text{then } x = 450.$$ The town's population a year ago was **450 people**.

<u>Example 40:</u> Over the past year, attendance at local high school basketball games has decreased by 18%. If the total attendance for this year is 5,330; then what was the attendance at local high school basketball games last year?

Solution: Think of the attendance last year as 100% and the decrease as 18% of the attendance last year. Then, the total attendance for this year is 100%−18% or 82% of the attendance last year. This gives the following results: 5,330 is equal to 82% of the attendance last year. Now, "5,330" is the *amount*, "82%" is the *percent* and "the attendance last year" is the *base*.

$$\frac{amount}{base} = \frac{percent}{100\%} \qquad \text{becomes}$$

$$\frac{5{,}330}{x} = \frac{82\%}{100\%}. \qquad \text{Reducing out the percent signs we get}$$

$$\frac{5{,}330}{x} = \frac{82\cancel{\%}}{100\cancel{\%}}. \qquad \text{Finding the cross products gives us}$$

$$82x = 5{,}330(100). \qquad \text{We divide both sides of the equation by 82 to isolate } x.$$

$$\frac{82x}{82} = \frac{5{,}330(100)}{82} \qquad \text{Reducing the left side we get}$$

$$\frac{\cancel{82}x}{\cancel{82}} = \frac{5{,}330(100)}{82}. \qquad \text{Since } 5{,}330(100) = 533{,}000 \text{ and using long division}$$

$$82\overline{)533{,}000}^{\,6{,}500}, \quad \text{then } x = 6{,}500. \qquad \text{The attendance at local high school basketball games last year was } \textbf{\underline{6,500 people}}.$$

Now try problem 57 from exercise set 2.3. (using method 2)

<u>Example 41:</u> A shirt is on sale for $7.80 and has been discounted 40%. What was the original price of the shirt?

Solution: Think of the original price as 100% and the discount as 40% of the original price. Then, the sale price is 100%−40% or 60% of the original price. This gives the following results: $7.80 is equal to 60% of the original price. Now, "$7.80" is the *amount*, "60%" is the *percent* and "the original price" is the *base*.

$$\frac{amount}{base} = \frac{percent}{100\%} \qquad \text{becomes}$$

$$\frac{\$7.80}{x} = \frac{60\%}{100\%}. \qquad \text{Reducing out the percent signs we get}$$

$$\frac{\$7.80}{x} = \frac{60\cancel{\%}}{100\cancel{\%}}. \qquad \text{Finding the cross products gives us}$$

$$60x = \$7.80(100). \qquad \text{We divide both sides of the equation by 60 to isolate } x.$$

$$\frac{60x}{60} = \frac{\$7.80(100)}{60} \qquad \text{Reducing both sides we get}$$

$$\frac{\cancel{60}x}{\cancel{60}} = \frac{\$7.80(10\cancel{0})}{6\cancel{0}}. \qquad \text{Since } \$7.80(10) = \$78 \text{ and using long division}$$

$$6\overline{)\$78}^{\,\$13}, \quad \text{then } x = \$13. \qquad \text{The original price of the shirt was } \textbf{\underline{\$13}}.$$

Problems involving multiple discounts.

Example 42: After Valentine's Day, a grocery store had some boxes of valentines regularly priced at $2.50 per box on sale for 20% off the regular price. A few days later the boxes of valentines that hadn't sold were clearanced for an additional 70% off the sale price. What was the final selling price of the remaining boxes of valentines?

Solution: Think of the regular price as 100% and the discount as 20% of the regular price.
Then, the sale price was 100%−20% or 80% of the regular price.
This gives the following results: The sale price was equal to 80% of $2.50.
Now, "the sale price" is the *amount*, "80%" is the *percent* and "$2.50" is the *base*.

$$\frac{amount}{base} = \frac{percent}{100\%}$$ becomes

$$\frac{x}{\$2.50} = \frac{80\%}{100\%}.$$ Reducing out the percent signs we get

$$\frac{x}{\$2.50} = \frac{80\cancel{\%}}{100\cancel{\%}}.$$ Finding the cross products gives us

$$100x = \$2.50(80).$$ We divide both sides of the equation by 100 to isolate x.

$$\frac{100x}{100} = \frac{\$2.50(80)}{100}$$ Reducing both sides we get

$$\frac{\cancel{100}x}{\cancel{100}} = \frac{\$2.50(8\cancel{0})}{10\cancel{0}}.$$ Since $\$2.50(8) = \$20,$ then $x = \dfrac{\$20}{10}.$

Dividing by 10 results in moving the decimal point one place to the left. Consequently, $x = \$2$ and the sale price was **$2**.

Next, we need to take an additional 70% off the sale price.
At this point, think of the sale price as 100% and the additional discount as 70% of the sale price.
This gives the following results: The final selling price was 100%−70% or 30% of $2.

Now, "the final selling price" is the *amount*, "30%" is the *percent* and "$2" is the *base*.

$$\frac{amount}{base} = \frac{percent}{100\%}$$ becomes

$$\frac{x}{\$2} = \frac{30\%}{100\%}.$$ Reducing out the percent signs we get

$$\frac{x}{\$2} = \frac{30\cancel{\%}}{100\cancel{\%}}.$$ Finding the cross products gives us

$$100x = \$2(30).$$ We divide both sides of the equation by 100 to isolate x.

$$\frac{100x}{100} = \frac{\$2(30)}{100}$$ Reducing both sides we get

$$\frac{\cancel{100}x}{\cancel{100}} = \frac{\$2(3\cancel{0})}{10\cancel{0}}.$$ Since $\$2(3) = \$6,$ then $x = \dfrac{\$6}{10}.$

Dividing by 10 results in moving the decimal point one place to the left. Consequently, $x = \$0.60$ and the final selling price of the remaining valentines was **$0.60** per box.

Now try problem 87 from exercise set 2.3. (using method 2)

Section 3 exercises.   Solve each of the following problems.

1.   A color television costs $250. If the sales tax rate is 7%, what is the amount of sales tax? What is the total cost of the television?

2.   A vacuum cleaner costs $375. If the sales tax rate is 6%, what is the amount of sales tax? What is the total cost of the vacuum cleaner?

3.   An electric toothbrush costs $80. If the sales tax on the toothbrush is $6.56, what is the sales tax rate?

4.   An electric saw costs $70. If the sales tax on the saw is $5.53, what is the sales tax rate?

5.   The sales tax on a book is $1.05, and the tax rate is 7.5%. What is the cost of the book? What is the total cost of the book including tax?

6.   The sales tax on a magazine is $0.34, and the tax rate is 8.5%. What is the cost of the magazine? What is the total cost of the magazine including tax?

7.   What amount of sales will produce a commission of $72 if the commission rate is 6%?

8.   What amount of sales will produce a commission of $104 if the commission rate is 8%?

9.   A sales person at a clothing store sells $1,230 worth of clothing in one week. If she is paid according to a 4.5% commission rate, what will her commission be for the week?

10.   A sales person at a furniture store sells $5,200 worth of furniture in one week. If he is paid according to a 12.5% commission rate, what will his commission be for the week?

11.   An employee receives $12 in commission on sales amounting to $300. According to what rate of commission is he being paid?

12.   An employee receives $30 in commission on sales amounting to $500. According to what rate of commission is she being paid?

13.   A salesman works for a base salary of $400 a month plus 7% commission on all the merchandise he sells beyond $5,000. If he sells $7,300 worth of merchandise in one month, what will his total income be for the month?

14.   A saleswoman works for a base salary of $600 a month plus 8% commission on all the merchandise she sells beyond $8,000. If she sells $12,400 worth of merchandise in one month, what will her total income be for the month?

15.   How many CDs will a salesperson need to sell to make $38.64 in commission if the commission rate is 7% and the CDs sell for $12 apiece?

16.   How many music cassettes will a salesperson need to sell to make $26.10 in commission if the commission rate is 5% and the music cassettes sell for $9 apiece?

17.   Sally's Super Spatula Store sold 1,800 spatulas in the month of September. In the month of October they increased their sales by 450 spatulas. By what percent did they increase their monthly sales of spatulas from September to October?

18.   Cory's Candy Counter sold 1,400 jawbreakers in the month of May. In the month of June they increased their sales by 588 jawbreakers. By what percent did they increase their monthly sales of jawbreakers from May to June?

19.   Last week Maria spent $15 on video rentals. This week she spent 35% more on video rentals than she did last week. By how much money did her video rental costs increase this week? What is her total video rental cost for this week?

20.   Last month Mark spent $25 on video game rentals. This month he spent 45% more on video game rentals than he did last month. By how much money did his video game rental costs increase this month? What is his total video game rental cost for this month?

21.   A rare manuscript increased in value 600% over the past 10 years. This was an increase of $1,500. What was the value of the manuscript 10 years ago? What is the value of the manuscript now?

22.   A stock increased in value 400% over the past 2 years. This was an increase of $300. What was the value of the stock 2 years ago? What is the value of the stock now?

23.   Veronica's Violin Village sold 200 violins in the month of July. In the month of August they decreased their sales by 24 violins. By what percent did they decrease their monthly sales of violins from July to August?

24.   Judy's Jeans Jamboree sold 1,200 pairs of jeans in the month of January. In the month of February they decreased their sales by 48 pairs of jeans. By what percent did they decrease their monthly sales of pairs of jeans from January to February?

25.   Last month Fred spent $54 on fast food to feed his family. This month his fast food bill decreased by 40%. By how much money did his fast food bill decrease this month? What is his total fast food bill for this month?

26.   Last year Joyce spent $140 on jellybeans to feed her sweet tooth. This year her jellybean bill decreased by 30%. By how much money did her jellybean bill decrease this year? What is her total jellybean bill for this year?

27.   A football player's rookie card decreased in value 65% over the past 20 years. This was a decrease of $156. What was the value of the card 20 years ago? What is the current value of the card?

28.   A certain stock decreased in value 18% over the past 4 years. This was a decrease of $6.84. What was the value of the stock 4 years ago? What is the current value of the stock?

29.   The price of silver went from $7.20 a troy ounce down to $6.12 a troy ounce during the past 6 months. This represents a decrease in price of what percent?

30.   The price of platinum went from $890 a troy ounce down to $863.30 a troy ounce during the past 5 months. This represents a decrease in price of what percent?

31.   A color printer regularly priced at $120 is on sale for 20% off. What is the amount of the discount? What is the sale price?

32.   A digital camera regularly priced at $450 is on sale for 30% off. What is the amount of the discount? What is the sale price?

33. A spindle of 100 blank DVDs is discounted $45, which is 60% off of the original price. What was the original price?

34. A package of 10 blank videotapes is discounted $6, which is 40% off of the original price. What was the original price?

35. A calculator regularly priced at $18 is on sale for $14.40. What is the discount rate?

36. A bookcase regularly priced at $24 is on sale for $15.60. What is the discount rate?

For the following problems, round money answers to the nearest cent and percents or rates to the nearest tenth of a percent if necessary.

37. A pair of dress pants is on sale for $29. If the sales tax rate is 7.9%, what is the amount of sales tax? What is the total cost of the pants?

38. A pair of shoes is on sale for $32. If the sales tax rate is 7.6%, what is the amount of sales tax? What is the total cost of the shoes?

39. What amount of sales will produce a commission of $61 if the commission rate is 7.4%?

40. What amount of sales will produce a commission of $79 if the commission rate is 6.3%?

41. A rare painting increased in value 1,500% over the past 50 years. This was an increase of $20,000. What was the value of the painting 50 years ago? What is the value of the painting now?

42. A rare vase increased in value 280% over the past 12 weeks. This was an increase of $800. What was the value of the vase 12 weeks ago? What is the value of the vase now?

43. The total cost of a color printer is $161.95 including tax. If the tax rate is 8%, what is the original cost of the color printer before adding the tax?

44. The total cost of a cordless drill is $52.99 including tax. If the tax rate is 6%, what is the original cost of the cordless drill before adding the tax?

45.   Last week Mickey spent $14 on cheese for his family. This week his son Pluto was away on a band trip, causing his cheese bill to decrease by 28.4%. By how much money did his cheese bill decrease this week? What is his total cheese bill for this week?

46.   Last term Tom spent $248 on college textbooks. This term the amount he spent on college textbooks decreased by 23.6%. By how much money did his textbook bill decrease this term? What is his total textbook bill for this term?

47.   A table lamp regularly priced at $12.59 is on sale for 30% off. What is the amount of the discount? What is the sale price?

48.   A hand held mixer regularly priced at $27.95 is on sale for 38% off. What is the amount of the discount? What is the sale price?

49. $14.99 is the price of a two-topping pizza. If the sales tax on the pizza is $1.24, what is the sales tax rate?

50. $3.29 is the price of a kid's meal at a local restaurant. If $0.26 is the sales tax on the meal, what is the sales tax rate?

51.   A tent is on sale for $32.49 and has been discounted 35%. What was the original price of the tent?

52.   A sleeping bag is on sale for $19.49 and has been discounted 25%. What was the original price of the sleeping bag?

53.   A tennis racket that regularly costs $50 is on sale for 20% off the regular price. If sales tax is applied to the sale price at a rate of 7%, what is the total cost of the tennis racket?

54.   A set of sheets that regularly costs $80 is on sale for 30% off the regular price. If sales tax is applied to the sale price at a rate of 6%, what is the total cost of the set of sheets?

55.   Last week Mary's Mini Mart sold 423 bags of ice. This week a local heat wave caused the sale of bags of ice to increase by 70%. By how many bags did the sale of ice increase this week? What is the total number of bags of ice sold this week? Round each answer to the nearest whole bag.

56.   Last week Carl's Cocoa Cafe sold 264 cups of cocoa. This week a local cold front caused the sale of cups of cocoa to increase by 40%. By how many cups did the sale of cocoa increase this week? What is the total number of cups of cocoa sold this week? Round each answer to the nearest whole cup.

57.   Over the past year, attendance at local baseball games has decreased by 18%. If the total attendance for this year is 12,179; then what was the attendance at local baseball games last year? Round the answer to the nearest whole person.

58.   Over the past year, attendance at local football games has decreased by 29%. If the total attendance for this year is 6,583; then what was the attendance at local football games last year? Round the answer to the nearest whole person.

59.   A salesman works for a base salary of $475 a month plus 12.4% commission on all the merchandise he sells beyond $5,000. If he sells $8,422 worth of merchandise in one month, what will his total income be for the month?

60.   A saleswoman works for a base salary of $565 a month plus 11.7% commission on all the merchandise she sells beyond $6,500. If she sells $9,538 worth of merchandise in one month, what will her total income be for the month?

61.   Jeff's Jumbo Jumpsuits sold 185 jumpsuits in the month of June. In the month of July they decreased their sales by 16 jumpsuits. By what percent did they decrease their monthly sales of jumpsuits from June to July?

62.   Harvey's Jalapeño Hotdogs sold 2,346 hotdogs in the month of August. In the month of September they decreased their sales by 347 hotdogs. By what percent did they decrease their monthly sales of hotdogs from August to September?

63.   A clock radio that is regularly priced at $35 is discounted $7. What is the discount rate on the clock radio?

64.   A cordless telephone that is regularly priced at $70 is discounted $21. What is the discount rate on the cordless telephone?

65.   Over the past several years, a city's population has been increasing at a rate of 12% per year. If the city's current population is 16,316 people, then what was the city's population a year ago? Round the answer to the nearest whole person.

66.   Over the past several months, a town's rabbit population has been increasing at a rate of 87% per month. If the town's current rabbit population is 2,848, then what was the town's rabbit population a month ago? Round the answer to the nearest whole rabbit.

67.   The sales tax on a dictionary is $1.38, and the tax rate is 7.4%. What is the cost of the dictionary? What is the total cost of the dictionary including tax?

68.   The sales tax on a 3-ring binder is $0.27, and the tax rate is 7.5%. What is the cost of the binder? What is the total cost of the binder including tax?

69.   A man working on commission makes $160 for selling $3,500 worth of merchandise. What is his commission rate?

70.   A woman working on commission makes $400 for selling $4,600 worth of merchandise. What is her commission rate?

71.   A sign on a rack of shirts said, "Sale price reflects a 40% savings." If the sale price of a shirt from the rack was $7.79, then what was its original price?

72.   An insert in a magazine advertises additional copies of the magazine for "$1.60 each-- SAVE 52%." How much does the magazine normally cost?

73.   Hamburger that regularly sells for $2.59 per pound has been reduced in price by $1.00 per pound. What is the discount rate?

74.   Candy that regularly sells for $3.79 per pound has been reduced in price by $1.00 per pound. What is the discount rate?

75.   4.2 inches of rain fell in the month of March. In the month of April, the amount of rain that fell increased by 1.5 inches. By what percent did the monthly amount of rainfall increase from March to April?

76.   16.8 inches of snow fell in the month of December. In the month of January, the amount of snow that fell increased by 6.1 inches. By what percent did the monthly amount of snowfall increase from December to January?

77.   The cost of 4 new college textbooks including tax is $210.04. If the tax rate is 8.8%, then what is the price of the textbooks before tax?

78.   The cost of 4 used college textbooks including tax is $157.87. If the tax rate is 8.8%, then what is the price of the textbooks before tax?

79.   A hockey player's rookie card decreased in value 35% over the past 6 years. This was a decrease of $4. What was the value of the card 6 years ago? What is the current value of the card?

80.   A basketball player's rookie card decreased in value 27% over the past 8 years. This was a decrease of $9. What was the value of the card 8 years ago? What is the current value of the card?

81.   A leather jacket is discounted $44, which is 15% off of the original price. What was the original price?

82.   A prom dress is discounted $43, which is 23% off of the original price. What was the original price?

83.   An item is on sale at 30% off the regular price. It is taxed at a rate of 7%. If the final sale price including tax is $44.94, then what is the sale price of the item without tax? What was the regular price of the item?

84.   An item is on sale at 40% off the regular price. It is taxed at a rate of 8%. If the final sale price including tax is $51.84, then what is the sale price of the item without tax? What was the regular price of the item?

85.   The price of a greeting card rose from 50¢ to $2.75 over the past 35 years. This represents an increase in price of what percent?

86.   The price of a loaf of bread rose from 15¢ to $1.50 over the past 50 years. This represents an increase in price of what percent?

87.   After Easter, a grocery store had some candy regularly priced at $3.50 per box on sale for 20% off the regular price. A few days later the boxes of candy that hadn't sold were clearanced for an additional 40% off the sale price. What was the final selling price of the remaining boxes of candy?

88.   After Halloween, a variety store had some costumes regularly priced at $18.80 on sale for 10% off the regular price. A few weeks later the costumes that hadn't sold were reduced an additional 50% off the sale price. What was the final selling price of the remaining costumes?

89.   An insurance company pays claims for bills from a chiropractor as follows: They take the actual bill, reduce it by 10% and then they pay 50% of the remaining amount. According to this policy, what percent of the original claim do they actually pay?

90.   An insurance company pays claims for bills from a physical therapist as follows: They take the actual bill, reduce it by 20% and then they pay 70% of the remaining amount. According to this policy, what percent of the original claim do they actually pay?

91.   You live across the street from a large shopping mall where the sales tax rate is 8.2%. 205 miles away in another state is a city that charges no sales tax. It costs 20 cents a mile to travel to the other city and back by car. How much merchandise, that is taxable in your city, would you have to buy in the other city to make it worth the cost of the trip?

92.   You live across the street from a large shopping mall where the sales tax rate is 8.8%. 150 miles away in another state is a city that charges no sales tax. It costs 22 cents a mile to travel to the other city and back by car. How much merchandise, that is taxable in your city, would you have to buy in the other city to make it worth the cost of the trip?

Writing:

93.   What do "percent of decrease" and "discount rate" have in common? How do they differ? Are they really both necessary? Why or why not?

94.   Explain why increasing an original amount by a certain percent and then decreasing the resulting amount by the same percent generally does not give you the original amount. Can you think of one example where this idea does give you the same original amount?

95.   If an item is advertised as "buy one, get one for half price" what is the average discount rate per item? Is this a good deal? Why or why not?

96.   If an item is advertised as "buy two, get one free" what is the average discount rate per item? Is this a good deal? Why or why not?

PERCENTS

Section 4: Interest

When you borrow money from a bank or a savings and loan institution, you pay them a fee for the privilege of borrowing their money. This fee is called **interest**. It is usually based on a percent of the amount of money borrowed from the institution. When you deposit money in a savings account at a bank, or a savings and loan institution, they pay you a fee for the privilege of borrowing your money. This fee is also called **interest**. The two scenarios described are basically the same one with the roles reversed.

Two kinds of interest will be discussed in this section, **simple interest** and **compound interest**.

Simple interest: To calculate simple interest on a loan or a savings account we need to find the following information. The **principal** is the amount of money to be borrowed or invested. The **rate** is the interest rate, which is generally expressed annually or yearly and is often referred to as the **A.P.R.**, or **annual percentage rate**. This is a percent used to calculate the amount of interest to be paid. Finally, **time** is the length of time (usually in years) that the money is to be borrowed or invested.

The simple interest formula is as follows:

$$\textit{Interest} \; = \; \textit{principal} \; \boldsymbol{\cdot} \; \textit{rate} \; \boldsymbol{\cdot} \; \textit{time}$$

or $$I \; = \; p \; \boldsymbol{\cdot} \; r \; \boldsymbol{\cdot} \; t$$ or simply $$I = prt$$

Example 1: How much simple interest is earned on $800 invested for 5 years at 6%?

Solution: I is the unknown, p is $800, r is 6% or 0.06, and t is 5 years.

$$I = prt \quad \text{becomes}$$

$$I \; = \; (\$800)(0.06)(5)$$

$$\text{or} \; I \; = \; \$240$$

The simple interest earned is **$240**.

Now try problem 3 from exercise set 2.4

<u>Example 2:</u> If Sarah deposits $1,000 in a savings account that pays 3% annually, how much money will she have in the account at the end of 1 year?

Solution: I is the unknown, p is $1,000, r is 3% or 0.03, and t is 1 year.

$$I = prt \quad \text{becomes}$$

$$I = (\$1,000)(0.03)(1)$$

$$\text{or} \quad I = \$30.$$

The simple interest earned will be $30. The amount of money in the account will be the $1,000 original deposit plus $30 interest, for a total of **$1,030**.

Now try problem 5 from exercise set 2.4

Note: The final answer could have been found by taking 100% of $1,000 plus 3% of $1,000 to get a total, which is 103% of $1,000, or $1,030.

<u>Example 3:</u> How much money would need to be deposited in a savings account with an annual interest rate of 4% in order to have $18 in interest at the end of 1 year?

Solution: I is $18, p is the unknown, r is 4% or 0.04, and t is 1 year.

$$I = prt \qquad \text{becomes}$$

$$\$18 = (p)(0.04)(1).$$ Rewriting the equation with the coefficient in front of the variable we get

$$\$18 = 0.04p.$$ We divide both sides of the equation by 0.04 to isolate p.

$$\frac{\$18}{0.04} = \frac{0.04p}{0.04}$$ Reducing the right side we get

$$\frac{\$18}{0.04} = \frac{\cancel{0.04}p}{\cancel{0.04}}.$$ So $\dfrac{\$18}{0.04} = p$ or $p = \dfrac{\$18}{0.04}.$

Using long division $0.04\overline{)\$18}$ becomes $4\overline{)\$1,800}$ with quotient $\$450$.

So, p = **$450** which is the amount of money that would need to be deposited.

Now try problem 13 from exercise set 2.4

<u>Example 4:</u> If you borrow $600 from a local savings and loan and at the end of 1 year you owe $624 including interest, what is the annual interest rate that is applied to your loan?

Solution: I is $624 - $600 = 24, p is $600, r is the unknown, and t is 1 year.

$$I = prt \qquad \text{becomes}$$

$24 \; = \; ($600)(r)(1) \quad$ or

$24 \; = \; $600r. \qquad$ We divide both sides of the equation by $600 to isolate p.

$$\frac{$24}{$600} = \frac{$600r}{$600} \qquad \text{Reducing both sides we get}$$

$$\frac{\cancel{$24}}{\cancel{$600}} = \frac{\cancel{$600}r}{\cancel{$600}}. \qquad \text{So} \quad \frac{24}{600} = r \quad \text{or} \quad r = \frac{24}{600}.$$

Using long division $\quad 600\overline{)24.00}^{\,0.04}$, $r = 0.04$.

But wait!! Don't forget that we need to convert 0.04 into a percent. 0.04 = 4%. So, **4%** is the annual interest rate that is applied to your loan.

Now try problem 15 from exercise set 2.4

<u>Example 5:</u> How long would you have to invest $400 in a savings account to accumulate $72 in simple interest if the annual interest rate is 3%?

Solution: I is $72, p is $400, r is 3% or 0.03, and t is the unknown.

$$I = prt \qquad \text{becomes}$$

$72 \; = \; ($400)(0.03)(t) \quad$ or

$72 \; = \; $12t. \qquad$ We divide both sides of the equation by $12 to isolate t.

$$\frac{$72}{$12} = \frac{$12t}{$12} \qquad \text{Reducing both sides we get}$$

$$\frac{\cancel{$72}}{\cancel{$12}} = \frac{\cancel{$12}t}{\cancel{$12}}. \qquad \text{So} \quad \frac{72}{12} = t \quad \text{or} \quad t = \frac{72}{12}.$$

Using long division $\quad 12\overline{)72}^{\,6}$, $t = $ **6 years**, which is the length of time you would need to invest the $400.

Now try problem 17 from exercise set 2.4

<u>Example 6</u>: How much simple interest is earned on $350 deposited in a bank for 7 months at 3%? Round to the nearest cent.

Solution: I is the unknown, p is $350, r is 3% or 0.03, and t is 7 months.

However, time must be expressed in years. Converting 7 months to years give us $(7 \text{ months})\left(\dfrac{1 \text{ year}}{12 \text{ months}}\right) = (7 \cancel{\text{ months}})\left(\dfrac{1 \text{ year}}{12 \cancel{\text{ months}}}\right)$

$= \dfrac{7}{12}$ of a year. Consequently, t is $\dfrac{7}{12}$ of a year.

$$I = prt \quad \text{becomes}$$

$$I = (\$350)(0.03)\left(\dfrac{7}{12}\right)$$

or $I = \$6.125$.

Rounding to the nearest cent, the simple interest earned is **$6.13**.

Now try problem 23 from exercise set 2.4

Note: Even though not all months are the same number of days in length, to make life simpler we will consider them all to be exactly 1/12th of a year.

<u>Example 7</u>: How much simple interest is earned on $570 deposited in a bank for 45 days at 4%? Round to the nearest cent.

Solution: I is the unknown, p is $570, r is 4% or 0.04, and t is 45 days.
However, time must be expressed in years. Converting 45 days to years give us $(45 \text{ days})\left(\dfrac{1 \text{ year}}{365 \text{ days}}\right) = (45 \cancel{\text{ days}})\left(\dfrac{1 \text{ year}}{365 \cancel{\text{ days}}}\right)$

$= \dfrac{45}{365}$ of a year. Consequently, t is $\dfrac{45}{365}$ of a year.

$$I = prt \quad \text{becomes}$$

$$I = (\$570)(0.04)\left(\dfrac{45}{365}\right).$$

Since $(\$570)(0.04)(45) = \$1{,}026$, then $I = \left(\dfrac{\$1026}{365}\right)$.

Using long division $365\overline{)\$1{,}026}$ and rounding to the nearest

cent we get $365\overline{)\$1{,}026.00}^{\,\$2.81}$ or $I = \$2.81$.

That is, the simple interest earned is **$2.81**.

Now try problem 27 from exercise set 2.4

Compound interest: Compound interest is interest that is paid on previously accumulated interest, as well as on the principal. Most savings accounts and investments pay this type of interest. To see how compound interest works let's look at an extension of example 2.

A bank pays 3% annual interest on all its savings accounts. If $1,000 is invested in one of these accounts, how much will be in the account at the end of 1 year? In bold type below example 2 we see that we can quickly get the final answer by taking 103% of $1,000 to get $1030. Written as an equation it is ($1,000)(1.03) = $1,030.

Let's see what happens when we leave the money in the bank for 3 years instead of just 1 year.

If we leave the $30 interest (from the first year) in the bank along with the $1,000 principal then during the second year there would be 3% interest on all of the $1,030. Written as an equation it is ($1,030)(1.03) = $1,060.90.

Again, if we leave all of the $1,060.90 in the bank during the third year at 3% interest the equation is ($1,060.90)(1.03) = $1,092.727 ($1,092.73 rounded to the nearest cent). At the end of the third year the account would contain $1,092.73.

This scenario would continue for as many years as the money was left in the bank. Each time the money in the account at the beginning of the year would be multiplied by 1.03 to get the amount in the account at the end of that year.

Another way of describing this situation is as follows:

Original deposit of $1,000   +   1st year's interest, which is **$30**   = $1,030

Balance at end of 1st year $1,030   +   2nd year's interest, which is **$30.90** = $1,060.90

Balance at end of 2nd year $1,060.90 + 3rd year's interest, which is **$31.827** = $1,092.727

Balance at end of 3rd year rounded to the nearest cent is $1,092.73

Notice how the interest amounts that are in bold type keep increasing each year. This is caused by the compounding interest.

If simple interest were applied for three years the interest would be just $90 instead of $92.73.

<u>Example 8:</u> A bank pays 5% annual interest compounded quarterly on all its savings accounts. If $1,000 is invested in one of these accounts, how much will be in the account at the end of 1 year?

Solution: I is the unknown, p is $1,000, r is 5% or 0.05, and t is quarterly or every 3 months. Since time must be expressed in years, we convert 3 months to years.

$$(3\ months)\left(\frac{1\ year}{12\ months}\right) = (3\ months)\left(\frac{1\ year}{12\ months}\right) = \frac{3}{12}\ of\ a\ year$$

which reduces to $\frac{1}{4}$ of a year. Consequently, t is $\frac{1}{4}$ of a year.

$$I = prt \quad becomes \quad I = (\$1,000)(0.05)\left(\frac{1}{4}\right) \quad or \quad I = \$12.50$$

The interest earned at the end of the first quarter is $12.50. This is left in the account and the new balance for the beginning of the second quarter is $1,000 + $12.50 or $1,012.50.

Now, $I = prt \quad becomes \quad I = (\$1,012.50)(0.05)\left(\frac{1}{4}\right) \quad or \quad I = \$12.65625$

which rounds to $12 66

The interest earned at the end of the second quarter is $12.66. This is left in the account and the new balance for the beginning of the third quarter is $1,012.50 + $12.66 or $1,025.16.

Now, $I = prt \quad becomes \quad I = (\$1,025.16)(0.05)\left(\frac{1}{4}\right) \quad or \quad I = \$12.8145$

which rounds to $12.81

The interest earned at the end of the third quarter is $12.81. This is left in the account and the new balance for the beginning of the fourth quarter is $1,025.16 + $12.81 or $1,037.97.

Now, $I = prt \quad becomes \quad I = (\$1,037.97)(0.05)\left(\frac{1}{4}\right) \quad or \quad I = \$12.974625$

which rounds to $12.97

The interest earned at the end of the fourth quarter is $12.97. Now at the end of the fourth quarter, that is, after 1 full year the new balance in the account is $1,037.97 + $12.97 or **$1,050.94**.

Now try problem 45 from exercise set 2.4

Note: $1,000 invested at 5% paid in simple interest at the end of the year would only produce $50 instead of $50.94.

<u>Example 9:</u> A bank pays 4% annual interest, compounded semiannually (twice a year), on all its savings accounts. If $5,000 is invested in one of these accounts, how much will be in the account at the end of 2 years?

Solution: I is the unknown, p is $5,000, r is 4% or 0.04, and t is semiannually or every 6 months. Since time must be expressed in years, we convert 6 months to years.

$$(6\ months)\left(\frac{1\ year}{12\ months}\right) = (6\ \cancel{months})\left(\frac{1\ year}{12\ \cancel{months}}\right) = \frac{6}{12}\ \text{of a year}$$

which reduces to $\frac{1}{2}$ of a year. Consequently, t is $\frac{1}{2}$ of a year.

$$\boldsymbol{I = prt} \quad \text{becomes} \quad I = (\$5,000)(0.04)\left(\frac{1}{2}\right) \quad \text{or} \quad I = \$100$$

The interest earned at the end of the first 6 months is $100. This is left in the account and the new balance for the beginning of the second 6 months is $5,000 + $100 or $5,100.

Now, $\boldsymbol{I = prt} \quad \text{becomes} \quad I = (\$5,100)(0.04)\left(\frac{1}{2}\right) \quad \text{or} \quad I = \$102$

The interest earned at the end of the second 6 months is $102. This is left in the account and the new balance for the beginning of the third 6 months is $5,100 + $102 or $5,202.

Now, $\boldsymbol{I = prt} \quad \text{becomes} \quad I = (\$5,202)(0.04)\left(\frac{1}{2}\right) \quad \text{or} \quad I = \$104.04$

The interest earned at the end of the third 6 months is $104.04. This is left in the account and the new balance for the beginning of the fourth 6 months is $5,202 + $104.04 or $5,306.04.

Now, $\boldsymbol{I = prt} \quad \text{becomes} \quad I = (\$5,306.04)(0.04)\left(\frac{1}{2}\right) \quad \text{or} \quad I = \$106.1208$

which rounds to $106.12

The interest earned at the end of the fourth 6 months is $106.12. At the end of the fourth 6 months, or 2 full years, the new balance in the account is $5,306.04 + $106.12 or **$5,412.16**.

Now try problem 49 from exercise set 2.4

Calculating compound interest can be very time consuming. A formula that can be used to determine the total amount in an account at the end of a given number of compoundings is called the **compound interest formula** and is as follows:

$$A = P\left(1 + \frac{r}{n}\right)^{nt}$$

Where A is the total amount in an account, P is the principal, r is the annual interest rate in decimal form, t is the amount of time in years, and n is the number of compoundings in one year.

 For problems more complex than the ones presented in this section, a calculator would be essential along with the compound interest formula.

Section 4 exercises.   Solve each of the following simple interest problems. Round money answers to the nearest cent and percents or rates to the nearest tenth of a percent if necessary.

1.   How much simple interest is earned on $6,000 deposited in a bank for 1 year at 4.3%?

2.   How much simple interest is earned on $7,000 deposited in a bank for 1 year at 3.4%?

3.   How much simple interest is made on an investment of $400 for 7 years at 9%?

4.   How much simple interest is made on an investment of $300 for 8 years at 7%?

5.   If $2,500 is deposited in a savings account that pays 3.5% annually, what will be the value of the account at the end of 1 year?

6.   If $5,700 is deposited in a savings account that pays 4.2% annually, what will be the value of the account at the end of 1 year?

7.   A businessman borrows $6,000 from a local savings and loan at 6.5%. How much money does he have to pay back at the end of 1 year if he decides to pay off the loan?

8.   A businesswoman borrows $2,000 from a local savings and loan at 5.6%. How much money does she have to pay back at the end of 1 year if she decides to pay off the loan?

9.   If $3,600 is invested at a bank that pays 4.6% annually, what will be the value of the investment at the end of 1 year?

10.   If $4,800 is invested at a bank that pays 3.9% annually, what will be the value of the investment at the end of 1 year?

11.   Charlie borrows $1,500 from a loan shark that charges 18.5% annually. If he pays off the loan in one lump sum at the end of a year, how much of that payment will be interest?

12.   Carol takes out a home equity loan for $3,500 to pay for some improvements. If the bank charges 4.5% annually, and Carol pays off the loan in one lump sum at the end of a year, how much of that payment will be interest?

13. In order to earn $26 in interest in 1 year's time, how much money would have to be deposited in a savings account with an annual interest rate of 3.6%?

14. In order to earn $47 in interest in 1 year's time, how much money would have to be deposited in a savings account with an annual interest rate of 5.4%?

15. By investing $750 in a savings account, after 1 year you have a total of $796. What is the annual interest rate that is being applied to your investment?

16. By depositing $4,550 in a bank account, after 1 year you have a balance of $4,832. What is the annual interest rate that is being applied to your deposit?

17. How many years would it take to make $50 simple interest on an investment of $650 if the annual rate of return was 3.2%? Round your answer to the nearest tenth of a year.

18. How many years would it take to make $67 simple interest on an investment of $460 if the annual rate of return was 2.8%? Round your answer to the nearest tenth of a year.

19. How many years would it take to make $500 simple interest on an investment of $500 if the annual rate of return was 6.7%? Round your answer to the nearest tenth of a year.

20. How many years would it take to make $800 simple interest on an investment of $800 if the annual rate of return was 8.9%? Round your answer to the nearest tenth of a year.

21. How many years would it take to double an investment if the annual simple interest rate is 5.3%? Round your answer to the nearest tenth of a year.

22. How many years would it take to double an investment if the annual simple interest rate is 4.7%? Round your answer to the nearest tenth of a year.

23. How much simple interest is earned on $350 deposited in a bank for 3 months at 3%?

24. How much simple interest is earned on $750 deposited in a bank for 9 months at 4%?

25. How much simple interest is earned on $400 deposited in a bank for 2 months at 7%?

26. How much simple interest is earned on $800 deposited in a bank for 10 months at 7%?

27.   How much simple interest is earned on $2,000 deposited in a bank for 75 days at 4%?

28.   How much simple interest is earned on $3,000 deposited in a bank for 65 days at 6%?

29.   How much simple interest is earned on $4,500 deposited in a bank for 40 days at 3.7%?

30.   How much simple interest is earned on $2,500 deposited in a bank for 50 days at 3.9%?

31.   Ben takes out a car loan for $6,000 at 7.2% annually from a local credit union. The loan is to be paid back over a 72-month period and the monthly payments are $103.

    a)   What amount of his first month's payment will be interest?

    b)   What amount of his first month's payment will be applied to the principal of the loan?

    c)   What percent of his first month's payment will be interest? Round your answer to the nearest percent.

32.   Sue takes out a car loan for $9,000 at 7.8% annually from a local credit union. The loan is to be paid back over a 72-month period and the monthly payments are $157.

    a)   What amount of her first month's payment will be interest?

    b)   What amount of her first month's payment will be applied to the principal of the loan?

    c)   What percent of her first month's payment will be interest? Round your answer to the nearest percent.

33.   Sean takes out a loan on an S.U.V. for $15,000 at 6.3% annually from a local credit union. The loan is to be paid back over a 60-month period and the monthly payments are $292.09.

    a)   What amount of his first month's payment will be interest?

    b)   What amount of his first month's payment will be applied to the principal of the loan?

34.   Jessica takes out a loan on a boat for $8,000 at 6.6% annually from a local credit union. The loan is to be paid back over a 60-month period and the monthly payments are $156.90.

   a)   What amount of her first month's payment will be interest?

   b)   What amount of her first month's payment will be applied to the principal of the loan?

35.   Joe buys a house that carries a $100,000 mortgage at 6.9% annually from a mortgage company. The loan is to be paid back over a 30-year period and the monthly payments are $658.60.

   a)   What amount of his first month's payment will be interest?

   b)   What amount of his first month's payment will be applied to the principal of the loan?

36.   Maria buys a house that carries a $100,000 mortgage at 7.5% annually from a mortgage company. The loan is to be paid back over a 30-year period and the monthly payments are $699.21.

   a)   What amount of her first month's payment will be interest?

   b)   What amount of her first month's payment will be applied to the principal of the loan?

37.   Carlton buys a house that carries a $150,000 mortgage at 5.4% annually from a mortgage company. The loan is to be paid back over a 15-year period and the monthly payments are $1,217.68.

   a)   What amount of his first month's payment will be interest?

   b)   What amount of his first month's payment will be applied to the principal of the loan?

38.   Harvey buys a house that carries a $150,000 mortgage at 5.1% annually from a mortgage company. The loan is to be paid back over a 15-year period and the monthly payments are $1,194.02.

   a)   What amount of his first month's payment will be interest?

   b)   What amount of his first month's payment will be applied to the principal of the loan?

39.   After a 3-month vacation in Europe, Sam has a huge credit card bill. His credit card has a 9% A.P.R. (annual percentage rate). After Sam makes a payment, what will be the interest charge on his next month's bill if he has a remaining balance of $8,000?

40.   After a 2-month vacation in South America, Lois has accumulated a large debt on her credit card. Her credit card has an 8.4% A.P.R. (annual percentage rate). After Lois makes a payment, what will be the interest charge on her next month's bill if she has a remaining balance of $6,600?

41.   A local business gives loans to help people get by until their next payday. If the business charges $15 interest per $100 borrowed over a period of half a month, what is the A.P.R. (annual percentage rate) of the loan?

42.   A local pawnshop is willing to loan $500 to a customer for 1 month with an interest charge of $43. What is the A.P.R. (annual percentage rate) of such a loan?

Solve each of the following compound interest problems. Round interest to the nearest cent after each compounding.

43.   A savings account pays 5% compounded annually. If $8,000 is deposited in the account, how much is in the account at the end of 2 years?

44.   A savings account pays 4% compounded annually. If $10,000 is deposited in the account, how much is in the account at the end of 2 years?

45.   If $6,000 is invested in a savings account that pays 4% compounded quarterly, how much is in the account at the end of 1 year?

46.   If $12,000 is invested in a savings account that pays 3% compounded quarterly, how much is in the account at the end of 1 year?

47.   If $9,000 is invested in a savings account that pays 5% compounded quarterly, how much is in the account at the end of 9 months?

48.   If $15,000 is invested in a savings account that pays 6% compounded quarterly, how much is in the account at the end of 9 months?

49.   If $2,800 is invested in a savings account that pays 4% compounded semiannually, how much is in the account at the end of $1\frac{1}{2}$ years?

50.   If $3,200 is invested in a savings account that pays 5% compounded semiannually, how much is in the account at the end of $1\frac{1}{2}$ years?

PERCENTS

Chapter Review

Section 1: Fractions, decimals and percents

Review Exercises: Change each fraction, mixed number or decimal to a percent. Give exact answers (don't round).

1. $\dfrac{2}{25}$ 2.   18.93   3. $2\dfrac{5}{6}$ 4.   12

5. $\dfrac{49}{20}$ 6. $6\dfrac{3}{4}$ 7.   0.0056   8. $\dfrac{7}{12}$

Change each percent into a decimal number. Give exact answers (don't round).

9.   19%   10.   0.076%   11. $5\dfrac{2}{3}\%$ 12. $0.\overline{7}\%$

Change each percent into a fraction or mixed number. Give exact answers (don't round).

13.   640%   14.   74.5%   15. $4\dfrac{5}{7}\%$ 16.   0.03%

Change each fraction or mixed number to a percent. Round answers to the nearest hundredth.

17. $\dfrac{2}{7}$ 18. $3\dfrac{4}{9}$ 19. $\dfrac{5}{6}$ 20. $7\dfrac{1}{3}$

21.   In a recent taste test 3 out of 8 people surveyed preferred diet cola over regular cola. What percent of the people surveyed did not prefer diet cola?

22.   Describe an easy way to find 20% of a number.

Section 2: Solving percent problems using equations

Review Exercises: Solve each of the following problems.

23.   What number is 48% of 630?

24.   0.068 is 0.4% of what number?

25.   215 is what percent of 50?

26. $\dfrac{3}{5}$% of 6,000 is what number?

27.   50% of what number is $\dfrac{2}{9}$?

28.   What percent of $5\dfrac{13}{15}$ is 1.76?

29.   On a recent utility bill, the water/sewer/garbage portion of the bill was $112.78. This consisted of 73% of the total bill. To the nearest cent, what was the total amount of the utility bill?

30.   Randy planted 80 radish seeds with a germination rate of 65%. How many radish seeds should he expect to germinate?

31.   Last year Natasha gave $31.25 a month to support local animal shelters. If she made $12,500 last year, what percent of her income did she give to support local animal shelters?

32.   Mark has to milk all the cows at the dairy once a day. If he milks 39 cows in the morning and the other 91 cows in the evening, what percent of the cows does he milk in the evening?

For the following 2 problems, give each answer to the nearest whole-number percent.

33.   If Joni earned 13 points out of 15 points on a homework assignment, what percent did she get correct?

34.   For breakfast Jessica ate the following: A piece of Razzleberry pie weighing 238 grams, 42 grams of which was fat; a pastry weighing 50 grams, 7 grams of which was fat; and a serving of orange juice weighing 71 grams, 0 grams of which was fat. What percent of Jessica's breakfast was fat?

Section 3: Applications of percents

Review Exercises: For the following problems, round money answers to the nearest cent and percents or rates to the nearest tenth of a percent if necessary.

35.   A pair of tennis shoes is on sale for $69. If the sales tax rate is 7.9%, what is the amount of sales tax? What is the total cost of the shoes?

36.   An electric blender regularly priced at $39.95 is on sale for 23% off. What is the amount of the discount? What is the sale price?

37.   Last week Mary's Mini Mart sold 783 Popsicles. This week a local heat wave caused the sale of Popsicles to increase by 40%. By what quantity did the sale of Popsicles increase this week? What is the total number of Popsicles sold this week? Round each answer to the nearest whole Popsicle.

38.   Over the past year attendance at local soccer games has decreased by 16%. If the total attendance for this year is 5,586, then what was the attendance at local soccer games last year?

39.   A salesman works for a base salary of $650 a month plus 8.6% commission on all the merchandise he sells beyond $5,000. If he sells $12,840 worth of merchandise in one month, what will his total salary be for the month?

40.   A telephone answering machine that is regularly priced at $48 is discounted $12. What is the discount rate on the answering machine?

41.   A woman working on commission makes $350 for selling $6,200 worth of clothing. What is her commission rate?

42.   6.4 inches of rain fell in the month of April. In the month of May, the amount of rain that fell increased by 1.8 inches. By what percent did the monthly amount of rainfall increase from April to May?

43.   A football player's rookie card decreased in value 28% over the past 8 years. This was a decrease of $14. What was the value of the card 8 years ago? What is the current value of the card?

44.   An item is on sale at 30% off the regular price. It is taxed at a rate of 8%. If the final sale price including tax is $22.68, then what is the sale price of the item without tax? What was the regular price of the item?

Section 4: Interest

Review Exercises: Solve each of the following simple interest problems. Round money answers to the nearest cent and percents or rates to the nearest tenth of a percent if necessary.

45.   How much simple interest is made on an investment of $600 for 9 years at 7%?

46.   If $3,500 is deposited in a savings account that pays 4.5% annually, what will be the value of the account at the end of 1 year?

47.   In order to earn $42.40 in interest in 1 year's time, how much money would have to be deposited in a savings account with an annual interest rate of 5.3%?

48.   By investing $640 in a savings account, after 1 year you have a total of $678. What is the annual interest rate that is being applied to your investment?

49.   How many years would it take to make $52 simple interest on an investment of $590 if the annual rate of return was 2.9%? Round your answer to the nearest tenth of a year.

50.   How much simple interest is earned on $750 deposited in a bank for 3 months at 4%?

51.   How much simple interest is earned on $2,000 deposited in a bank for 70 days at 3.8%?

Solve each of the following compound interest problems. Round interest to the nearest cent after each compounding.

52.   A savings account pays 4% compounded annually. If $16,000 is deposited in the account, how much is in the account at the end of 3 years?

53.   If $10,000 is invested in a savings account that pays 5% compounded quarterly, how much is in the account at the end of 9 months?

54.   If $15,000 is invested in a savings account that pays 6% compounded semiannually, how much is in the account at the end of $1\frac{1}{2}$ years?

PERCENTS

Chapter Test

Change each fraction, mixed number or decimal to a percent. Give exact answers (don't round).

1. $\dfrac{7}{20}$

2. $8\dfrac{1}{6}$

3. 0.047

Change each percent into a decimal number. Give exact answers (don't round).

4. $7\dfrac{4}{9}\%$

5. $0.0\overline{5}\%$

Change each percent into a fraction or mixed number. Give exact answers (don't round).

6. $2\dfrac{2}{3}\%$

7. 0.6%

Change each fraction or mixed number to a percent. Round answers to the nearest hundredth.

8. $\dfrac{5}{7}$

9. $7\dfrac{7}{11}$

Solve each of the following problems.

10. In a recent taste test 7 out of 16 people surveyed preferred coffee over tea. What percent of the people surveyed did not prefer coffee?

11. $\dfrac{4}{5}\%$ of 9,000 is what number?

12. What percent of $3\dfrac{11}{15}$ is 2.24?

Solve each of the following problems.

13. On a recent phone bill, the long distance portion of the bill was $36.71. This consisted of 62% of the total bill. To the nearest cent, what was the total amount of the phone bill?

14. Lonnie's Lawn Service mowed 68 lawns on Friday and 102 lawns on Saturday. What percent of the lawns did they mow on Saturday?

For the following problems, round money answers to the nearest cent and percents or rates to the nearest tenth of a percent if necessary.

15. A swimsuit regularly priced at $44.99 is on sale for 37% off. What is the amount of the discount? What is the sale price?

16. Over the past year attendance at local band concerts has decreased by 26%. If the total attendance for this year is 629, then what was the attendance at local band concerts last year?

17. A salesman works for a base salary of $800 a month plus 9.4% commission on all the merchandise he sells beyond $5,000. If he sells $15,438 worth of merchandise in one month, what will his total salary be for the month?

18. 7.8 inches of rain fell in the month of June. In the month of July, the amount of rain that fell increased by 2.4 inches. By what percent did the monthly amount of rainfall increase from June to July?

19. An item is on sale at 20% off the regular price. It is taxed at a rate of 8%. If the final sale price including tax is $103.68, then what is the sale price of the item without tax? What was the regular price of the item?

For the following problem, give the answer to the nearest whole-number percent.

20.   Micah wants to calculate his overall homework grade midway through the quarter. On the five assignments that were graded he earned the following scores: 18 out of 23, 17 out of 26, 15 out of 20, 14 out of 16, and 7 out of 10. Assuming that all points on homework have equal value, what overall percent does Micah have on his homework?

Solve each of the following simple interest problems. Round money answers to the nearest cent and percents or rates to the nearest tenth of a percent if necessary.

21.   If $4,300 is deposited in a savings account that pays 3.8% annually, what will be the value of the account at the end of 1 year?

22.   In order to earn $38.44 in interest in 1 year's time, how much money would have to be deposited in a savings account with an annual interest rate of 6.2%?

23.   By investing $275 in a savings account, after 1 year you have a total of $288. What is the annual interest rate that is being applied to your investment?

24.   How much simple interest is earned on $950 deposited in a bank for 4 months at 6%?

Solve the following compound interest problem. Round interest to the nearest cent after each compounding.

25.   If $20,000 is invested in a savings account that pays 4% compounded quarterly, how much is in the account at the end of 9 months?

CHAPTER 3
AN INTRODUCTION TO ALGEBRA

Section 1: Signed Numbers

Absolute Value
Opposites
Addition of Signed Numbers
Subtraction of Signed Numbers
Multiplication of Signed Numbers
Multiplication by Zero
Division of Signed Numbers
Division by Zero
Order of Operations
Evaluating Algebraic Expressions

Section 2: Properties of Real Numbers

Commutative Properties
Associative Properties
Identity Properties
Multiplication Property of Zero
Inverse Properties
Distributive Property

Section 3: Simplifying Variable Expressions

Combining Like Terms

Section 4: Solving First-Degree Equations

Addition Property of Equality
Multiplication Property of Equality

Section 5: Solving Complex First-Degree Equations

Eliminating Fractions and Decimals

Section 6: Solving General First-Degree Equations

Section 7: Translating Between Mathematical Terminology and Algebraic Expressions

Section 8: Application Problems

AN INTRODUCTION
TO ALGEBRA

Section 1: Signed Numbers

In real life situations we encounter both positive and negative numbers. We can have a positive or negative balance of dollars in our checking account (though a negative balance is not recommended). The temperature outside can be a positive or a negative number of degrees.

A number line is another example of how positive and negative numbers can be expressed. On the number line positive numbers are to the right of zero and negative numbers are to the left of zero.

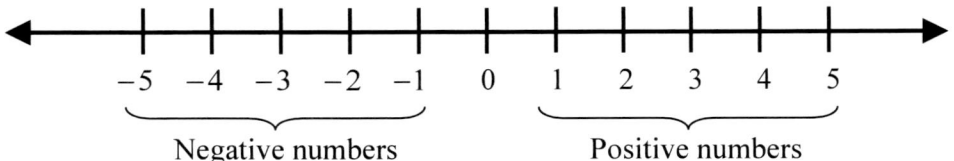

You can move in a positive direction or a negative direction on a number line. The actual distance you move however, is considered to be a positive amount. In the case of no movement, it is considered to be zero amount. This leads to a concept involving distance called **absolute value**.

> **Absolute Value: The absolute value of a number is the distance from zero to that number on the number line. An absolute value is never a negative amount. Two vertical bars, one on each side of a number, are used to indicate that we wish to find the absolute value of a number. For example, $\left|-3\right|$ implies that we wish to find the absolute value of -3.**

Example 1: Find the following absolute value: $\left|-3\right|$

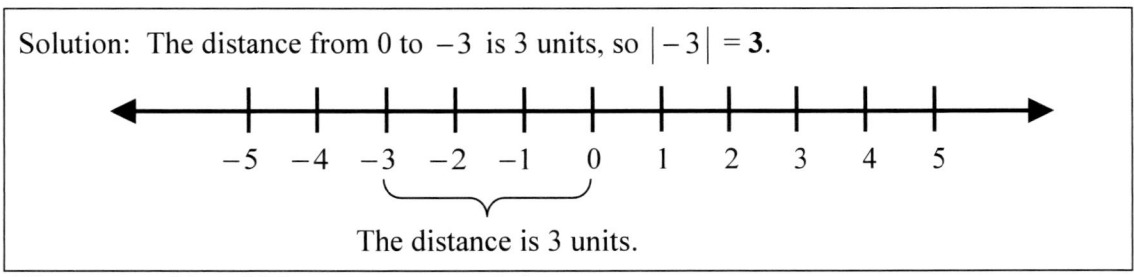

Now try problem 13 from exercise set 3.1

Example 2: Find the following absolute value: $\left|4\right|$

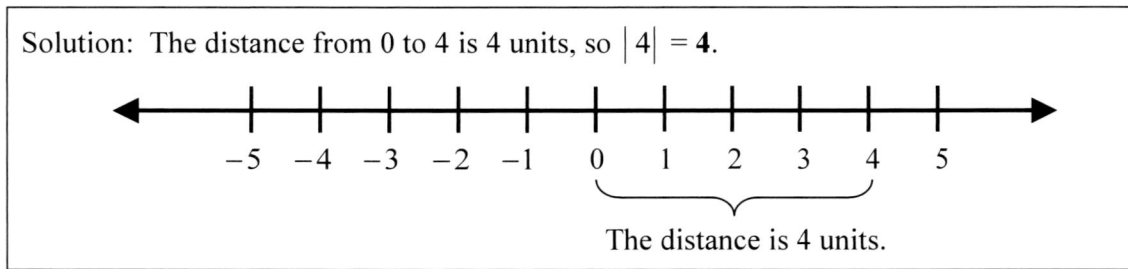

Now try problem 19 from exercise set 3.1

Example 3: Find the absolute value of each of the following numbers: $6,\ -5,\ 0.2,\ -\dfrac{3}{5},\ 0$.

> Solution: Find the distance from zero to the given number on the number line.
>
> | Number | Absolute value |
> |:---:|:---:|
> | 6 | $\lvert 6 \rvert = \mathbf{6}$ |
> | -5 | $\lvert -5 \rvert = \mathbf{5}$ |
> | 0.2 | $\lvert 0.2 \rvert = \mathbf{0.2}$ |
> | $-\dfrac{3}{5}$ | $\left\lvert -\dfrac{3}{5} \right\rvert = \dfrac{\mathbf{3}}{\mathbf{5}}$ |
> | 0 | $\lvert 0 \rvert = \mathbf{0}$ |

Now try problems 1 through 11 from exercise set 3.1

Opposites: **Two numbers that are the same distance from zero on a number line, but on opposite sides of zero, are called opposites.**

Example 4: Find the opposite of 2.

> Solution: The distance from 0 to 2 is 2 units.
>
>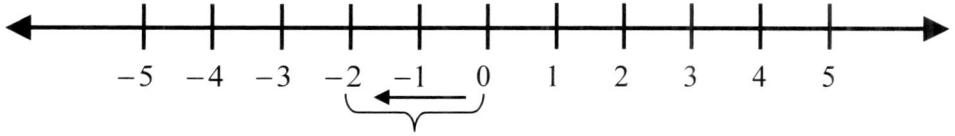
>
> The distance is 2 units.
>
> If we travel 2 units from 0 in the opposite direction, we will reach the opposite of 2.
>
> Traveling 2 units in the opposite direction we arrive at -2.
>
> **The opposite of 2 is -2.**

Now try problem 33 from exercise set 3.1

Note: -2 and 2 have the same absolute value because they are the same distance from zero on the number line.

Example 5: Find the opposite of -4.

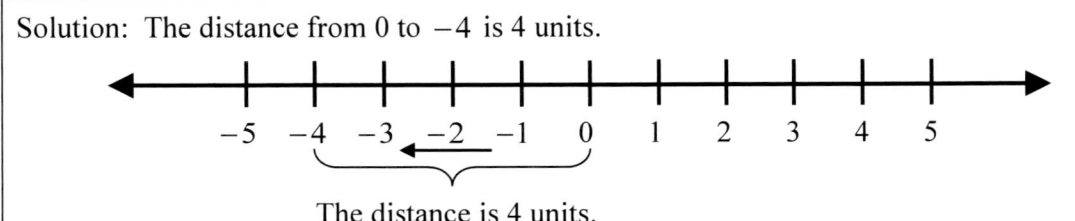

Solution: The distance from 0 to -4 is 4 units.

The distance is 4 units.

If we travel 4 units from 0 in the opposite direction we will reach the opposite of -4.

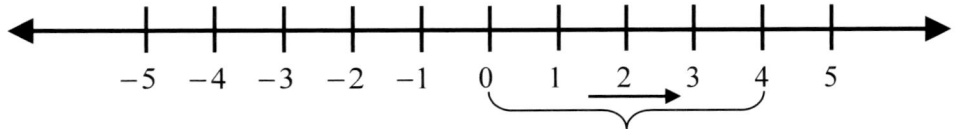

Traveling 4 units in the opposite direction we arrive at 4.

The opposite of -4 is 4.

Now try problem 35 from exercise set 3.1

Another way of determining the opposite of a number is by applying a negative sign to the number. The opposite of 6 is -6. The opposite of 12 is -12. The opposite of -4 is $-(-4)$. However, as we see from example 5, the opposite of -4 is 4. So, $-(-4) = 4$. Or, in general, the opposite of a negative number is a positive number.

Warning!! Be careful not to say that two negatives make a positive. This could imply that $-3+(-4) = 7$, which is not true. Multiplying or dividing two negative numbers however, does result in a positive answer.

Example 6: Find the opposite of each of the following numbers: $6, -5, 0.2, -\dfrac{3}{5}, 0.$

Solution: Apply a negative sign to each number and then simplify.

Number	Opposite
6	$-(6) = \mathbf{-6}$
-5	$-(-5) = \mathbf{5}$
0.2	$-(0.2) = \mathbf{-0.2}$
$-\dfrac{3}{5}$	$-\left(-\dfrac{3}{5}\right) = \dfrac{\mathbf{3}}{\mathbf{5}}$
0	$-(0) = \mathbf{0}$

Now try problem 33 through 39 from exercise set 3.1

Note: The $-$ symbol can be used to indicate a negative number, the opposite of a number, or the operation of subtraction.

Addition of signed numbers: To add signed numbers, apply the following rules.

1. To add two numbers with the same sign, add their absolute values and attach their common sign to the resulting sum. If both numbers are positive, then the final answer is positive. If both numbers are negative, then the final answer is negative.

2. To add two numbers with opposite signs, subtract the smaller absolute value from the larger absolute value. Then attach the sign of the number with the larger absolute value to the resulting difference in order to get the final answer.

Example 7: Find the sum: $-0.3 + (-1.4)$

Solution: When adding two numbers with the same sign, (in this case both numbers are negative) add their absolute values.

$$|-0.3| + |-1.4| =$$

$$0.3 \; + \; 1.4 \; =$$

$$1.7 \qquad \text{Now, attach their common sign (negative) to the resulting sum.}$$

$$-1.7 \qquad -0.3 + (-1.4) = \mathbf{-1.7}$$

Now try problem 65 from exercise set 3.1

Example 8: Find the sum: $-\dfrac{1}{4} + \left(-\dfrac{2}{3}\right)$

Solution: In order to add or subtract two fractions we must first get a common denominator. In this case the common denominator is 12. Now we must build each fraction such that it has 12 as a denominator.

$$-\frac{1}{4} + \left(-\frac{2}{3}\right) = -\frac{1}{4}\left(\frac{3}{3}\right) + \left(-\frac{2}{3}\right)\left(\frac{4}{4}\right) = -\frac{3}{12} + \left(-\frac{8}{12}\right)$$

Now, we are ready to add the two fractions.

When adding two numbers with the same sign, (in this case both numbers are negative) add their absolute values.

$$\left|-\frac{3}{12}\right| + \left|-\frac{8}{12}\right| = \frac{3}{12} + \frac{8}{12} = \frac{11}{12}$$

Now, attach their common sign (negative) to the resulting sum.

$$-\frac{11}{12} \qquad\qquad -\frac{1}{4} + \left(-\frac{2}{3}\right) = -\frac{\mathbf{11}}{\mathbf{12}}$$

Now try problem 79 from exercise set 3.1

Example 9: Find the sum: $-8+3$

Solution: When adding two numbers with opposite signs, subtract the smaller absolute value from the larger absolute value.

$|-8|=8$ and $|3|=3$.

Since 3 is smaller than 8, we subtract it from 8. $8-3=5$

Now, attach the sign of the number with the larger absolute value to the resulting difference. Since -8 has the larger absolute value, attach a negative sign to the 5 and the final answer becomes -5. $-8+3=\mathbf{-5}$

Now try problem 61 from exercise set 3.1

Example 10: Find the sum: $12+(-9)$

Solution: When adding two numbers with opposite signs, subtract the smaller absolute value from the larger absolute value.

$|12|=12$ and $|-9|=9$.

Since 9 is smaller than 12, we subtract it from 12. $12-9=3$

Now, attach the sign of the number with the larger absolute value to the resulting difference. Since 12 has the larger absolute value, attach a positive sign to the 3 and the final answer becomes +3 or just 3. $12+(-9)=\mathbf{3}$

Now try problem 57 from exercise set 3.1

Subtraction of signed numbers: **To subtract signed numbers, apply the following rule.**

To subtract two numbers, add the first number and the opposite of the second number.

Or, in symbolic form: $a-b=a+(-b)$

Another way of describing the situation is to say; subtracting a number is like adding its opposite.

Example 11: Find the difference: $4-12$

Solution: First, rewrite the problem as addition of the opposite.

$4-12$ becomes $4+(-12)$.

Now, applying the rule for adding two numbers with opposite signs, subtract the smaller absolute value from the larger absolute value.

$|4|=4$ and $|-12|=12$.

Since 4 is smaller than 12, we subtract it from 12. $12-4=8$

Now, attach the sign of the number with the larger absolute value to the resulting difference. Since -12 has the larger absolute value, attach a negative sign to the 8 and the final answer becomes -8. $4-12=\mathbf{-8}$

Now try problem 101 from exercise set 3.1

<u>Example 12</u>: Find the difference: $-\dfrac{2}{5}-\dfrac{1}{5}$

Solution: First, rewrite the problem as addition of the opposite.

$$-\dfrac{2}{5}-\dfrac{1}{5} \text{ becomes } -\dfrac{2}{5}+\left(-\dfrac{1}{5}\right).$$

Now, applying the rule for adding two numbers with the same sign we add their absolute values.

$$\left|-\dfrac{2}{5}\right|+\left|-\dfrac{1}{5}\right|=\dfrac{2}{5}+\dfrac{1}{5}=\dfrac{3}{5}$$

Now, attach their common sign (negative) to the resulting sum.

$$-\dfrac{3}{5} \qquad\qquad -\dfrac{2}{5}-\dfrac{1}{5}=-\dfrac{3}{5}$$

<u>Example 13</u>: Find the difference: $0.6-(-0.3)$

Solution: First, rewrite the problem as addition of the opposite.

$0.6-(-0.3)$ becomes $0.6+(+0.3)$ or simply $0.6 + 0.3$.

Since adding two positive numbers produces a positive result, $0.6 + 0.3 = \mathbf{0.9}$.

<u>Example 14</u>: Find the difference: $-4-(-7)$

Solution: First, rewrite the problem as addition of the opposite.

$-4-(-7)$ becomes $-4+(+7)$ or simply $-4+7$.

Now, applying the rule for adding two numbers with opposite signs, subtract the smaller absolute value from the larger absolute value.

$$|-4|=4 \text{ and } |7|=7.$$

Since 4 is smaller than 7, we subtract it from 7. $7-4=3$

Now, attach the sign of the number with the larger absolute value to the resulting difference. Since 7 has the larger absolute value, attach a positive sign to the 3 and the final answer becomes +3 or simply 3. $-4-(-7)=\mathbf{3}$

Now try problem 125 from exercise set 3.1

Multiplication of signed numbers: When multiplying two numbers, apply the following rules.

1. If the signs of the numbers are the same, both positive or both negative, then their product is a positive number.

2. If the signs of the numbers are opposites, one positive and one negative, then their product is a negative number.

Example 15: Multiply: $4(-3)$

> Solution: The signs are opposites, therefore the product is negative.
>
> $$4(-3) = -12$$

Now try problem 141 from exercise set 3.1

Example 16: Multiply: $-8(-6)$

> Solution: The signs are the same, therefore the product is positive.
>
> $$-8(-6) = 48$$

Now try problem 145 from exercise set 3.1

Example 17: Multiply: $(-x)(6)$

> Solution: The signs are opposites, therefore the product is negative.
>
> $$(-x)(6) = -6x$$
>
> Note: We write the final answer with the coefficient in front of the variable.

Example 18: Multiply: $(-y)(-4)$

> Solution: The signs are the same, therefore the product is positive.
>
> $$(-y)(-4) = 4y$$
>
> Note: We write the final answer with the coefficient in front of the variable.

Multiplication by zero: Multiplying a number by zero always results in a product of zero.

Example 19: Multiply: $-6(0)$

> Solution: Even though one of the factors is negative, since the other factor is zero, the product is **zero**. Zero is neither positive nor negative in sign.

Now try problem 157 from exercise set 3.1

Division of signed numbers: When dividing two numbers, apply the following rules.

1.   If the signs of the numbers are the same, both positive or both negative, then their quotient is a positive number.

2.   If the signs of the numbers are opposites, one positive and one negative, then their quotient is a negative number.

Example 20: Divide: $8 \div (-2)$

> Solution: The signs are opposites, therefore the quotient is negative.
> $$8 \div (-2) = -4$$

Now try problem 165 from exercise set 3.1

Example 21: Divide: $-15 \div (-3)$

> Solution: The signs are the same, therefore the quotient is positive.
> $$-15 \div (-3) = 5$$

Now try problem 169 from exercise set 3.1

Example 22: Divide: $-\dfrac{2}{3} \div \dfrac{5}{6}$

> Solution: The signs are opposites, therefore the quotient is negative. However, in order to divide by a fraction, we multiply by its reciprocal instead.
>
> $-\dfrac{2}{3} \div \dfrac{5}{6}$ becomes
>
> $-\dfrac{2}{3}\left(\dfrac{6}{5}\right).$ Now, reducing out common factors we get
>
> $-\dfrac{2}{\cancel{3}}\left(\dfrac{2\cdot\cancel{3}}{5}\right) = -\dfrac{4}{5}.$ $\qquad -\dfrac{2}{3} \div \dfrac{5}{6} = -\dfrac{4}{5}$

Now try problem 181 from exercise set 3.1

Division by zero: Dividing by zero is not possible. Therefore, division by zero is undefined.

Example 23: Divide: $-15 \div (0)$

> Solution: Even though the numerator is negative, since the denominator is zero, the answer is **undefined**.

Order of operations: When simplifying a mathematical expression, use the following order of operations.

1.   Perform all calculations within grouping symbols, such as parentheses, brackets, braces or absolute value bars. Also simplify above and below any fraction bars.

2.   Evaluate all exponential expressions.

3.   Do all multiplication and division in order from left to right.

4.   Do all addition and subtraction in order from left to right.

Example 24: Simplify the expression: $3 + 6(4)$

Solution:	
$3 + 6(4)$	First multiply.
$3 + 24$	Then add.
27	

Example 25: Simplify the expression: $(3 + 6)(4)$

Solution:	
$(3 + 6)(4)$	First perform all calculations within parentheses.
$(9)(4)$	Then multiply.
36	

Example 26: Simplify the expression: $(3+6)^2(4)$

Solution:	
$(3+6)^2(4)$	First perform all calculations within parentheses.
$(9)^2(4)$	Then evaluate the exponential expression.
$81(4)$	Finally, multiply.
324	

Example 27: Simplify the expression: $\left|2-3(2)^2\right|+3(8\div2\cdot5)$

Solution:

$\left\|2-3(2)^2\right\|+3(8\div2\cdot5)$	Perform all calculations within grouping symbols, such as parentheses or absolute value bars.
	Start within the absolute value bars.
$\left\|2-3(2)^2\right\|+3(8\div2\cdot5)$	First evaluate the exponential expression.
$\left. 2-3(4)\right\|+3(8\div2\cdot5)$	Then multiply.
$\left\|2-12\right\|+3(8\div2\cdot5)$	Next subtract.
$\left\|-10\right\|+3(8\div2\cdot5)$	Finally, take the absolute value of -10.
$10+3(8\div2\cdot5)$	
	Now simplify within the set of parentheses.
$10+3(8\div2\cdot5)$	Do all multiplication and division in order from left to right.
$10+3(4\cdot5)$	
$10+3(20)$	Now that the contents of the parentheses have been simplified, do the multiplication.
$10+60$	Finally, add.
70	

Evaluating algebraic expressions: **When numbers and variables are combined using operations such as multiplication, division, addition, and/or subtraction, these combinations are called algebraic expressions. When we know the numerical value of the variables in these expressions, we substitute the numbers in place of the variables. This allows us to determine the value of the algebraic expression. This process is called "evaluating algebraic expressions."**

Example 28: Evaluate the expression for the given value of the variable: $2x+3$, where $x=4$

Solution:

$2x+3$	Substitute 4 in the place of x.
$2(4)+3$	Then evaluate the expression using order of operations.
$2(4)+3$	First multiply.
$8+3$	Then add.
11	

Example 29: Evaluate the expression for the given value of the variable: $\dfrac{4(2y-3)}{y+3}$, where $y = 5$

Solution:

$\dfrac{4(2y-3)}{y+3}$ Substitute 5 in the place of y.

$\dfrac{4(2(5)-3)}{(5)+3}$ Then evaluate the expression using order of operations.

Start by simplifying within the parentheses of the numerator.

$\dfrac{4(2(5)-3)}{(5)+3}$ First multiply.

$\dfrac{4(10-3)}{(5)+3}$ Then subtract.

$\dfrac{4(7)}{(5)+3}$ Now that the contents of the parentheses have been simplified, do the multiplication of the entire numerator.

$\dfrac{28}{(5)+3}$ Now simplify the denominator by doing the addition.

$\dfrac{28}{8}$ Finally, simplify the fraction by reducing out common factors.

$\dfrac{7\cdot\cancel{4}}{2\cdot\cancel{4}}$ The final answer is

$\dfrac{7}{2}$.

Example 30: Evaluate the expression for the given values of the variables: $-3x^2 + 2y$, where $x = -2$ and $y = -4$

Solution:

$-3x^2 + 2y$ Substitute -2 in the place of x and -4 in the place of y.

$-3(-2)^2 + 2(-4)$ Then evaluate the expression using order of operations.

First evaluate the exponential expression.

$-3(4) + 2(-4)$ Then multiply.

$-12 + (-8)$ Finally, add.

-20

Now try problem 97 from exercise set 3.1

Section 1 exercises. Find the absolute value of each number.

1.   2   **2.**   7   **3.** -5 **4.** -3

5. $\dfrac{1}{7}$ **6.** $\dfrac{2}{9}$ **7.** -3.6 **8.** -5.2

9. $-4\dfrac{1}{4}$ **10.** $-6\dfrac{2}{5}$ **11.**   0.08   **12.**   0.35

Evaluate.

13. $|-6|$ **14.** $|-9|$ **15.** $-|6|$ **16.** $-|12|$

17. $|-3.7|$ **18.** $|9.8|$ **19.** $|4.5|$ **20.** $|-3.6|$

21. $-|-5|$ **22.** $-|-4|$ **23.** $-\left|-\dfrac{7}{9}\right|$ **24.** $-\left|-\dfrac{3}{8}\right|$

Evaluate the expression for the given value of the variable.

25. $|x|$ for $x=-2$ **26.** $|x|$ for $x=-6$ **27.** $|-x|$ for $x=3$

28. $|-x|$ for $x=7$ **29.** $-|-x|$ for $x=5$ **30.** $-|-x|$ for $x=8$

31. $-|-y|$ for $y=-7$ **32.** $-|-y|$ for $y=-3$

Find the opposite of each quantity.

33.   6   **34.**   3   **35.** -2 **36.** -4

37. -0.3 **38.** -8.4 **39.** $3\dfrac{1}{2}$ **40.** $5\dfrac{1}{6}$

41. a **42.** b **43.** $-c$ **44.** $-d$

Simplify.

45. $-(-5)$ **46.** $-(-7)$ **47.** $-(3)$ **48.** $-(4)$

49. $-(-0.8)$ **50.** $-(-0.4)$ **51.** $-(-x)$ **52.** $-(-y)$

53. $-(z)$ **54.** $-(w)$ **55.** $-\left(-2\dfrac{1}{2}\right)$ **56.** $-\left(-3\dfrac{1}{8}\right)$

Add.

57. $6+(-2)$ **58.** $5+(-3)$ **59.** $-7.3+4.2$ **60.** $-8.5+5.6$

61. $-12+3$ **62.** $-9+5$ **63.** $\dfrac{12}{5}+\left(-\dfrac{3}{5}\right)$ **64.** $\dfrac{9}{7}+\left(-\dfrac{5}{7}\right)$

65. $-12+(-3)$ **66.** $-9+(-5)$ **67.** $-7+0$ **68.** $-6+0$

69. $-5\dfrac{3}{7}+3\dfrac{1}{7}$ **70.** $-6\dfrac{2}{3}+5\dfrac{1}{3}$ **71.** $4+(-19)$ **72.** $5+(-11)$

73. $9+(-9)$ **74.** $6+(-6)$ **75.** $0+(-18)$ **76.** $0+(-3)$

77. $-10+10$ **78.** $-3+3$ **79.** $-\dfrac{12}{5}+\left(-\dfrac{9}{4}\right)$ **80.** $-\dfrac{18}{5}+\left(-\dfrac{6}{7}\right)$

81. $7+(-8)+(-2)$ **82.** $6+(-5)+(-9)$ **83.** $-3+4+(-4)$

84. $-4+6+(-6)$ **85.** $9.2+(-6.1)+4.8$ **86.** $5.6+(-8.3)+7.5$

87. $\dfrac{4}{9}+\left(-\dfrac{3}{9}\right)+\dfrac{7}{9}$ **88.** $\dfrac{2}{7}+\left(-\dfrac{4}{7}\right)+\dfrac{8}{7}$ **89.** $2\dfrac{5}{8}+\left(-3\dfrac{1}{4}\right)+9$

90. $6\dfrac{1}{4}+\left(-7\dfrac{1}{8}\right)+3$ **91.** $-\dfrac{2}{5}+(-0.7)+8$ **92.** $-\dfrac{3}{4}+(-0.6)+3$

Evaluate the expression for the given values of the variables.

93. $x + y$ for $x = -3$ and $y = -8$ **94.** $x + y$ for $x = -6$ and $y = -7$

95. $-2x + 7y$ for $x = -4$ and $y = -2$ **96.** $-6x + 3y$ for $x = -2$ and $y = -8$

97. $-3x^2 + y^2$ for $x = -2$ and $y = -5$ **98.** $-5x^2 + 2y^2$ for $x = -3$ and $y = -5$

99. $-x^2 + 4y^2$ for $x = -\dfrac{2}{3}$ and $y = -\dfrac{1}{2}$ **100.** $-x^2 + 6y^2$ for $x = -\dfrac{1}{2}$ and $y = -\dfrac{1}{3}$

Subtract.

101. $6 - 9$ **102.** $7 - 12$ **103.** $4 - 11$ **104.** $3 - 8$

105. $3.7 - 9.6$ **106.** $8.9 - 12.7$ **107.** $6.5 - 11.4$ **108.** $2.7 - 8.3$

109. $\dfrac{3}{7} - \dfrac{9}{6}$ **110.** $\dfrac{8}{9} - \dfrac{12}{7}$ **111.** $\dfrac{6}{5} - \dfrac{11}{4}$ **112.** $\dfrac{2}{7} - \dfrac{8}{3}$

113. $-11 - 4$ **114.** $-8 - 3$ **115.** $-9 - 6$ **116.** $-12 - 17$

117. $-11.4 - 6.5$ **118.** $-8.3 - 2.7$ **119.** $-9.6 - 3.7$ **120.** $-12.7 - 8.9$

121. $-3\dfrac{1}{4} - 7\dfrac{1}{2}$ **122.** $-5\dfrac{2}{5} - 9\dfrac{3}{10}$ **123.** $-6\dfrac{5}{6} - 2\dfrac{1}{3}$ **124.** $-8\dfrac{1}{4} - 2\dfrac{1}{2}$

125. $-7 - (-12)$ **126.** $-6 - (-9)$ **127.** $-8 - (-3)$ **128.** $-11 - (-4)$

129. $-5 - 6 - (-7)$ **130.** $-5 - 4 - (-3)$ **131.** $7 - (-7) - 5$ **132.** $5 - (-5) - 7$

Evaluate the expression for the given values of the variables.

133. $x - y$ for $x = -4$ and $y = -6$

134. $x - y$ for $x = -6$ and $y = -9$

135. $-7x - 2y$ for $x = -4.6$ and $y = 2.3$

136. $-3x - 6y$ for $x = -2.5$ and $y = 8.9$

137. $-x^2 - 3y^2$ for $x = -1$ and $y = -2$

138. $-2x^2 - 5y^2$ for $x = -1$ and $y = -3$

139. $-4x^2 - y^2$ for $x = -\dfrac{2}{3}$ and $y = -\dfrac{1}{2}$

140. $-6x^2 - y^2$ for $x = -\dfrac{1}{2}$ and $y = -\dfrac{1}{3}$

Multiply.

141. $5(-9)$ **142.** $3(-8)$ **143.** $7(-4)$ **144.** $6(-2)$

145. $-9.6(-7.3)$ **146.** $-6.9(-3.7)$ **147.** $-8.5(4.2)$ **148.** $-8.7(4.9)$

149. $-\dfrac{2}{3}\left(\dfrac{6}{7}\right)$ **150.** $-\dfrac{3}{5}\left(\dfrac{10}{13}\right)$ **151.** $-\dfrac{7}{5}\left(-\dfrac{15}{14}\right)$ **152.** $-\dfrac{4}{3}\left(-\dfrac{9}{8}\right)$

153. $-6(-9)(5)$ **154.** $3(-5)(7)$ **155.** $4(-3)(2)$ **156.** $-8(-6)(4)$

157. $-7(-6)(0)(-5)$ **158.** $-3(-5)(-9)(0)$

Evaluate the expression for the given values of the variables.

159. xy for $x = -3$ and $y = -7$

160. xy for $x = -5$ and $y = -9$

161. $-7xy$ for $x = -4.3$ and $y = 2.7$

162. $-3xy$ for $x = -2.9$ and $y = 8.4$

163. $-x^2 y^2$ for $x = -1$ and $y = -2$

164. $-2x^2 y^2$ for $x = -1$ and $y = -3$

Divide.

165. $6 \div (-3)$ **166.** $8 \div (-4)$ **167.** $12 \div (-3)$ **168.** $15 \div (-5)$

169. $-16 \div (-4)$ **170.** $-24 \div (-6)$ **171.** $-36 \div (-9)$ **172.** $-45 \div (-9)$

173. $4 \div (-1.6)$ **174.** $8.5 \div (-0.5)$ **175.** $5 \div (-1.5)$ **176.** $4 \div (-1.2)$

177. $\dfrac{25}{-5}$ **178.** $\dfrac{35}{-5}$ **179.** $\dfrac{-70}{-14}$ **180.** $\dfrac{-60}{-12}$

181. $\dfrac{2}{5} \div \left(-\dfrac{4}{15}\right)$ **182.** $\dfrac{4}{9} \div \left(-\dfrac{8}{15}\right)$ **183.** $-\dfrac{3}{7} \div \left(-\dfrac{14}{15}\right)$ **184.** $-\dfrac{2}{7} \div \left(-\dfrac{21}{8}\right)$

Evaluate the expression for the given values of the variables.

185. $x \div y$ for $x = 27$ and $y = -3$ **186.** $x \div y$ for $x = 42$ and $y = -7$

187. $\dfrac{-3x}{y}$ for $x = -1.5$ and $y = -6$ **188.** $\dfrac{-4x}{y}$ for $x = -2.6$ and $y = -8$

189. $x \div (-y)$ for $x = -1$ and $y = -2$ **190.** $x \div (-y)$ for $x = -1$ and $y = -3$

Simplify the expression.

191. $2 \cdot 3 + 8 \div 0$ **192.** $8 \cdot 4 + 10 \div 0$ **193.** $4 + 2(7 - 3)$

194. $6 + 3(9 - 5)$ **195.** $9 \cdot 7 - (4 - 8)^2$ **196.** $6 \cdot 12 - (3 - 7)^2$

197. $12 \div 3(2 - 7)^2$ **198.** $15 \div 5(6 - 9)^2$ **199.** $-1(-2)^2(-3)^3$

200. $-4(-3)^2(-2)^3$ **201.** $(0.6 - 0.8)(0.8 - 6)^2$ **202.** $(0.3 - 0.7)(0.7 - 3)^2$

Simplify the expression.

203. $8 \div 4 \cdot 2 \cdot 10 \div 5$

204. $12 \div 3 \cdot 6 \cdot 2 \div 4$

205. $7 + (-3) - 4 - (-6)$

206. $8 + (-5) - 3 - (-9)$

207. $2[3 - (6-8)^2 + 4]^2$

208. $3[4 - (5-8)^2 + 9]^2$

209. $(8 \div 2)^2 - 8 \div 2^2$

210. $(12 \div 2)^2 - 12 \div 2^2$

211. $6 - 2 \cdot 8$

212. $4 - 3 \cdot 7$

213. $5(8 + 4 \cdot 3)$

214. $7(9 + 5 \cdot 6)$

215. $6 \cdot 3^2 + 18 \div 2 - 4^2$

216. $7 \cdot 2^3 + 24 \div 6 - 3^2$

217. $7 + 3[4 + 5(2-6)]$

218. $8 + 5[3 + 2(7-12)]$

219. $|-6 + 0.3|$

220. $|-9 + 0.4|$

221. $-3|-6 + 9|$

222. $-4|-3 + 5|$

223. $|-3 - 4|$

224. $|-9 - 2|$

225. $|-4 - (-9)|$

226. $|-3 - (-8)|$

227. $-5^2 + 5^2$

228. $-7^2 + 7^2$

229. $-[-(-3 + 6) + 7] + 2$

230. $-[-(-8 + 11) + 4] + 9$

231. $\left|-\dfrac{7}{8}\right| \cdot |-3 + 7|$

232. $\left|-\dfrac{6}{7}\right| \cdot |-5 + 12|$

233. $\left|-6^2 + 4^2 - \dfrac{5}{6}\right|$

234. $\left|-5^2 + 3^2 - \dfrac{8}{9}\right|$

235. $\dfrac{4^2 - 3^2}{5^2 - 2^2}$

236. $\dfrac{6^2 - 4^2}{7^2 - 3^2}$

237. $\dfrac{-11 - (-3)}{2 - 6}$

238. $\dfrac{-13 - (-4)}{7 - 10}$

239. $\dfrac{-2(-8) + (-1)^2}{7^2 - 10^2}$

240. $\dfrac{-8(-3) + (-1)^2}{3^2 - 2^2}$

Evaluate the expression for the given values of the variables.

241. $6x^2y - 4x$, where $x = -\dfrac{2}{3}$ and $y = \dfrac{3}{4}$

242. $5xy^2 - 8y$, where $x = \dfrac{4}{5}$ and $y = -\dfrac{2}{3}$

243. $x^2 - 4x + y$, where $x = -3$ and $y = -7$

244. $x^2 + 3x - y$, where $x = -2$ and $y = -4$

245. $\dfrac{3x^2 - 4y}{3y^2 - 4x}$, where $x = -\dfrac{2}{5}$ and $y = -\dfrac{1}{5}$

246. $\dfrac{2x^2 - 5y}{5y^2 - 2x}$, where $x = -\dfrac{3}{10}$ and $y = -\dfrac{1}{10}$

247. $4(2x - y)^2 + 7z$, where $x = -2$, $y = -5$, and $z = -1$

248. $5(3x + y)^2 + 8z$, where $x = -4$, $y = -2$, and $z = -3$

249. $x^3 - y^2 + z$, where $x = -2$, $y = -3$, and $z = -4$

250. $x^2 + y^3 - z$, where $x = -5$, $y = 3$, and $z = 10$

AN INTRODUCTION TO ALGEBRA

Section 2: Properties of Real Numbers

The properties of real numbers describe the way operations on numbers can be carried out.

THE COMMUTATIVE PROPERTY OF ADDITION:

For any real numbers a and b,

$$a + b = b + a.$$

Two numbers can be added in any order and the sum will be the same.

Example 1: Show by example that addition is commutative.

Solution: $3 + 5 = 8$ and $5 + 3 = 8$. Therefore, $3 + 5 = 5 + 3$.

Conclusion: The order in which numbers are added does not change the resulting sum. This is an example showing that **addition is commutative**.

THE COMMUTATIVE PROPERTY OF MULTIPLICATION:

For any real numbers a and b,

$$a \cdot b = b \cdot a.$$

Two numbers can be multiplied in any order and the product will be the same.

Example 2: Show by example that multiplication is commutative.

Solution: $3 \cdot 7 = 21$ and $7 \cdot 3 = 21$. Therefore, $3 \cdot 7 = 7 \cdot 3$.

Conclusion: The order in which numbers are multiplied does not change the resulting product. This is an example showing that **multiplication is commutative**.

THE ASSOCIATIVE PROPERTY OF ADDITION:

For any real numbers a, b, and c,

$$(a + b) + c = a + (b + c).$$

When three or more numbers are added together, the way in which they are grouped does not change the resulting sum.

Example 3: Show by example that addition is associative.

Solution: Following order of operations,

$(3 + 4) + 5 = 7 + 5 = 12$ and $3 + (4 + 5) = 3 + 9 = 12$.

Therefore, $(3 + 4) + 5 = 3 + (4 + 5)$.

Conclusion: When three or more numbers are added together, the way in which they are grouped does not change the resulting sum. This is an example showing that **addition is associative**.

THE ASSOCIATIVE PROPERTY OF MULTIPLICATION:

For any real numbers a, b, and c,

$$(a \cdot b) \cdot c = a \cdot (b \cdot c).$$

When three or more numbers are multiplied together, the way in which they are grouped does not change the resulting product.

Example 4: Show by example that multiplication is associative.

Solution: Following order of operations,

$(3 \cdot 4) \cdot 5 = 12 \cdot 5 = 60$ and $3 \cdot (4 \cdot 5) = 3 \cdot 20 = 60$.

Therefore, $(3 \cdot 4) \cdot 5 = 3 \cdot (4 \cdot 5)$.

Conclusion: When three or more numbers are multiplied together, the way in which they are grouped does not change the resulting product. This is an example showing that **multiplication is associative**.

THE IDENTITY PROPERTY OF ADDITION:

For any real number a,

$$a + 0 = a \quad \text{and} \quad 0 + a = a .$$

If 0 is added to any real number a, the sum is a.

Note: The number 0 is called the <u>additive identity</u>.

<u>Example 5:</u> Show an example of the identity property of addition.

Solution: $7 + 0 = 7$ and $0 + 7 = 7$.

Conclusion: **Adding 0 to a number does not change the number's original value.**

THE IDENTITY PROPERTY OF MULTIPLICATION:

For any real number a,

$$a \cdot 1 = a \quad \text{and} \quad 1 \cdot a = a .$$

If 1 is multiplied by any real number a, the product is a.

Note: The number 1 is called the <u>multiplicative identity</u>.

<u>Example 6:</u> Show an example of the identity property of multiplication.

Solution: $4 \cdot 1 = 4$ and $1 \cdot 4 = 4$.

Conclusion: **Multiplying 1 by a number does not change the number's original value.**

THE MULTIPLICATION PROPERTY OF ZERO:

For any real number a,

$$a \cdot 0 = 0 \quad \text{and} \quad 0 \cdot a = 0 .$$

If 0 is multiplied by any real number a, the product is 0.

<u>Example 7:</u> Show an example of the multiplication property of zero.

Solution: $7 \cdot 0 = 0$ and $0 \cdot 7 = 0$.

Conclusion: **Multiplying 0 by a number or multiplying a number by 0 produces a product that is 0.**

THE ADDITIVE INVERSE PROPERTY:

For any real number a,

$$a + (-a) = 0 \quad \text{and} \quad -a + a = 0.$$

The sum of a number and its additive inverse (opposite) equals the additive identity 0.

Note: <u>Additive inverse</u> is another name for opposite.

Example 8: Show an example of the additive inverse property.

Solution: $7 + (-7) = 0$ and $-7 + 7 = 0$.

Conclusion: **7 and -7 are additive inverses**.

THE MULTIPLICATIVE INVERSE PROPERTY:

For any real number a,

$$a \cdot \frac{1}{a} = 1 \quad \text{and} \quad \frac{1}{a} \cdot a = 1 \quad \text{if } a \neq 0.$$

The product of a number and its multiplicative inverse (reciprocal) equals the multiplicative identity 1.

Note: <u>Multiplicative inverse</u> is another name for reciprocal.

Example 9: Show an example of the multiplicative inverse property.

Solution: $5 \cdot \frac{1}{5} = 1$ and $\frac{1}{5} \cdot 5 = 1$.

Conclusion: **5 and $\frac{1}{5}$ are multiplicative inverses**.

THE DISTRIBUTIVE PROPERTY:

For any real numbers a, b, and c,

$$a \cdot (b+c) = a \cdot b + a \cdot c$$

and

$$a \cdot (b-c) = a \cdot b - a \cdot c.$$

Multiplying a group by any real number a is equivalent to multiplying each term of the group by the number a.

Example 10: Show an example of the distributive property.

Solution: Following order of operations,

$$3(6+5) = 3(11) = 33.$$

Using the distributive property,

$$3(6+5) = 3 \cdot 6 + 3 \cdot 5 = 18 + 15 = 33.$$

Conclusion: **Distributing across a grouping symbol gives the same results as multiplying by the entire group all at once.**

Since real numbers can be represented by variables, properties of real numbers can be used to simplify expressions, which contain variables.

Example 11: Simplify: $-8x + 5 + 8x$

Solution:

$-8x + 5 + 8x$	Use the commutative property of addition to rewrite the problem as
$-8x + 8x + 5.$	Use the associative property of addition to rewrite the problem as
$(-8x + 8x) + 5.$	Use the additive inverse property to rewrite the problem as
$0 + 5.$	Use the identity property of addition to rewrite the problem as
$5.$	

Now try problem 29 from exercise set 3.2

Example 12: Simplify: $\frac{1}{4} \cdot (x \cdot 4)$

Solution:

$\frac{1}{4} \cdot (x \cdot 4)$	Use the commutative property of multiplication to rewrite the problem as
$\frac{1}{4} \cdot (4 \cdot x)$.	Use the associative property of multiplication to rewrite the problem as
$\left(\frac{1}{4} \cdot 4\right) \cdot x$.	Use the multiplicative inverse property to rewrite the problem as
$1 \cdot x$.	Use the identity property of multiplication to rewrite the problem as
x.	

*Now try problem 35 from exercise set 3.2

Example 13: Simplify: $x \cdot (-5y + 5y)$

Solution:

$x \cdot (-5y + 5y)$	Use the additive inverse property to rewrite the problem as
$x \cdot (0)$.	Use the multiplication property of zero to rewrite the problem as
0.	

Example 14: Simplify: $4(x + y)$

Solution:

$4(x + y)$	Use the distributive property.
$4 \cdot x + 4 \cdot y$	Simplify further.
$4x + 4y$	

*Now try problem 67 from exercise set 3.2

Example 15: Simplify: $-3\left(2x-\dfrac{1}{3}\right)$

Solution:

$-3\left(2x-\dfrac{1}{3}\right)$	Use the distributive property.
$(-3)(2x)+(-3)\left(-\dfrac{1}{3}\right)$	Following order of operations, multiply from left to right. First, use the associative property of multiplication to rewrite the problem as
$(-3\cdot 2)x+(-3)\left(-\dfrac{1}{3}\right).$	Second, multiply -3 and 2.
$-6x+(-3)\left(-\dfrac{1}{3}\right)$	Third, use the multiplicative inverse property to rewrite the problem as
$-6x+1.$	

The following are examples of simplifying algebraic expressions without listing the properties being used in the simplification process.

Example 16: Simplify: $4y+6+(-4y)$

Solution:

$4y+6+(-4y)=$

$4y+(-4y)+6=$

$0+6=$

6

Now try problem 45 from exercise set 3.2

Example 17: Simplify: $\dfrac{2}{3}\cdot\left(x\cdot\dfrac{3}{2}\right)$

Solution:

$\dfrac{2}{3}\cdot\left(x\cdot\dfrac{3}{2}\right)=$

$\left(\dfrac{2}{3}\cdot\dfrac{3}{2}\right)\cdot x=$

$1\cdot x=$

x

Example 18: Simplify: $6y(3x - 3x)$

Solution:

$6y(3x - 3x) =$

$6y[3x + (-3x)] =$

$6y(0) =$

0

Example 19: Simplify: $6x(-y)$

Solution:

$6x(-y) =$

$6x(-1y) =$

$[6(-1)](x \cdot y) =$

$-6xy$

Now try problem 33 from exercise set 3.2

Example 20: Simplify: $(-3x)(-4x)$

Solution:

$(-3x)(-4x) =$

$[(-3)(-4)](x \cdot x) =$

$12x^2$

Now try problem 57 from exercise set 3.2

Example 21: Simplify: $-(x - 4y + 6z - 4)$

Solution:

$-(x - 4y + 6z - 4) =$

$-x - (-4y) - 6z - (-4) =$

$-x + 4y - 6z + 4$

Now try problem 85 from exercise set 3.2

Example 22: Simplify: $-4(x - 3y + z)$

Solution:

$-4(x - 3y + z) =$

$-4(x) - 4(-3y) - 4(z) =$

$-4(x) + [(-4)(-3)]y - 4(z) =$

$-4x + 12y - 4z$

Now try problem 89 from exercise set 3.2

Section 2 exercises. Identify which property is being used to transform the left side of each equation into the right side.

1. $x \cdot \dfrac{1}{x} = \dfrac{1}{x} \cdot x$

2. $7 + (3 + x) = (7 + 3) + x$

3. $9 \cdot 0 = 0$

4. $8 + (-8) = -8 + 8$

5. $x \cdot \dfrac{1}{x} = 1$

6. $0 + 6 = 6$

7. $6(7x) = (6 \cdot 7)x$

8. $2x \cdot 1 = 2x$

9. $8 + (-8) = 0$

10. $6(x + 4) = 6x + 24$

11. $-2x + (2x + 7) = (-2x + 2x) + 7$

12. $0y = 0$

13. $6(x + 4) = 6(4 + x)$

14. $6(x + 4) = (x + 4)6$

15. $z + 0 = z$

16. $6\big(4 + (-4)\big) = 6(0)$

17. $-8(x - 4) = -8x + 32$

18. $\dfrac{1}{7}(7) = 1$

19. $1 \cdot x^2 = x^2$

20. $(xy)z = x(yz)$

Simplify each expression.

21. $10x + (-10x)$

22. $6y + (-6y)$

23. $4(2x)$

24. $6(3x)$

25. $-2(5w)$

26. $-9(3r)$

27. $\left(\dfrac{1}{5}x\right)(10x)$

28. $\left(\dfrac{1}{2}y\right)(4y)$

29. $3x + 7 + (-3x)$

30. $8z - 11 + (-8z)$

31. $\dfrac{2}{3}(9y)$

32. $\dfrac{3}{5}(10y)$

33. $(-3x)(-5y)$

34. $(-4x)(-7y)$

35. $\left(-\dfrac{3}{4}x\right)\left(-\dfrac{4}{3}\right)$

36. $\left(-\dfrac{5}{7}y\right)\left(-\dfrac{7}{5}\right)$

37. $-4w - 4w - 12$

38. $-9x + 9x + 6$

39. $(0.7r) \cdot 3$

40. $(0.9k) \cdot 4$

41. $-\dfrac{2}{7}(14x)$

42. $-\dfrac{4}{9}(18y)$

43. $7\left(\dfrac{1}{7}w\right)$

44. $4\left(\dfrac{1}{4}z\right)$

45. $0.4 + 0.7y - 0.7y$

46. $0.3 - 0.2w + 0.2w$

47. $(5p)(6p)$

48. $(4w)(7w)$

49. $-\dfrac{8}{9}(-12w)$

50. $-\dfrac{3}{14}(-21z)$

51. $3w(-7)$

52. $4y(-6)$

53. $-6 + 4x + 6$

54. $-8 + 3x + 8$

55. $(-0.6x) \cdot 5$

56. $(-0.7n) \cdot 6$

57. $(-5x)(7x)$

58. $(-3w)(6w)$

59. $(7m)(6n)$

60. $(4p)(8q)$

Simplify each expression by using the distributive property.

61. $4(3x+7)$

62. $5(6x+8)$

63. $0.3(2x-9)$

64. $0.7(4x-5)$

65. $-8(y+2)$

66. $-6(y+7)$

67. $4(2m+3n)$

68. $3(4x+5y)$

69. $-(3a+b)$

70. $-(4w+x)$

71. $-(-2y-6)$

72. $-(-4y-11)$

73. $5(2y+3z-4)$

74. $7(y+4z-6)$

75. $-(5x-6)$

76. $-(7x-9)$

77. $-7(-3z+8)$

78. $-4(-6w+3)$

79. $-9(-5c-6)$

80. $-10(-6h-7)$

81. $4(3x+2y+5)$

82. $6(4x+3y+2)$

83. $3(4a-b-0.5)$

84. $2(3c-d-0.7)$

85. $-(-5x+3a-4m)$

86. $-(-6y+5b-8n)$

87. $-3x(2x-4y)$

88. $-6(-a+b-c)$

89. $-8(-x+y-z)$

90. $-6x(3x-5y)$

91. $-0.5(-3m-n+0.4)$

92. $-0.4(-6w-x+0.3)$

93. $-5(3a-4)$

94. $-(4a+3b-9c)$

95. $-(6x+7y-3z)$

96. $-6(8b-3)$

97. Give an example to show that division is not commutative.

98. Give an example to show that division is not associative.

99. Give an example to show that subtraction is not commutative.

100. Give an example to show that subtraction is not associative.

AN INTRODUCTION
TO ALGEBRA

Section 3: Simplifying Variable Expressions

Variable expressions consist of a certain number of **terms**. These terms are separated by addition signs. For example, the expression $5x + 4$ contains two terms. $5x$ is the first term and 4 is the second term. The expression $3x + y + 8$ contains three terms. $3x$ is the first term, y is the second term and 8 is the third term. If terms are separated by addition signs, then what about the expression $-x - 4y$? How many terms does this expression contain and what are these terms? We solve this problem by rewriting the subtraction part of the expression as addition of the opposite. $-x - 4y$ becomes $-x + (-4y)$. Now we see that the expression has two terms. $-x$ is the first term and $-4y$ is the second term.

In the expression $5x + 4$, the first term is $5x$, and is called the **variable term**. x is the **variable** and 5 is called the **numerical coefficient** of the variable. When a number and a variable are being multiplied together, it is customary to put the number or numerical coefficient in front of the variable. The coefficient of the variable tells how much of that variable we have. The second term is 4, and is called a **constant term**, or just a **constant** since the term contains no variable.

Example 1: For the algebraic expression, $3.4x - 8y + 4 - z$, list each term. Tell whether it is a variable term or a constant term. If it is a variable term, also list its numerical coefficient.

Solution:

1st term: $3.4x$; variable term; the numerical coefficient is 3.4

2nd term: $-8y$; variable term; the numerical coefficient is -8

3rd term: 4; constant term

4th term: $-z$; variable term; the numerical coefficient is -1

Now try problem 7 from exercise set 3.3

Example 2: For the algebraic expression, $-2xy + \dfrac{8y}{3} + z^2 - 7$, list each term. Tell whether it is a variable term or a constant term. If it is a variable term, also list its numerical coefficient.

Solution:

1st term: $-2xy$; variable term; the numerical coefficient is -2

2nd term: $\dfrac{8y}{3}$; variable term; the numerical coefficient is $\dfrac{8}{3}$

3rd term: z^2; variable term; the numerical coefficient is 1

4th term: -7; constant term

Now try problem 3 from exercise set 3.3

Combining like terms: Terms in an algebraic expression that contain the same variables with the same exponents are called **like terms**. These like terms can be added or subtracted depending on the signs of their numerical coefficients. For instance, $2x + 3x$ can be written as $5x$. Since both terms $2x$ and $3x$ contain the single variable x, we combine them by adding their numerical coefficients. This process can be done by using the distributive property in the reverse direction from what we've done before.

$$2x + 3x = (2 + 3)x = 5x$$

or in general, $ac + bc = (a + b)c$
where a, b and c are real numbers

The expression $4x - 7x$ can be simplified as follows: $4x - 7x = (4 - 7)x = -3x$.

By using the distributive property in the above manner, in combination with other proprieties, we can simplify variable expressions.

Example 3: Simplify: $\dfrac{4x}{5} + 3 + \dfrac{5x}{8} - 7$

Solution:

$\dfrac{4x}{5} + 3 + \dfrac{5x}{8} - 7$ Rewrite the subtraction part of the expression as addition of the opposite.

$= \dfrac{4x}{5} + 3 + \dfrac{5x}{8} + (-7)$ Use the commutative property of addition to put like terms together.

$= \dfrac{4x}{5} + \dfrac{5x}{8} + 3 + (-7)$ Use the distributive property to add like terms.

$= \left(\dfrac{4}{5} + \dfrac{5}{8}\right)x + 3 + (-7)$ Find a common denominator in order to add the fractions.

$= \left(\dfrac{32}{40} + \dfrac{25}{40}\right)x + 3 + (-7)$ Simplify further.

$= \dfrac{57}{40}x - 4$

Now try problem 27 from exercise set 3.3

Note: All constant terms are "like terms."

Note: $\dfrac{4x}{5}$ **is equivalent to** $\dfrac{4}{5}x$ **and** $\dfrac{5x}{8}$ **is equivalent to** $\dfrac{5}{8}x$.

Example 4: Simplify: $-3.7x + 6 - 2y + 5.2x$

Solution:	
$-3.7x + 6 - 2y + 5.2x$	Rewrite the subtraction part of the expression as addition of the opposite.
$= -3.7x + 6 + (-2y) + 5.2x$	Use the commutative property of addition to put like terms together.
$= -3.7x + 5.2x + 6 + (-2y)$	Use the distributive property to add like terms.
$= (-3.7 + 5.2)x + 6 + (-2y)$	Simplify further.
$= 1.5x + 6 - 2y$	It is common practice to put variable terms first (in alphabetical order) followed by constant terms. This is done by using the commutative property of addition.
$= 1.5x - 2y + 6$	

Now try problem 45 from exercise set 3.3

Example 5: Simplify: $3(x - 4) - 5(2x + 7)$

Solution:	
$3(x - 4) - 5(2x + 7)$	Use the distributive property to remove parentheses.
$= 3x - 12 - 10x - 35$	Rewrite the subtraction part of the expression as addition of the opposite.
$= 3x + (-12) + (-10x) + (-35)$	Use the commutative property of addition to put like terms together.
$= 3x + (-10x) + (-12) + (-35)$	Use the distributive property to add like terms.
$= [3 + (-10)]x + (-12) + (-35)$	Simplify further.
$= -7x - 47$	

Now try problem 55 from exercise set 3.3

The following are examples where descriptions of each step are not listed.

Example 6: Simplify: $\dfrac{4}{3}x - 6y + 8 - \dfrac{7}{2}x$ Example 7: Simplify: $3.6x + 4x^2 - 7.3x + 5$

Solution:

$$\dfrac{4}{3}x - 6y + 8 - \dfrac{7}{2}x$$

$$= \dfrac{4}{3}x - \dfrac{7}{2}x - 6y + 8$$

$$= \dfrac{8}{6}x - \dfrac{21}{6}x - 6y + 8$$

$$= -\dfrac{13}{6}x - 6y + 8$$

Solution:

$$3.6x + 4x^2 - 7.3x + 5$$

$$= 3.6x - 7.3x + 4x^2 + 5$$

$$= -3.7x + 4x^2 + 5$$

It is common practice to put terms with the same variable in order of descending powers of the variable from left to right. This is called **standard form**. With this in mind, the final simplification is made.

$$= 4x^2 - 3.7x + 5$$

Now try problem 47 from exercise set 3.3

Example 8: Simplify: $4xy^2 + 8x^2y - 2y^2 + 6xy^2 - 8$

Solution:

$$4xy^2 + 8x^2y - 2y^2 + 6xy^2 - 8$$

$$= 4xy^2 + 6xy^2 + 8x^2y - 2y^2 - 8$$

$$= 10xy^2 + 8x^2y - 2y^2 - 8$$

When arranging terms containing more than one variable, there is no set rule concerning the order. However, in future math courses you will encounter situations where it will be advantageous to put the terms in order of descending powers for "one" of the variables. For instance, if we use "x" as the variable of choice,

$$10xy^2 + 8x^2y - 2y^2 - 8 \text{ becomes}$$

$$= \quad 8x^2y \quad + \quad 10xy^2 \quad - \quad 2y^2 \quad - \quad 8.$$

$$\uparrow \qquad\qquad \uparrow \qquad\qquad \uparrow \qquad\qquad \uparrow$$

$$x^2 \text{ term} \qquad x \text{ term} \qquad \text{no } x \text{ term} \qquad \text{constant term}$$

Now try problem 75 from exercise set 3.3

Example 9: Simplify:

$-(2x+3y)-4(5y-6)+7(x-3)$

Solution:

$-(2x+3y)-4(5y-6)+7(x-3)$

$=-2x-3y-20y+24+7x-21$

$=-2x+7x-3y-20y+24-21$

$=5x-23y+3$

Now try problem 73 from exercise set 3.3

Example 10: Simplify:

$8x^2+2[x-3(x+4)+5(x^2-3)+x]$

Solution:

$8x^2+2[x-3(x+4)+5(x^2-3)+x]$

$=8x^2+2[x-3x-12+5x^2-15+x]$

$=8x^2+2[5x^2+x-3x+x-12-15]$

$=8x^2+2[5x^2-x-27]$

$=8x^2+10x^2-2x-54$

$=18x^2-2x-54$

It isn't necessary to put like terms next to each other in order to combine them. The following examples combine like terms without grouping them together first.

Example 11: Simplify:

$7x-4y+6z+8x-3y-8z$

Solution:

$7x-4y+6z+8x-3y-8z$

$=15x-7y-2z$

Example 13: Simplify:

$6+[3(x-4)-2(x^2+x)]+x^2$

Solution:

$6+[3(x-4)-2(x^2+x)]+x^2$

$=6+[3x-12-2x^2-2x]+x^2$

$=6+[-2x^2+x-12]+x^2$

$=6-2x^2+x-12+x^2$

$=-x^2+x-6$

Example 12: Simplify:

$-4(3x-7)-(4x+6)$

Solution:

$-4(3x-7)-(4x+6)$

$=-12x+28-4x-6$

$=-16x+22$

Example 14: Simplify:

$4.3-2(7.3x-5.6)+3x$

Solution:

$4.3-2(7.3x-5.6)+3x$

$=4.3-14.6x+11.2+3x$

$=-11.6x+15.5$

Section 3 exercises. For the algebraic expressions below, list each term. Tell whether it is a variable term or a constant term. If it is a variable term, also list its numerical coefficient.

1. $x - y + 6$

2. $-a + b - 4$

3. $3x^2 - \dfrac{2}{3}y + 8z$

4. $4x^2 - \dfrac{3}{4}y + 6z$

5. $a - 3$

6. $b + 6$

7. $-0.1a + 5.7b - 25$

8. $2.6w - 4.9x + 187$

9. $8ab^2 + 40 - 6b^2c$

10. $7w^2x - 12 + 9xy^2$

11. $4 - x$

12. $9 - y$

Simplify each algebraic expression.

13. $4x + 9x$

14. $2p + 8p$

15. $8x - 3x$

16. $-5b + 5b$

17. $7y - 12y$

18. $9w - 4w$

19. $-6a + 6a$

20. $4m - 7m$

21. $x - 4x$

22. $y - 3y$

23. $\dfrac{1}{3}x + \dfrac{2}{3}x$

24. $\dfrac{1}{4}y + \dfrac{3}{4}y$

25. $\dfrac{2}{3}a - \dfrac{5}{3}a$

26. $\dfrac{3}{5}b - \dfrac{8}{5}b$

27. $\dfrac{4x}{5} + \dfrac{3x}{4}$

28. $\dfrac{5w}{6} + \dfrac{3w}{5}$

29. $\dfrac{3y}{7} - \dfrac{2y}{9}$

30. $\dfrac{6p}{7} - \dfrac{7p}{9}$

Simplify each algebraic expression.

31. $4.2x - 2.9x$

32. $6.8y - 3.9y$

33. $-1.7a + 0.8a$

34. $-3.6b + 0.9b$

35. $7w + 3m - 2w$

36. $3m - 8y + 6m$

37. $-8 + 8x - 5$

38. $-6 + 6y - 3$

39. $4a - 6b + 8a + 12b$

40. $5x - 3w + 7x + 11w$

41. $6m - 3 + 4x - 7m$

42. $5n + 4 - 3y - 8n$

43. $17x - 8 + 4x - 7$

44. $9y - 3 + 8y - 9$

45. $6.3x + 8.3y - 6.1y - 12.3x$

46. $4.2m - 7.3a + 8.7a - 5.2m$

47. $4x^2 - 3x + 8x^2 - 7x$

48. $12y + 8y^2 - 3y^2 - 19y$

49. $7mn - 8 + 9mn + 3$

50. $12xy - 4 - 8xy + 7$

51. $\dfrac{2}{3}x - \dfrac{4}{5}y + \dfrac{3}{5}x + \dfrac{4}{3}y$

52. $\dfrac{1}{6}a - \dfrac{3}{4}b + \dfrac{1}{4}a + \dfrac{5}{6}b$

53. $3x^2 + 7 - 3x^2 - 7$

54. $8 + 5y^2 - 8 - 5y^2$

55. $3(x + 8) - 4(2x - 6)$

56. $5(y + 3) - 7(4y - 2)$

57. $6m - (3m + 2) - 7$

58. $8w - (4 - 3w) + 8$

59. $7 - 3(x + 7) + (2x - 9)$

60. $9 - 6(x - 8) + (7x + 2)$

Simplify each algebraic expression.

61. $(3m - 2n + p) + (6n - 4p - 3m)$

62. $(3x + 5y - 7z) + (5z - 2x - 5y)$

63. $(6x - 3y + 4z) - (4z + 6x - 3y)$

64. $(7m + 3n - 2p) - (3n - 2p + 7m)$

65. $(4a^2 + 2a - 7) + (3a^2 - 4a + 5)$

66. $(6b^2 - 5b + 6) + (7b^2 + 8b - 4)$

67. $2(3x^2 - x + 8) - 4(x + 5 - x^2)$

68. $6(4y - 3y^2 - 9) - 3(y^2 - y + 4)$

69. $7(1.6x + 2.4y) - 9(6.3y - 2.1x)$

70. $5(2.8m + 4.2n) - 7(9.2n - 3.5m)$

71. $\dfrac{2}{3}(7x - 3y) + \dfrac{3}{5}(10x - 6y)$

72. $\dfrac{2}{7}(5x - 14w) + \dfrac{4}{5}(15x - 7w)$

73. $(2x + 3y) - (4z - 6x) + (8y - 7z)$

74. $(a - 4b) - (2c - 8a) + (12b - 6c)$

Simplify. Put the final answers in order of descending powers, in terms of the variable "x."

75. $-7xy^2 + 5x^2y + 3y^2 + 6x^2y + 10$

76. $12xz - 8x^2z - 5 - 9z^2 + 4xz$

77. $12y(3 - x) + x^2y$

78. $5z(5 + 2x) + x^2z$

79. $y[5(x - 2) + x(x + 4)]$

80. $z[3(x - 7) + x(x + 1)]$

AN INTRODUCTION TO ALGEBRA

Section 4: Solving First-Degree Equations

An equation contains two mathematical expressions set equal to each other. Consequently, an equation contains an = sign. In this section we will explore techniques for solving first-degree equations. That is, variables involved in each equation will be 1st degree such as x or y as opposed to x^2 or y^3. Also, the equations in this chapter will be limited to just one variable. In a different chapter we will consider equations with two different variables. In solving an equation we are trying to determine what number can replace the variable and make the statement true. That is, make the left side of the equation equal to the right side of the equation. In order to solve an equation, the variable must be isolated, or by itself. Sometimes solving an equation requires removing a constant term from the same side of the equation that contains the variable. To do this, we use what is called **The Addition Property of Equality**.

THE ADDITION PROPERTY OF EQUALITY:

When a, b, and c are real numbers, the following is true:

$$\text{If} \quad a = b \quad \text{then} \quad a + c = b + c .$$

If the same quantity is added to both sides of an equation, the new equation is equivalent to the old equation. That is, both equations have the same solution.

<u>Example 1:</u> Solve: $x - 4 = 12$

Solution:	
$x - 4 = 12$	To remove the constant term, -4, from the left side of the equation, use the addition property of equality. Do this by adding the opposite of -4, which is 4, to both sides of the equation.
$x - 4 + 4 = 12 + 4$	Use the additive inverse property to simplify the left side of the equation.
$x + 0 = 12 + 4$	Use the identity property of addition to simplify further.
$x = 16$	To verify the solution, substitute it back into the original equation in place of the variable.
$x - 4 = 12$	becomes
$16 - 4 \overset{?}{=} 12$	which further simplifies to
$12 \overset{\checkmark}{=} 12 .$	The statement is true, therefore the solution is correct.

Now try problem 3 from exercise set 3.4

Example 2: Solve: $y + 8 = 15$

Solution:

$y + 8 = 15$	To remove the constant term, 8, from the left side of the equation, use the addition property of equality. Do this by adding the opposite of 8, which is -8, to both sides of the equation.
$y + 8 + (-8) = 15 + (-8)$	Use the additive inverse property to simplify the left side of the equation.
$y + 0 = 15 + (-8)$	Use the identity property of addition to simplify further.
$y = 7$	To verify the solution, substitute it back into the original equation in place of the variable.
$y + 8 = 15$	becomes
$7 + 8 \overset{?}{=} 15$	which further simplifies to
$15 \overset{\checkmark}{=} 15$.	The statement is true, therefore the solution is correct.

Now try problem 1 from exercise set 3.4

Because subtraction can be defined as addition of the opposite, we can use the addition property of equality to justify the following.

When a, b, and c are real numbers, the following is true:

$$\text{If} \quad a = b \quad \text{then} \quad a - c = b - c.$$

In other words, if the same quantity is subtracted from both sides of an equation, the new equation is equivalent to the old equation. That is, both equations have the same solution.

Example 3: Solve: $10 = x + 4$

Solution:

$10 = x + 4$	To remove the constant term, 4, from the right side of the equation, subtract it from both sides of the equation.
$10 - 4 = x + 4 - 4$	Use the additive inverse property.
$10 - 4 = x + 0$	Simplify further.
$6 = x$	It is preferred to write the final answer with the variable on the left side of the equation. Rewrite it as
$x = 6$.	To verify the solution, substitute it back into the original equation in place of the variable.
$10 = x + 4$	becomes
$10 \overset{?}{=} 6 + 4$	which further simplifies to
$10 \overset{\checkmark}{=} 10$.	The statement is true, therefore the solution is correct.

Now try problem 5 from exercise set 3.4

<u>Example 4:</u> Solve: $x + \dfrac{2}{5} = \dfrac{4}{7}$

Solution:	
$x + \dfrac{2}{5} = \dfrac{4}{7}$	To remove the constant term, $\dfrac{2}{5}$, from the left side of the equation, subtract it from both sides of the equation.
$x + \dfrac{2}{5} - \dfrac{2}{5} = \dfrac{4}{7} - \dfrac{2}{5}$	Use the additive inverse property.
$x + 0 = \dfrac{4}{7} - \dfrac{2}{5}$	Simplify further and get a common denominator in order to subtract the fractions.
$x = \dfrac{20}{35} - \dfrac{14}{35}$	Subtract the fractions.
$x = \dfrac{6}{35}$	To verify the solution, substitute it back into the original equation in place of the variable.
$x + \dfrac{2}{5} = \dfrac{4}{7}$	becomes
$\dfrac{6}{35} + \dfrac{2}{5} \stackrel{?}{=} \dfrac{4}{7}$	which further simplifies to
$\dfrac{6}{35} + \dfrac{14}{35} \stackrel{?}{=} \dfrac{4}{7}$.	Then,
$\dfrac{20}{35} \stackrel{?}{=} \dfrac{4}{7}$	which reduces to
$\dfrac{4}{7} \stackrel{\checkmark}{=} \dfrac{4}{7}$.	The statement is true, therefore the solution is correct.

Now try problem 39 from exercise set 3.4

<u>Example 5:</u> Solve: $m - 1.25 = -6.31$

Solution:	
$m - 1.25 = -6.31$	To isolate m, add 1.25 to both sides of the equation.
$m - 1.25 + 1.25 = -6.31 + 1.25$	Simplify.
$m = -5.06$	To verify the solution, substitute it back into the original equation in place of the variable.
$m - 1.25 = -6.31$	becomes
$-5.06 - 1.25 \stackrel{?}{=} -6.31$	which further simplifies to
$-6.31 \stackrel{\checkmark}{=} -6.31$.	The statement is true, therefore the solution is correct.

Now try problem 29 from exercise set 3.4

Example 6: Solve: $7 + x - 9 = 3$

Solution:	
$7 + x - 9 = 3$	Combine like terms to simplify the left side of the equation.
$x - 2 = 3$	To isolate x, add 2 to both sides of the equation.
$x - 2 + 2 = 3 + 2$	Simplify.
$x = 5$	To verify the solution, substitute it back into the original equation in place of the variable.
$7 + x - 9 = 3$	becomes
$7 + 5 - 9 \overset{?}{=} 3$	which further simplifies to
$3 \overset{\checkmark}{=} 3$.	The statement is true, therefore the solution is correct.

Now try problem 27 from exercise set 3.4

Example 7: Solve: $4x + 7 - 3x = 15$

Solution:	
$4x + 7 - 3x = 15$	Combine like terms to simplify the left side of the equation.
$x + 7 = 15$	To isolate x, subtract 7 from both sides of the equation.
$x + 7 - 7 = 15 - 7$	Simplify.
$x = 8$	To verify the solution, substitute it back into the original equation in place of the variable.
$4x + 7 - 3x = 15$	becomes
$4(8) + 7 - 3(8) \overset{?}{=} 15$	which further simplifies to
$32 + 7 - 24 \overset{?}{=} 15$.	Then,
$15 \overset{\checkmark}{=} 15$.	The statement is true, therefore the solution is correct.

Now try problem 25 from exercise set 3.4

Sometimes solving an equation requires removing a coefficient in order to isolate the variable. To do this we use what is called **The Multiplication Property of Equality**.

THE MULTIPLICATION PROPERTY OF EQUALITY:

When a, b, and c are real numbers with $c \neq 0$, the following is true:

$$\text{If} \quad a = b \quad \text{then} \quad a \cdot c = b \cdot c.$$

If the same non-zero quantity is multiplied by both sides of an equation, the new equation is equivalent to the old equation. That is, both equations have the same solution.

<u>Example 8:</u> Solve: $3x = 12$

Solution:	
$3x = 12$	To remove the coefficient of x, which is 3, from the left side of the equation, use the multiplication property of equality. Do this by multiplying both sides of the equation by the reciprocal of 3, which is $\frac{1}{3}$.
$\frac{1}{3} \cdot 3x = \frac{1}{3} \cdot 12$	Use the multiplicative inverse property to simplify the left side of the equation.
$1 \cdot x = \frac{1}{3} \cdot 12$	Use the identity property of multiplication to simplify further.
$x = 4$	To verify the solution, substitute it back into the original equation in place of the variable.
$3x = 12$	becomes
$3(4) \overset{?}{=} 12$	which further simplifies to
$12 \overset{\checkmark}{=} 12$.	The statement is true, therefore the solution is correct.

Now try problem 41 from exercise set 3.4

<u>Example 9:</u> Solve: $\frac{2}{5}x = 16$

Solution:	
$\frac{2}{5}x = 16$	To remove the coefficient of x, which is $\frac{2}{5}$, from the left side of the equation, use the multiplication property of equality. Do this by multiplying both sides of the equation by the reciprocal of $\frac{2}{5}$, which is $\frac{5}{2}$.
$\frac{5}{2} \cdot \frac{2}{5}x = \frac{5}{2} \cdot 16$	Use the multiplicative inverse property to simplify the left side of the equation.
$1 \cdot x = \frac{5}{2} \cdot 16$	Use the identity property of multiplication to simplify further.
$x = 40$	To verify the solution, substitute it back into the original equation in place of the variable.
$\frac{2}{5}x = 16$	becomes
$\frac{2}{5} \cdot 40 \overset{?}{=} 16$	which further simplifies to
$16 \overset{\checkmark}{=} 16$.	The statement is true, therefore the solution is correct.

Now try problem 67 from exercise set 3.4

Because division can be rewritten in terms of multiplication (dividing by a number is equivalent to multiplying by its reciprocal) we can use the multiplication property of equality to justify the following.

When a, b, and c are real numbers with $c \neq 0$, the following is true:

$$\text{If} \quad a = b \quad \text{then} \quad \frac{a}{c} = \frac{b}{c}.$$

In other words, if both sides of an equation are divided by the same non-zero number, the new equation is equivalent to the old equation. That is, both equations have the same solution.

Example 10: Solve: $4.2x = -7.14$

Solution:	
$4.2x = -7.14$	To remove the coefficient of x, which is 4.2, from the left side of the equation, divide both sides of the equation by the 4.2, which is the coefficient of the variable.
$\dfrac{4.2x}{4.2} = \dfrac{-7.14}{4.2}$	Reduce.
$x = -1.7$	To verify the solution, substitute it back into the original equation in place of the variable.
$4.2x = -7.14$	becomes
$4.2(-1.7) \overset{?}{=} -7.14$	which further simplifies to
$-7.14 \overset{\checkmark}{=} -7.14.$	The statement is true, therefore the solution is correct.

Now try problem 65 from exercise set 3.4

Note: As a general rule, if the coefficient of the variable is an integer or a decimal number, then divide both sides of the equation by that number. If the coefficient of the variable is a fraction, then multiply both sides of the equation by that number's reciprocal.

Example 11: Solve: $\dfrac{4}{7}x = \dfrac{5}{14}$

Solution:

$\dfrac{4}{7}x = \dfrac{5}{14}$	To remove the coefficient of x, which is $\dfrac{4}{7}$, from the left side of the equation, multiply both sides of the equation by $\dfrac{7}{4}$, which is the reciprocal of the coefficient of the variable.
$\dfrac{7}{4} \cdot \dfrac{4}{7}x = \dfrac{7}{4} \cdot \dfrac{5}{14}$	Reduce.
$x = \dfrac{5}{8}$	To verify the solution, substitute it back into the original equation in place of the variable.
$\dfrac{4}{7}x = \dfrac{5}{14}$	becomes
$\dfrac{4}{7} \cdot \dfrac{5}{8} \overset{?}{=} \dfrac{5}{14}$	which further simplifies to
$\dfrac{5}{14} \overset{\checkmark}{=} \dfrac{5}{14}$.	The statement is true, therefore the solution is correct.

*Now try problem 75 from exercise set 3.4

Example 12: Solve: $3x - 12x = 18$

Solution:

$3x - 12x = 18$	Combine like terms to simplify the left side of the equation.
$-9x = 18$	To remove the coefficient of x, which is -9, from the left side of the equation, divide both sides of the equation by the -9, which is the coefficient of the variable.
$\dfrac{-9x}{-9} = \dfrac{18}{-9}$	Reduce.
$x = -2$	To verify the solution, substitute it back into the original equation in place of the variable.
$3x - 12x = 18$	becomes
$3(-2) - 12(-2) \overset{?}{=} 18$	which further simplifies to
$-6 + 24 \overset{?}{=} 18$.	Then
$18 \overset{\checkmark}{=} 18$.	The statement is true, therefore the solution is correct.

*Now try problem 83 from exercise set 3.4

Section 4 exercises. Solve by using the addition property of equality.

1. $x+5=12$

2. $x+9=14$

3. $y-3=10$

4. $m-7=16$

5. $7=x+4.6$

6. $18=y+11.3$

7. $6=a-3$

8. $9=w-4$

9. $z-5=-9$

10. $x-3=-7$

11. $4.2+y=-6$

12. $8.7+a=-9$

13. $-4+w=8$

14. $-6+c=7$

15. $12+n=7.5$

16. $14+k=3.4$

17. $x+9=-6$

18. $y+4=-8$

19. $-10=w+4$

20. $-1=x+5$

21. $-6=y-6$

22. $-9=z-9$

23. $-4=5+a$

24. $-6=9+m$

25. $3a+8-2a=-6$

26. $6x+3-5x=-12$

27. $5+y-9=4$

28. $7+n-12=8$

29. $8.7=-12.6+x$

30. $6.4=-9.3+w$

31. $-7m+10+8m=6$

32. $-9y-4+10y=-6$

33. $x-\dfrac{3}{4}=\dfrac{3}{4}$

34. $y - \dfrac{2}{3} = \dfrac{2}{3}$

35. $w + \dfrac{7}{8} = \dfrac{3}{8}$

36. $z + \dfrac{5}{6} = \dfrac{1}{6}$

37. $\dfrac{1}{2} + x = \dfrac{2}{9}$

38. $\dfrac{2}{3} + y = \dfrac{3}{7}$

39. $a + \dfrac{2}{3} = -\dfrac{4}{5}$

40. $m + \dfrac{4}{7} = -\dfrac{8}{9}$

Solve by using the multiplication property of equality.

41. $3x = 15$

42. $4x = 20$

43. $9y = -27$

44. $12z = -48$

45. $-6a = 25$

46. $-3b = 28$

47. $-4m = -56$

48. $-8n = -56$

49. $-x = 7$

50. $-y = 9$

51. $4a = 0$

52. $5c = 0$

53. $42 = 9m$

54. $70 = 8n$

55. $42 = -0.6w$

56. $32 = -0.4x$

57. $-15 = 54y$

58. $-15 = 48z$

59. $-a = -6$

60. $-c = -10$

61. $-1.4 = -42m$

62. $-1.6 = -48n$

63. $-8x = 0$

64. $-9y = 0$

65. $4.8w = 1.2$

66. $8.4m = 2.1$

67. $\dfrac{3}{4}x = 9$

68. $\dfrac{4}{5}y = 12$

69. $\dfrac{6}{7}z = -20$

70. $\dfrac{8}{9}w = -14$

71. $-\dfrac{3}{5}x = 10$

72. $-\dfrac{3}{7}y = 14$

73. $\dfrac{-a}{6} = -5$

74. $\dfrac{-m}{3} = -8$

75. $\dfrac{5}{9}x = \dfrac{10}{3}$

76. $\dfrac{4}{7}y = \dfrac{2}{21}$

77. $\dfrac{-7}{12} = \dfrac{-21}{2}p$

78. $\dfrac{-8}{3} = \dfrac{-4}{9}n$

79. $7.5 = \dfrac{3}{7}x$

80. $4.8 = \dfrac{3}{11}x$

81. $0 = \dfrac{2}{9}a$

82. $0 = \dfrac{1}{7}h$

83. $12x - 15x = -11 + 2$

84. $8m - 9m = -10 + 8$

85. $6y - y = 3 - 8$

86. $7w - 3w = 8 - 12$

87. $\dfrac{1}{2}x + \dfrac{1}{3}x = \dfrac{1}{4}$

88. $\dfrac{1}{3}y + \dfrac{1}{4}y = \dfrac{1}{5}$

89. $4.2y - 5.7y = 6$

90. $3.8n - 5.2n = 7$

AN INTRODUCTION
TO ALGEBRA

Section 5: Solving Complex First-Degree Equations

In this section we will solve equations that require the use of both the addition property of equality and the multiplication property of equality.

<u>Example 1</u>: Solve: $2x - 5 = 13$

Solution:	
$2x - 5 = 13$	To remove the constant term -5, from the left side of the equation, use the addition property of equality. Do this by adding the opposite of -5, which is 5, to both sides of the equation.
$2x - 5 + 5 = 13 + 5$	Use the additive inverse property to simplify the left side of the equation.
$2x + 0 = 13 + 5$	Use the identity property of addition to simplify further.
$2x = 18$	To remove the coefficient of x, which is 2, from the left side of the equation, use the multiplication property of equality. Do this by multiplying both sides of the equation by the reciprocal of 2, which is $\dfrac{1}{2}$.
$\dfrac{1}{2} \cdot 2x = \dfrac{1}{2} \cdot 18$	Use the multiplicative inverse property to simplify the left side of the equation.
$1 \cdot x = \dfrac{1}{2} \cdot 18$	Use the identity property of multiplication to simplify further.
$\mathbf{x = 9}$	To verify the solution, substitute it back into the original equation in place of the variable.
$2x - 5 = 13$	becomes
$2(9) - 5 \overset{?}{=} 13$.	Follow order of operations.
$18 - 5 \overset{?}{=} 13$	Simplify further.
$13 \overset{\checkmark}{=} 13$	The statement is true, therefore the solution is correct.

Now try problem 1 from exercise set 3.5

<u>Example 2</u>: Solve: $16 = 7 - \dfrac{3}{4}y$

Solution:

$16 = 7 - \dfrac{3}{4}y$ | To remove the constant term 7, from the right side of the equation, use the addition property of equality. Do this by subtracting 7 from both sides of the equation.

$16 - 7 = 7 - 7 - \dfrac{3}{4}y$ | Simplify both sides of the equation.

$9 = -\dfrac{3}{4}y$ | To remove the coefficient of y, which is $-\dfrac{3}{4}$, from the right side of the equation, use the multiplication property of equality. Do this by multiplying both sides of the equation by the reciprocal of $-\dfrac{3}{4}$, which is $-\dfrac{4}{3}$.

$-\dfrac{4}{3} \cdot 9 = -\dfrac{4}{3}\left(-\dfrac{3}{4}y\right)$ | Simplify by reducing both sides of the equation.

$-12 = y$ | Rewrite the equation with the variable on the left side.

$\mathbf{y = -12}$ | To verify the solution, substitute it back into the original equation in place of the variable.

$16 = 7 - \dfrac{3}{4}y$ | becomes

$16 \stackrel{?}{=} 7 - \dfrac{3}{4}(-12).$ | Follow order of operations.

$16 \stackrel{?}{=} 7 + 9$ | Simplify further.

$16 \stackrel{\checkmark}{=} 16$ | The statement is true, therefore the solution is correct.

Now try problem 59 from exercise set 3.5

<u>Example 3</u>: Solve: $5x + 3 - 2x + 8 = 7 - 2$

Solution: $5x + 3 - 2x + 8 = 7 - 2$	Combine like terms on both sides of the equation.
$3x + 11 = 5$	Subtract 11 from both sides of the equation.
$3x + 11 - 11 = 5 - 11$	Simplify both sides of the equation.
$3x = -6$	Divide both sides of the equation by 3.
$\dfrac{3x}{3} = \dfrac{-6}{3}$	Simplify by reducing both sides of the equation.
$\mathbf{x = -2}$	To verify the solution, substitute it back into the original equation in place of the variable.
$5x + 3 - 2x + 8 = 7 - 2$	becomes
$5(-2) + 3 - 2(-2) + 8 \overset{?}{=} 7 - 2.$	Follow order of operations.
$-10 + 3 + 4 + 8 \overset{?}{=} 7 - 2$	Simplify further.
$5 \overset{\checkmark}{=} 5$	The statement is true, therefore the solution is correct.

Now try problem 43 from exercise set 3.5

<u>Example 4</u>: The cost of renting a car for one day can be determined by using the formula $C = 0.25m + 30$, where m is the number of miles driven and C is the total cost of the car rental in dollars. How far was the car driven in one day if the total cost of the car rental was \$112?

Solution: $C = 0.25m + 30$	Replace C in the formula with \$112, since it represents the total cost of renting the car.
$112 = 0.25m + 30$	Now, solve the formula for the variable m in order to determine the number of miles driven.
	Subtract 30 from both sides of the equation.
$112 - 30 = 0.25m + 30 - 30$	Simplify both sides of the equation.
$82 = 0.25m$	Divide both sides of the equation by 0.25.
$\dfrac{82}{0.25} = \dfrac{0.25m}{0.25}$	Simplify by reducing both sides of the equation.
$328 = m$ or $m = 328$	**The car was driven 328 miles.**
	To verify the solution, substitute it back into the original equation in place of the variable.
$112 = 0.25m + 30$	becomes
$112 \overset{?}{=} 0.25(328) + 30.$	Follow order of operations.
$112 \overset{?}{=} 82 + 30$	Simplify further.
$112 \overset{\checkmark}{=} 112$	The statement is true, therefore the solution is correct.

Now try problem 69 from exercise set 3.5

Section 5 exercises. Solve.

1. $4x + 3 = 11$

2. $5y + 9 = 24$

3. $9 = 4 + 5a$

4. $37 = 2 + 7c$

5. $-8x - 5 = 35$

6. $-12y - 7 = 29$

7. $8 - 6z = -34$

8. $7 - 4a = -21$

9. $-8x + 24 = 0$

10. $-9y + 45 = 0$

11. $6h - 7 = 2$

12. $10k - 3 = 12$

13. $6 = 3 + 2m$

14. $12 = 8 + 6n$

15. $6 - 3y = 6$

16. $8 - 5z = 8$

17. $6n - \dfrac{2}{7} = \dfrac{40}{7}$

18. $8m - \dfrac{3}{5} = \dfrac{37}{5}$

19. $\dfrac{2}{3}w - 8 = 4$

20. $\dfrac{4}{5}z - 7 = 13$

21. $8 = 4 - \dfrac{y}{7}$

22. $9 = 6 - \dfrac{x}{4}$

23. $\dfrac{4}{9}x + \dfrac{1}{5} = \dfrac{4}{5}$

24. $\dfrac{5}{8}y + \dfrac{5}{6} = \dfrac{13}{6}$

25. $18.28 = 4.5 - 2.6w$

26. $19.74 = 4.8 - 8.3z$

27. $\dfrac{k}{2} - \dfrac{1}{3} = \dfrac{1}{4}$

28. $\dfrac{p}{5} - \dfrac{3}{4} = \dfrac{2}{3}$

29. $8w - 5 = 27$

30. $3z - 8 = 13$

31. $8x - 7 + 6x = -5$

32. $4y + 3 - 2y = -1$

33. $-6h + 5 = 53$

34. $-2k + 9 = 31$

35. $4 - w = 9$

36. $6 - x = 0$

37. $6 - 18 = 3w - 5 - 9w$

38. $3 - 9 = 4z + 8 - 10z$

39. $-17 = 4 - 3h$

40. $-19 = 7 - 13k$

41. $4w + 9 = 12$

42. $5z + 4 = 10$

43. $7a - 4 + 3a - 6 = 3 + 27$

44. $6b - 7 - 2b + 18 = 7 + 38$

45. $-3x - 10 = -6$

46. $-8y - 7 = -4$

47. $-7 = 8 + 10x$

48. $-13 = 9 + 3k$

49. $-3m + 8 + 7m = -5$

50. $-n + 6 - 5n = -18$

51. $7x - \dfrac{8}{9} = \dfrac{13}{9}$

52. $5y - \dfrac{1}{4} = \dfrac{29}{4}$

53. $\dfrac{3}{7}a + 9 = 6$

54. $\dfrac{5}{6}k + 4 = -6$

55. $-5k = 16 - 4.5$

56. $-4a = 7 - 17.4$

57. $\dfrac{2}{3}m + \dfrac{1}{2} = -\dfrac{1}{5}$

58. $\dfrac{1}{3}n + \dfrac{1}{5} = -\dfrac{1}{2}$

59. $6 - \dfrac{2}{9}m = -8$

60. $7 - \dfrac{3}{5}n = -14$

61. $4.8x - 2.3 = 7.78$

62. $3.5y - 5.9 = 16.5$

63. $-9 - 7m = 4$

64. $3.2x - 7.2 + 9.4x = 18$

65. $4.8k - 9.2 + 6.3k = 13$

66. $-2 - 8n = 13$

The cost of a long distance phone call using Company A's calling plan can be found by using the formula $C = 0.35m + 2.50$, where m is the length of the call in minutes and C is the total cost of the call in dollars.

67.   How long was a long distance phone call made using Company A's calling plan if the total cost was $8.80?

68.   How long was a long distance phone call made using Company A's calling plan if the total cost was $12.65?

The cost of renting a car from Company B for one day can be found by using the formula $C = 0.43m + 28$, where m is the number of miles driven and C is the total cost of the car rental in dollars.

69.   How far was the car driven in one day if the total cost of the car rental was $141.52?

70.   How far was the car driven in one day if the total cost of the car rental was $108.41?

The monthly cost of natural gas from a local gas company can be found by using the formula $C = 1.28T + 4$, where T is the number of therms (a unit used to measure heat) used and C is the total monthly cost in dollars.

71.   How much natural gas was used in a month if the total cost was $165.28?

72.   How much natural gas was used in a month if the total cost was $119.20?

The monthly cost of electricity from a local power company can be found by using the formula $C = 0.035k + 4.75$, where k is the number of kilowatt-hours of electricity used and C is the total monthly cost in dollars.

73.   How much electricity was used in a month if the total cost was $19.10?

74.   How much electricity was used in a month if the total cost was $18.61?

The perimeter of a rectangle can be found by using the formula $P = 2L + 2W$, where P is the perimeter, L is the length, and W is the width of the rectangle.

75.   Find the length of a rectangle with a perimeter of 38 inches and a width of 8 inches.

76.   Find the width of a rectangle with a perimeter of 46 inches and a length of 14 inches.

AN INTRODUCTION
TO ALGEBRA

Section 6: Solving General First-Degree Equations

In this section we will solve equations that contain variable terms on both sides of the equation. As we did with constant terms in the previous section, we will use the addition property of equality to eliminate variable terms from one side of the equation. We will also solve equations that involve the use of the distributive property. Finally, we will look at techniques to eliminate fractions and decimals from equations in order to make the solving process easier.

Example 1: Solve: $5x = 3x + 4$

Solution:

$5x = 3x + 4$	Decide which side of the equation to isolate the variable on. Since it is preferred to give the final answer in the form: variable = constant, isolate the variable on the left side of the equation.
$5x = 3x + 4$	To remove the variable term $3x$, from the right side of the equation, use the addition property of equality. Do this by subtracting $3x$ from both sides of the equation.
$5x - 3x = 3x - 3x + 4$	Combine like terms on both sides of the equation.
$2x = 4$	Divide both sides of the equation by 2.
$\dfrac{2x}{2} = \dfrac{4}{2}$	This reduces to
$\boldsymbol{x = 2}$.	To verify the solution, substitute it back into the original equation in place of the variable.
$5x = 3x + 4$	becomes
$5(2) \overset{?}{=} 3(2) + 4.$	Follow order of operations.
$10 \overset{?}{=} 6 + 4$	Simplify further.
$10 \overset{\checkmark}{=} 10$	The statement is true, therefore the solution is correct.

Now try problem 21 from exercise set 3.6

<u>Example 2:</u> Solve: $6x - 7 = 3 - 2x$

Solution:

$6x - 7 = 3 - 2x$	Decide which side of the equation to isolate the variable on. Since it is preferred to give the final answer in the form: variable = constant, isolate the variable on the left side of the equation.
$6x - 7 = 3 - 2x$	To remove the variable term $-2x$, from the right side of the equation, use the addition property of equality. Do this by adding $2x$ to both sides of the equation.
$6x + 2x - 7 = 3 - 2x + 2x$	Combine like terms on both sides of the equation.
$8x - 7 = 3$	To remove the constant term -7, from the left side of the equation, use the addition property of equality. Do this by adding 7 to both sides of the equation.
$8x - 7 + 7 = 3 + 7$	Combine like terms on both sides of the equation.
$8x = 10$	Divide both sides of the equation by 8.
$\dfrac{8x}{8} = \dfrac{10}{8}$	This reduces to
$\mathbf{x = \dfrac{5}{4}}$.	To verify the solution, substitute it back into the original equation in place of the variable.
$6x - 7 = 3 - 2x$	becomes
$6\left(\dfrac{5}{4}\right) - 7 \overset{?}{=} 3 - 2\left(\dfrac{5}{4}\right)$.	Follow order of operations.
$\dfrac{15}{2} - 7 \overset{?}{=} 3 - \dfrac{5}{2}$	Find a common denominator in order to combine fractions.
$\dfrac{15}{2} - \dfrac{14}{2} \overset{?}{=} \dfrac{6}{2} - \dfrac{5}{2}$	Simplify further.
$\dfrac{1}{2} \overset{\checkmark}{=} \dfrac{1}{2}$	The statement is true, therefore the solution is correct.

Now try problem 17 from exercise set 3.6

<u>Example 3:</u> Solve: $4y + 6 - 7y = 2y - 8 + 3y$

Solution:

$4y + 6 - 7y = 2y - 8 + 3y$	Simplify both sides of the equation by combining like terms.
$-3y + 6 = 5y - 8$	Since it is preferred to give the final answer in the form: variable = constant, isolate the variable on the left side of the equation.
	To remove the variable term $5y$, from the right side of the equation, use the addition property of equality. Do this by subtracting $5y$ from both sides of the equation.
$-3y - 5y + 6 = 5y - 5y - 8$	Combine like terms on both sides of the equation.
$-8y + 6 = -8$	To remove the constant term 6, from the left side of the equation, use the addition property of equality. Do this by subtracting 6 from both sides of the equation.
$-8y + 6 - 6 = -8 - 6$	Combine like terms on both sides of the equation.
$-8y = -14$	Divide both sides of the equation by -8.
$\dfrac{-8y}{-8} = \dfrac{-14}{-8}$	This reduces to
$y = \dfrac{7}{4}$.	To verify the solution, substitute it back into the original equation in place of the variable.
$4y + 6 - 7y = 2y - 8 + 3y$	becomes
$4\left(\dfrac{7}{4}\right) + 6 - 7\left(\dfrac{7}{4}\right) \overset{?}{=} 2\left(\dfrac{7}{4}\right) - 8 + 3\left(\dfrac{7}{4}\right)$.	Follow order of operations.
$\dfrac{28}{4} + 6 - \dfrac{49}{4} \overset{?}{=} \dfrac{14}{4} - 8 + \dfrac{21}{4}$	Find a common denominator in order to combine fractions.
$\dfrac{28}{4} + \dfrac{24}{4} - \dfrac{49}{4} \overset{?}{=} \dfrac{14}{4} - \dfrac{32}{4} + \dfrac{21}{4}$	Simplify further.
$\dfrac{3}{4} \overset{\checkmark}{=} \dfrac{3}{4}$	The statement is true, therefore the solution is correct.

*Now try problem 35 from exercise set 3.6

Using the distributive property to solve equations:

Example 4: Solve: $4 - 3(2x - 3) = 5(6 - x) + 1$

Solution:

$4 - 3(2x - 3) = 5(6 - x) + 1$	We must simplify both sides of the equation. First, apply the distributive property.
$4 - 6x + 9 = 30 - 5x + 1$	Then, combine like terms on each side of the equation.
$-6x + 13 = -5x + 31$	Since it is preferred to give the final answer in the form: variable = constant, isolate the variable on the left side of the equation.
	To remove the variable term $-5x$, from the right side of the equation, use the addition property of equality. Do this by adding $5x$ to both sides of the equation.
$-6x + 5x + 13 = -5x + 5x + 31$	
	Combine like terms on both sides of the equation.
$-x + 13 = 31$	To remove the constant term 13, from the left side of the equation, use the addition property of equality. Do this by subtracting 13 from both sides of the equation.
$-x + 13 - 13 = 31 - 13$	Combine like terms on both sides of the equation.
$-x = 18$	Divide both sides of the equation by -1.
$\dfrac{-x}{-1} = \dfrac{18}{-1}$	This reduces to
$\mathbf{x = -18}.$	To verify the solution, substitute it back into the original equation in place of the variable.
$4 - 3(2x - 3) = 5(6 - x) + 1$	Becomes
$4 - 3[2(-18) - 3] \stackrel{?}{=} 5[6 - (-18)] + 1.$	Follow order of operations.
$4 - 3[-36 - 3] \stackrel{?}{=} 5[6 + 18] + 1$	Simplify further.
$4 - 3[-39] \stackrel{?}{=} 5[24] + 1$	This becomes
$4 + 117 \stackrel{?}{=} 120 + 1.$	And finally,
$121 \stackrel{\checkmark}{=} 121.$	The statement is true, therefore the solution is correct.

*Now try problem 57 from exercise set 3.6

Using the least common denominator to eliminate fractions in an equation:

Example 5: Solve: $\dfrac{1}{2}x + \dfrac{2}{3} = \dfrac{3}{4}$

Solution: $\dfrac{1}{2}x + \dfrac{2}{3} = \dfrac{3}{4}$	To eliminate the fractions, multiply both sides of the equation by the least common denominator of all the fractions contained within the equation. Since the least common denominator is 12, multiply both sides of the equation by 12.
$12\left(\dfrac{1}{2}x + \dfrac{2}{3}\right) = 12\left(\dfrac{3}{4}\right)$	Use the distributive property.
$12\left(\dfrac{1}{2}x\right) + 12\left(\dfrac{2}{3}\right) = 12\left(\dfrac{3}{4}\right)$	Reduce both sides of the equation.
$6x + 8 = 9$	**Notice that all the fractions have been reduced out of the equation.** Subtract 8 from both sides of the equation.
$6x + 8 - 8 = 9 - 8$	Combine like terms on both sides of the equation.
$6x = 1$	Divide both sides of the equation by 6.
$\dfrac{6x}{6} = \dfrac{1}{6}$	This reduces to
$x = \dfrac{1}{6}$.	**Note: Even though we previously eliminated fractions from the equation, a fraction can still appear as the final answer.**
	To verify the solution, substitute it back into the original equation in place of the variable.
$\dfrac{1}{2}x + \dfrac{2}{3} = \dfrac{3}{4}$	becomes
$\dfrac{1}{2}\left(\dfrac{1}{6}\right) + \dfrac{2}{3} \overset{?}{=} \dfrac{3}{4}$.	Follow order of operations.
$\dfrac{1}{12} + \dfrac{2}{3} \overset{?}{=} \dfrac{3}{4}$	Find a common denominator in order to combine the fractions.
$\dfrac{1}{12} + \dfrac{8}{12} \overset{?}{=} \dfrac{3}{4}$	Simplify further.
$\dfrac{9}{12} \overset{?}{=} \dfrac{3}{4}$	Reduce the left side of the equation.
$\dfrac{3}{4} \overset{\checkmark}{=} \dfrac{3}{4}$	The statement is true, therefore the solution is correct.

Now try problem 73 from exercise set 3.6

Example 6: Solve: $\dfrac{1}{2} = \dfrac{1}{x} + \dfrac{1}{3}$

Solution:

$\dfrac{1}{2} = \dfrac{1}{x} + \dfrac{1}{3}$ | To eliminate the fractions, multiply both sides of the equation by the least common denominator of all the fractions contained within the equation. Since the least common denominator is $6x$, multiply both sides of the equation by $6x$.

$6x\left(\dfrac{1}{2}\right) = 6x\left(\dfrac{1}{x} + \dfrac{1}{3}\right)$ | Use the distributive property.

$6x\left(\dfrac{1}{2}\right) = 6x\left(\dfrac{1}{x}\right) + 6x\left(\dfrac{1}{3}\right)$ | Reduce both sides of the equation.

$3x = 6 + 2x$ | **Notice that all the fractions have been reduced out of the equation.**

Subtract $2x$ from both sides of the equation.

$3x - 2x = 6 + 2x - 2x$ | Combine like terms on both sides of the equation.

$\boldsymbol{x = 6}$ | To verify the solution, substitute it back into the original equation in place of the variable.

$\dfrac{1}{2} = \dfrac{1}{x} + \dfrac{1}{3}$ | becomes

$\dfrac{1}{2} \overset{?}{=} \dfrac{1}{6} + \dfrac{1}{3}.$ | Find a common denominator in order to combine the fractions.

$\dfrac{1}{2} \overset{?}{=} \dfrac{1}{6} + \dfrac{2}{6}$ | becomes

$\dfrac{1}{2} \overset{?}{=} \dfrac{3}{6}.$ | Reduce the right side of the equation.

$\dfrac{1}{2} \overset{\checkmark}{=} \dfrac{1}{2}$ | The statement is true, therefore the solution is correct.

Now try problem 75 from exercise set 3.6

Using a power of 10 to eliminate decimals in an equation:

Example 7: Solve: $4.7x + 1.5 = 1.2x - 2.7$

Solution:

$4.7x + 1.5 = 1.2x - 2.7$	To eliminate the decimals, multiply both sides of the equation by a power of 10. In this case the decimal point needs to move 1 place to the right. So, multiply by 10.
$10(4.7x + 1.5) = 10(1.2x - 2.7)$	Use the distributive property.
$10(4.7x) + 10(1.5) = 10(1.2x) - 10(2.7)$	
	Multiply.
$47x + 15 = 12x - 27$	**Notice that all the decimals have been eliminated from the equation.**
	Subtract $12x$ from both sides of the equation.
$47x - 12x + 15 = 12x - 12x - 27$	Combine like terms on both sides of the equation.
$35x + 15 = -27$	Subtract 15 from both sides of the equation.
$35x + 15 - 15 = -27 - 15$	Combine like terms on both sides of the equation.
$35x = -42$	Divide both sides of the equation by 35.
$\dfrac{35x}{35} = \dfrac{-42}{35}$	This reduces to
$x = -\dfrac{6}{5}.$	Even though $-\dfrac{6}{5}$ is a correct answer, since the original equation contains decimal numbers, it would be most appropriate to give the final answer as a decimal number. Therefore, divide -6 by 5 to get -1.2. The final answer is
$x = -1.2.$	

Note: Even though we previously eliminated decimals from the equation, a decimal can still appear as the final answer.

	To verify the solution, substitute it back into the original equation in place of the variable.
$4.7x + 1.5 = 1.2x - 2.7$	becomes
$4.7(-1.2) + 1.5 \overset{?}{=} 1.2(-1.2) - 2.7.$	Follow order of operations.
$-5.64 + 1.5 \overset{?}{=} -1.44 - 2.7$	Simplify further.
$-4.14 \overset{\checkmark}{=} -4.14$	The statement is true, therefore the solution is correct.

Now try problem 83 from exercise set 3.6

<u>Example 8:</u> Solve: $3.8y + 2.06 = 2.48y + 8$

$3.8y + 2.06 = 2.48y + 8$	To eliminate the decimals, multiply both sides of the equation by a power of 10. In this case the decimal point needs to move 2 places to the right. So, multiply by 100.
$100(3.8y + 2.06) = 100(2.48y + 8)$	Use the distributive property.
$100(3.8y) + 100(2.06) = 100(2.48y) + 100(8)$	
	Multiply.
$380y + 206 = 248y + 800$	**Notice that all the decimals have been eliminated from the equation.**
	Subtract $248y$ from both sides of the equation.
$380y - 248y + 206 = 248y - 248y + 800$	
	Combine like terms on both sides of the equation.
$132y + 206 = 800$	Subtract 206 from both sides of the equation.
$132y + 206 - 206 = 800 - 206$	Combine like terms on both sides of the equation.
$132y = 594$	Divide both sides of the equation by 132.
$\dfrac{132y}{132} = \dfrac{594}{132}$	This reduces to
$y = \dfrac{9}{2}$.	Even though $\dfrac{9}{2}$ is a correct answer, since the original equation contains decimal numbers, it would be most appropriate to give the final answer as a decimal number. Therefore, divide 9 by 2 to get 4.5. The final answer is
$\mathbf{y = 4.5}$.	To verify the solution, substitute it back into the original equation in place of the variable.
$3.8y + 2.06 = 2.48y + 8$	becomes
$3.8(4.5) + 2.06 \overset{?}{=} 2.48(4.5) + 8.$	Follow order of operations.
$17.1 + 2.06 \overset{?}{=} 11.16 + 8$	Simplify further.
$19.16 \overset{\checkmark}{=} 19.16$	The statement is true, therefore the solution is correct.

Now try problem 85 from exercise set 3.6

As shown in previous examples, there can be quite a few steps involved in solving a first-degree equation. Here is a list of all the steps that can be used to solve such an equation. You won't always have to use all the steps listed, but it is important that you do the necessary steps in the order that they appear.

Step 1: **To eliminate any fractions, multiply both sides of the equation by the least common denominator. To eliminate any decimals, multiply both sides of the equation by the necessary power of 10.**

Step 2: **Use the distributive property to remove any parentheses.**

Step 3: **Combine like terms on each side of the equation.**

Step 4: **Use the addition property of equality to get all variable terms on one side of the equation and all constant terms on the other side of the equation. Then, combine like terms.**

Step 5: **Use the multiplication property of equality to get the variable by itself on one side of the equation.**

Step 6: **Verify the solution by substituting it back into the original equation in place of the variable.**

Example 9: Solve: $3(2x-4)=18$

Solution: $3(2x-4)=18$

Step 1: Since there are no fractions or decimals to eliminate, step 1 can be skipped.

Step 2: Use the distributive property to remove any parentheses. $6x-12=18$

Step 3: Since there are no like terms to be combined at this time, step 3 can be skipped.

Step 4: To remove the constant term -12, from the left side of the equation, use the addition property of equality. Do this by adding 12 to both sides of the equation.

$6x-12+12=18+12$ Then, combine like terms. $6x=30$

Step 5: Use the multiplication property of equality to get the variable by itself on one side of the equation. Do this by dividing both sides of the equation by 6.

$\dfrac{6x}{6}=\dfrac{30}{6}$ This reduces to $x=5$.

Step 6: Verify the solution by substituting it back into the original equation in place of the variable.

$3(2x-4)=18$ becomes $3[2(5)-4]=18$.   Follow order of operations.

$3[10-4]\overset{?}{=}18$ Simplify further. $3[6]=18$ Continue to simplify further.

$18\overset{\checkmark}{=}18$ The statement is true, therefore the solution is correct.

Now try problem 37 from exercise set 3.6

Example 10: Solve: $\dfrac{3}{4} = \dfrac{1}{x} - \dfrac{3}{2}$

Solution: $\dfrac{3}{4} = \dfrac{1}{x} - \dfrac{3}{2}$

Step 1: To eliminate any fractions, multiply both sides of the equation by the least common denominator, $4x$.

$$4x\left(\dfrac{3}{4}\right) = 4x\left(\dfrac{1}{x} - \dfrac{3}{2}\right)$$

Step 2: Use the distributive property to remove any parentheses.

$$4x\left(\dfrac{3}{4}\right) = 4x\left(\dfrac{1}{x}\right) - 4x\left(\dfrac{3}{2}\right) \qquad \text{Reduce both sides of the equation.} \qquad 3x = 4 - 6x$$

Step 3: Since there are no like terms to be combined at this time, step 3 can be skipped.

Step 4: Use the addition property of equality to get all variable terms on one side of the equation and all constant terms on the other side of the equation. Do this by adding $6x$ to both sides of the equation.

$$3x + 6x = 4 - 6x + 6x \qquad \text{Then, combine like terms.} \qquad 9x = 4$$

Step 5: Use the multiplication property of equality to get the variable by itself on one side of the equation. Do this by dividing both sides of the equation by 9.

$$\dfrac{9x}{9} = \dfrac{4}{9} \qquad \text{This reduces to} \qquad x = \dfrac{4}{9}.$$

Step 6: Verify the solution by substituting it back into the original equation in place of the variable.

$\dfrac{3}{4} = \dfrac{1}{x} - \dfrac{3}{2}$ becomes

$\dfrac{3}{4} \overset{?}{=} \dfrac{1}{\frac{4}{9}} - \dfrac{3}{2}.$ Since $\dfrac{1}{\frac{4}{9}} = 1 \div \dfrac{4}{9} = 1 \cdot \dfrac{9}{4} = \dfrac{9}{4}$, the equation can be rewritten as

$\dfrac{3}{4} \overset{?}{=} \dfrac{9}{4} - \dfrac{3}{2}.$ Find a common denominator in order to combine the fractions.

$\dfrac{3}{4} \overset{?}{=} \dfrac{9}{4} - \dfrac{6}{4}$ becomes

$\dfrac{3}{4} \overset{\checkmark}{=} \dfrac{3}{4}.$ The statement is true, therefore the solution is correct.

Now try problem 79 from exercise set 3.6

<u>Section 6 exercises.</u> Determine and explain the mistakes in the solution process of the following equations. Then, solve each equation using the correct process. Be sure to check your solutions.

1. $2x+6=10$

$$\frac{2x}{2}+6=\frac{10}{2}$$

$x+6=5$

$x+6-6=5-6$

$x=-1$

2. $3(x+2)-4=9$

$3x+6-12=9$

$3x-6=9$

$3x-6+6=9+6$

$3x=15$

$$\frac{3x}{3}=\frac{15}{3}$$

$x=5$

3. $3x=10$

$3x-3=10-3$

$x=7$

4. $x+4=10$

$x+4+4=10+4$

$x=14$

Solve the following equations.

5. $3x+2=x+10$

6. $4y+6=y+33$

7. $6m-8=2m-20$

8. $7n-3=2n-28$

9. $12w-5=8w+7$

10. $9z-4=6z+17$

11. $5a+6=12+a$

12. $10c+9=19+6c$

13. $4x-7=3-6x$

14. $10y-4=7-y$

15. $8m+3=4m-11$

16. $n+17=5n-1$

17. $4w+9=12-2w$

18. $15z+7=15-z$

19. $4-6a=10a$

20. $9-8c=10c$

21. $3x=5+6x$

22. $y=7+4y$

23. $4-3m=6m-5$

24. $13-4n=10n-1$

25. $-3w=7-4w$

26. $-5z=8-3z$

27. $6-3x=6+3x$

28. $9-5y=9+4y$

29. $4m + 3 - 5m = 7m + 8$

30. $6n - 8 + 9n = 3n - 4$

31. $-3w + 5 - 4w = 7w - 9$

32. $-4z + 12 - 3z = 9z - 4$

33. $3x - 2 + 4x = 7 + 5x - 9$

34. $7y + 8 - 2y = 11 - 3y + 5$

35. $-5m + 8 - 6m = 7m - 12 - 3m$

36. $-8n - 1 - 3n = 5n + 7 - 6n$

37. $2(3w - 4) = 7$

38. $4(5h - 3) = 13$

39. $6(7k + 3) = -12k$

40. $8(4x + 9) = -4x$

41. $-5(2y - 7) = 15$

42. $-3(8z - 9) = 3$

43. $7 - (3m + 2) = 2m$

44. $6 - (7n + 8) = 3n$

45. $3(2a + 1) - 5 = 16$

46. $4(5c + 8) + 19 = 11$

47. $-6(2x + 3) + 4x = 0$

48. $-7(3y + 5) + 6y = 0$

49. $7w + 8(w + 1) = 38$

50. $3z + 5(z + 8) = 16$

51. $6 + 2(2m - 3) = 10$

52. $12 + 4(5n - 3) = 6$

53. $4h - 5(h - 6) = 7$

54. $2k - 3(k - 5) = 6$

55. $4(3x - 7) = 5x + 35$

56. $7(2y - 3) = 6y + 11$

57. $3 - 2(3w - 4) = 7(w - 4)$

58. $5 - 5(2z - 7) = 4(z + 3)$

59. $6 - (7 - a) + 3 = 10a - 5$

60. $9 - (3 - c) + 8 = 12c - 2$

61. $-3h + 5 = 12 - 4(6h - 2)$

62. $-5k + 9 = 3 - 2(8k - 7)$

63. $7x - 3(2x + 7) = x - (3x + 7) - 4$

64. $6y - 5(3y + 4) = 2y - (8y + 9) - 3$

65. $(2x + 3) - (4x - 5) = (6x + 4) + (8x - 7)$

66. $(2y + 5) + (8y - 3) = (7y - 2) - (y - 9)$

67. $5k - 3 = 12 - (7 - k)$

68. $6h - 7 = 9 - (4 - 2h)$

Solve the following equations by first eliminating the fractions.

69. $\dfrac{1}{4}m - 3 = \dfrac{3}{4}$

70. $\dfrac{1}{6}n - 5 = \dfrac{5}{6}$

71. $\dfrac{2}{5}x - \dfrac{7}{2} = \dfrac{3}{5}$

72. $\dfrac{5}{7}w - \dfrac{2}{3} = \dfrac{2}{7}$

73. $\dfrac{1}{3}x + \dfrac{1}{4} = \dfrac{1}{6}$

74. $\dfrac{1}{5}z + \dfrac{1}{4} = \dfrac{1}{2}$

75. $7 - \dfrac{1}{x} = \dfrac{1}{3}$

76. $\dfrac{1}{y} + \dfrac{2}{5} = 6$

77. $\dfrac{1}{y} + \dfrac{5}{2} = \dfrac{3}{y}$

78. $\dfrac{1}{x} + \dfrac{7}{3} = \dfrac{2}{x}$

79. $\dfrac{2}{a} + \dfrac{1}{2} = \dfrac{1}{3}$

80. $\dfrac{2}{3} + \dfrac{2}{c} = \dfrac{2}{5}$

Solve the following equations by first eliminating the decimals.

81. $8.6x - 2.9 = 1.4$

82. $12.5x - 7.4 = 2.6$

83. $6.2y + 4 = 22.6$

84. $4.9y - 6 = 8.7$

85. $9.22m - 1.2 = 3.8m + 9.64$

86. $7.27n + 6.2 = 5.2n + 12.41$

87. $4.6x - 2.3 + 8x = 30.5 - 0.2x + 12$

88. $9.1w - 4.4 + 6w = 41.2 - 0.5w + 9$

89. $4.7x - 10.81 = 0$

90. $3.9y + 24.96 = 0$

AN INTRODUCTION
TO ALGEBRA

Section 7: Translating Between Mathematical
Terminology and Algebraic Expressions

In this section we will look at translating between mathematical terminology and algebraic expressions. First, we will consider algebraic expressions involving just one operation, starting with **addition**.

Example 1: List several different ways of writing the expression $x + 4$, using mathematical terminology.

Some possible solutions are:	
x plus four	*the sum of* x and four
x increased by four	four *more than* x
four *added to* x	the *total* of x and four

Next, we will consider algebraic expressions involving **subtraction**.

Example 2: List several different ways of writing the expression $y - 6$, using mathematical terminology.

Some possible solutions are:	
y minus six	*the difference of* y and six
y decreased by six	six *less than* y
six *subtracted from* y	y *less* six
the difference between y and six	

Now try problem 1 from exercise set 3.7

Now, we will consider algebraic expressions involving **multiplication**.

Example 3: List several different ways of writing the expression $2x$, using mathematical terminology.

Some possible solutions are:	
two *times* x	*the product of* two and x
two *multiplied by* x	*twice* x

Finally, we will consider algebraic expressions involving **division**.

Example 4: List several different ways of writing the expression $\dfrac{x}{5}$, using mathematical terminology.

Some possible solutions are:
x divided by five   **the *quotient of*** *x* and five
five *divided into* *x*

Now, we will consider algebraic expressions involving more than one operation.

Example 5: List several different ways of writing the expression $4x + 9$, using mathematical terminology.

Some possible solutions are:
four *times x plus* nine   nine *more than the product of* four and *x*
nine *added to* four *x*   **the sum of** four *x* and nine
four *x* *increased by* nine

Now try problem 5 from exercise set 3.7

Example 6: List several different ways of writing the expression $\dfrac{y}{3} - 2$, using mathematical terminology.

Some possible solutions are:
y divided by three, ***decreased by*** two
two ***less than the quotient of*** *y* and three

Now try problem 11 from exercise set 3.7

Example 7: List several different ways of writing the expression $4(x + 9)$, using mathematical terminology.

Some possible solutions are:
four ***times the sum of*** *x* and nine
four ***times the quantity*** *x **plus*** nine

Now try problem 7 from exercise set 3.7

Example 8: List several different ways of writing the expression $\dfrac{x+9}{4}$, using mathematical terminology.

> Some possible solutions are:
>
> > four *divided into the sum of* x and nine
> >
> > *the quantity of* x *plus* nine, *divided by* four

Now try problem 17 from exercise set 3.7

Application problems often require translating mathematical terminology into algebraic expressions. Consider the following examples. In each case we will use the letter x to represent the variable.

Example 9: Translate "seven less than twice a number" into an algebraic expression.

> Solution: "seven less than twice a number"
>
> Sort through the given phrase looking for key words that indicate mathematical operations.
>
> | seven | less than | twice | a number |
> |-------|-----------|-------|----------|
> | 7 | subtract from | multiply by two | the unknown "x" |
>
> Use these key words to write an algebraic expression.
>
> Twice a number becomes: $2x$
>
> Seven less than twice a number becomes: $\mathbf{2x-7}$

Now try problem 23 from exercise set 3.7

Example 10: Translate "the difference of seven and twice a number" into an algebraic expression.

> Solution: "the difference of seven and twice a number"
>
> Sort through the given phrase looking for key words that indicate mathematical operations.
>
> | the difference of | seven and | twice | a number |
> |-------------------|-----------|-------|----------|
> | subtract from | 7 | multiply by two | the unknown "x" |
>
> Use these key words to write an algebraic expression.
>
> Twice a number becomes: $2x$
>
> The difference of seven and twice a number becomes: $\mathbf{7-2x}$

Now try problem 21 from exercise set 3.7

<u>Example 11</u>: Translate "three times the sum of a number and five" into an algebraic expression.

Solution: "three times the sum of a number and five"

Sort through the given phrase looking for key words that indicate mathematical operations.

three times	the sum of	a number	and five
multiply by three	add together	the unknown "x"	5

Use these key words to write an algebraic expression.

The sum of a number and five becomes: $x + 5$

Three times the sum of a number and five becomes: $3(x + 5)$

Now try problem 45 from exercise set 3.7

<u>Example 12</u>: Translate "the sum of three times a number and five" into an algebraic expression.

Solution: "the sum of three times a number and five"

Sort through the given phrase looking for key words that indicate mathematical operations.

the sum of	three times	a number	and five
add together	multiply by three	the unknown "x"	5

Use these key words to write an algebraic expression.

Three times a number becomes: $3x$

The sum of three times a number and five becomes: $3x + 5$

Now try problem 39 from exercise set 3.7

Note: In example 11, the three is being multiplied by the entire sum of a number and five. Whereas, in example 12, the three is being multiplied by just a number and then the resulting product is added to five.

Example 13: Translate "four times a number divided by the sum of the number and six" into an algebraic expression.

Solution: "four times a number divided by the sum of the number and six"

Sort through the given phrase looking for key words that indicate mathematical operations.

four times	a number	divided by	the sum of	the number	and six
multiply by four	the unknown "x"	division	add together	the unknown "x"	6

Use these key words to write an algebraic expression.

Four times a number becomes: $4x$

The sum of a number and six becomes: $x+6$

Four times a number divided by the sum of the number and six becomes: $\dfrac{4x}{x+6}$

Example 14: Translate "two less than the product of six and the sum of a number and ten" into an algebraic expression. Then simplify the expression.

Solution: "two less than the product of six and the sum of a number and ten"

Sort through the given phrase looking for key words that indicate mathematical operations.

two less than	the product of	six and	the sum of	a number	and ten
subtract two	multiply together	6	add together	the unknown "x"	10

Use these key words to write an algebraic expression.

The sum of a number and ten becomes: $x+10$

The product of six and the sum of a number and ten becomes: $6(x+10)$

Two less than the product of six and the sum of a number and ten becomes: $6(x+10)-2$

Now, simplify the expression. $6(x+10)-2 = 6x+60-2 = \mathbf{6x+58}$

Now try problem 59 from exercise set 3.7

Sometimes a problem has more than one unknown quantity. Quite often it is possible to express several unknowns in terms of just one variable.

Example 15: The sum of two numbers is fifteen. If x is used to represent the smaller number, then how could the larger number be represented in terms of x?

Solution: The sum of two numbers is fifteen. This leads to the following equation:

The smaller number + the larger number = 15.   Since the smaller number is x we can rewrite the equation as

x + the larger number = 15.   By subtracting x from both sides of the equation we get

$x - x +$ the larger number $= 15 - x$.   This simplifies to

the larger number $= \mathbf{15 - x}$.

Now try problem 69 from exercise set 3.7

Example 16: The sum of two numbers is twenty-eight. If x is used to represent the smaller number, translate "four more than twice the larger number" into an algebraic expression written in terms of x. Then simplify the expression.

Solution: The sum of two numbers is twenty-eight. This leads to the following equation:

The smaller number + the larger number = 28.   Since the smaller number is x we can rewrite the equation as

x + the larger number = 28.   By subtracting x from both sides of the equation we get

$x - x +$ the larger number $= 28 - x$.   This simplifies to

the larger number $= 28 - x$.

Now we know the larger number is $28 - x$.

Twice the larger number becomes $2(28 - x)$.

Four more than twice the larger number becomes: $2(28 - x) + 4$

Now, simplify the expression. $2(28 - x) + 4 = 56 - 2x + 4 = \mathbf{-2x + 60}$

Now try problem 85 from exercise set 3.7

<u>Example 17:</u> Jim is five years older than Maria. If a is used to represent Maria's age in years, then how could Jim's age be represented in terms of a?

> Solution:
>
> **Maria's age:** a
>
>   **Jim's age:** $a + 5$

Now try problem 81 from exercise set 3.7

<u>Example 18:</u> The white horse is three inches shorter than the black horse. If h is used to represent the height of the black horse in inches, then how could the white horse's height be represented in terms of h?

> Solution:
>
> **Height of the black horse:** h
>
> **Height of the white horse:** $h - 3$

Now try problem 71 from exercise set 3.7

<u>Example 19:</u> The length of a rectangle is six less than four times its width. If w is used to represent the width of the rectangle, then how could the length of the rectangle be represented in terms of W?

> Solution:
>
> **Width of the rectangle:** W
>
> **Length of the rectangle:** $4W - 6$

Now try problem 73 from exercise set 3.7

<u>Example 20:</u> The value of a quarter is twenty-five cents. If q is used to represent the number of quarters that a person has, then how could the total value of the quarters be represented in cents, in terms of q?

> Solution:
>
>   **Number of quarters:** q
>
> **Total value of quarters:** $25q$

Now try problem 77 from exercise set 3.7

Section 7 exercises. Translate each algebraic expression into words using mathematical terminology.

1. $x - 7$

2. $y - 5$

3. $4 + x$

4. $8 + w$

5. $2x - 4$

6. $5w - 3$

7. $2(x - 4)$

8. $5(w - 3)$

9. $7 - x$

10. $5 - y$

11. $\dfrac{w}{9} + 1$

12. $\dfrac{m}{3} + 2$

13. $4(2x - 5) + 3$

14. $7(4y - 2) + 8$

15. $4 - \dfrac{2x}{9}$

16. $8 - \dfrac{5n}{7}$

17. $\dfrac{m + 3}{6}$

18. $\dfrac{k + 6}{2}$

Translate each phrase into an algebraic expression. In each case use the letter x to represent the variable.

19.   a number increased by six

20.   the product of four and a number

21.   the difference of three and a number

22.   eight less than three times a number

23.   seven more than twice a number

24.   the difference of one and a number

25.   the product of nine and a number

26.   the quotient of a number and eight

27.   the quotient of a number and two

28.   a number increased by three

29.   a number decreased by fourteen

30.   negative seven less a number

31.   negative five less a number

32.   a number decreased by eighty

33.   eighty more than the product of six and a number

34.   fifty less than the quotient of nine and a number

35.   three less than the product of four and a number

36.   sixteen more than the quotient of a number and twelve

37.   the difference between six times a number and seventeen

38.   the sum of twelve times a number and six

39.   the sum of nine times a number and thirty

40.   the difference between ten and three times a number

Translate each phrase into an algebraic expression. In each case use the letter x to represent the variable. Then simplify the algebraic expression.

41.   four times the difference of a number and three

42.   the sum of a number and five, minus the sum of the same number and two

43.   the sum of a number divided by two and the same number divided by four

44.   the product of a number and ten added to the product of the same number and seventeen

45.   five multiplied by the sum of a number and six

46.   eleven more than the difference of a number and fifty

47.   twice the difference of eight times a number and three

48.   negative four multiplied by the sum of nine and a number

49.   the sum of a number and two, minus the sum of the same number and five

50.   six times the difference of a number and eight

51.   the product of a number and four added to the product of the same number and seven

52.   sixty minus the sum of a number and fifty

53.   a number decreased by the difference between negative five and the same number

54.   the sum of a number divided by three and the same number divided by six

55.   a number subtracted from the product of two and the same number

56.   a number decreased by the difference between negative three and the same number

57.   negative three multiplied by the sum of eight and a number

58.   a number subtracted from the product of five and the same number

59.   ten more than the product of four and the difference of seven and a number

60.   three multiplied by the sum of a number and twenty

61.   two more than the difference of a number and seventeen

62.   the sum of a number and four, added to the difference between the same number and nine

63.   three times the quotient of a number and three

64.   eight more than the product of three and the difference of two and a number

65.   sixteen minus the sum of a number and fourteen

66.   twice the difference of five times a number and seven

67.   the sum of a number and five, added to the difference between the same number and two

68.   four times the quotient of a number and negative four

More translation problems:

69.   The sum of two numbers is twenty-five. If n is used to represent the smaller number, then how could the larger number be represented in terms of n?

70.   The sum of two numbers is thirty-six. If n is used to represent the smaller number, then how could the larger number be represented in terms of n?

71.   John is three years younger than Frank. If a is used to represent Frank's age in years, then how could John's age be represented in terms of a?

72.   Julie is seven years younger than Fiona. If a is used to represent Fiona's age in years, then how could Julie's age be represented in terms of a?

73.   The length of a rectangle is five less than three times its width. If W is used to represent the width of the rectangle, then how could the length of the rectangle be represented in terms of W?

74.   The length of a rectangle is eight less than seven times its width. If W is used to represent the width of the rectangle, then how could the length of the rectangle be represented in terms of W?

75.   The sum of two numbers is forty-eight. If n is used to represent the larger number, then how could the smaller number be represented in terms of n?

76.   The sum of two numbers is sixty-four. If n is used to represent the larger number, then how could the smaller number be represented in terms of n?

77.   The value of a nickel is five cents. If n is used to represent the number of nickels that a person has, then what is the total value of the nickels in cents, in terms of n?

78.   The value of a dime is ten cents. If d is used to represent the number of dimes that a person has, then what is the total value of the dimes in cents, in terms of d?

79.   The length of a rectangle is five more than six times its width. If W is used to represent the width of the rectangle, then how could the length of the rectangle be represented in terms of W?

80.   The length of a rectangle is ten more than two times its width. If W is used to represent the width of the rectangle, then how could the length of the rectangle be represented in terms of W?

81.   Gwen is five years older than Arthur. If a is used to represent Arthur's age in years, then how could Gwen's age be represented in terms of a?

82.   Samson is eighteen years older than Delilah. If a is used to represent Delilah's age in years, then how could Samson's age be represented in terms of a?

83.   The width of a rectangle is seven less than one-half the length. If L is used to represent the length of the rectangle, then how could the width of the rectangle be represented in terms of L?

84.   The width of a rectangle is three less than one-third the length. If L is used to represent the length of the rectangle, then how could the width of the rectangle be represented in terms of L?

Translate and simplify:

85. The sum of two numbers is twenty-six. If n is used to represent the smaller number, translate "five less than three times the larger number" into an algebraic expression written in terms of n. Then simplify the expression.

86. The sum of two numbers is sixteen. If n is used to represent the smaller number, translate "eleven more than four times the larger number" into an algebraic expression written in terms of n. Then simplify the expression.

87. Joyce is seven years older than Tammy. If a is used to represent Tammy's age in years, translate "three years more than twice Joyce's age" into an algebraic expression written in terms of a. Then simplify the expression.

88. Brian is nine years older than Margaret. If a is used to represent Margaret's age in years, translate "six years less than five times Brian's age" into an algebraic expression written in terms of a. Then simplify the expression.

89. The length of a rectangle is twice as long as the width. If W is used to represent the width of the rectangle, translate "four less than three times the length" into an algebraic expression written in terms of W. Then simplify the expression.

90. The length of a rectangle is four times as long as the width. If W is used to represent the width of the rectangle, translate "seven less than twice the length" into an algebraic expression written in terms of W. Then simplify the expression.

91. Mike has three more nickels than he has dimes. If d is used to represent the number of dimes that he has, translate the "total value of the nickels" in cents into an algebraic expression written in terms of d. Then simplify the expression. Don't forget that a nickel is worth five cents!

92. Tim has six more quarters than he has dimes. If d is used to represent the number of dimes that he has, translate "the total value of the quarters" in cents into an algebraic expression written in terms of d. Then simplify the expression. Don't forget that a quarter is worth twenty-five cents!

AN INTRODUCTION TO ALGEBRA

Section 8: Application Problems

Many of the concepts taught in this chapter will be used in this section to help the process of solving applications, or story problems, as they are often called. A story or descriptive paragraph is translated into an equation. Solving the equation portion will then lead to answering the questions that are being asked in the descriptive paragraph. This process is broken down into six steps, which are as follows:

Six Steps for Solving Story Problems

Step 1: **What information is being requested?**

Step 2: **Assign a variable to the unknown quantity that is being asked for. If there is more than one unknown quantity, describe them all in terms of the same variable.**

Step 3: **Translate the story into an equation using the variable from step 2.**

Step 4: **Solve the equation.**

Step 5: **Answer the question(s) being asked (be sure to include any necessary units such as miles or feet).**

Step 6: **Check your work to verify that the information found is correct.**

<u>Example 1</u>: The sum of twice a number and six is thirty-four. Find the number.

Solution:

Step 1: What information is being requested?

We are to "find the number."

Step 2: Assign a variable to the unknown quantity that is being asked for.

Call "the number" x.

Step 3: Translate the story into an equation using the variable from step 2.

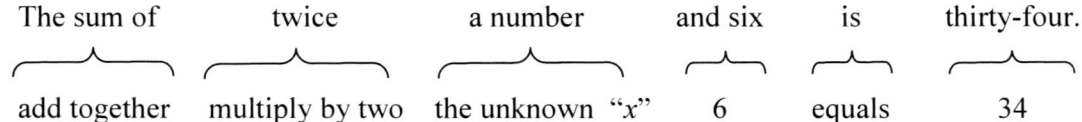

The sum of	twice	a number	and six	is	thirty-four.
add together	multiply by two	the unknown "x"	6	equals	34

Twice a number becomes: $2x$

The sum of twice a number and six becomes: $2x+6$

The sum of twice a number and six is thirty-four becomes: $2x+6=34$

Step 4: Solve the equation.

$2x+6=34$ 　　　Subtract 6 from both sides of the equation.

$2x+6-6=34-6$ 　　Simplify.

$2x=28$ 　　　Divide both sides of the equation by 2.

$\dfrac{2x}{2}=\dfrac{28}{2}$ 　　Reduce both sides of the equation.

$x=14$

Step 5: Answer the question being asked.

Since the unknown number is being represented by x, and since $x=14$, **the number is 14**.

Step 6: Check your work to verify that the information found is correct.

To verify the solution, substitute 14 in the place of x in the original equation.

$2x+6=34$ 　　　becomes

$2(14)+6\stackrel{?}{=}34$. 　　Follow order of operations.

$28+6\stackrel{?}{=}34$ 　　Simplify further.

$34\stackrel{\checkmark}{=}34$ 　　The statement is true, therefore the solution is correct.

Now try problem 7 from exercise set 3.8

Example 2: The sum of two numbers is twenty-six. Twice the larger number is equal to two more than three times the smaller number. Find the numbers.

Solution:

Step 1: What information is being requested?

We are to "find the numbers."

Step 2: Assign a variable to one of the unknown quantities that are being asked for. Describe the other unknown quantity in terms of the same variable.

Call "the larger number" x.

Call "the smaller number" $26 - x$.

Step 3: Translate the story into an equation using the variable from step 2.

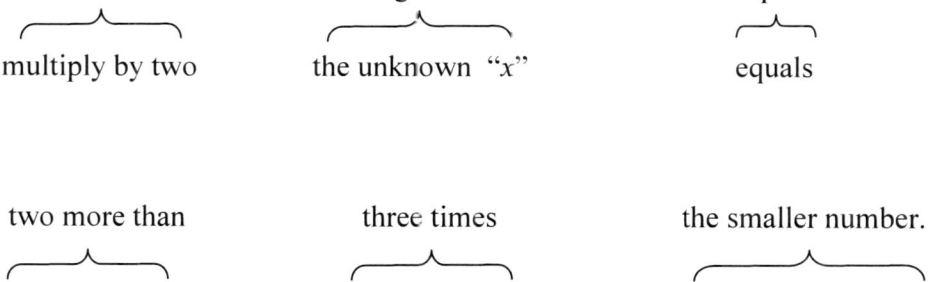

Twice	the larger number	is equal to
multiply by two	the unknown "x"	equals

two more than	three times	the smaller number.
add two	multiply by three	the unknown "$26-x$"

Twice the larger number becomes: $2x$

Three times the smaller number becomes: $3(26-x)$

Two more than three times the smaller number becomes: $3(26-x)+2$

Twice the larger number is equal to two more than three times the smaller number becomes:

$2x = 3(26-x)+2$ **Problem continued on next page.**

Problem continued from previous page.

Step 4: Solve the equation.

$2x = 3(26 - x) + 2$	Simplify the right side by using the distributive property.
$2x = 78 - 3x + 2$	Combine like terms on the right side.
$2x = 80 - 3x$	Add $3x$ to both sides of the equation.
$2x + 3x = 80 - 3x + 3x$	Combine like terms on both sides of the equation.
$5x = 80$	Divide both sides of the equation by 5.
$\dfrac{5x}{5} = \dfrac{80}{5}$	Reduce both sides of the equation.
$x = 16$	

Step 5: Answer the questions being asked.

Since the unknown larger number is being represented by x, and since $x = 16$,

the larger number is 16.

Since the smaller number is being represented by $26 - x$, and since $26 - x = 26 - 16 = 10$,

the smaller number is 10.

Step 6: Check your work to verify that the information found is correct.

To verify the solutions, substitute 16 in the place of x in the original equation.

$2x = 3(26 - x) + 2$	becomes
$2(16) \overset{?}{=} 3[26 - (16)] + 2$.	Follow order of operations.
$32 \overset{?}{=} 3[10] + 2$	Simplify further.
$32 \overset{?}{=} 30 + 2$	And finally,
$32 \overset{\checkmark}{=} 32$	The statement is true, therefore the solution is correct.

Now try problem 13 from exercise set 3.8

<u>Example 3</u>: The sum of two numbers is forty-two. The larger number is equal to twice the smaller number. Find the numbers.

Solution:

Step 1: **What information is being requested?**

We are to "find the numbers."

Step 2: **Assign a variable to one of the unknown quantities that are being asked for. Describe the other unknown quantity in terms of the same variable.**

Call "the larger number" x.

Call "the smaller number" $42 - x$.

Step 3: **Translate the story into an equation using the variable from step 2.**

The larger number	is equal to	twice	the smaller number
the unknown "x"	equals	multiply by two	the unknown "$42 - x$"

The larger number becomes: x

Twice the smaller number becomes: $2(42 - x)$

The larger number is equal to twice the smaller number becomes:

$x = 2(42 - x)$ **Problem continued on next page.**

Problem continued from previous page.

Step 4: Solve the equation.

$x = 2(42 - x)$ Simplify the right side by using the distributive property.

$x = 84 - 2x$ Add $2x$ to both sides of the equation.

$x + 2x = 84 - 2x + 2x$ Combine like terms on both sides of the equation.

$3x = 84$ Divide both sides of the equation by 3.

$\dfrac{3x}{3} = \dfrac{84}{3}$ Reduce both sides of the equation.

$x = 28$

Step 5: Answer the questions being asked.

Since the unknown larger number is being represented by x, and since $x = 28$,

the larger number is 28.

Since the smaller number is being represented by $42 - x$, and since $42 - x = 42 - 28 = 14$,

the smaller number is 14.

Step 6: Check your work to verify that the information found is correct.

To verify the solutions, substitute 28 in the place of x in the original equation.

$x = 2(42 - x)$ becomes

$(28) \stackrel{?}{=} 2[42 - (28)]$.   Follow order of operations.

$28 \stackrel{?}{=} 2[14]$ Simplify further.

$28 \stackrel{\checkmark}{=} 28$ The statement is true, therefore the solution is correct.

Now try problem 15 from exercise set 3.8

<u>Example 4:</u> Ben is twenty-nine years older than his daughter Jessica. In five years, the sum of their ages will be seventy-seven. How old are they now?

Solution:

Step 1: What information is being requested?

"How old are they now?"

Step 2: Assign a variable to one of the unknown quantities that are being asked for. Describe the other unknown quantity in terms of the same variable.

Call "Jessica" x.

Call "Ben" $x+29$.

Step 3: Translate the story into an equation using the variable from step 2.

To help us in writing the equation we will use the following table:

	Now	In five years
Ben	$x + 29$	$x + 34$
Jessica	x	$x + 5$

Because the sum of their ages five years from now is seventy-seven, the equation becomes:

Ben's age in five years	plus	Jessica's age in five years	equals	seventy-seven	or
$(x+34)$	$+$	$(x+5)$	$=$	77	or

$$(x+34)+(x+5)=77$$

<u>Problem continued on next page.</u>

Problem continued from previous page.

Step 4: **Solve the equation.**

$(x+34)+(x+5)=77$	Remove parentheses.
$x+34+x+5=77$	Combine like terms on the left side.
$2x+39=77$	Subtract 39 from both sides of the equation.
$2x+39-39=77-39$	Combine like terms on both sides of the equation.
$2x=38$	Divide both sides of the equation by 2.
$\dfrac{2x}{2}=\dfrac{38}{2}$	Reduce both sides of the equation.
$x=19$	

Step 5: **Answer the questions being asked.**

Since Jessica's present age is being represented by x, and since $x=19$,

Jessica is 19 years old.

Since Ben's present age is being represented by $x+29$, and since $x+29=19+29=48$,

Ben is 48 years old.

Step 6: **Check your work to verify that the information found is correct.**

To verify the solutions, substitute 19 in the place of x in the original equation.

$(x+34)+(x+5)=77$	becomes
$[(19)+34]+[(19)+5]\overset{?}{=}77$.	Follow order of operations.
$[53]+[24]\overset{?}{=}77$	Simplify further.
$77\overset{\checkmark}{=}77$	The statement is true, therefore the solutions are correct.

Now try problem 21 from exercise set 3.8

Example 5: The length of a rectangle is twice its width. The perimeter is 30 feet. Find the length and the width.

Solution:

Step 1: What information is being requested?

We are to "find the length and the width."

Step 2: Assign a variable to one of the unknown quantities that are being asked for. Describe the other unknown quantity in terms of the same variable.

Call "the width" x.

Call "the length" $2x$.

length = $2x$

width = x

Make a sketch of the problem if it will help you to visualize what is being described.

Step 3: Translate the story into an equation using the variable from step 2.

In this situation we will use the formula for finding the perimeter of a rectangle which is: $P = 2L + 2W$. The perimeter (P) is 30 feet, the width (W) is x, and the length (L) is $2x$. We make the following substitutions into the perimeter formula.

$$P \ = \ 2L \ + \ 2W \quad \text{becomes}$$

$$30 \ = \ 2(2x) + 2(x)$$

Problem continued on next page.

Problem continued from previous page.

Step 4: **Solve the equation.**

$30 = 2(2x) + 2(x)$ Multiply.

$30 = 4x + 2x$ Combine like terms on the right side.

$30 = 6x$ Divide both sides of the equation by 6.

$\dfrac{30}{6} = \dfrac{6x}{6}$ Reduce both sides of the equation.

$x = 5$

Step 5: **Answer the questions being asked.**

Since the width is being represented by x, and since $x = 5$,

The width is 5 feet.

Since the length is being represented by $2x$, and since $2x = 2(5) = 10$,

The length is 10 feet.

Step 6: **Check your work to verify that the information found is correct.**

To verify the solutions, substitute 5 in the place of x in the original equation.

$30 = 2(2x) + 2x$ becomes

$30 \overset{?}{=} 2[2(5)] + 2(5)$.   Follow order of operations.

$30 \overset{?}{=} 20 + 10$ Simplify further.

$30 \overset{\checkmark}{=} 30$ The statement is true, therefore the solutions are correct.

Now try problem 31 from exercise set 3.8

Example 6: Brian has $3.10 in dimes and nickels. If he has seven more dimes than nickels, how many of each coin does he have?

Solution:

Step 1: What information is being requested?

"How many of each coin does he have?"

Step 2: Assign a variable to one of the unknown quantities that are being asked for. Describe the other unknown quantity in terms of the same variable.

Call "the number of nickels" x.

Call "the number of dimes" $x + 7$.

Step 3: Translate the story into an equation using the variable from step 2.

To help us in writing the equation we will use the following table:

	Number of	Total value of (in cents)
Nickels	x	$5x$
Dimes	$x + 7$	$10(x + 7)$

Because the sum of the coins' total values are $3.10, the equation becomes:

The total value of the nickels   plus   the total value of the dimes   equals $3.10.

There is still a problem, or an inconsistency, however. The value of the nickels and dimes are given in cents, whereas the value of the sum is given in dollars. We can fix this by changing $3.10 into 310 cents. Now the equation becomes:

The total value of the nickels   plus   the total value of the dimes   equals   310¢ or

$5x$ + $10(x + 7)$ =   310   or

$$5x + 10(x + 7) = 310$$

Problem continued on next page.

Problem continued from previous page.

Step 4: **Solve the equation.**

$5x + 10(x + 7) = 310$	Simplify the left side by using the distributive property.
$5x + 10x + 70 = 310$	Combine like terms on the left side.
$15x + 70 = 310$	Subtract 70 from both sides of the equation.
$15x + 70 - 70 = 310 - 70$	Combine like terms on both sides of the equation.
$15x = 240$	Divide both sides of the equation by 15.
$\dfrac{15x}{15} = \dfrac{240}{15}$	Reduce both sides of the equation.
$x = 16$	

Step 5: **Answer the questions being asked.**

Since the number of nickels is being represented by x, and since $x = 16$,

Brian has 16 nickels.

Since the number of dimes is being represented by $x + 7$, and since $x + 7 = 16 + 7 = 23$,

Brian has 23 dimes.

Step 6: **Check your work to verify that the information found is correct.**

To verify the solutions, substitute 16 in the place of x in the original equation.

$5x + 10(x + 7) = 310$	becomes
$5(16) + 10[(16) + 7] \overset{?}{=} 310$.	Follow order of operations.
$5(16) + 10[23] \overset{?}{=} 310$	Simplify further.
$80 + 230 \overset{?}{=} 310$	And finally,
$310 \overset{\checkmark}{=} 310$.	The statement is true, therefore the solutions are correct.

Now try problem 39 from exercise set 3.8

Example 7: A car rental company charges $20 per day and 32 cents per mile for their cars. If a car was rented for one day and the total cost of the rental was $47.52, how many miles was the car driven?

Solution:

Step 1: What information is being requested?

"How many miles was the car driven?"

Step 2: Assign a variable to the unknown quantity that is being asked for.

Call "the number of miles" x.

Step 3: Translate the story into an equation using the variable from step 2.

To help us in writing the equation we will use the following table:

	Number of	Cost per total (in cents)
Miles driven	x	$32x$

The total cost of the miles driven   plus   the daily charge for one day   equals $47.52.

There is still a problem, or an inconsistency, however. The total cost of miles driven is given in cents, whereas the value of the daily charge for one day is given in dollars. The total cost of the rental is also given in dollars. We can fix this by changing 32 cents into $0.32. Now the table looks like this:

	Number of	Cost per total (in dollars)
Miles driven	x	$0.32x$

And the equation becomes:

The total cost of the miles driven   plus   the daily charge for one day   equals $47.52.   or

$$0.32x \qquad + \qquad 20 \qquad = \qquad 47.52 \quad \text{or}$$

$$0.32x + 20 = 47.52$$

Problem continued on next page.

Problem continued from previous page.

Step 4: **Solve the equation.**

$0.32x + 20 = 47.52$ Subtract 20 from both sides of the equation.

$0.32x + 20 - 20 = 47.52 - 20$ Combine like terms on both sides of the equation.

$0.32x = 27.52$ Divide both sides of the equation by 0.32.

$\dfrac{0.32x}{0.32} = \dfrac{27.52}{0.32}$ Reduce the left side of the equation.

$x = \dfrac{27.52}{0.32}$ Using long division

$0.32\overline{)27.52}$ becomes $32\overline{)2752}^{86}$.   Consequently,

$x = 86.$

Step 5: **Answer the question being asked.**

Since the number of miles driven is being represented by x, and since $x = 86$,

The car was driven 86 miles.

Step 6: **Check your work to verify that the information found is correct.**

To verify the solutions, substitute 86 in the place of x in the original equation.

$0.32x + 20 = 47.52$ becomes

$0.32(86) + 20 \overset{?}{=} 47.52$.   Follow order of operations.

$27.52 + 20 \overset{?}{=} 47.52$ Simplify further.

$47.52 \overset{\checkmark}{=} 47.52$ The statement is true, therefore the solutions are correct.

Now try problem 47 from exercise set 3.8

<u>Section 8 exercises.</u> Use the "Six Steps for Solving Story Problems" to solve the following story problems.

NUMBER PROBLEMS

1. If four times a number is decreased by three, the result is thirty-three. Find the number.

2. If seven times a number is decreased by five, the result is thirty-seven. Find the number.

3. Nine more than the product of six and a number is thirty-three. Find the number.

4. Eight more than the product of three and a number is twenty-three. Find the number.

5. Twice the sum of a number and four is negative two. Find the number.

6. Three times the sum of a number and seven is three. Find the number.

7. The difference of seven and twice a number is negative thirteen. Find the number.

8. The difference of twelve and twice a number is negative six. Find the number.

9. Three less than twice a number is equal to the difference of five times the same number and fifteen. Find the number.

10. The difference of six times a number and seven is equal to the sum of four times the same number and five. Find the number.

11.   One-third of a number plus one-half of the same number equals one-fourth of the same number. Find the number.

12.   One-fourth of a number minus one-fifth of the same number is equal to one-sixth of the same number. Find the number.

13.   The sum of two numbers is twenty-two. Three times the smaller number is four less than twice the larger number. Find the numbers.

14.   The sum of two numbers is thirty-one. Three times the smaller number is three more than twice the larger number. Find the numbers.

15.   The sum of two numbers is forty-five. Two times the larger number is three times the smaller number. Find the numbers.

16.   The sum of two numbers is fifty-six. Four more than the larger number is twice the smaller number. Find the numbers.

17.   The sum of two numbers is two. Four times the smaller number is negative three times the larger number. Find the numbers.

18.   The sum of two numbers is eight. Negative four times the smaller number is two more than twice the larger number. Find the numbers.

19.   The sum of two numbers is four-fifths. Six times the smaller number is twice the larger number. Find the numbers.

20.   The sum of two numbers is two-thirds. Five times the smaller number is the larger number. Find the numbers.

AGE PROBLEMS

21.   Jan is thirty-one years older than her son Isa. In six years, the sum of their ages will be seventy-five. How old are they now? A table has been provided to help you get started.

	Now	In six years
Jan		
Isa	x	

22.   Nancy is thirty-two years older than her son Ben. In six years, the sum of their ages will be one hundred forty. How old are they now? A table has been provided to help you get started.

	Now	In six years
Nancy		
Ben	x	

23.   Joe is twice as old as Martin. Three years ago, the sum of their ages was thirty-six. How old are they now?

24.   Mary is three times as old as Susan. Two years ago, the sum of their ages was twenty. How old are they now?

25.   Todd is five years younger than his brother Max. In four years, the sum of their ages will be forty-five. How old are they now?

26.   Eric is seven years younger than his brother Jeff. In eight years, the sum of their ages will be sixty-nine. How old are they now?

27.   John is three years less than twice as old as Mike. In four years, the sum of their ages will be thirty-five. How old are they now?

28.   Mark is four years more than twice as old as Doug. In six years, the sum of their ages will be forty-nine. How old are they now?

29. Pete is three times as old as Joel. In seven years, Pete will be twice as old as Joel. How old are they now?

30. Darren is four times as old as Tabitha. In twenty years, Darren will be twice as old as Tabitha. How old are they now?

GEOMETRY PROBLEMS

31. The length of a rectangle is twice its width. The perimeter is 72 inches. Find the length and the width.

32. The length of a rectangle is three times its width. The perimeter is 72 feet. Find the length and the width.

33. The width of a rectangle is four centimeters less than its length. If the perimeter is 40 centimeters, what is the width?

34. The width of a rectangle is eight yards less than its length. If the perimeter is 40 yards, what is the width?

35. The length of a rectangle is five inches less than three times its width. The perimeter is 62 inches. Find the length and the width.

36. The length of a rectangle is three meters less than five times its width. The perimeter is 66 meters. Find the length and the width.

37. The length of a rectangle is four feet more than six times its width. The perimeter is 78 feet. Find the length and the width.

38. The length of a rectangle is six inches more than four times its width. The perimeter is 82 inches. Find the length and the width.

COIN PROBLEMS

39.   Reba has $2.40 in nickels and quarters. If she has six more nickels than quarters, how many of each coin does she have? A table has been provided to help you get started.

	Number of	Total value of (in cents)
Nickels		
Quarters	x	

40.   Ronald has $3.15 in nickels and quarters. If he has nine less nickels than quarters, how many of each coin does he have? A table has been provided to help you get started.

	Number of	Total value of (in cents)
Nickels		
Quarters	x	

41.   Harvey has $3.05 in dimes and quarters. If he has eight less dimes than quarters, how many of each coin does he have?

42.   Heather has $2.10 in nickels and dimes. If she has six more nickels than dimes, how many of each coin does she have?

43.   Jim has $3.28 in pennies and dimes. If the number of pennies is six more than four times the number of dimes, how many of each coin does he have?

44.   Joan has $7.39 in pennies and nickels. If the number of pennies is nine more than five times the number of nickels, how many of each coin does she have?

45.   Sam has $1.50 in nickels, dimes and quarters. If he has twice as many nickels as dimes and three less quarters than the number of dimes, how many of each coin does he have?

46.   Sarah has $5.00 in nickels, dimes and quarters. If she has four times as many nickels as quarters and five less dimes than the number of quarters, how many of each coin does she have?

MISCELLANEOUS PROBLEMS

47.   A car rental company charges $37 per day and 28 cents per mile for their cars. If a car was rented for one day and the total cost of the rental was $77.88, how many miles was the car driven?

48.   A car rental company charges $42 per day and 27 cents per mile for their cars. If a car was rented for one day and the total cost of the rental was $78.45, how many miles was the car driven?

49.   A car rental company charges $34 per day and 26 cents per mile for their cars. If a car was rented for two days and the total cost of the rental was $130.66, how many miles was the car driven?

50.   A car rental company charges $29 per day and 29 cents per mile for their cars. If a car was rented for three days and the total cost of the rental was $199.23, how many miles was the car driven?

51.   Using Company A's calling plan, the cost of an overseas phone call is a $1.25 connection fee plus 23 cents per minute. If the total cost of the call is $5.39, how long is the phone call?

52.   Using Company B's calling plan, the cost of an overseas phone call is a $0.95 connection fee plus 38 cents per minute. If the total cost of the call is $11.21, how long is the phone call?

53.   The monthly cost of electricity from a local power company consists of a $4.75 billing charge plus 3.5 cents per kilowatt-hour of electricity used. If the total cost of a month's electric bill is $30.72, how much electricity was used that month?

54.   The monthly cost of electricity from a local power company consists of a $4.75 billing charge plus 3.5 cents per kilowatt-hour of electricity used. If the total cost of a month's electric bill is $34.99, how much electricity was used that month?

AN INTRODUCTION TO ALGEBRA

Chapter Review

Section 1: Signed Numbers

Review Exercises: Subtract.

Find the opposite of the quantity.

1. $-3\dfrac{1}{4} - 2\dfrac{1}{2}$

2. -4.8

Divide.

Simplify the expression.

3. $-\dfrac{4}{9} \div \left(-\dfrac{14}{15}\right)$

4. $\left| -3^2 + 4^2 - \dfrac{5}{7} \right|$

Evaluate the expression for the given value(s) of the variable(s).

5. $-|-x|$ for $x = 9$

6. $-3x + 6y$ for $x = -8$ and $y = -2$

7. $-5xy$ for $x = 2.4$ and $y = -8.9$

8. $\dfrac{2x^2 - 5y}{3y^2 - 4x}$ for $x = -\dfrac{3}{10}$ and $y = -\dfrac{1}{5}$

Section 2: Properties of Real Numbers

Review Exercises: Identify which property is being used to transform the left side of each equation into the right side.

9. $\dfrac{1}{y} \cdot y = y \cdot \dfrac{1}{y}$

10. $1 \cdot (7x) = (1 \cdot 7)x$

11. $(-2x + 2x) + 7 = (0) + 7$

12. $-8(7 + m) = -8(m + 7)$

Simplify each expression.

13. $-3n-6+3n$

14. $-(-7w-15)$

15. $0.6(8x-4)$

16. $-\dfrac{8}{3}y\left(-\dfrac{3}{8}\right)$

Section 3: Simplifying Variable Expressions

Review Exercises: For the algebraic expressions below, list each term. Tell whether it is a variable term or a constant term. If it is a variable term, also list its numerical coefficient.

17. $a-m-5$

18. $30-8b^2d+4ac^2$

Simplify each algebraic expression.

19. $3.6x+3.8y-1.6y-13.2x$

20. $\dfrac{2}{3}x+\dfrac{4}{5}y-\dfrac{3}{5}x+\dfrac{4}{3}y$

21. $\dfrac{2}{3}(7x-3y)+\dfrac{4}{5}(15x-7y)$

22. $(3x+2y)+(6z-4x)-(7y-8z)$

Simplify. Put the final answers in order of descending powers, in terms of the variable "*x*."

23. $-xy^2-4x^2y-3y^2+9x^2y-18$

24. $y[5(x+4)+x(x-3)]$

Section 4: Solving First-Degree Equations

Review Exercises: Solve by using the addition property of equality.

25. $-8 = m - 8$

26. $7x + 8 - 6x = -6$

27. $6.4 = -12.6 + y$

28. $a + \dfrac{9}{7} = \dfrac{2}{7}$

Solve by using the multiplication property of equality.

29. $-n = 12$

30. $\dfrac{-7}{12} = \dfrac{-14}{3}x$

31. $9.6 = \dfrac{3}{7}x$

32. $\dfrac{1}{4}m + \dfrac{1}{5}m = \dfrac{1}{6}$

Section 5: Solving Complex First-Degree Equations

Review Exercises: Solve.

33. $6w + 7 = 25$

34. $16 - 8x = 0$

35. $-7 = 3 - \dfrac{a}{6}$

36. $9y + 6 - 3y + 8 = 14 - 26$

37. $8.4k - 2.6 + 3.6k = 31$

38. $\dfrac{k}{5} - \dfrac{1}{3} = -\dfrac{1}{4}$

The cost of renting a car from Company B for one day can be found by using the formula $C = 0.43m + 28$, where m is the number of miles driven and C is the total cost of the car rental in dollars.

39.   How far was the car driven in one day if the total cost of the car rental was $93.36?

The monthly cost of natural gas from a local gas company can be found by using the formula $C = 1.28T + 4$, where T is the number of therms (a unit used to measure heat) used and C is the total monthly cost in dollars.

40.   How much natural gas was used in a month if the total cost was $295.84?

Section 6: Solving General First-Degree Equations

Review Exercises: Solve the following equations.

41. $5w - 12 = -9 - 3w$

42. $5m - 8 + 6m = -7m + 12 + 3m$

43. $(3x + 2) - (5x - 4) = (4x + 6) + (7x - 8)$

44. $-4(3x + 2) + 6x = 0$

Solve the following equations by first eliminating the fractions.

45. $\dfrac{2}{5}x + \dfrac{3}{2} = -\dfrac{7}{5}$

46. $\dfrac{3}{x} + \dfrac{2}{3} = \dfrac{4}{5}$

Solve the following equations by first eliminating the decimals.

47. $2.6y - 4 = 24.6$

48. $3.2x - 6.1 + 9x = 65.3 - 1.4x + 17$

Section 7: Translating Between Mathematical Terminology and Algebraic Expressions

Review Exercises: Translate each algebraic expression into words using mathematical terminology.

49. $6(5x - 7) + 4$

50. $3 - \dfrac{4y}{7}$

Translate each phrase into an algebraic expression. In each case use the letter x to represent the variable. Then simplify the algebraic expression.

51.   a number decreased by the difference between negative six and the same number

52.   negative seven multiplied by the sum of five and a number

53.   twelve more than the product of five and the difference of three and a number

54.   eighteen minus the sum of a number and twelve

Translate and simplify:

55.   Joyce is eight years older than Tammy. If a is used to represent Tammy's age in years, translate "six years more than four times Joyce's age" into an algebraic expression written in terms of a. Then simplify the expression.

56.   The length of a rectangle is five times as long as the width. If W is used to represent the width of the rectangle, translate "three less than four times the length" into an algebraic expression written in terms of W. Then simplify the expression.

Section 8: Application Problems

Review Exercises: Use the "Six Steps for Solving Story Problems" to solve the following story problems.

57.   The difference of five times a number and three is equal to the sum of four times the same number and six. Find the number.

58.   The sum of two numbers is twenty-eight. Two times the larger number is five times the smaller number. Find the numbers.

59.   Ralph is two years more than three times as old as Kerry. In four years, the sum of their ages will be eighteen. How old are they now?

60.   Seth is three times as old as Leroy. In six years, Seth will be twice as old as Leroy. How old are they now?

61.   The width of a rectangle is seven centimeters less than its length. If the perimeter is 38 centimeters, what is the width?

62.   The length of a rectangle is five inches less than three times its width. The perimeter is 54 inches. Find the length and the width.

63.   Simon has $1.66 in pennies, dimes and quarters. If he has three times as many pennies as dimes and four less quarters than the number of dimes, how many of each coin does he have?

64.   A car rental company charges $28 per day and 31 cents per mile for their cars. If a car was rented for two days and the total cost of the rental was $187.13, how many miles was the car driven?

AN INTRODUCTION TO ALGEBRA

Chapter Test

Subtract.

Simplify the expression.

1. $-7\dfrac{1}{8}-5\dfrac{3}{4}$

2. $\left| 6^2 - \dfrac{7}{9} - 4^2 \right|$

Evaluate the expression for the given value(s) of the variable(s).

3. $-\left|-m\right|$ for $m=-8$

4. $\dfrac{5x^2 - 3y}{7y^2 - x}$ for $x = -\dfrac{2}{5}$ and $y = -\dfrac{3}{7}$

Identify which property is being used to transform the left side of each equation into the right side.

5. $\left(\dfrac{2}{3}\cdot\dfrac{3}{2}\right)x = (1)x$

6. $-3(mn) = -3(nm)$

Simplify each expression.

7. $4-8w+4+8w$

8. $-0.5(3y-6)$

For the algebraic expression below, list each term. Tell whether it is a variable term or a constant term. If it is a variable term, also list its numerical coefficient.

9. $17x^2 y - 6 + z$

Simplify each algebraic expression.

10.　$4.5x - 6.1y - 2.7y - 3.2x$

11.　$\dfrac{3}{5}(4x - 5y) - \dfrac{1}{4}(8x - 3y)$

Simplify. Put the final answer in order of descending powers, in terms of the variable "x."

12.　$8xy + 3y - 4x^2 y + 8 - 5y$

Solve by using the addition property of equality.

13.　$4 = 4 + w$

14.　$x - \dfrac{4}{9} = \dfrac{5}{9}$

Solve by using the multiplication property of equality.

15.　$\dfrac{-8}{15} = \dfrac{-14}{25}k$

16.　$8.4 = \dfrac{4}{9}m$

Solve.

17.　$7p - 8 = 41$

18.　$-6 = 13 - \dfrac{x}{9}$

19.　$-8m + 7 + 3m - 12 = 4 - 18$

The monthly cost of natural gas from a local gas company can be found by using the formula $C = 1.36T + 6$, where T is the number of therms (a unit used to measure heat) used and C is the total monthly cost in dollars.

20. How much natural gas was used in a month if the total cost was \$370.48?

Solve the following equations.

21. $(4x - 2) - (5 - x) = (3x - 7) + (9x - 2)$ **22.** $-8(7x - 3) - 4x = 0$

Solve the following equations by first eliminating the fractions or decimals.

23. $\dfrac{5}{x} + \dfrac{1}{3} = \dfrac{-6}{7}$ **24.** $3.7y - 5 = 43.1$

Translate the algebraic expression into words using mathematical terminology.

25. $-3(2y - 8) - 7$

Translate the phrase into an algebraic expression. Use the letter x to represent the variable. Then simplify the algebraic expression.

26. a number decreased by the sum of negative twelve and the same number

Translate and simplify:

27. George is three years younger than Lou. If a is used to represent Lou's age in years, translate "eight years more than five times George's age" into an algebraic expression written in terms of a. Then simplify the expression.

Use the "Six Steps for Solving Story Problems" to solve the following story problems.

28.   The sum of two numbers is thirty-six. Two times the larger number is two more than three times the smaller number. Find the numbers.

29.   Rhonda is five years more than twice as old as Jayne. Four years ago, the sum of their ages was eighteen. How old are they now?

30.   The length of a rectangle is seven inches less than three times its width. The perimeter is 58 inches. Find the length and the width.

31.   Steven has $2.29 in pennies, nickels and quarters. If he has eight times as many pennies as nickels and three less quarters than the number of nickels, how many of each coin does he have?

32.   A car rental company charges $33 per day and 29 cents per mile for their cars. If a car was rented for three days and the total cost of the rental was $221.09, how many miles was the car driven?

CHAPTER 4
FORMULAS & GRAPHING

Section 1: Geometric Formulas

Perimeter and Area of Composite Figures
Surface Area of Spheres
Surface Area of Right Circular Cylinders
Volume of Spheres
Volume of Right Circular Cylinders

Section 2: Solving Formulas

Section 3: Graphing Ordered Pairs

Section 4: Ordered Pairs as Solutions to Equations

Section 5: Graphing Linear Equations

FORMULAS & GRAPHING

Section 1: Geometric Formulas

In Chapter 1 we found the perimeter and area of geometric figures such as a square or a triangle. Sometimes a figure is a combination of several geometric shapes. This is called a **composite figure**. When finding the area of a composite figure, we find the area of each separate shape and then add them all together. When finding the perimeter, however, we only add up the distance around the outside of the entire composite figure, not the distance around each separate shape. (The geometric formulas from Chapter 1 are all listed on the inside of the back cover of this book.)

Example 1: Find the perimeter and the area of the following composite figure. Give both exact answers and approximations using the fact that $\pi \approx 3.14$.

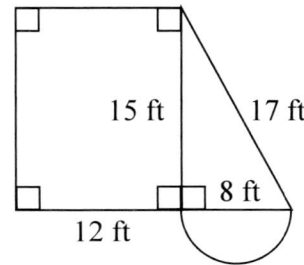

Solution: To find the perimeter of the composite figure, we need to determine the missing dimensions of the rectangle, as well as the perimeter (or circumference) of the semi-circle. Since opposite sides of a rectangle are equal, the top of the rectangle is 12 ft and the left side is 15 ft. Since the diameter of the semi-circle is 8 feet, then the radius is 4 feet. Using the formula for the circumference of a circle:

$C = 2\pi r$, we get $C = 2\pi(4\text{ft})$ or $C = 8\pi$ ft. However, since it is a semi-circle, the circumference is half of that, or just 4π ft. Filling in the missing dimensions we get:

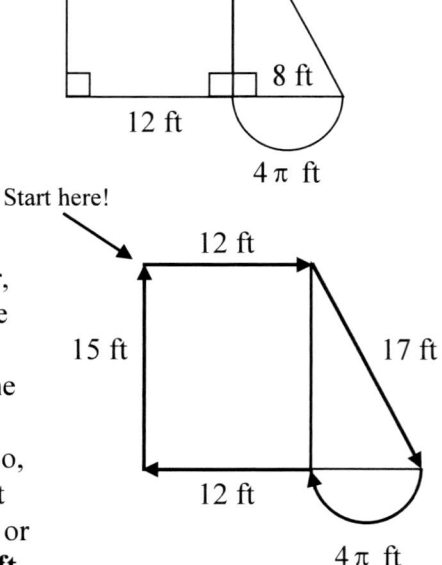

Now we can calculate the perimeter of the entire composite figure by adding the lengths of all the outside edges. Starting at the upper left of the figure and moving in a clockwise manner, we get 12 ft + 17 ft + 4π ft + 12 ft + 15 ft. To write an exact answer we must leave π in its exact form. Combine all the terms without π separately from the term that contains π. This gives us a total of 56 ft + 4π ft which we can write as $(56 + 4\pi)$ ft. So, **the exact perimeter is $(56 + 4\pi)$ ft**. Using the fact that $\pi \approx 3.14$, $(56 + 4\pi)$ ft becomes $(56 + 12.56)$ ft or 68.56 ft. So, **the approximate perimeter is 68.56 ft.**

Problem continued on next page.

Problem continued from previous page.

To find the exact area of the composite figure, we find the area of each separate shape and then add them all together.

Using the formula for the area of a rectangle: $A = LW$
we get $A = (15 \text{ ft})(12 \text{ ft})$ or $A = 180 \text{ ft}^2$.

15 ft

$A = \boxed{180 \text{ ft}^2}$

12 ft

Using the formula for the area of a triangle: $A = \frac{1}{2}bh$

we get $A = \dfrac{1}{2}(8 \text{ ft})(15 \text{ ft})$ or $A = 60 \text{ ft}^2$.

15 ft   17 ft

$A = \boxed{60 \text{ ft}^2}$

8 ft

Using the formula for the area of a circle: $A = \pi r^2$
we get $A = \pi (4 \text{ ft})^2$ or $A = 16\pi \text{ ft}^2$.

However, since it is a semi-circle,
the area is half of that, or just $8\pi \text{ ft}^2$.

8 ft

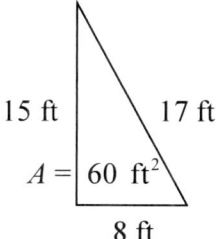

$A = 8\pi \text{ ft}^2$

Adding the area of each figure we get:

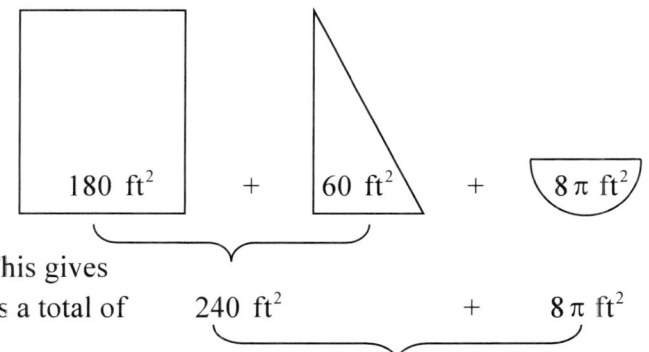

180 ft²   +   60 ft²   +   8π ft²

To write an exact answer we must leave π in its exact form. Combine the terms without π separately from the term that contains π.

This gives
us a total of   240 ft²   +   8π ft²   which we can write as

$$A = (240 + 8\pi) \text{ ft}^2.$$ So,

the exact area of the composite figure is $(240 + 8\pi) \text{ ft}^2$.

Using the fact that $\pi \approx 3.14$,

$A \approx (240 + 8(3.14)) \text{ ft}^2$.   Since $(240 + 8(3.14)) \text{ ft}^2 = (240 + 25.12) \text{ ft}^2 = 265.12 \text{ ft}^2$ then,

$A \approx 265.12 \text{ ft}^2$.   Consequently,

the approximate area of the composite figure is 265.12 ft^2.

Now try problem 3 from exercise set 4.1

Next, we will consider formulas for the surface area of **spheres** and **right circular cylinders**.

A sphere is an object with a round ball-like shape.

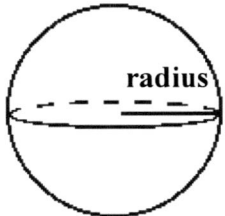

In the formula for the surface area of a sphere, "*r*" stands for the length of the radius of the sphere. The radius of a sphere is a line from the center to a point on the sphere.

FORMULA FOR THE SURFACE AREA OF A SPHERE:

$$SA = 4\pi r^2$$

<u>Example 2</u>: Find the surface area of the following sphere in square inches. Give both the exact answer and an approximation using the fact that $\pi \approx 3.14$.

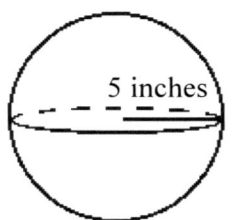

Solution: The length of the radius of the sphere is 5 in. Using the formula for the surface area of a sphere,

$SA = 4\pi r^2$ gives us

$SA = 4\pi (5 \text{ in.})^2$.   Following order of operations, we get

$SA = 4\pi (25 \text{ in.}^2)$ or $SA = 100\pi \text{ in.}^2$.   So,

the exact surface area of the sphere is 100π square inches or 100π in.^{2} .

Using the fact that $\pi \approx 3.14$,

$SA \approx (100)(3.14) \text{ in.}^2$.   Since $(100)(3.14) \text{ in.}^2 = 314 \text{ in.}^2$ then,

$SA \approx 314 \text{ in.}^2$.   Consequently,

the approximate surface area of the sphere is 314 square inches or 314 in.^{2} .

A right circular cylinder is an object that is shaped like a can. The top and bottom are circles that are perpendicular to the side of the cylinder.

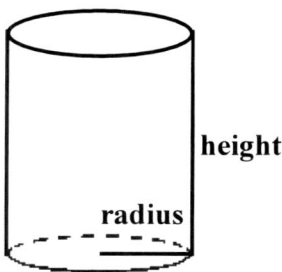

We determine the surface area of a cylinder by finding the sum of the areas of the top and bottom that are circles and of the side, which when laid flat or unrolled is a rectangle.

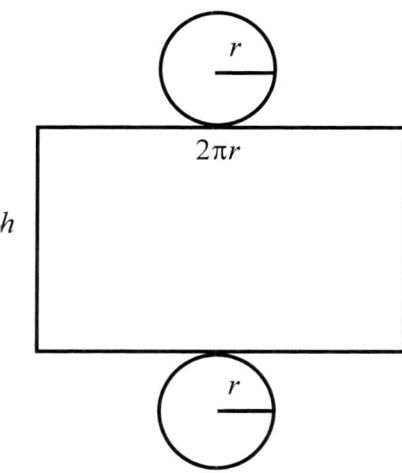

Note that in the above diagram, the top and the bottom each have the same area, which consists of πr^2. The dimensions of the rectangle in the middle consist of the circumference of the top of the cylinder times the height of the cylinder. That is, $2\pi rh$. Adding these three parts together leads to the formula below.

In the formula for the surface area of a right circular cylinder, "r" stands for the length of the radius of the circle on the top or the bottom of the cylinder and "h" stands for the height that corresponds to the side of the cylinder.

FORMULA FOR THE SURFACE AREA OF A RIGHT CIRCULAR CYLINDER:

$$SA = 2\pi r^2 + 2\pi rh$$

Example 3: Find the surface area of the following cylinder in square inches. Give both the exact answer and an approximation using the fact that $\pi \approx 3.14$.

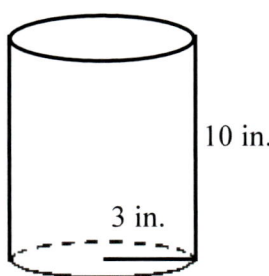

10 in.

3 in.

Solution: The length of the radius of the cylinder is 3 in. and the height is 10 in. Using the formula for the surface area of a right circular cylinder,

$SA = 2\pi r^2 + 2\pi rh$	gives us
$SA = 2\pi(3 \text{ in.})^2 + 2\pi(3 \text{ in.})(10 \text{ in.})$.	Following order of operations we get
$SA = 2\pi(9 \text{ in.}^2) + 2\pi(3 \text{ in.})(10 \text{ in.})$	which simplified further becomes
$SA = 18\pi \text{ in.}^2 + 60\pi \text{ in.}^2$	and finally becomes
$SA = 78\pi \text{ in.}^2$.	So,

the exact surface area of the cylinder is 78π square inches or 78π in.^{2}.

Using the fact that $\pi \approx 3.14$,

$SA \approx (78)(3.14) \text{ in.}^2$.	Since $(78)(3.14) \text{ in.}^2 = 244.92 \text{ in.}^2$ then,
$SA \approx 244.92 \text{ in.}^2$.	Consequently,

the approximate surface area of the cylinder is 244.92 square inches or 244.92 in.^{2}.

How did Sir Cumference meet Lady Diameter?

They travel in all the same social circles.

Why was Sir Cumference upset with Lady Diameter?

Because she crossed him one too many times.

As previously mentioned, a sphere is an object with a round ball-like shape.

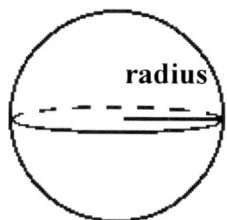

In the formula for the volume of a sphere "V" stands for volume and "r" stands for the length of the radius of the sphere. The radius of a sphere is a line from the center to a point on the sphere.

FORMULA FOR THE VOLUME OF A SPHERE:

$$V = \frac{4}{3}\pi r^3$$

<u>Example 4:</u> Find the volume of the following sphere in cubic inches. Give both the exact answer and an approximation using the fact that $\pi \approx 3.14$.

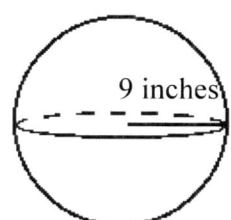

Solution: The length of the radius of the sphere is 9 in. Using the formula for the volume of a sphere,

$V = \frac{4}{3}\pi r^3$ gives us

$V = \frac{4}{3}\pi\,(9\text{ in.})^3$.   Following order of operations we get

$V = \frac{4}{3}\pi\,(729\text{ in.}^3)$ which simplified further becomes

$V = 972\pi\text{ in.}^3$.   So,

the exact volume of the sphere is 972π cubic inches or 972π in.^{3}.

Using the fact that $\pi \approx 3.14$,

$V = (972)(3.14)\text{ in.}^3$.   Since $(972)(3.14)\text{ in.}^3 = 3{,}052.08\text{ in.}^3$ then,

$V = 3{,}052.08\text{ in.}^3$.   Consequently,

the approximate volume of the sphere is 3,052.08 cubic inches or 3,052.08 in.^{3}.

Now try problem 5 from exercise set 4.1. (Find the volume.) See example 2 for the surface area.

As previously mentioned, a right circular cylinder is an object that is shaped like a can. The top and bottom are circles that are perpendicular to the side of the cylinder.

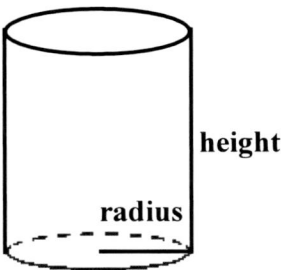

height

radius

In the formula for the volume of a right circular cylinder "V" stands for volume, "r" stands for the length of the radius of the circle on the top or the bottom of the cylinder, and "h" stands for the height that corresponds to the side of the cylinder.

FORMULA FOR THE VOLUME OF A RIGHT CIRCULAR CYLINDER:

$$V = \pi r^2 h$$

Example 5: Find the volume of the following cylinder in cubic inches. Give both the exact answer and an approximation using the fact that $\pi \approx 3.14$.

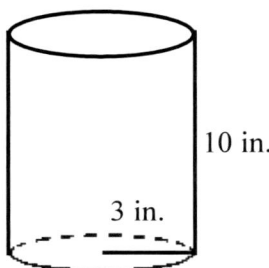

10 in.

3 in.

Solution: The length of the radius of the cylinder is 3 in. and the height is 10 in. Using the formula for the volume of a right circular cylinder,

$V = \pi r^2 h$ gives us

$V = \pi \, (3 \text{ in.})^2 (10 \text{ in.})$.   Following order of operations we get

$V = \pi \, (9 \text{ in.}^2)(10 \text{ in.})$ which simplified further becomes

$V = 90\pi \text{ in.}^3$.   So,

the exact volume of the cylinder is 90π cubic inches or $90\pi \text{ in.}^3$.

Using the fact that $\pi \approx 3.14$,

$V \approx (90)(3.14) \text{ in.}^3$.   Since $(90)(3.14) \text{ in.}^3 = 282.6 \text{ in.}^3$ then,

$V \approx 282.6 \text{ in.}^3$.   Consequently,

the approximate volume of the cylinder is 282.6 cubic inches or 282.6 in.^3.

Now try problem 9 from exercise set 4.1. (Find the volume.) See example 3 for the surface area.

<u>Section 1 exercises.</u> Find the perimeter and area of each composite figure.

1.

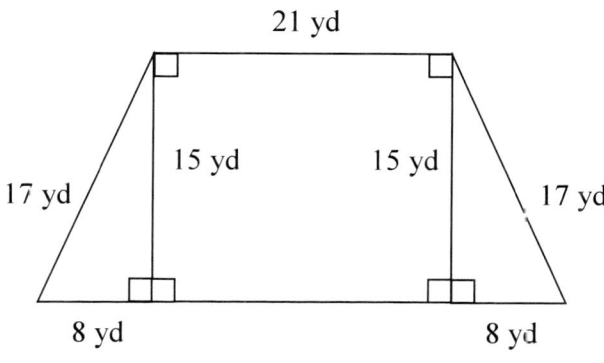

2.

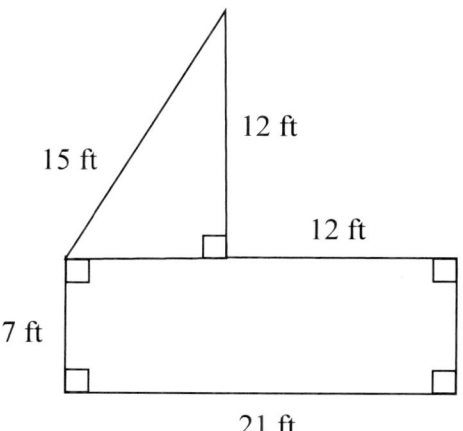

Find the perimeter and area of each composite figure. Give the exact answers and the approximations using the fact that $\pi \approx 3.14$.

3.

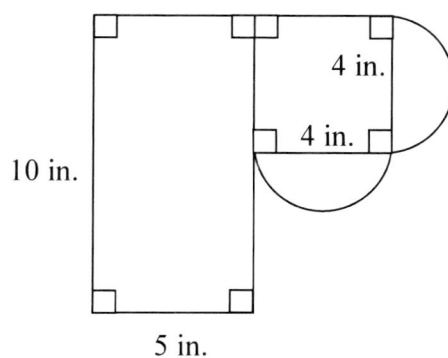

4.

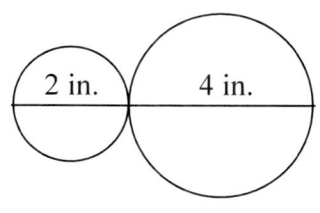

Find the surface area and the volume of each figure. Give the exact answers and the approximations using the fact that $\pi \approx 3.14$.

5.

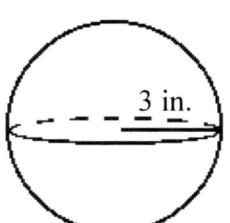

6.

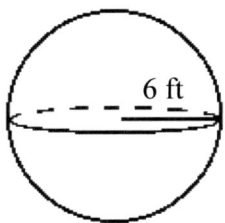

7.

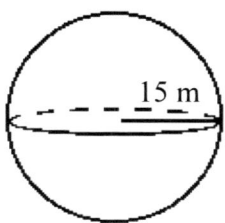

8.

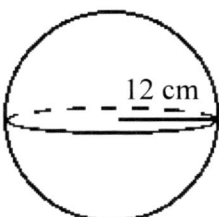

9.

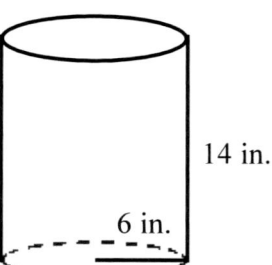

10.

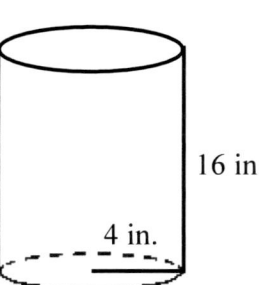

11.

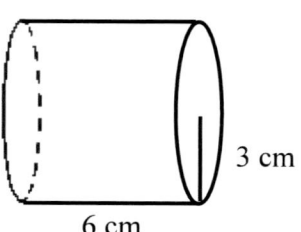

12.

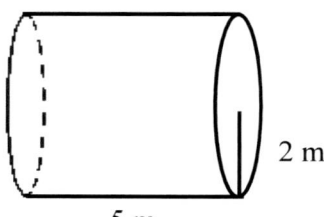

13.

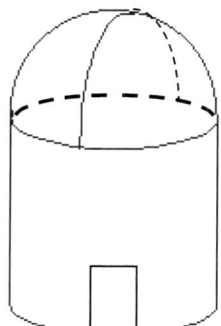

A farmer builds a grain silo on a flat concrete floor. The silo consists of a cylindrical base, which is 20 feet high and has a diameter of 12 feet, and a hemisphere shaped roof. (A hemisphere is half of a sphere.)

a)   If the farmer wishes to paint the outside of his silo including the roof and door, how many square feet will he need to paint? Give both the exact answer and an approximation using the fact that $\pi \approx 3.14$.

b)   How many cubic feet of grain can he store in his silo if he fills it to the top? Give both the exact answer and an approximation using the fact that $\pi \approx 3.14$.

14.

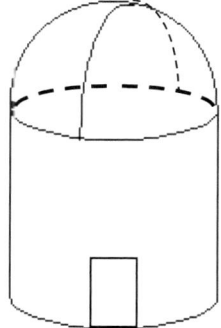

A farmer builds a grain silo on a flat wooden floor. The silo consists of a cylindrical base, which is 5 meters high and has a diameter of 3 meters, and a hemisphere shaped roof. (A hemisphere is half of a sphere.)

a)   If the farmer wishes to paint the outside of his silo including the roof and door, how many square meters will he need to paint? Give both the exact answer and an approximation using the fact that $\pi \approx 3.14$.

b)   How many cubic meters of grain can he store in his silo if he fills it to the top? Give both the exact answer and an approximation using the fact that $\pi \approx 3.14$.

FORMULAS
& GRAPHING

Section 2: Solving Formulas

In this section, we will focus on solving equations that are **formulas**.

Formula: **A formula is an equation that contains at least two different variables.**

The equation $A = LW$, which tells how to find the area of a rectangle, is an example of a formula. If numerical values for two of the three variables in this formula are known, we can use the formula to find the numerical value of the third variable.

Example 1: The area A of a rectangle is 60 square feet. If the length L is 10 feet, find the width.

Solution:	First, substitute 60 in place of A and 10 in place of L.
$A = LW$	becomes
$60 = 10W$.	Now, solve for W. Divide both sides of the equation by 10.
$\dfrac{60}{10} = \dfrac{10W}{10}$	Reduce both sides of the equation.
$W = 6$	Therefore, the width is 6 feet.

Now try problem 5 from exercise set 4.2

Example 2: The perimeter P of a rectangle is 60 feet. If the length L is 20 feet, find the width.

Solution: First, substitute 60 in place of P and 20 in place of L.	
$P = 2L + 2W$	becomes
$60 = 2(20) + 2W$.	Simplify the right side of the equation.
$60 = 40 + 2W$	Now, solve for W. Subtract 40 from both sides of the equation.
$60 - 40 = 40 - 40 + 2W$	Simplify both sides of the equation.
$20 = 2W$	Divide both sides of the equation by 2.
$\dfrac{20}{2} = \dfrac{2W}{2}$	Reduce both sides of the equation.
$W = 10$	Therefore, the width is 10 feet.

Now try problem 9 from exercise set 4.2

<u>Example 3</u>: Find y when $x = 6$ in the formula $5x + 2y = 38$.

Solution: First, substitute 6 in place of x.

$5x + 2y = 38$ becomes

$5(6) + 2y = 38$.   Simplify the left side of the equation.

$30 + 2y = 38$ Now, solve for y. Subtract 30 from both sides of the equation.

$30 - 30 + 2y = 38 - 30$ Simplify both sides of the equation.

$2y = 8$ Divide both sides of the equation by 2.

$\dfrac{2y}{2} = \dfrac{8}{2}$ Reduce both sides of the equation.

$y = 4$

Now try problem 17 from exercise set 4.2

Now, consider examples of formulas where numerical values aren't given for any of the variables. Our goal will be to solve the formula for one of its variables. To accomplish this we must isolate one of the variables on either side of the equation. At the same time, all other variables and constants must be on the other side of the equation.

<u>Example 4</u>: Solve $A = LW$ for the variable W.

Solution: In order to solve for the variable w, we must isolate it. Since in the formula $A = LW$, L is being multiplied by W, we must separate them by using division. In other words, divide both sides of the equation by L.

$A = LW$ becomes

$\dfrac{A}{L} = \dfrac{LW}{L}$.   Reduce both sides of the equation.

$\dfrac{A}{L} = W$ or, $W = \dfrac{A}{L}$.

Now try problem 31 from exercise set 4.2

Example 5: Solve $P = 2L + 2W$ for the variable W.

Solution: In order to solve for the variable W, we must isolate it. The formula $P = 2L + 2W$ contains 3 terms, which are P, $2L$ and $2W$. In order to isolate W, we will start by isolating the term that contains W. This is done by subtracting $2L$ from both sides of the equation.

$P = 2L + 2W$ becomes

$P - 2L = 2L - 2L + 2W$.   Simplify both sides of the equation.

$P - 2L = 2W$ Divide both sides of the equation by 2.

$\dfrac{P - 2L}{2} = \dfrac{2W}{2}$ Reduce both sides of the equation.

$\dfrac{P - 2L}{2} = W$ or, $W = \dfrac{P - 2L}{2}$.

A slightly different form of the answer can be obtained by splitting the right side of the equation into two separate fractions and then reducing.

$W = \dfrac{P - 2L}{2}$ becomes

$W = \dfrac{P}{2} - \dfrac{2L}{2}$ which reduces to

$W = \dfrac{P}{2} - L$ or, $W = \dfrac{1}{2}P - L$.

Now try problem 43 from exercise set 4.2

Example 6: Solve $5x + 4y = 12$ for the variable y.

Solution: In order to solve for the variable y, we must isolate it. In order to isolate y, we will start by isolating the term that contains y. This is done by subtracting $5x$ from both sides of the equation.

$5x + 4y = 12$ becomes

$5x - 5x + 4y = 12 - 5x$.   Simplify both sides of the equation.

$4y = 12 - 5x$ Rewrite the right side of the equation so that the term with the variable is first, followed by the constant term.

$4y = -5x + 12$ Divide both sides of the equation by 4.

$\dfrac{4y}{4} = \dfrac{-5x + 12}{4}$ Split the right side of the equation into two separate fractions.

$\dfrac{4y}{4} = -\dfrac{5x}{4} + \dfrac{12}{4}$ Reduce both sides of the equation.

$y = -\dfrac{5}{4}x + 3$

Now try problem 59 from exercise set 4.2

Example 7: Solve $\dfrac{x}{3} + \dfrac{y}{2} = 1$ for the variable y.

Solution: Since this equation contains several fractions, we will start by eliminating them from the original equation. This is done by multiplying both sides of the equation by 6, since this is the least common denominator of all the fractions in the equation.

$\dfrac{x}{3} + \dfrac{y}{2} = 1$ becomes

$6\left(\dfrac{x}{3} + \dfrac{y}{2}\right) = 6(1)$.   Use the distributive property.

$6\left(\dfrac{x}{3}\right) + 6\left(\dfrac{y}{2}\right) = 6(1)$ Reduce or simplify both sides of the equation.

$2x + 3y = 6$ In order to solve for the variable y, we must isolate it. In order to isolate y, we will start by isolating the term that contains y. This is done by subtracting $2x$ from both sides of the equation.

$2x + 3y = 6$ becomes

$2x - 2x + 3y = 6 - 2x$.   Simplify both sides of the equation.

$3y = 6 - 2x$ Rewrite the right side of the equation so that the term with the variable is first, followed by the constant term.

$3y = -2x + 6$ Divide both sides of the equation by 3.

$\dfrac{3y}{3} = \dfrac{-2x + 6}{3}$ Split the right side of the equation into two separate fractions.

$\dfrac{3y}{3} = -\dfrac{2x}{3} + \dfrac{6}{3}$ Reduce both sides of the equation.

$y = -\dfrac{2}{3}x + 2$

Now try problem 67 from exercise set 4.2

Note: Even though we could have used $y = \dfrac{-2x + 6}{3}$ as the final answer, the form

$y = -\dfrac{2}{3}x + 2$ **will be easier to work with when doing graphing in future algebra courses.**

Several of the problems in this section contain the variables x and y.   When solving these equations for the variable y, put them in the form where the right side of the equation is split into two separate terms, as is done in the solutions of examples 6 and 7.

<u>Section 2 exercises.</u> Use the formula $A = LW$ to find the length of a rectangle under the given conditions.

1.   The width is 20 inches and the area is 500 square inches.

2.   The width is 35 yards and the area is 1,400 square yards.

3.   The width is 31 feet and the area is 1,209 square feet.

4.   The width is 17 meters and the area is 476 square meters.

Use the formula $A = LW$ to find the width of a rectangle under the given conditions.

5.   The length is 56 meters and the area is 1,904 square meters.

6.   The length is 47 feet and the area is 1,645 square feet.

7.   The length is 4.2 yards and the area is 14.7 square yards.

8.   The length is 5.2 inches and the area is 23.4 square inches.

Use the formula $P = 2L + 2W$ to find the width of a rectangle under the given conditions.

9.   The length is 18 inches and the perimeter is 68 inches.

10.   The length is 29 yards and the perimeter is 86 yards.

11.   The length is 14.2 feet and the perimeter is 36 feet.

12.   The length is 6.4 meters and the perimeter is 20.8 meters.

Use the formula $P = 2L + 2W$ to find the length of a rectangle under the given conditions.

13.   The width is $3\frac{1}{2}$ meters and the perimeter is $17\frac{2}{5}$ meters.

14.   The width is $5\frac{1}{4}$ inches and the perimeter is $25\frac{1}{2}$ inches.

15.   The width is 2 yards and the perimeter is 16 yards.

16.   The width is 4 feet and the perimeter is 26 feet.

Use the formula $6x + 4y = 12$ to find y under the given conditions.

17. $x = 4$ **18.** $x = 6$ **19.** $x = -6$ **20.** $x = -4$

Use the formula $4x - 5y = 40$ to find x under the given conditions.

21. $y = 2$ **22.** $y = 0$ **23.** $y = -8$ **24.** $y = -6$

Use the formula $y = 3x + 2$ to find y under the given conditions.

25. $x = -2$ **26.** $x = -1$ **27.** $x = 0$ **28.** $x = 1$

Solve each of the following formulas for the indicated variable.

29. $P = 4s$ for s **30.** $C = \pi d$ for d

31. $d = rt$ for r **32.** $d = rt$ for t

33. $C = 2\pi r$ for r **34.** $A = LW$ for L

35. $A = \frac{1}{2}bh$ for h

36. $A = \frac{1}{2}bh$ for b

37. $V = LWH$ for W

38. $V = LWH$ for H

39. $V = \pi r^2 h$ for h

40. $V = \pi r^2 h$ for r^2

41. $P = a + b + c$ for b

42. $P = a + b + c$ for a

43. $P = 2L + 2W$ for L

44. $SA = 2\pi r^2 + 2\pi rh$ for h

45. $V = \frac{4}{3}\pi r^3$ for r^3

46. $V = \frac{1}{3}\pi r^2 h$ for h

47. $s = \dfrac{a + b + c}{2}$ for b

48. $z = \dfrac{x - y}{3}$ for x

49. $m = \dfrac{F}{a}$ for a

50. $h = \dfrac{2a}{b}$ for b

51. $x - 5y = -7$ for x

52. $x + 6y = 3$ for x

53. $3x - 5y = 7$ for x

54. $8x + 3y = 5$ for x

Solve each formula for *y*.

55. $-5x + y = 9$ **56.** $6x + y = -18$

57. $4x - y = 7$ **58.** $3x - y = 10$

59. $3x + 2y = 12$ **60.** $4x + 6y = -12$

61. $5x + 4y = -20$ **62.** $7x + 4y = 28$

63. $2x - 5y = 3$ **64.** $5x - 7y = 6$

65. $7 - 3y = 8x$ **66.** $9 - 4y = 3x$

67. $\dfrac{x}{4} + \dfrac{y}{5} = 1$ **68.** $\dfrac{x}{6} + \dfrac{y}{4} = 1$

69. $\dfrac{x}{3} - \dfrac{y}{8} = 1$ **70.** $\dfrac{x}{7} - \dfrac{y}{5} = 1$

71. $-\dfrac{1}{3}x + \dfrac{1}{5}y = 1$ **72.** $-\dfrac{1}{12}x + \dfrac{1}{5}y = 1$

FORMULAS & GRAPHING

Section 3: Graphing Ordered Pairs

Have you ever been lost in a big city where you were trying to locate a street on a map? Typically, on the back of a map, street names are listed in alphabetical order. Next to each street name is a letter followed by a number. For example, Jones St. D-4. On the front of the map, around the outside edges are a series of letters and numbers. The letters, starting with A, go down the left edge of the map from the top to the bottom. The numbers, starting with 1, go across the top edge from left to right. By using both pieces of information listed with the street name, that is, the D and the 4, we are able to pinpoint the location of Jones Street on the map.

Back of map

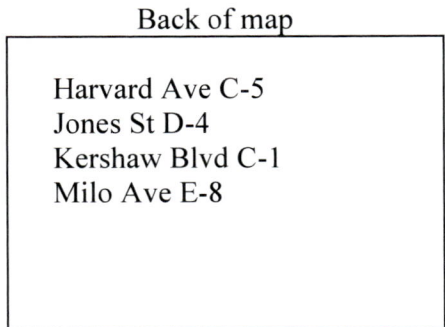

Front of map

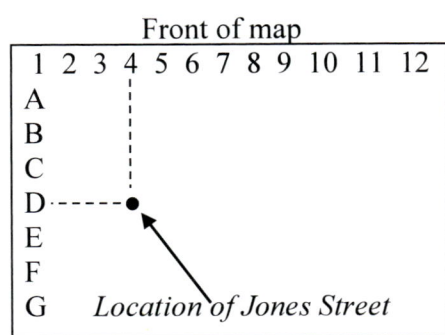

The process used to locate and plot points on a grid is called **graphing**. This section will focus on graphing ordered pairs, or plotting points. The solution, or picture, that is formed by the plotting of points is called the **graph**. The process of graphing is very similar to the above example where we located a point on a map or grid using two pieces of information. This grid is called the **rectangular coordinate system**. It consists of two number lines that intersect. One of these lines, called the **x-axis**, goes from left to right, or horizontally (think of the horizon). On the x-axis the numbers get larger as we move to the right and smaller as we move to the left. The other line is vertical, or goes up and down, and is called the **y-axis**. On the y-axis the numbers get larger as we move up and smaller as we move down. The point on the grid where the two axes intersect is called the **origin**. When locating (or graphing) a point on the rectangular coordinate system, we start at the origin and then move from there, based on information that is given to us. The x-axis and y-axis form a two-dimensional **plane**, or grid, that extends infinitely out on all sides. The x-axis and y-axis divide this plane into four regions called **quadrants**, which are numbered counterclockwise using the Roman Numerals I, II, III and IV.

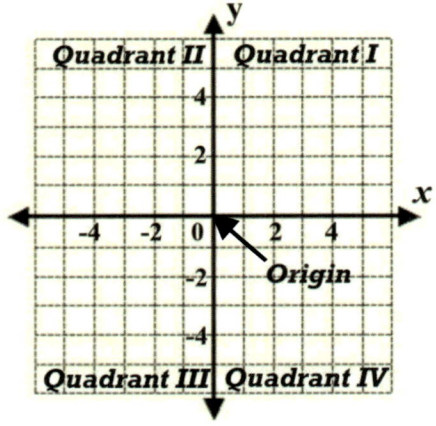

In order to locate or plot a point on the rectangular coordinate system we need two pieces of information. First, we need to know the location of the point in terms of the *x*-axis. This number is called the **x-coordinate** of the point. Second, we need to know the location of the point in terms of the *y*-axis. This number is called the **y-coordinate** of the point. The two numbers that represent the *x*-coordinate and the *y*-coordinate are written in a form known as an **ordered pair**. The *x*-coordinate comes first, followed by the *y*-coordinate. The ordered pair (x, y) is used to locate a point on a grid and is called the **coordinates** of the point.

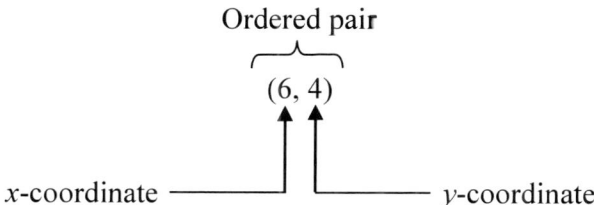

To graph an ordered pair (x, y), start at the origin and move "*x*" units to the right or left depending on whether "*x*" is a positive or negative number. Then move "*y*" units up or down depending on whether "*y*" is a positive or negative number. The dot drawn at the coordinates of a point in the plane is the graph of that ordered pair (x, y).

<u>Example 1:</u> Graph the ordered pair: $(3, -2)$

Solution:

The *x*-coordinate is a positive 3, so we start at the origin and move 3 units to the right along the *x*-axis.

Then, since the y-coordinate is a negative 2, start at the place we left off along the *x*-axis and move down 2 units.

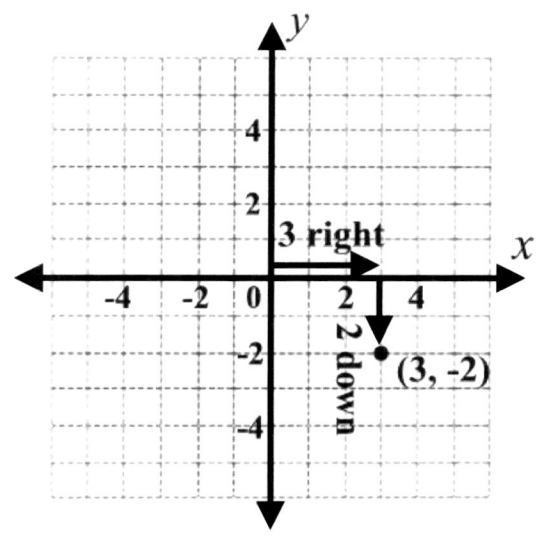

<u>Example 2:</u> Graph the ordered pair: $(5, 0)$

Solution:

The *x*-coordinate is a positive 5, so we start at the origin and move 5 units to the right along the *x*-axis.

Then, since the y-coordinate is a 0, starting at the place we left off along the *x*-axis, we don't move at all up or down. That is, we move 0 units.

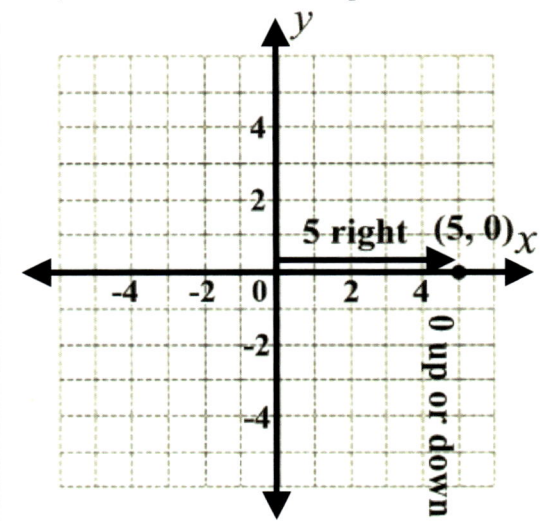

When graphing points, the extra arrows are not needed. These arrows are provided as guides to help you understand where to graph the given point.

<u>Example 3:</u> Graph all of the following ordered pairs on the same graph: $(-4, 2)$, $(4, 3)$, $(0, 5)$ and $(-2, -5)$

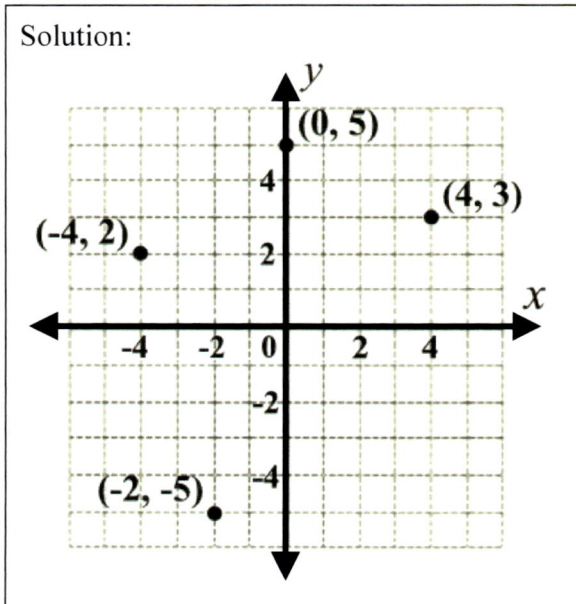

The numbers directly below the *x*-axis, and immediately to the left of the *y*-axis, indicate the **scale** of each axis. For these graphs, both the *x*-axis and the *y*-axis have a scale where 1 side of each square on the grid stands for 1 unit. Much of the graphing that we will do in this chapter will use this scale. However, there are times when it is necessary to use a different scale than this. In fact, sometimes the scale on the *x*-axis needs to be different than the scale on the *y*-axis.

Now try problem 11 from exercise set 4.3

Plotting points is a way of showing the relationship between two variables. There are many types of these relationships and they are used in a variety of applications. Some examples of these applications are the following:

A market analyst wants to know the relationship between the price per pound of coffee and the amount of coffee that can be sold at that price.

A dentist wants to know the relationship between the frequency that his patients receive fluoride treatments and the decrease in the number of cavities they get as a result of these treatments.

Once data of this type is collected, the relationships between the two variables form sets of ordered pairs. These ordered pairs are then plotted on a graph. This graph is called a **scatterplot**. In the area of mathematics known as statistics, the information on a scatterplot is studied by means of **regression analysis**. This process determines the best way to use the information to make future predictions based on the given data. At this time however, we will limit ourselves to the making of scatterplots and save the regression analysis for a later course.

The following table gives data comparing the number of calories in a 12 fluid ounce serving of a soft drink and the milligrams of sodium also contained in that serving.

Calories per serving, x	160	140	150	140	170	160	140	140	170	150	0
Mg of sodium per serving, y	60	50	55	70	35	50	75	60	45	35	35

The scatterplot for this set of data looks as follows:

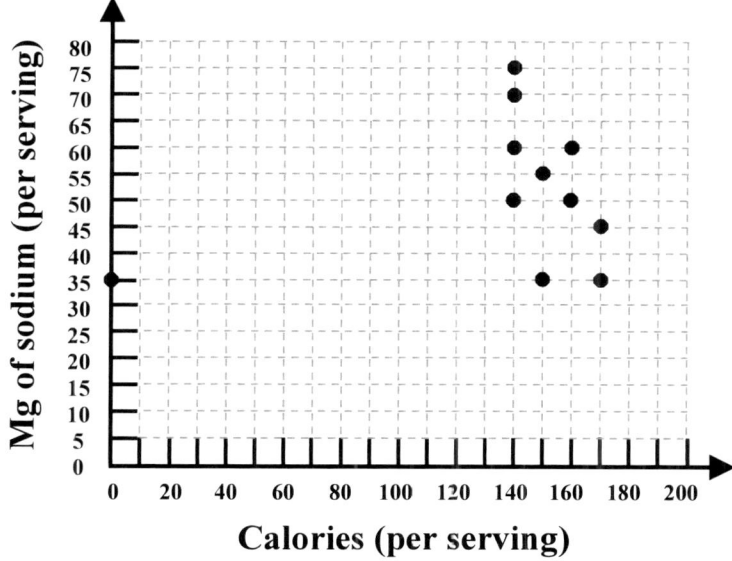

Each ordered pair in the table represents the sodium content and the calorie content of a serving of a different kind of soft drink. For example (170, 35) indicates a soft drink with 170 calories and 35 mg of sodium. This also corresponds to the point on the scatterplot that has the coordinates (170, 35).

What do you think is different about the soft drink represented by the ordered pair (0, 35)?

<u>Example 4:</u> A physician collects data on the age of people and their corresponding weights. The data are recorded in the following table. Graph the scatterplot that corresponds to the table.

Age in years, x	16	19	13	17	14	18	15	17	15	20
Weight in pounds, y	120	110	95	125	100	130	100	130	120	135

Solution:

Graph the ordered pairs on the rectangular coordinate system. The x-axis becomes "Age in years" and the y-axis becomes "Weight in pounds."

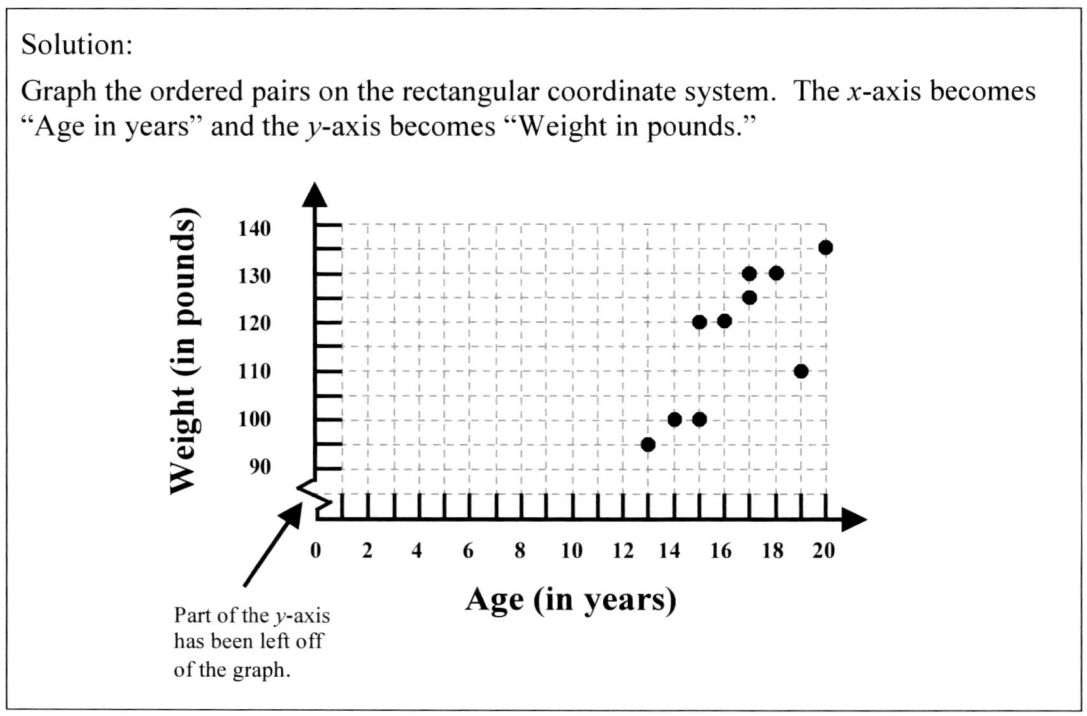

Part of the y-axis has been left off of the graph.

Now try problem 39 from exercise set 4.3

<u>Example 5:</u> To determine the relationship between a newborn baby's weight in pounds and length in inches, a nurse gathered data, illustrated in the scatterplot below. The weight of one of the newborn babies was 7.75 pounds. What was the length of this newborn baby?

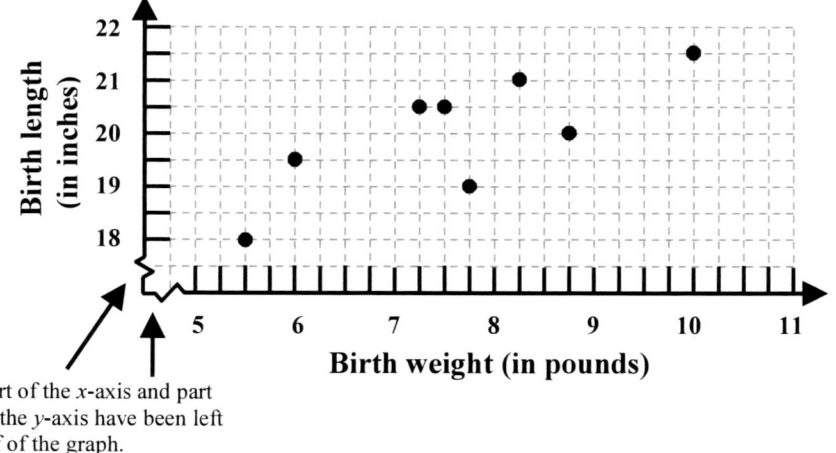

Part of the x-axis and part of the y-axis have been left off of the graph.

Solution:

Locate 7.75 pounds on the x-axis and then follow the vertical line up to the point on the scatterplot. Next follow the horizontal line that passes through the point until you reach the y-axis. This gives a y-coordinate of 19 inches. The coordinates of the point are $(7.75, 19)$ and **the length of the newborn baby is 19 inches**.

Section 3 exercises.

1.   What are the signs of the coordinates of any point located in Quadrant I?

2.   What are the signs of the coordinates of any point located in Quadrant II?

3.   What are the signs of the coordinates of any point located in Quadrant III?

4.   What are the signs of the coordinates of any point located in Quadrant IV?

In which quadrant is each point located?

5. $(4, -6)$ 6. $(-6, 4)$ 7. $(7, 1)$

8. $(-5, -4)$ 9. $(0, 2)$ 10. $(-3, 0)$

Graph each set of ordered pairs on a different graph.

11. $(2, 5)$, $(2, -4)$, $(-2, 5)$, and $(-2, -4)$.   12. $(6, 1)$, $(-3, -1)$, $(1, -6)$, and $(-1, 6)$.

13. $(-4, -4)$, $(0, 0)$, $(2, \frac{3}{2})$, and $(-5, 3)$.   14. $(0, -3)$, $(4, 4)$, $(3, \frac{1}{2})$, and $(-1, 5)$.

15. $(2, -1.5)$, $(5, -3)$, $(3, 6)$, and $(0, 3)$.   16. $(1.5, -2)$, $(1, -1)$, $(6, 2)$, and $(2, 0)$.

17. $(-\frac{3}{2}, -5)$, $(0, -4)$, $(-3, -2)$, and $(6, 4)$.   18. $(-\frac{5}{2}, 2)$, $(0, 0)$, $(5, -4)$, and $(2, 3)$.

19. $(-6, 5)$, $(-2, 0)$, $(1, -3)$, and $(-1, 4)$.   20. $(3, -5)$, $(-5, 0)$, $(4, -3)$, and $(-6, 3)$.

For exercises 21-30, list the ordered pair that corresponds to each numbered point on the graph below.

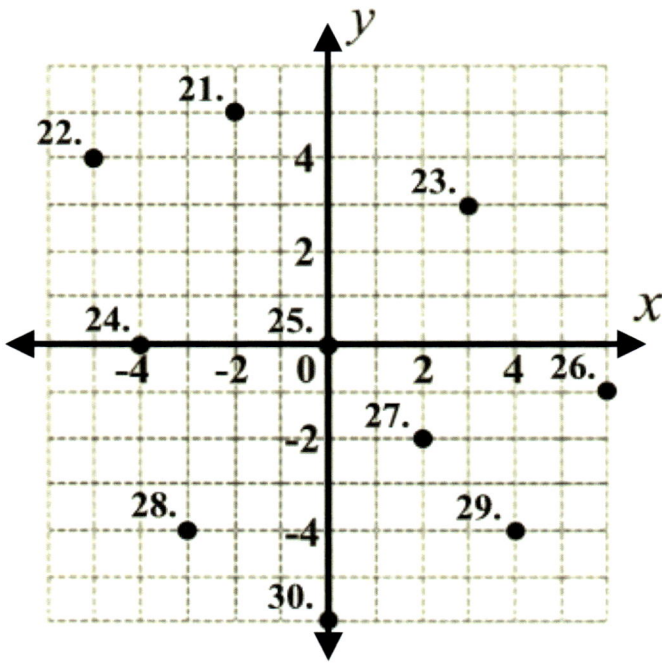

Plot the points $(5, 4)$ and $(-1, 1)$ on the same graph and then draw a straight line that passes through both of them. Now, answer the following questions.

31.   Does the point $(1, 2)$ lie on the line?

32.   Does the point $(-3, 0)$ lie on the line?

33.   Does the point $(0, -3)$ lie on the line?

34.   Does the point $(-5, 2)$ lie on the line?

Plot the points $(-2, 5)$ and $(2, -3)$ on the same graph and then draw a straight line that passes through both of them. Now, answer the following questions.

35.   Does the point $(0, 0)$ lie on the line?

36.   Does the point $(1, -1)$ lie on the line?

37.   Does the point $(0, 1)$ lie on the line?

38.   Does the point $(-1, -3)$ lie on the line?

39. The following table gives data comparing the number of calories in a serving of breakfast cereal and the number of grams of total carbohydrate also contained in that serving.

Calories per serving, x	120	200	130	130	190	120	100	130	110	110	150
Grams of total carbohydrate per serving, y	28	35	26	30	44	25	22	24	23	26	27

On a piece of graph paper, reproduce the scatterplot below and graph the ordered pairs from the table above.

40. The following table gives data comparing the engine size of cars (in liters) and their highway gas mileage (in miles per gallon).

Engine size (in liters), x	1.5	1.5	1.8	3.4	2.7	3.8	2.0	2.2	2.4	2.5	2.4	3.5
Highway gas mileage (in miles per gallon), y	38	35	36	32	29	29	34	34	24	22	27	24

On a piece of graph paper, reproduce the scatterplot below and graph the ordered pairs from the table above.

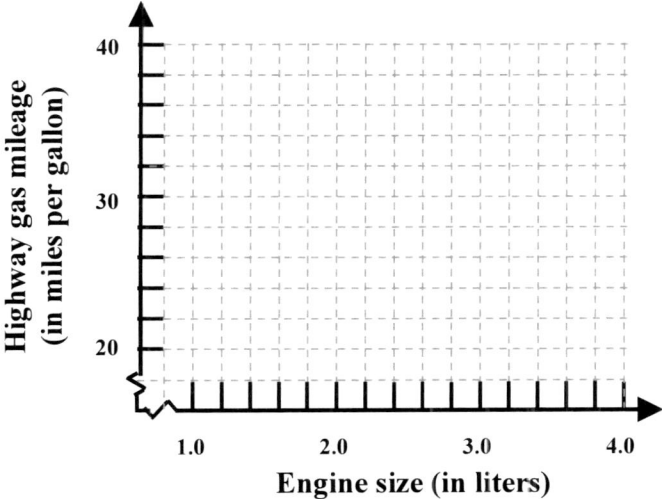

41.   The following table gives data comparing the size of a color television (in inches) and its price (in dollars).

Color television size (in inches), x	15	27	24	15	20	20	13	13	20	14	20	17
Price (in dollars), y	250	250	175	225	400	100	50	75	350	75	125	300

On a piece of graph paper, reproduce the scatterplot below and graph the ordered pairs from the table above.

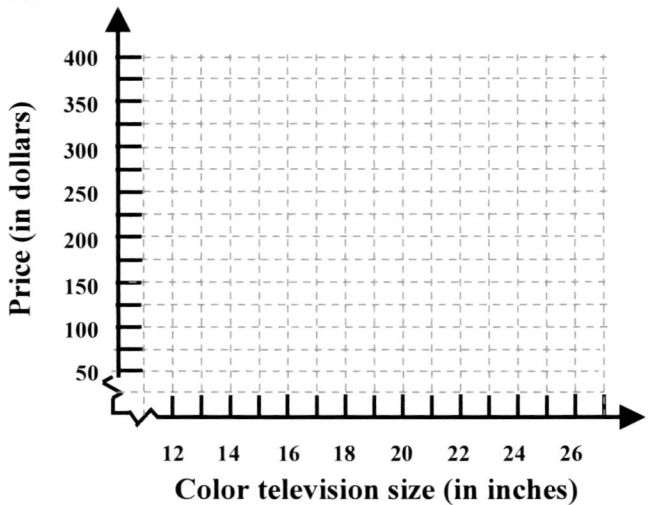

42.   The following table gives data comparing the calendar years from 1990 to 1998 with the average price of a gallon of gas (in dollars per gallon).

Calendar year, x	'90	'91	'92	'93	'94	'95	'96	'97	'98
Average price of a gallon of gas (in dollars per gallon), y	1.09	1.15	1.10	1.22	1.21	1.23	1.32	1.33	1.16

On a piece of graph paper, reproduce the scatterplot below and graph the ordered pairs from the table above.

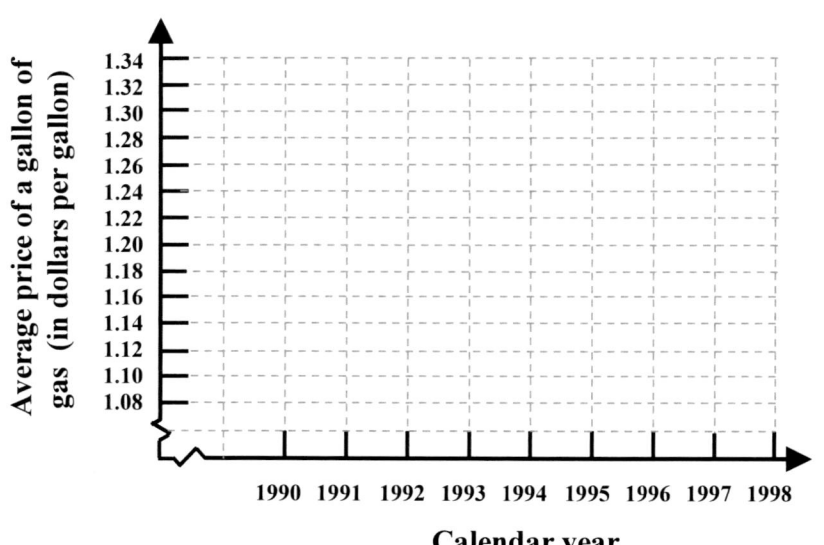

43.   The scatterplot below shows a comparison of the calendar years from 1980 to 1990 with the average price of white bread (in cents per pound).

a)   During what calendar year(s) was the average price of white bread 54 cents per pound?

b)   During what calendar year(s) was the average price of white bread 61 cents per pound?

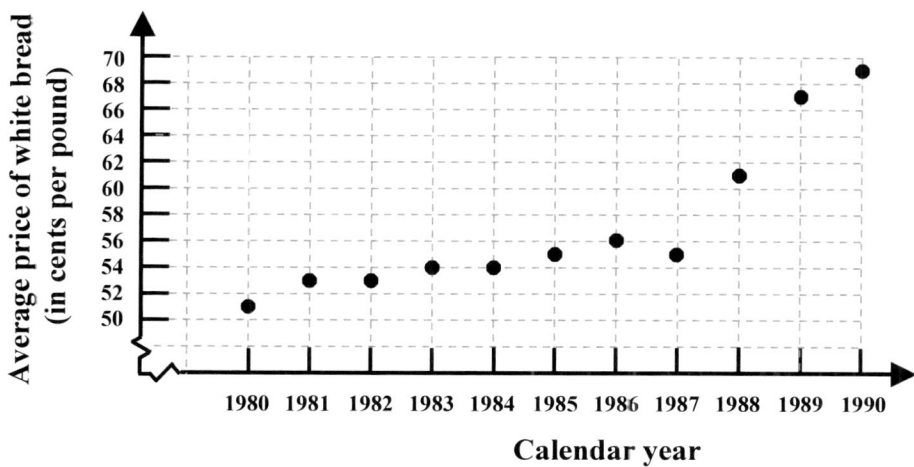

44.   The scatterplot below shows a comparison of the calendar years from 1990 to 1998 with the average cost of electricity (in cents per kilowatt-hour).

a)   During what calendar year(s) was the average price of electricity 8.7 cents per kilowatt-hour?

b)   During what calendar year(s) was the average price of electricity 8.8 cents per kilowatt-hour?

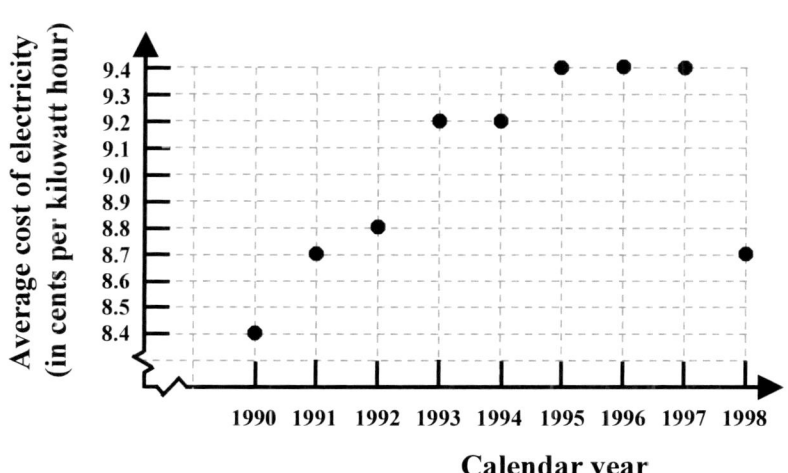

Writing:

For each of the following problems, use a piece of graph paper to create a scatterplot complete with labels and a scale for each axis. Then, using this scatterplot, graph the ordered pairs from each table provided. Explain how you determined what scale to use on each axis

45.   The following table gives data comparing the calendar years from 1996 to 2005 with the average price of red delicious apples (in dollars per pound).

Calendar year, x	'96	'97	'98	'99	'00	'01	'02	'03	'04	'05
Average price of red delicious apples (in dollars per pound), y	0.88	0.91	0.92	0.86	0.95	0.81	0.88	0.98	1.02	0.97

46.   The following table gives data comparing the calendar years from 1997 to 2006 with the average price of whole milk (in dollars per gallon).

Calendar year, x	'97	'98	'99	'00	'01	'02	'03	'04	'05	'06
Average price of whole milk (in dollars per gallon), y	2.68	2.63	2.94	2.79	2.85	2.81	2.69	2.88	3.30	3.20

47.   The following table gives data comparing the time (in minutes) for beginning algebra students to complete a math test and the score they received on that test (as a percent).

Time to complete test (in minutes), x	20	23	25	25	26	29	35	35	40	23	26	28	29	35	40	20
Score on test (as a percent), y	75	72	80	86	80	79	76	79	84	90	90	81	88	88	88	81

48.   The following table gives data comparing the time (in minutes) for intermediate algebra students to complete a math test and the score they received on that test (as a percent).

Time to complete test (in minutes), x	54	47	46	44	43	53	55	50	40	47	52	54	47	46	49	51
Score on test (as a percent), y	97	85	91	86	92	86	83	78	88	94	93	78	80	94	75	84

FORMULAS
& GRAPHING

Section 4: Ordered Pairs as Solutions to Equations

This section will focus on the idea of completing ordered pairs by use of an equation. In section 2 we used the equation $y = 3x + 2$ to find the values of y under the given conditions. (See problems 25-28 on page 333). These conditions were $x = -2$, $x = -1$, $x = 0$, and $x = 1$. As each new x-value was substituted into the same equation, a new y-value resulted. These combinations of x-value inputs and y-value outputs are, in fact, ordered pairs. By continuing to put different values for x into the equation $y = 3x - 2$, we could get an infinite set of ordered pairs as solutions of the equation.

Example 1: For the equation $y = 5x - 4$, complete the ordered pairs: $(2, \quad)$, $(-3, \quad)$, $(\quad , -4)$

Solution:

Since the x-coordinate of the first ordered pair is 2, we replace x in the equation $y = 5x - 4$ with a 2.   The equation then becomes

$y = 5(2) - 4$ which simplifies to

$y = 6$.   Thus, **the first ordered pair is (2, 6)**.

Since the x-coordinate of the second ordered pair is -3, we replace x in the equation $y = 5x - 4$ with a -3.   The equation then becomes

$y = 5(-3) - 4$ which simplifies to

$y = -19$.   Thus, **the second ordered pair is (−3, −19)**.

Since the y-coordinate of the third ordered pair is -4, we replace y in the equation $y = 5x - 4$ with a -4.   The equation then becomes

$-4 = 5x - 4$.   In order to isolate x we add 4 to both sides of the equation.

$-4 + 4 = 5x - 4 + 4$ becomes

$0 = 5x$.   Dividing both sides of the equation by 5, we get

$\dfrac{0}{5} = \dfrac{5x}{5}$ which simplifies to

$0 = x$ or $x = 0$.   Thus, **the third ordered pair is (0, −4)**.

Now try problem 1 from exercise set 4.4

<u>Example 2:</u> For the equation $3x + 2y = 6$, complete the given table.

x	y
3	
	0
	−6

Solution: Filling the table is the same as completing the ordered pairs, $(3,\ )$, $(\ ,0)$, $(\ ,-6)$. So, we will proceed as in example 1. Since the x-coordinate of the first ordered pair is 3, we replace x in the equation $3x + 2y = 6$ with a 3. The equation then becomes

$3(3) + 2y = 6$ which simplifies to

$9 + 2y = 6$.   In order to isolate y, we subtract 9 from both sides of the equation.

$9 - 9 + 2y = 6 - 9$ becomes

$2y = -3$.   Now, dividing both sides of the equation by 2 we get

$\dfrac{2y}{2} = \dfrac{-3}{2}$ which simplifies to

$y = -\dfrac{3}{2}$.   So, **the first ordered pair is** $\left(3, -\dfrac{3}{2}\right)$.

Since the y-coordinate of the second ordered pair is 0, we replace y in the equation $3x + 2y = 6$ with a 0.   The equation then becomes

$3x + 2(0) = 6$ which simplifies to

$3x = 6$.   Dividing both sides of the equation by 3, we get

$\dfrac{3x}{3} = \dfrac{6}{3}$ which simplifies to

$x = 2$.   So, **the second ordered pair is** $(2, 0)$.

Since the y-coordinate of the third ordered pair is -6, we replace y in the equation $3x + 2y = 6$ with a -6.   The equation then becomes

$3x + 2(-6) = 6$ which simplifies to

$3x - 12 = 6$.   In order to isolate x, we add 12 to both sides of the equation.

$3x - 12 + 12 = 6 + 12$ becomes

$3x = 18$.   Dividing both sides of the equation by 3, we get

$\dfrac{3x}{3} = \dfrac{18}{3}$ which simplifies to

$x = 6$.   So, **the third ordered pair is** $(6, -6)$.

The completed table is as follows:

x	y
3	−3/2
2	0
6	−6

<u>Example 3:</u> Which of the following ordered pairs $(-2, -6)$, $(-1, 2)$, $(-3, -10)$, and $(0, 6)$ are solutions of the equation $y = 4x + 2$?

Solution: The way to determine if an ordered pair is a solution of an equation is to substitute the ordered pair into the equation and see if it makes the resulting equation a true statement.

To test the ordered pair $(-2, -6)$, substitute -2 in the place of x and -6 in the place of y.

$y = 4x + 2$ becomes

$(-6) = 4(-2) + 2$ which simplifies to

$-6 = -6$. Since this is a true statement, **$(-2, -6)$ is a solution**.

To test the ordered pair $(-1, 2)$, substitute -1 in the place of x and 2 in the place of y.

$y = 4x + 2$ becomes

$(2) = 4(-1) + 2$ which simplifies to

$2 = -2$. Since this is a false statement, **$(-1, 2)$ is not a solution**.

To test the ordered pair $(-3, -10)$, substitute -3 in the place of x and -10 in the place of y.

$y = 4x + 2$ becomes

$(-10) = 4(-3) + 2$ which simplifies to

$-10 = -10$. Since this is a true statement, **$(-3, -10)$ is a solution**.

To test the ordered pair $(0, 6)$, substitute 0 in the place of x and 6 in the place of y.

$y = 4x + 2$ becomes

$(6) = 4(0) + 2$ which simplifies to

$6 = 2$. Since this is a false statement, **$(0, 6)$ is not a solution**.

*Now try problem 27 from exercise set 4.4

Section 4 exercises.

For each of the following equations, complete the given ordered pairs.

1. $4x + y = 12$ $(0, \ )$, $(-3, \ )$, $(\ , -8)$

2. $6x - y = 10$ $(1, \ )$, $(0, \ )$, $(\ , 8)$

3. $5x + 3y = 15$ $(0, \ )$, $(\ , 0)$, $(\ , -5)$

4. $7x + 2y = 14$ $(2, \ )$, $(\ , -7)$, $(0, \ )$

5. $y = 3x - 5$ $(4, \ )$, $(\ , 4)$, $(\ , 0)$

6. $y = 4x + 3$ $(-2, \ )$, $(\ , 0)$, $(\ , -9)$

7. $x = 3y - 4$ $(\ , 0.6)$, $(-1.6, \ )$, $(0, \ )$

8. $x = 2y + 5$ $(0, \ )$, $(-0.8, \ )$, $(\ , 0.7)$

9. $y = \dfrac{2}{3}x - 4$ $(6, \ )$, $(-3, \ )$, $(\ , -8)$

10. $y = \dfrac{1}{2}x + 5$ $(-4, \ )$, $(8, \ )$, $(\ , 0)$

11. $x = 4$ $(\ , 7)$, $\left(\ , -\dfrac{1}{3} \right)$, $(\ , 0)$

12. $y = -3$ $(-5, \ )$, $(0, \ )$, $\left(\dfrac{1}{2}, \ \right)$

13. $y + 2x = 8$ $(0, \ )$, $(\ , 0)$, $(3, \ )$

14. $y - 5x = 12$ $(\ , 0)$, $(-2, \ )$, $(1, \ )$

For each of the following equations, complete the given table.

15. $y = 2x$

x	y
3	
-4	
	-4
	8

16. $y = -3x$

x	y
-5	
0	
	12
	-6

17. $y = -4x$

x	y
0	
	2
-3	
	-16

18. $y = 5x$

x	y
-2	
	0
4	
	1

19. $x = -y$

x	y
	2
	-3
-5	
6	

20. $x = 3y$

x	y
	4
	6
-12	
0	

21. $x - y = 10$

x	y
5	
-3	
7	
	4

22. $x + y = 6$

x	y
0	
2	
-8	
	-4

23. $3x - 4y = 12$

x	y
0	
	0
	6
-4	

24. $2x - 5y = 10$

x	y
-5	
	6
	0
0	

25. $y = -3x - 7$

x	y
-2	
	0
1/2	
	4

26. $y = -6x + 2$

x	y
5	
	0
-3/4	
	4

For each of the following equations, tell which of the given ordered pairs are solutions.

27. $y + 3x = -7$ $(-2, -1)$, $(-7, 0)$, $\left(\dfrac{3}{4}, -\dfrac{37}{4}\right)$

28. $y + 2x = -5$ $(-3, 1)$, $\left(\dfrac{9}{16}, -\dfrac{49}{8}\right)$, $(-1, -7)$

29. $y = 4x$ $(2, 8)$, $(0, 0)$, $(-3, 12)$

30. $y = -6x$ $(0, 0)$, $(3, 18)$, $(2, -12)$

31. $y = \dfrac{4}{5}x - 3$ $(10, 5)$, $(2.5, -1)$, $(20, -13)$

32. $y = \dfrac{2}{7}x - 4$ $(14, 0)$, $\left(\dfrac{14}{3}, \dfrac{8}{3}\right)$, $(21, 2)$

33. $y = 6$ $(-2, -6)$, $(6, 3)$, $(2, 6)$

34. $x = -5$ $(-5, 3)$, $(4, -5)$, $\left(-5, \dfrac{2}{3}\right)$

35. $x - y = 0$ $(-3, 3)$, $(4, 4)$, $\left(\dfrac{2}{3}, \dfrac{3}{2}\right)$

36. $x + y = 10$ $(7, 3)$, $(5, -5)$, $(3.5, 6.5)$

FORMULAS & GRAPHING

Section 5: Graphing Linear Equations

In previous sections we looked at graphing ordered pairs on the rectangular coordinate system, as well as creating ordered pairs from a given equation. In this section we will put the two ideas together by graphing the ordered pairs, or solutions, created from given equations.

Example 1: For the equation $x + y = 3$, complete the ordered pairs: $(0, \quad)$, $(2, \quad)$, $(4, \quad)$, $(6, \quad)$ Then, graph the ordered pairs on the rectangular coordinate system.

Solution:	
Since the x-coordinate of the first ordered pair is 0, replace x in the equation $x + y = 3$ with a 0. The equation then becomes	
$0 + y = 3$	which simplifies to
$y = 3$.	Thus, the first ordered pair is $(0, 3)$.
The x-coordinate of the second ordered pair is 2, so replace x in the equation $x + y = 3$ with a 2. The equation then becomes	
$2 + y = 3$.	In order to isolate y, subtract 2 from both sides of the equation.
$2 - 2 + y = 3 - 2$	becomes
$y = 1$.	Thus, the second ordered pair is $(2, 1)$.
The x-coordinate of the third ordered pair is 4, so replace x in the equation $x + y = 3$ with a 4. The equation then becomes	
$4 + y = 3$.	In order to isolate y, subtract 4 from both sides of the equation.
$4 - 4 + y = 3 - 4$	becomes
$y = -1$.	Thus, the third ordered pair is $(4, -1)$.
The x-coordinate of the fourth ordered pair is 6, so replace x in the equation $x + y = 3$ with a 6. The equation then becomes	
$6 + y = 3$.	In order to isolate y, subtract 6 from both sides of the equation.
$6 - 6 + y = 3 - 6$	becomes
$y = -3$.	Thus, the fourth ordered pair is $(6, -3)$.
<div align="center">**Problem continued on next page.**</div>	

Problem continued from previous page.

Next, graph these ordered pairs $(0,3)$, $(2,1)$, $(4,-1)$, and $(6,-3)$ on the rectangular coordinate system.

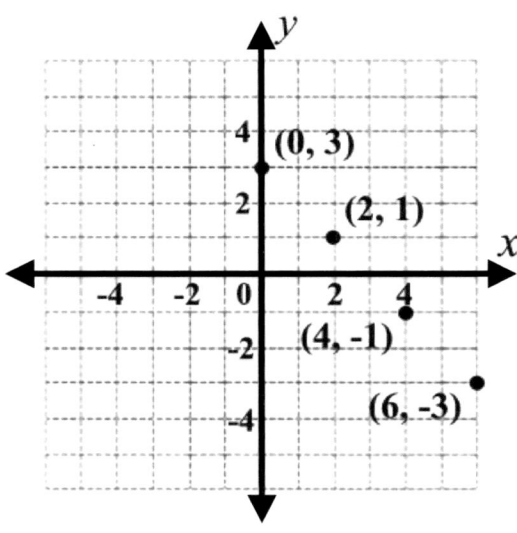

Do you notice anything about the four ordered pair solutions? It is not a coincidence that they form a straight line. In fact, if we were to find all the ordered pairs that are solutions of the equation $x + y = 3$ and then plot them on the same graph, they would form a solid straight line.

Here is the complete set of solutions to the equation $x + y = 3$.

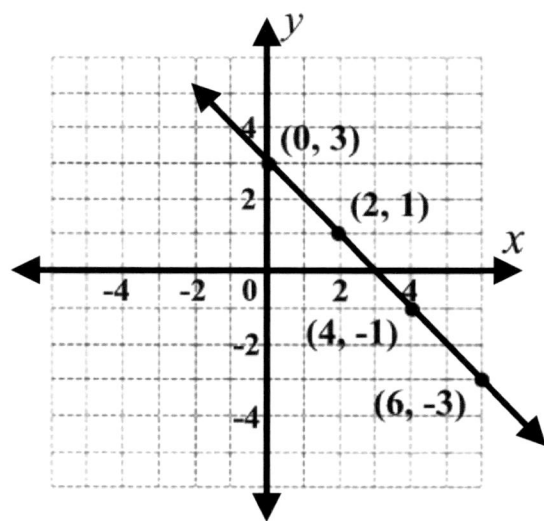

Because of the fact that the solution set of points for the equation $x + y = 3$ forms a straight line, this type of equation is known as a **linear equation in two variables**.

Now try problem 13 from exercise set 4.5

A **linear equation in two variables** is any equation that can be written in the form $ax + by = c$ where a, b, and c are real numbers and a and b are not both 0. The graph of a linear equation is a straight line.

Example 2: Which of the following equations are linear and consequently produce a graph that is a straight line?

a) $y = 2x - 5$

b) $3y = 4x^2 + 7$

c) $y = 3$

d) $y = \dfrac{1}{x + 4}$

e) $2x - 3y = -1$

Solution:

a) $y = 2x - 5$ **is a linear equation.** By subtracting $2x$ from both sides of the equation we get $-2x + y = -5$. a is -2, b is 1, and c is -5.

b) $3y = 4x^2 + 7$ **is not a linear equation.** The variable x has an exponent of 2. All linear equation variables must have an exponent of 1.

c) $y = 3$ **is a linear equation.** a is 0, b is 1, and c is 3. (Think $0x + y = 3$.)

d) $y = \dfrac{1}{x + 4}$ **is not a linear equation.** The variable x is in the denominator and therefore the equation can't be written as $ax + by = c$.

e) $2x - 3y = -1$ **is a linear equation.** a is 2, b is -3, and c is -1.

Now try problem 1 from exercise set 4.5

Steps for drawing the straight-line solution to a linear equation:

Step 1: Find three ordered pair solutions to the given linear equation.

Step 2: Graph the three ordered pairs found in step 1 on the rectangular coordinate system.

Step 3: Draw a straight line through the three points graphed in step 2.

Example 3: Graph the equation: $2x + 3y = 12$

Solution: **Step 1:** To graph the equation we must find three ordered pairs. We can choose any value of x, or any value of y, and then complete the ordered pairs. If we complete the following table, we will have all the information we need to form the graph.

x	y
0	
	0
-3	

Since the x-coordinate of the first ordered pair is 0, we replace x in the equation $2x + 3y = 12$ with a 0. The equation then becomes

$2(0) + 3y = 12$ which simplifies to

$3y = 12$.   Dividing both sides of the equation by 3, we get

$\dfrac{3y}{3} = \dfrac{12}{3}$ which simplifies to

$y = 4$.   Thus, the first ordered pair is **(0, 4)**.

The y-coordinate of the second ordered pair is 0, so replace y in the equation $2x + 3y = 12$ with a 0.   The equation then becomes

$2x + 3(0) = 12$.   which simplifies to

$2x = 12$.   Dividing both sides of the equation by 2, we get

$\dfrac{2x}{2} = \dfrac{12}{2}$ which simplifies to

$x = 6$.   Thus, the second ordered pair is **(6, 0)**.

The x-coordinate of the third ordered pair is -3, so replace x in the equation $2x + 3y = 12$ with a -3.   The equation then becomes

$2(-3) + 3y = 12$.   which simplifies to

$-6 + 3y = 12$.   In order to isolate y, we add 6 to both sides of the equation.

$-6 + 6 + 3y = 12 + 6$ becomes

$3y = 18$.   Dividing both sides of the equation by 3, we get

$\dfrac{3y}{3} = \dfrac{18}{3}$ which simplifies to

$y = 6$.   Thus, the third ordered pair is **(−3, 6)**.

Problem continued on next page.

Problem continued from previous page.

The completed table is as follows:

x	y
0	4
6	0
−3	6

Step 2: Plot the points on the graph.

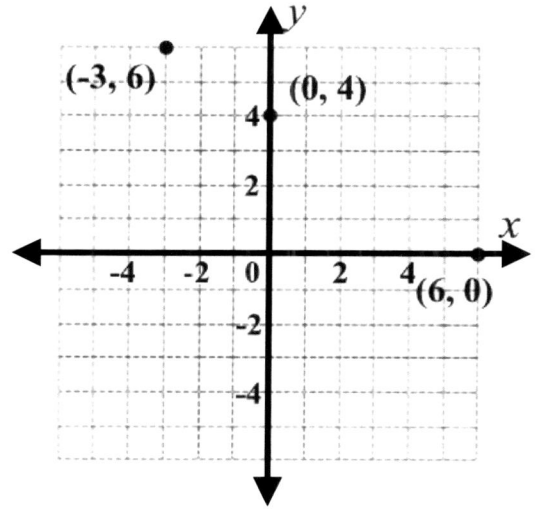

Step 3: Draw a line through the points.

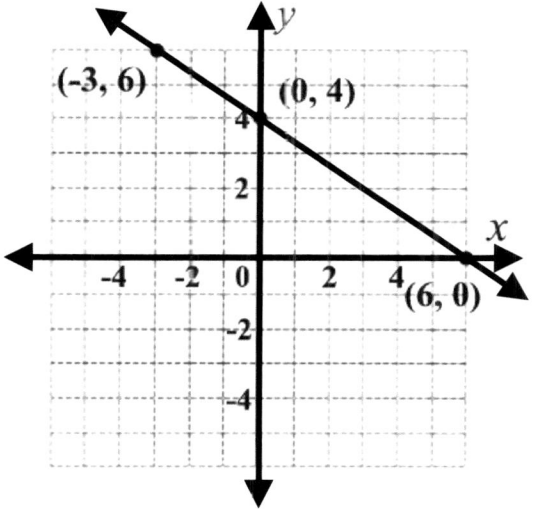

Now try problem 43 from exercise set 4.5

Example 4: Graph the equation: $y = \dfrac{1}{2}x + 4$

Solution: **Step 1:** To graph the equation we must find three ordered pairs. We can choose any value of x, or any value of y, and then complete the ordered pairs. Since this equation is in a form where y is isolated, it would be easier to choose x-values to start with and then solve for the corresponding y-values. Also, because the coefficient of the x term is a fraction, $\dfrac{1}{2}$, it would be best to choose x-values that are multiples of 2. When the right side of the equation is simplified each time, it will produce an integer instead of a fraction. This will make it easier to graph.

x	y
0	
2	
4	

Since the x-coordinate of the first ordered pair is 0, replace x in the equation $y = \dfrac{1}{2}x + 4$ with a 0. The equation then becomes

$y = \dfrac{1}{2}(0) + 4$ which simplifies to

$y = 4$. Thus, the first ordered pair is $(0, 4)$.

The x-coordinate of the second ordered pair is 2, so replace y in the equation $y = \dfrac{1}{2}x + 4$ with a 2.   The equation then becomes

$y = \dfrac{1}{2}(2) + 4$ which simplifies to

$y = 1 + 4$. This simplifies further to

$y = 5$. Thus, the second ordered pair is $(2, 5)$.

The x-coordinate of the third ordered pair is 4, so replace x in the equation $y = \dfrac{1}{2}x + 4$ with a 4.   The equation then becomes

$y = \dfrac{1}{2}(4) + 4$ which simplifies to

$y = 2 + 4$. This simplifies further to

$y = 6$. Thus, the third ordered pair is $(4, 6)$.

Problem continued on next page.

Problem continued from previous page.

The completed table is as follows:

x	y
0	4
2	5
4	6

Step 2: Plot the points on the graph.

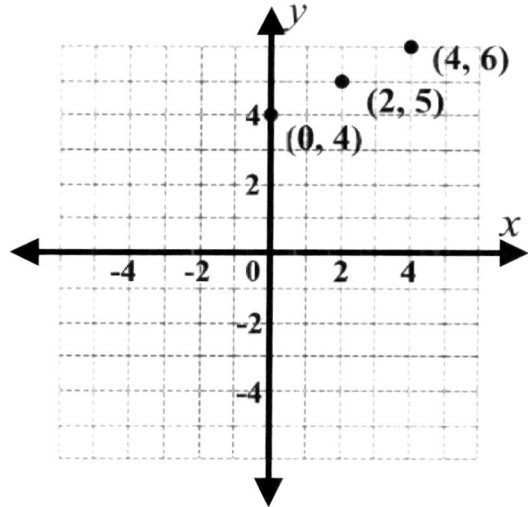

Step 3: Draw a line through the points.

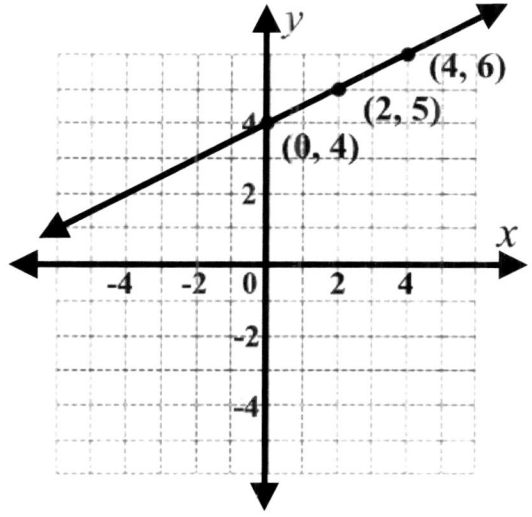

Now try problem 37 from exercise set 4.5

Example 5: Graph the equation: $x = -4$

Solution: To graph the equation we must find three ordered pairs. No matter what value of y we choose, x will still be equal to -4. If we complete the following table, we will have all the information we need to form the graph.

x	y
-4	
-4	
-4	

becomes

x	y
-4	1
-4	3
-4	5

and the graph is a vertical line.

Now try problem 39 from exercise set 4.5

Example 6: Graph the equation: $y = 3$

Solution: To graph the equation we must find three ordered pairs. No matter what value of x we choose, y will still be equal to 3. If we complete the following table, we will have all the information we need to form the graph.

x	y
	3
	3
	3

becomes

x	y
-4	3
-2	3
-5	3

and the graph is a horizontal line.

Now try problem 45 from exercise set 4.5

<u>Example 7:</u> Graph the equation: $2x - 3y = 6$

Solution: **<u>Step 1:</u>** To graph the equation we must find three ordered pairs. We can choose any value of x, or any value of y, and then complete the ordered pairs. However, if we first put the equation in the form where y is isolated, it will be easier to choose x-values to start with and then solve for the corresponding y-values.

$2x - 3y = 6$ In order to isolate y, we subtract $2x$ from both sides of the equation.

$2x - 2x - 3y = -2x + 6$ becomes

$-3y = -2x + 6$.   Dividing both sides of the equation by -3, we get

$\dfrac{-3y}{-3} = \dfrac{-2x}{-3} + \dfrac{6}{-3}$ which simplifies to

$y = \dfrac{2}{3}x - 2$.   Since the coefficient of the x term is a fraction, $\dfrac{2}{3}$, it will be best to choose x-values that are multiples of 3. In doing so, when the right side of the equation is simplified each time, it will produce an integer instead of a fraction. This will be easier to graph.

x	y
-3	
0	
3	

Since the x-coordinate of the first ordered pair is -3, we replace x in the equation $y = \dfrac{2}{3}x - 2$ with a -3.

The equation then becomes

$y = \dfrac{2}{3}(-3) - 2$ which simplifies to

$y = -2 - 2$.   This simplifies further to

$y = -4$ Thus, the first ordered pair is **$(-3, -4)$**.

The x-coordinate of the second ordered pair is 0, so replace x in the equation $y = \dfrac{2}{3}x - 2$ with a 0.

The equation then becomes

$y = \dfrac{2}{3}(0) - 2$ which simplifies to

$y = -2$.   Thus, the second ordered pair is **$(0, -2)$**.

The x-coordinate of the third ordered pair is 3, so replace x in the equation $y = \dfrac{2}{3}x - 2$ with a 3.

The equation then becomes

$y = \dfrac{2}{3}(3) - 2$ which simplifies to

$y = 2 - 2$.   This simplifies further to

$y = 0$.   Thus, the third ordered pair is **$(3, 0)$**.

<u>Problem continued on next page.</u>

Problem continued from previous page.

The completed table is as follows:

x	y
-3	-4
0	-2
3	0

Step 2: Plot the points on the graph.

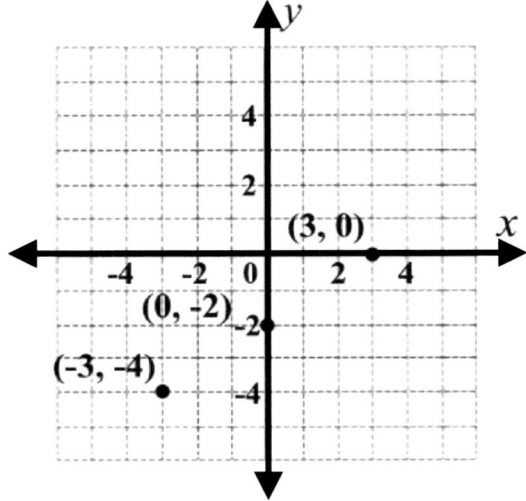

Step 3: Draw a line through the points.

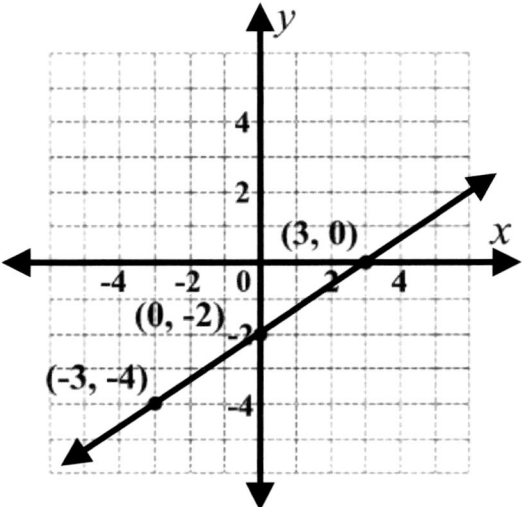

Now try problem 29 from exercise set 4.5

<u>Example 8:</u> For the given graph, what is the value of *y* when *x* is 3?

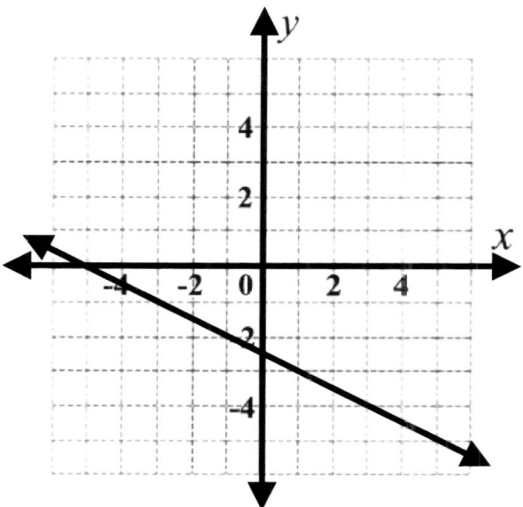

Solution: Locate 3 on the *x*-axis. Next, follow a vertical line from 3 to the point of the graph. Now follow a horizontal line from that point to the *y*-axis. The number where the horizontal line crosses the *y*-axis is the *y*-value corresponding to the *x*-value of 3.

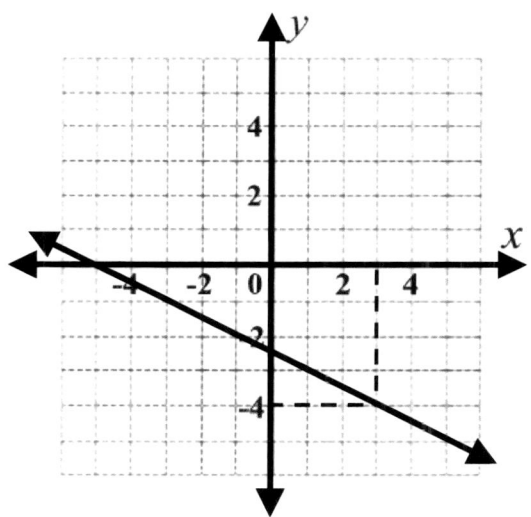

The value of *y* is -4 when *x* is 3.

Now try problem 49 from exercise set 4.5

Section 5 exercises.

Which of the following equations are linear and consequently produce a graph that is a straight line?

1. $y = x^2 + 7x + 4$ **2.** $-4x + 5y = 21$ **3.** $3x = 4 - 8y$

4. $2y = \dfrac{5}{x-9}$ **5.** $3x = 8$ **6.** $y = -\dfrac{4}{7}x + 5$

7. $y = \dfrac{3}{5}x - 6$ **8.** $-4y = 23$ **9.** $y^2 = 2x^2 - 5$

10. $x + y = -3$ **11.** $4 - y = -7x$ **12.** $x = 2y^3 - 8$

Use each equation to complete the given ordered pairs. Then use the ordered pairs to draw the graph of the equation.

13. $x + y = 5$ $(-1,\ )$, $(2,\ )$, $(\ ,4)$

14. $x - y = 6$ $(0,\ )$, $(2,\ )$, $(\ ,-5)$

15. $x - y = 7$ $(6,\ )$, $(\ ,-4)$, $(2,\ )$

16. $x + y = 2$ $(1,\ )$, $(\ ,-1)$, $(-3,\ )$

17. $y = x$ $(-2,\ )$, $(0,\ )$, $(\ ,3)$

18. $y = -x$ $(-3,\ )$, $(0,\ )$, $(\ ,2)$

19. $y = \dfrac{2}{3}x + 2$ $(-3,\ )$, $(0,\ )$, $(3,\ )$

20. $y = -\dfrac{3}{2}x - 2$ $(-2,\ )$, $(0,\ )$, $(2,\ )$

21. $2x + 3y = 6$ $(0,\ )$, $(\ ,0)$, $(\ ,4)$

22. $4x - 2y = -8$ $(0,\ )$, $(\ ,0)$, $(\ ,2)$

23. $y = 4$ $(-4,\ )$, $(2,\ )$, $(3,\ )$

24. $x = -3$ $(\ ,-3)$, $(\ ,0)$, $(\ ,5)$

25. $y = -2x + 5$ $(0,\ )$, $(\ ,0)$, $(1,\ )$

26. $y = 3x - 2$ $(0,\ )$, $(\ ,0)$, $(-1,\ )$

27. $x = 3y$ $(0,\ )$, $(\ ,-2)$, $(3,\ )$

28. $x = 2y$ $(0,\ )$, $(\ ,2)$, $(-4,\ )$

For the following problems:

a) Solve each equation for y.

b) Complete the given ordered pairs using the equation formed in part a).

c) Use the ordered pairs to graph the equation.

29. $3x + 5y = 10$ $(-5, \ )$, $(0, \ )$, $(5, \ )$

30. $5x + 3y = 12$ $(0, \ )$, $(3, \ )$, $(6, \ )$

31. $3x - 4y = 8$ $(-4, \ )$, $(0, \ )$, $(4, \ )$

32. $3x - 2y = 6$ $(-2, \ )$, $(0, \ )$, $(2, \ )$

33. $2y - x = 8$ $(-2, \ )$, $(0, \ )$, $(2, \ )$

34. $3y - x = 9$ $(-3, \ )$, $(0, \ )$, $(3, \ )$

Find three solutions to each equation. Then, use these solutions to graph the equation.

35. $y = 4x + 1$ **36.** $y = -2x + 3$

37. $y = -\dfrac{1}{3}x$ **38.** $y = 2x$

39. $x = 4$ **40.** $y = -4$

41. $2x - y = 1$ **42.** $3x - y = -1$

43. $3x - 5y = 10$ **44.** $5x + 3y = -3$

45. $y = 0$ **46.** $x = -1$

47.   For the given graph, what is the value of *y* when *x* is 0?

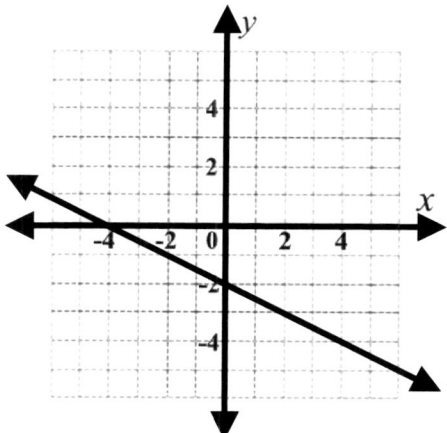

48.   For the given graph, what is the value of *y* when *x* is −2?

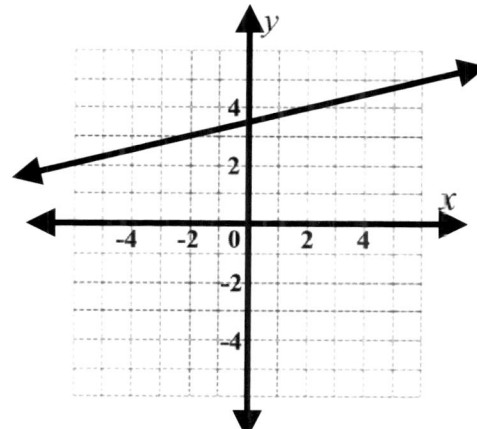

49.   For the given graph, what is the value of *y* when *x* is −4?

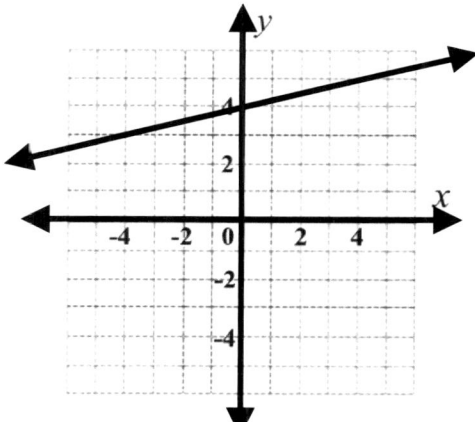

50.   For the given graph, what is the value of *y* when *x* is 5?

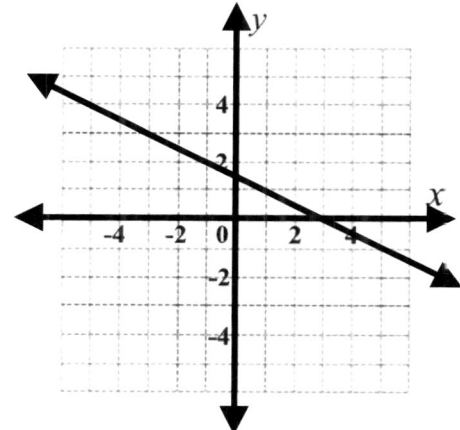

51.   For the given graph, what is the value of *y* when *x* is 2?

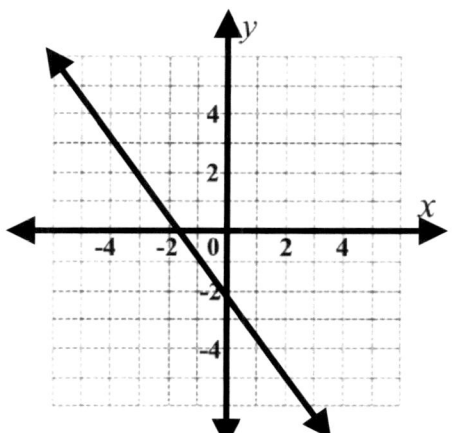

52.   For the given graph, what is the value of *y* when *x* is −3?

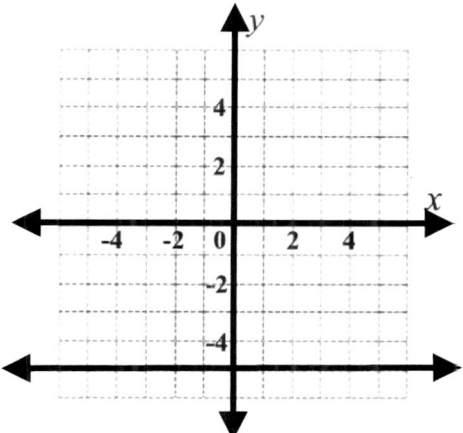

53.   For the given graph, what is the value of x when y is -1?

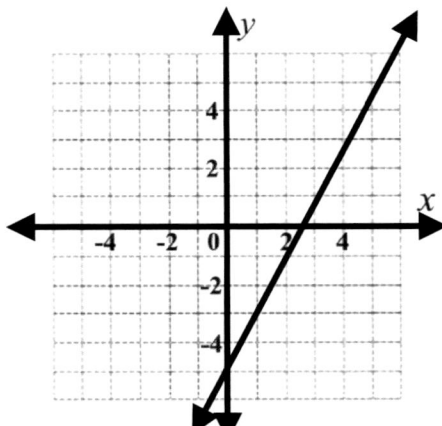

54.   For the given graph, what is the value of x when y is 4?

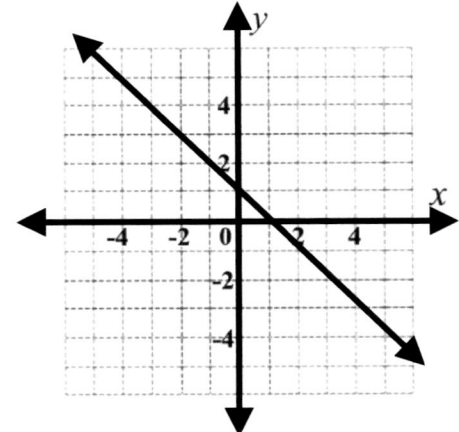

55.   For the given graph, what is the value of x when y is 3?

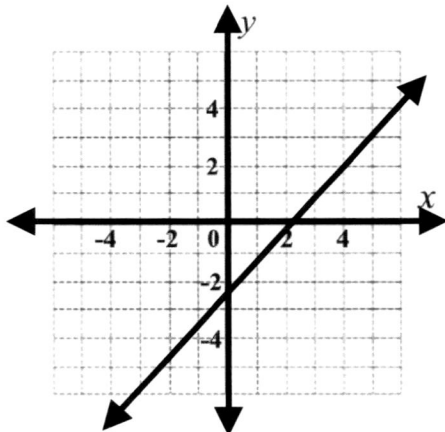

56.   For the given graph, what is the value of x when y is 0?

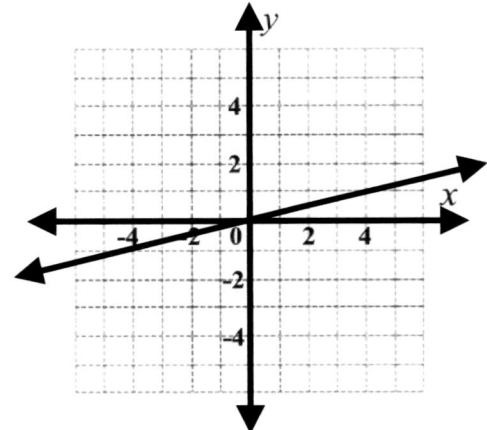

57.   For the given graph, what is the value of x when y is 5?

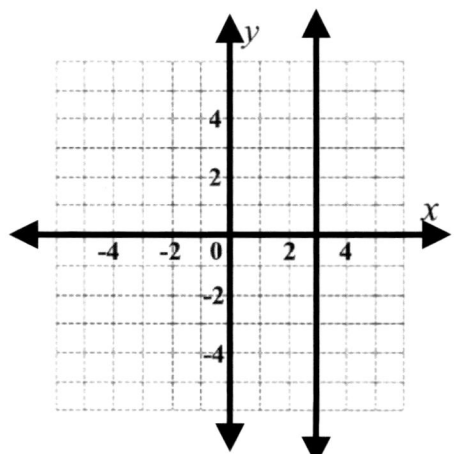

58.   For the given graph, what is the value of x when y is -6?

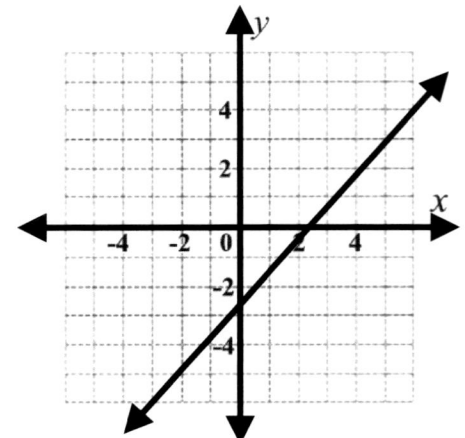

FORMULAS & GRAPHING

Chapter Review

Section 1: Geometric Formulas

Review Exercises:

1.   Find the perimeter and area of the composite figure. Give the exact answers and the approximations using the fact that $\pi \approx 3.14$.

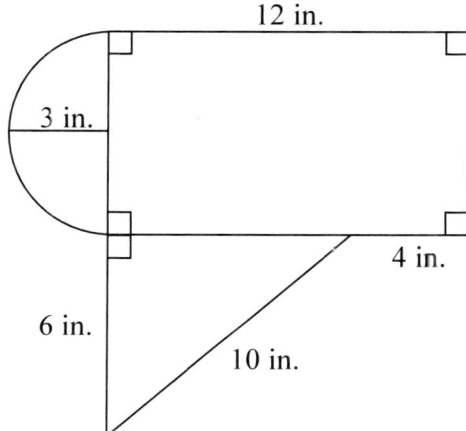

Find the surface area and the volume of each figure. Give the exact answers and the approximations using the fact that $\pi \approx 3.14$.

2.

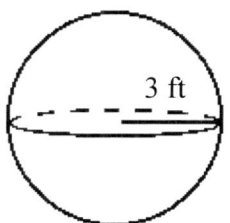

3.

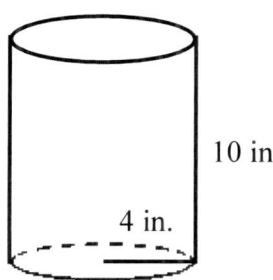

Section 2: Solving Formulas

Review Exercises:

4.   Use the formula $A = LW$ to find the length of a rectangle if the width is 16 meters and the area is 560 square meters.

5.   Use the formula $A = LW$ to find the width of a rectangle if the length is 6.5 yards and the area is 53.3 square yards.

6.   Use the formula $P = 2L + 2W$ to find the width of a rectangle if the length is 22 inches and the perimeter is 70 inches.

7.   Use the formula $P = 2L + 2W$ to find the length of a rectangle if the width is $6\frac{1}{4}$ inches and the perimeter is $32\frac{1}{2}$ inches.

8.   Use the formula $4x - 2y = -8$ to find x when $y = -6$.

9.   Use the formula $y = -3x + 5$ to find y when $x = 2$.

Solve each of the following formulas for the indicated variable.

10. $s = \dfrac{a+b+c}{2}$ for c

11. $x = -\dfrac{b}{2a}$ for a

12. $2x + 3y = 12$ for y

13. $\dfrac{x}{5} + \dfrac{y}{4} = 1$ for y

Section 3: Graphing Ordered Pairs

Review Exercises: In which quadrant is each point located?

14. $(-3, 7)$ **15.** $(3, 0)$

Graph each set of ordered pairs on a different graph.

16. $(-2, 1.5)$, $(-1, 1)$, $(2, 6)$, and $(0, 2)$.

17. $(-5, -\frac{3}{2})$, $(-4, 0)$, $(-2, -3)$, and $(4, 6)$.

Plot the points $(4, 5)$ and $(1, -1)$ on the same graph and then draw a straight line that passes through both of them. Now, answer the following questions.

18.   Does the point $(1, 2)$ lie on the line?

19.   Does the point $(0, -3)$ lie on the line?

20.   The scatterplot below shows a comparison of the calendar years from 1982 to 1990 with the average cost of electricity (in cents per kilowatt-hour).

    a)   During what calendar year(s) was the average price of electricity 7.8 cents per kilowatt-hour?

    b)   During what calendar year(s) was the average price of electricity 8.4 cents per kilowatt-hour?

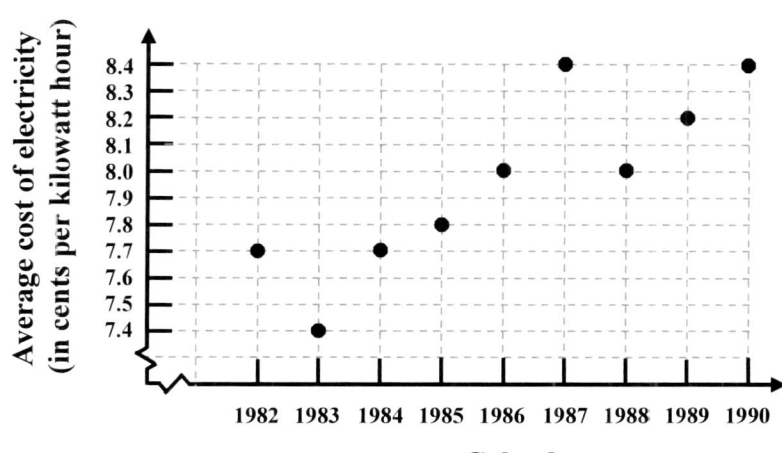

21.   The following table gives data comparing the number of calories in a nutrition bar and the number of grams of total fat also contained in that nutrition bar.

Calories per nutrition bar, x	200	220	230	340	280	180	400	250
Grams of total fat per nutrition bar, y	6	7	2	10	6	4.5	14	6

On a piece of graph paper, reproduce the scatterplot below and graph the ordered pairs from the table above.

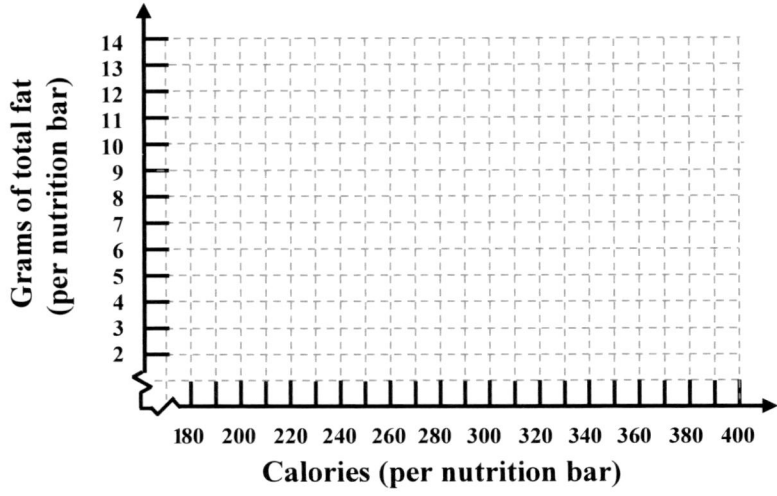

Section 4: Ordered Pairs as Solutions to Equations

Review Exercises: For each of the following equations, complete the given ordered pairs.

22. $x + 4y = 12$ (0,) , (−4,) , (,8)

23. $3x − y = 5$ (,− 0.8) , (−2.6,) , (0,)

24. $x = −7$ (,4) , $\left(,\dfrac{2}{5}\right)$, (,0)

For each of the following equations, complete the given table.

25. $y = -4.2x$

x	y
-3	
-4	
	-12.6
	-14.7

26. $2x + 5y = 12$

x	y
-4	
0	
	12
	-6

27. $y = -2x + 8$

x	y
0	
	-2
	16

For each of the following equations, tell which of the given ordered pairs are solutions.

28. $y + 3x = -7$ $\qquad (-3,2)$, $\left(\dfrac{9}{4}, -\dfrac{55}{4}\right)$, $(0,7)$

29. $y = -8$ $\qquad (-8,0)$, $(0,-8)$, $(-1,8)$

30. $x - y = 3$ $\qquad (-3,3)$, $(4,1)$, $\left(\dfrac{7}{3}, -\dfrac{2}{3}\right)$

Section 5: Graphing Linear Equations

Review Exercises: Which of the following equations are linear and consequently produce a graph that is a straight line?

31. $x = \dfrac{2}{3}y - 7$ $\qquad$ **32.** $17 = -3x$ $\qquad$ **33.** $2x = y^3 + 6$

Use each equation to complete the given ordered pairs. Then use the ordered pairs to draw the graph of the equation.

34. $3x + 2y = -6$ $(0, \ )$, $(\ ,0)$, $(\ ,3)$

35. $y = 5$ $(-3, \ )$, $(2, \ )$, $(0, \ )$

36. $x = 4y$ $(0, \ )$, $(\ ,-1)$, $(2, \ )$

For the following problems:

a) Solve each equation for y.

b) Complete the given ordered pairs using the equation formed in part a).

c) Use the ordered pairs to graph the equation.

37. $3x + 4y = 8$ $(-4, \ )$, $(0, \ )$, $(4, \ )$

38. $3y + x = 9$ $(-3, \ )$, $(0, \ )$, $(3, \ )$

Find three solutions to each equation. Then, use these solutions to graph the equation.

39. $y = -3x + 2$ **40.** $x = 0$ **41.** $3x + 5y = -5$

42.   For the given graph, what is the value of y when x is -5?

43.   For the given graph, what is the value of x when y is 2?

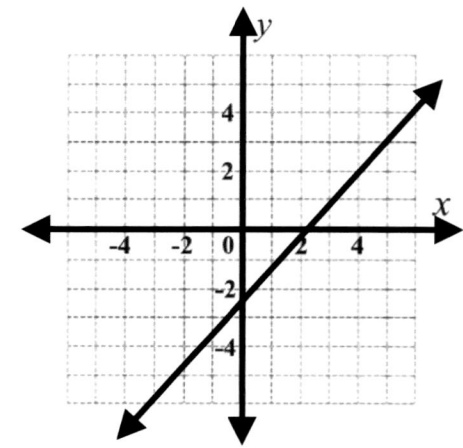

FORMULAS
& GRAPHING

Chapter Test

Find the perimeter and area of the composite figure.

1.

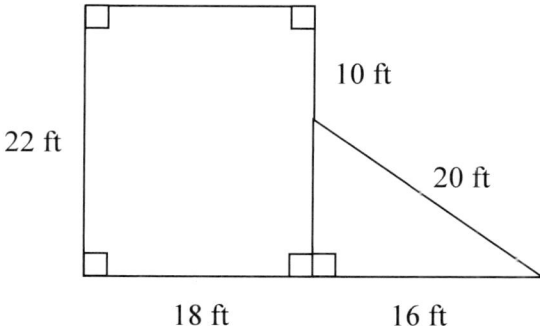

Find the surface area and the volume of the figure. Give the exact answers and the approximations using the fact that $\pi \approx 3.14$.

2.

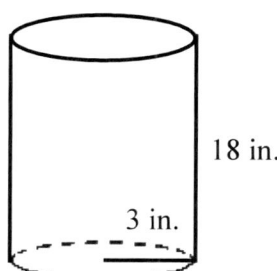

3.   Use the formula $A = LW$ to find the width of a rectangle if the length is 14.4 centimeters and the area is 180 square centimeters.

4.   Use the formula $P = 2L + 2W$ to find the length of a rectangle if the width is 10 feet and the perimeter is $48\frac{2}{5}$ feet.

5.   Use the formula $y = -\dfrac{1}{2}x - 6$ to find y when $x = \dfrac{2}{3}$.

Solve each of the following formulas for the indicated variable.

6. $y = mx + b$ for x **7.** $\dfrac{x}{3} + \dfrac{y}{7} = 1$ for y

In which quadrant is the point located?

8. $(3.6, -4.3)$

Graph the set of ordered pairs on the same rectangular coordinate system.

9. $\left(-\frac{5}{2}, -4\right)$, $(3, 0)$, $(-1.5, 3)$, and $(2, 6)$.

Plot the points $(-4, -2)$ and $(5, 1)$ on the same graph and then draw a straight line that passes through both of them. Now, answer the following questions.

10.   Does the point $(0, 2)$ lie on the line?

11.   Does the point $(-1, -1)$ lie on the line?

12.   The following table gives data comparing the calendar years from 1973 to 1980 with the federal minimum wage rates (in dollars per hour).

Calendar year, x	'73	'74	'75	'76	'77	'78	'79	'80
Federal minimum wage (in dollars per hour), y	1.60	2.00	2.10	2.30	2.30	2.65	2.90	3.10

On a piece of graph paper, reproduce the scatterplot below and graph the ordered pairs from the table above.

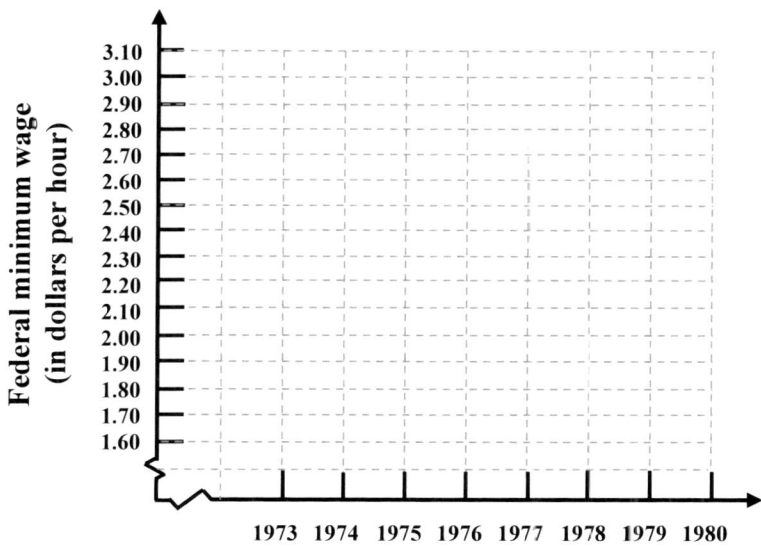

For each of the following equations, complete the given ordered pairs.

13. $x + \dfrac{2}{3}y = 12$ $(0, \quad)$, $(-4, \quad)$, $(\quad, 9)$

14. $x = \dfrac{2}{5}$ $(\quad, -0.3)$, $\left(\quad, \dfrac{7}{3}\right)$, $(\quad, 18)$

For the following equation, complete the given table.

15. $2x = 3y$

x	y
-3	
-6	
	6
	7

For each of the following equations, tell which of the given ordered pairs are solutions.

16. $-2y + 4x = 6$ $(-3,3)$, $\left(\dfrac{7}{5}, \dfrac{1}{5}\right)$, $(1,-1)$

17. $y = -2$ $(-2,0)$, $(3,-2)$, $(-1,-2)$

Use the equation to complete the given ordered pairs. Then use the ordered pairs to draw the graph of the equation.

18. $2x + 4y = 6$ $(0,\ )$, $(\ ,0)$, $(\ ,3)$

For the following problem:

a) Solve the equation for y.

b) Complete the given ordered pairs using the equation formed in part a).

c) Use the ordered pairs to graph the equation.

19. $3x + 2y = -2$ $(-2,\ )$, $(0,\ )$, $(2,\ )$

Find three solutions to each equation. Then, use these solutions to graph the equation.

20. $y = 3 - 2x$ **21.** $2x - y = 4$

22.   For the given graph, what is the value of x when y is -3?

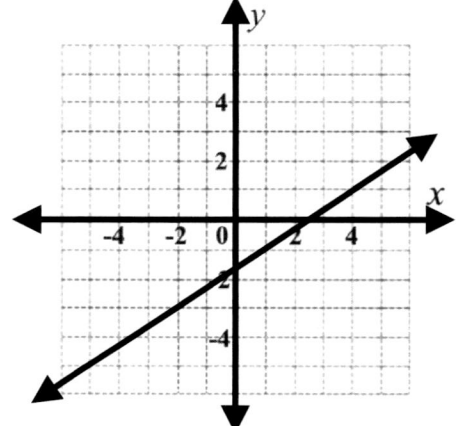

Ratios, proportions, & measurements: Section 1 answers

1.   rate   **3.**   ratio   **5.**   unit rate   **7.**   unit price

9. $\dfrac{3}{7}$ **11.** $\dfrac{19}{24}$ **13.** $\dfrac{31}{24}$ **15.** $\dfrac{10}{67}$

17. $\dfrac{5}{3}$ **19.** $\dfrac{5}{12}$ **21.** $\dfrac{3}{5}$ **23.** $\dfrac{1}{3}$

25. $\dfrac{1}{3}$ **27.** $\dfrac{7}{2}$ **29.** $\dfrac{4\ cups}{5\ minutes}$ **31.** $\dfrac{\$10}{3\ dolls}$

33. $\dfrac{3\ bags}{2\ dozen}$ **35.** $\dfrac{5\ inches}{6\ hours}$ **37.** $\dfrac{\$50}{13\ dozen}$

39. $\dfrac{2.5\ kids}{1\ family}$ or $\dfrac{2\frac{1}{2}\ kids}{1\ family}$ **41.** $\dfrac{15\ houses}{1\ city\ block}$

43. $\dfrac{3.75\ countries}{1\ week}$ or $\dfrac{3\frac{3}{4}\ countries}{1\ week}$ **45.** $\dfrac{58\ miles}{1\ hour}$

47. $\dfrac{43.75\ bales}{1\ acre}$ or $\dfrac{43\frac{3}{4}\ bales}{1\ acre}$ **49.** $\dfrac{\$15.60}{1\ game}$ **51.** $\dfrac{\$2.75}{1\ yard}$

53. $\dfrac{2.4¢}{1\ ounce}$ **55.** $\dfrac{\$7.40}{1\ hour}$ **57.** $\dfrac{\$0.35}{1\ candy\ bar}$ or $\dfrac{35¢}{1\ candy\ bar}$

59. $\dfrac{8}{3}$ **61.** $\dfrac{6}{5}$ **63.** $\dfrac{1}{5}$ **65.** $\dfrac{7\ blouses}{2\ stores}$

67. $\dfrac{25\ pages}{1\ day}$ **69.** $\dfrac{5,100\ words}{1\ hour}$ **71.** $\dfrac{0.125\ mile}{1\ minutes}$ or $\dfrac{\frac{1}{8}\ mile}{1\ minute}$; $\dfrac{8\ minutes}{1\ mile}$

Ratios, proportions, & measurements: Section 1 answers continued

73. $\dfrac{14.8¢}{1\,ounce}$ **75.** $\dfrac{12.8¢}{1\,ounce}$ **77.** $\dfrac{8.0¢}{1\,ounce}$ **79.** $\dfrac{\$1.59}{1\,pound}$

81. **a)** $\dfrac{22.8¢}{1\,ounce}$; $\dfrac{17.9¢}{1\,ounce}$; $\dfrac{20.0¢}{1\,ounce}$ **b)**   The 15 ounce size is the best buy.

83. **a)** $\dfrac{20.0¢}{1\,ounce}$; $\dfrac{16.2¢}{1\,ounce}$; $\dfrac{10.1¢}{1\,ounce}$ **b)**   The 64 ounce size is the best buy.

85. **a)** $\dfrac{15.8¢}{1\,fluid\,ounce}$; $\dfrac{17.4¢}{1\,fluid\,ounce}$ **b)**   The 12 fluid ounce size is the best buy.

87. **a)** $\dfrac{7.9¢}{1\,fluid\,ounce}$; $\dfrac{7.8¢}{1\,fluid\,ounce}$ **b)**   The 16 fluid ounce size is the best buy.

89. **a)** $\dfrac{132.5¢}{1\,quart}$ or $\dfrac{\$1.325}{1\,quart}$; $\dfrac{139.8¢}{1\,quart}$ or $\dfrac{\$1.398}{1\,quart}$

   b)   The 2 quart size is the best buy.

91. $\dfrac{49.0\,miles}{1\,hour}$ **93.** $\dfrac{4.7\,gallons}{1\,minute}$

Ratios, proportions, & measurements: Section 2 answers

1. extremes: 3, 100; means: 25, 12   **3.**   extremes: 6.2, 18; means: 9.3, 12

5. extremes: $\dfrac{4}{7}$, 21; means: $\dfrac{6}{5}$, 10

7. extremes: 6 possums, 18 skunks; means: 9 skunks, 12 possums

9. Yes   **11.** No   **13.** No   **15.** Yes

Ratios, proportions, & measurements: Section 2 answers continued

17. Yes   **19.** Yes   **21.** $x = 90$ **23.** $x = 17.5$

25. $x = 3\dfrac{3}{50}$ or $x = \dfrac{153}{50}$ or $x = 3.06$ **27.** $x = -14$ **29.** $x = 1.82$

31. $x = 1\dfrac{2}{3}$ **33.** $x = 11.25$ or $x = 11\dfrac{1}{4}$ or $x = \dfrac{45}{4}$ **35.** $x = -3$

37. $x = 0.625$ or $x = \dfrac{5}{8}$ **39.** $x = 5.\overline{4}$ or $x = 5\dfrac{4}{9}$ or $x = \dfrac{49}{9}$

41. $x = 3.675$ **43.** $x = -\dfrac{1}{7}$ **45.** Several possible answers are:

$$\frac{5\ hours}{170\ miles} = \frac{12\ hours}{x}; \qquad \frac{170\ miles}{x} = \frac{5\ hours}{12\ hours}; \qquad \frac{x}{170\ miles} = \frac{12\ hours}{5\ hours}$$

47. Several possible answers are:

$$\frac{515\ customers}{9\ weeks} = \frac{x}{45\ weeks};$$

$$\frac{9\ weeks}{45\ weeks} = \frac{515\ customers}{x}; \qquad \frac{45\ weeks}{9\ weeks} = \frac{x}{515\ customers}$$

49. 48 times   **51.** \$450; $\dfrac{\$4.50}{sq.\ ft.}$ **53.** \$2,076   **55.** 79 feet

57. 19.5 grams   **59.** 48 acres   **61.** 1 cup   **63.** approximately 69 kilometers

65. 26 minutes   **67.** 12   **69.** 120

71. **a)** $\dfrac{7}{20}$ **b)** $\dfrac{13}{20}$ **c)** 2,100 students   **73.** $x = 5\dfrac{5}{7}$ m; $y = 15$ m

Ratios, proportions, & measurements: Section 2 answers continued

75. $x = 15.4\,\text{in.};\quad y = 14\,\text{in.}$ **77.**   The perimeter of the small triangle is $19\frac{1}{6}\,\text{yd}.$

The perimeter of the large triangle is $32\frac{6}{7}\,\text{yd}.$

79.   24 feet   **81.**   41.6 meters   **83.**   4 feet   **85.**   35 feet

Ratios, proportions, & measurements: Section 3 answers

1.   42 inches   **3.** $3\frac{3}{4}$ feet or 3.75 feet   **5.**   92 inches

7.   4 feet   **9.** $13\frac{1}{2}$ feet or 13.5 feet

11. $15\frac{2}{3}$ yards or $15.\overline{6}$ yards   **13.**   15,840 feet

15. $1\frac{3}{4}$ miles or 1.75 miles   **17.**   129.6 inches   **19.** $3\frac{1}{2}$ yards or 3.5 yards

21.   3,520 yards   **23.** $4\frac{1}{2}$ miles or 4.5 miles   **25.**   31,680 inches

27.   2 miles   **29.** $432\,\text{in.}^2$ **31.** $5\frac{3}{4}\,\text{ft}^2$ or $5.75\,\text{ft}^2$

33. $55\frac{4}{5}\,\text{ft}^2$ or $55.8\,\text{ft}^2$ **35.** $2\frac{7}{9}\,\text{yd}^2$ or $2.\overline{7}\,\text{yd}^2$

37. $3,240\,\text{in.}^2$ **39.** $4\frac{1}{4}\,\text{yd}^2$ or $4.25\,\text{yd}^2$ **41.**   3,328 acres

Ratios, proportions, & measurements: Section 3 answers continued

43. $2\frac{3}{5}$ mi^2 or 2.6 mi^2 **45.**   5,324 yd^2 **47.**   130,680 ft^2

49.   5,184 in.^{3} **51.**   162 ft^3 **53.**   3 yd^3

55. $61\frac{1}{3}$ fl oz or $61.\overline{3}$ fl oz   **57.**   3 cups   **59.**   10 cups

61. $7\frac{1}{2}$ pints or 7.5 pints   **63.** $9\frac{3}{4}$ pints or 9.75 pints

65.   3 quarts   **67.**   6 quarts   **69.** $3\frac{3}{4}$ gallons or 3.75 gallons

71.   40 fluid ounces   **73.** $2\frac{1}{2}$ pints or 2.5 pints

75.   10 cups   **77.** $5\frac{1}{2}$ quarts or 5.5 quarts   **79.**   16 pints

81. $5\frac{1}{4}$ gallons or 5.25 gallons   **83.**   96 fluid ounces

85. $3\frac{1}{8}$ quarts or 3.125 quarts   **87.**   66 cups

89. $2\frac{1}{2}$ gallons or 2.5 gallons   **91.**   384 fluid ounces

93. $1\frac{1}{2}$ gallons or 1.5 gallons   **95.** $53\frac{1}{3}$ ounces or $53.\overline{3}$ ounces

Ratios, proportions, & measurements: Section 3 answers continued

97. $76\frac{4}{5}$ ounces or 76.8 ounces

99. $2\frac{5}{8}$ pounds or 2.625 pounds

101.   3,400 pounds

103. $2\frac{1}{4}$ tons or 2.25 tons

105.   64,000 ounces

107. $1\frac{3}{4}$ tons or 1.75 tons

109.   900 seconds

111.   8 minutes   113.   144 minutes

115. $3\frac{1}{3}$ hours or $3.\overline{3}$ hours

117.   72 hours

119. $1\frac{1}{4}$ days or 1.25 days

121.   42 days   123.   54 months

125. $1\frac{5}{12}$ years or $1.41\overline{6}$ years

127.   12,600 seconds

129. $1\frac{3}{10}$ hours or 1.3 hours

131.   720 minutes

133. $1\frac{3}{4}$ days or 1.75 days

135.   546 hours   137.   86,400 seconds

139. $1\frac{1}{5}$ days or 1.2 days

141.   20,160 minutes

143.   302,400 seconds

145.   88 feet/second

147.   45 miles/hour

149.   70 miles/hour

Ratios, proportions, & measurements: Section 3 answers continued

151. $2\dfrac{38}{125}$ tons/ft^2 or

2.304 tons/ft^2

153. $13\dfrac{8}{9}$ pounds/in.^{2} or

$13.\overline{8}$ pounds/in.^{2}

155. 30 pounds/in.^{2}

157. $19,800$ feet / pint

159. 2 yards/quart

161. 8 yards / pint

163. $\dfrac{1}{2}$ gallon for $\$2.65$

165. 64 ounces for $\$4.39$

167. 5 pounds for $\$12.50$

169. 61 feet 9 inches

171. 11 pounds 4 ounces

173. 6 feet 10 inches

175. 2 **177.** 48

179. $1\dfrac{5}{16}$ gallons or 1.3125 gallons

181. $P = 28$ in.; $A = 45$ in.^{2}

183. $P = 28$ ft; $A = 49$ ft^2

185. $P = 36$ ft; $A = 54$ ft^2

187. $P = 12$ ft; $A = 8.75$ ft^2

189. $P = 20$ ft; $A = 24.4375$ ft^2 or $24\dfrac{7}{16}$ ft^2

191. $P = 34$ ft; $A = 72.25$ ft^2 or $72\dfrac{1}{4}$ ft^2

193. $P = 16$ yd; $A = 15.\overline{5}$ yd^2 or $15\dfrac{5}{9}$ yd^2

195. $P = 144$ in. or 12 ft or 4 yd; $A = 864$ in.^{2} or 6 ft^2 or $\dfrac{2}{3}$ yd^2 or $0.\overline{6}$ yd^2

Ratios, proportions, & measurements: Section 3 answers continued

197. $C = 2\pi$ ft ; $C \approx 6.28$ ft
        $A = \pi$ ft^2; $A \approx 3.14$ ft^2

199. $C = 6\pi$ in.; $C \approx 18.84$ in.
        $A = 9\pi$ in.^{2}; $A \approx 28.26$ in.^{2}

201. $SA = 888$ ft^2; $V = 1,728$ ft^3

203. $SA = 150$ in.^{2}; $V = 125$ in.^{3}

205.   **a)** $704   **b)** $429   **c)** $25   **d)** $1,158

207.   **a)**   The 16 inch pizza for $9.49   **b)**   The 18 inch pizza for $12.49

209. $A \approx 113.04$ in.^{2}

Ratios, proportions, & measurements: Section 4 answers

1.   420 centimeters

3.   6,570 deciliters

5.   98 grams

7.   478 dekameters

9.   0.03 kiloliter

11.   1,600 dekagrams

13.   12.3 meters

15.   890,600 centiliters

17.   26 milligrams

19.   0.3465 hectometer

21.   31,400 deciliters

23.   48,600 milligrams

25.   7 centimeters

27.   0.00040404 hectoliter

29.   57,130 dekagrams

31.   0.01 meter

33.   0.0028 hectoliter

35.   7.5 dm^2

Ratios, proportions, & measurements: Section 4 answers continued

37. $3{,}600 \text{ dm}^2$ **39.** 0.6 dm^3

41. $5{,}600 \text{ cm}^3$ **43.**   2,600 kilograms

45.   20 hectoliters   **47.**   7,400 meters

49.   0.00405 dekagram   **51.**   569.2 hectoliters

53.   0.00045 centimeter   **55.**   76,489,200 centigrams

57.   354,000 deciliters   **59.**   3,100,000 millimeters

61.   2,960 decigrams   **63.**   0.69273 dekaliter

65.   0.236 dekameter   **67.**   0.29 kilogram

69.   77,700 milliliters   **71.**   0.0051 kilometer

73.   1,230 grams   **75.**   9.426 deciliters

77.   791.59 decimeters   **79.**   50,000 centigrams

81.   0.00003587 kiloliter   **83.**   9.652 kilometers

85.   0.000439 kilogram   **87.**   50 cubic centimeters

89.   12 liters   **91.**   0.1 kilogram

93.   13.5 grams   **95.**   0.38 gram

97.   1.215 grams   **99.**   85 milligrams

Ratios, proportions, & measurements: Section 4 answers continued

101. 0.045 liter

103. 12 centimeters

105. 1 serving

107. 1 hectare

109. $P = 38$ m; $A = 84\,\text{m}^2$

111. $P = 24$ mm; $A = 36\,\text{mm}^2$

113. $P = 36$ cm; $A = 54\,\text{cm}^2$

115. $P = 4$ m or 40 dm or 400 cm; $A = 0.6\,\text{m}^2$ or $60\,\text{dm}^2$ or $6{,}000\,\text{cm}^2$

117. $C = 2\pi$ m; $C \approx 6.28$ m; $A = \pi\,\text{m}^2$; $A \approx 3.14\,\text{m}^2$

119. $C = 6\pi$ cm; $C \approx 18.84$ cm; $A = 9\pi\,\text{cm}^2$; $A \approx 28.26\,\text{cm}^2$

121. $SA = 888\,\text{m}^2$; $V = 1{,}728{,}000{,}000\,\text{cm}^3$

123. $SA = 0.00015\,\text{m}^2$; $V = 0.125\,\text{cm}^3$

Ratios, proportions, & measurements: Section 5 answers

1. a meter

3. an inch

5. a kilogram

7. a cup

9. a liter

11. a gallon

13. 25°F

15. 350°F

17. 60°C

19. 18 cm

21. 220 mm

23. 72 cm

25. 2 m

27. 15 mm

29. 300 g

31. 500 mg

33. 640,000 kg

35. 70 L

37. 350 mL

39. 0.03 mL

41. -5°C

43. 180°C

45. 38°C

47. 4.36 yards

49. 8.86 kilometers

51. 55.76 feet

53. 66.04 centimeters

Ratios, proportions, & measurements: Section 5 answers continued

55. 3,703 meters

57. 1.64 yards

59. 1.35 kilometers

61. 179.4 inches

63. 60 centimeters

65. 2.72 kilograms

67. 4.2 ounces

69. 1.42 kilograms

71. 1,225.8 grams

73. 11.36 liters

75. 7.42 quarts

77. 2.84 liters

79. 405.6 fluid ounces

81. 7,570 milliliters

83. 4.45 quarts

85. 2.84 dekaliters

87. 27,040 fluid ounces

89. $25.\overline{5}°C$

91. 115.16°F

93. $-26.\overline{6}°C$

95. 16.88°F

97. 1.37 inches

99. 88.55 kilometers per hour

101. 3

103. 300 grams for $2.29

105. 26.83 meters per second

107. The runner who ran 1 mile

109. 10.63 kilometers per liter

111. 8.33 pounds per gallon

113. An ounce of prevention is worth a pound of cure.

115. I'd like a quarter pounder with cheese.

117. $P \approx 50.8 \, \text{cm}$; $A = 24 \, \text{in.}^2$

119. $P \approx 91.44 \, \text{cm}$; $A = 54 \, \text{in.}^2$

121. $C \approx 1.88 \, \text{m}$; $A \approx 3.14 \, \text{ft}^2$

Ratios, proportions, & measurements: Chapter review answers

1. $\dfrac{9}{10}$ 2. $\dfrac{1}{3}$ 3. $\dfrac{1}{9}$ 4. $\dfrac{13\ inches}{6\ days}$

5. $\dfrac{\$4}{3\ cups}$ 6. $\dfrac{3.4\ dogs}{1\ kennel}$ 7. $\dfrac{2.25\ states}{1\ day}$ 8. $\dfrac{780\ documents}{1\ hour}$

9. $\dfrac{1.25\ window\ frames}{1\ hour}$; $\dfrac{0.8\ hour}{1\ window\ frame}$ 10. $\dfrac{6.1\ gallons}{1\ minute}$

11. $\dfrac{\$3.37}{1\ quart}$

12. a) $\dfrac{59.8¢}{1\ pound}$; $\dfrac{52.9¢}{1\ pound}$; $\dfrac{53.6¢}{1\ pound}$ b)   The 10 pound size is the best buy.

13. extremes: $\dfrac{3}{5}$, 3.5; means: 1.5, $1\dfrac{2}{5}$ 14. No

15. Yes   16. $x = 1\dfrac{2}{3}$ 17. $x = -3$

18. $\dfrac{7\ hours}{13\ gallons} = \dfrac{12\ hours}{x}$; $\dfrac{13\ gallons}{x} = \dfrac{7\ hours}{12\ hours}$; $\dfrac{x}{13\ gallons} = \dfrac{12\ hours}{7\ hours}$

19. $\$1,903$ 20. 20 grams   21. 2 cups of sugar

22. approximately 112 miles   23. $x = 10.5\ \text{ft}$; $y = 16.5\ \text{ft}$ 24. 28 feet

25. 6 feet   26. $3\dfrac{1}{4}$ yards or 27. $4{,}212\ \text{in.}^2$ 28. $7{,}744\ \text{yd}^2$
3.25 yards

Ratios, proportions, & measurements: Chapter review answers continued

29.   192 fluid ounces

30. $4\frac{1}{8}$ pounds or 4.125 pounds

31.   9,000 seconds

32.   22 feet/second

33.   1 ounce for 19¢

34.   5 feet 10 inches

35.   52

36. $P = 36$ ft; $A = 54 \, \text{ft}^2$

37. $P = 72$ ft; $A = 224 \, \text{ft}^2$

38. $SA = 664 \, \text{in.}^2$; $V = 1{,}120 \, \text{in.}^3$

39. $SA = 1{,}176 \, \text{in.}^2$; $V = 2{,}744 \, \text{in.}^3$

40. $6\frac{3}{4}$ feet or 6.75 feet

41.   470 hectometers

42.   940,300 centiliters

43.   67 decigrams

44.   0.000376 dekaliters

45.   5,300 kilograms

46.   0.000023 centimeters

47.   26,510,000 decimeters

48.   0.92 kilograms

49.   4.032 liters

50.   9.3 liters

51.   1.8 grams

52.   300 milligrams

53.   25 hectares

54. $C = 20\pi$ mm; $C \approx 62.8$ mm; $A = 100\pi \, \text{mm}^2$; $A \approx 314 \, \text{mm}^2$

55.   5,152 meters

56.   1.64 feet

57.   140 ounces

58.   1,679.8 grams

59.   11,355 milliliters

60.   105 pints

61. $-8.\overline{4}°\text{C}$

62.   18.86°F

63.   3 kilograms for $23.99

64.   8.50 kilometers per liter

Ratios, proportions, & measurements: Chapter test answers

1. $\dfrac{9}{5}$ 2. $\dfrac{4}{7}$ 3. $\dfrac{3\ inches}{2\ hours}$ 4. $\dfrac{6.4\ gallons}{1\ minute}$

5. $x = -\dfrac{1}{7}$ 6. $x = -6$ 7. $\dfrac{2}{3}$ tablespoon of baking soda

8. approximately 65.8 kilometers   9. $x = 17.6\,\text{ft};$ $y = 16\,\text{ft}$ 10. $5\dfrac{3}{4}$ yards or 5.75 yards

11. $396\,\text{in.}^2$ 12. 160 fluid ounces   13. 9 inches

14. 72   15. $P = 48\text{ft};$ $A = 96\,\text{ft}^2$

16. $C = 18\pi\,\text{cm};$ $C \approx 56.52\,\text{cm};$ $A = 81\pi\,\text{cm}^2;$ $A \approx 254.34\,\text{cm}^2$

17. $SA = 2{,}520\,\text{m}^2;$ $V = 8{,}100\,\text{m}^3$ 18. 86,700 centiliters

19. 4,580 decigrams   20. 0.72 liters

21. 0.000056 kilograms   22. 35.68 liters

23. 2.09 grams   24. 450 milligrams

25. 245 ounces   26. 73.5 pints

27. $-33.\overline{6}\,°\text{C}$ 28. 98.6°F

29. 3 gallons of milk for $5.97   30. 70.40 miles per gallon

Percents: Section 1 answers

1. 700%   3. 12%   5. 620%   7. 23%

9. 60%   11. 70%   13. 4,300%   15. 147.5% or $147\frac{1}{2}$%

17. 1,064%   19. 75%   21. 0.478%   23. $66\frac{2}{3}$% or $65.\overline{6}$%

25. 85%   27. 11.4%   29. 60%   31. 275%

33. 12.5% or $12\frac{1}{2}$%   35. $41.\overline{7}$%   37. $466.\overline{6}$% or $466\frac{2}{3}$%

39. $116.\overline{6}$% or $116\frac{2}{3}$%   41. 910.4%   43. $28\frac{4}{7}$% or $28.\overline{571428}$%

45. $587\frac{1}{2}$% or 587.5%   47. $31\frac{1}{4}$% or 31.25%

49. 101.03%   51. $516.\overline{6}$% or $516\frac{2}{3}$%   53. 0.069

55. 0.17   57. 0.01   59. $0.04\overline{3}$ 61. 0.00314

63. $0.00\overline{4}$ 65. $\frac{37}{5}$ or $7\frac{2}{5}$ 67. $\frac{8}{125}$ 69. $\frac{14}{25}$

71. $\frac{61}{700}$ 73. $\frac{3}{500}$ 75. $\frac{109}{250}$ 77. 33.33%

79. 216.67%   81. 428.57%   83. 244.44%   85. 0.9; 90%

Percents: Section 1 answers continued

87.   0.0075; $\dfrac{3}{400}$ **89.** $\dfrac{2}{5}$; 40%   **91.**   0.6; 60%

93.   1.55; $\dfrac{31}{20}$ **95.** $\dfrac{7}{8}$; 87.5%   **97.**   0.04; 4%   **99.**   0.005; $\dfrac{1}{200}$

101. $41\dfrac{2}{3}$% or 41.$\overline{6}$%   **103.**   **a)** 30%   **b)** 20%   **c)** 24%

105.   42.5% or $42\dfrac{1}{2}$%   **107.**   64%   **109.**   20%

111.   15%   **113.**   3.5% or $3\dfrac{1}{2}$%   **115.**   1.25% or $1\dfrac{1}{4}$%

117.   22.7%   **119.**   12.5%   **121.**   0.143   **123.**   63%

125.   200%   **127.**   42%   **129.**   107%

Percents: Section 2 answers

1.   196   **3.** $66\dfrac{2}{3}$ or 66.$\overline{6}$ **5.**   40%

7.   6,000   **9.**   70%   **11.**   0.068 or $\dfrac{17}{250}$

13.   1.9$\overline{4}$% or $1\dfrac{17}{18}$%   **15.**   0.512 or $\dfrac{64}{125}$ **17.**   7.375 or $7\dfrac{3}{8}$

19.   0.56 or $\dfrac{14}{25}$ **21.** $\dfrac{5}{6}$ or 0.8$\overline{3}$ **23.**   40%

Percents: Section 2 answers continued

25. 2,000   **27.** $39\dfrac{13}{33}\%$ or $39.\overline{39}\%$ **29.** 18

31. 400%   **33.** 215   **35.** $187\dfrac{1}{2}$ or 187.5

37. 21   **39.** $128.25   **41.** 12   **43.** 37.5% or $37\dfrac{1}{2}\%$

45. 52   **47.** $23.36   **49.** 40%   **51.** 28.8% or $28\dfrac{4}{5}\%$

53. $4,305   **55.** 35   **57.** 40%   **59.** 2,500mg

61. 57   **63.** 72%   **65.** 64%   **67.** 86%

69. 71%   **71.** 91%   **73.** **a)** 11%   **b)** 9%   **c)** 8%   **d)** 9%

Percents: Section 3 answers

1. $17.50; $267.50   **3.** 8.2%   **5.** $14; $15.05   **7.** $1,200

9. $55.35   **11.** 4%   **13.** $561   **15.** 46

17. 25%   **19.** $5.25; $20.25   **21.** $250; $1,750   **23.** 12%

25. $21.60; $32.40   **27.** $240; $84   **29.** 15%   **31.** $24; $96

33. $75   **35.** 20%   **37.** $2.29; $31.29   **39.** $824.32

41. $1,333.33; $21,333.33   **43.** $149.95   **45.** $3.98; $10.02

Percents: Section 3 answers continued

47. $3.78; $8.81   **49.** 8.3%   **51.** $49.98   **53.** $42.80

55. 296; 719   **57.** 14,852   **59.** $899.33   **61.** 8.6%

63. 20%   **65.** 14,568   **67.** $18.65; $20.03

69. 4.6%   **71.** $12.98   **73.** 38.6%   **75.** 35.7%

77. $193.05   **79.** $11.43; $7.43   **81.** $293.33   **83.** $42; $60

85. 450%   **87.** $1.68   **89.** 45%   **91.** $1,000

Percents: Section 4 answers

1. $258   **3.** $252   **5.** $2,587.50   **7.** $6,390

9. $3,765.60   **11.** $277.50   **13.** $722.22   **15.** 6.1%

17. 2.4 years   **19.** 14.9 years   **21.** 18.9 years   **23.** $2.63

25. $4.67   **27.** $16.44   **29.** $18.25

31. a) $36   b) $67   c)   35%

33. a) $78.75   b) $213.34   **35.** a) $575   b) $83.60

37. a) $675   b) $542.68   **39.** $60   **41.** 360%

43. $8,820   **45.** $6,243.63   **47.** $9,341.74   **49.** $2,971.38

Percents: Chapter review answers

1. 8%

2. 1,893%

3. $283\frac{1}{3}$% or $283.\overline{3}$%

4. 1,200%

5. 245%

6. 675%

7. 0.56%

8. $58\frac{1}{3}$% or $58.\overline{3}$%

9. 0.19

10. 0.00076

11. $0.05\overline{6}$

12. $0.00\overline{7}$

13. $6\frac{2}{5}$

14. $\dfrac{149}{200}$

15. $\dfrac{33}{700}$

16. $\dfrac{3}{10,000}$

17. 28.57%

18. 344.44%

19. 83.33%

20. 733.33%

21. $62\frac{1}{2}$% or 62.5%

22. Move the decimal point one place to the left and multiply the results by two.

23. 302.4

24. 17

25. 430%

26. 36

27. $\dfrac{4}{9}$

28. 30%

29. $154.49

30. 52

31. 3%

32. 70%

33. 87%

34. 14%

35. $5.45; $74.45

36. $9.19; $30.76

37. 313; 1,096

38. 6,650

39. $1,324.24

40. 25%

41. 5.6%

42. 28.1%

43. $50; $36

44. $21; $30

45. $378

46. $3,657.50

Percents: Chapter review answers continued

47. $800   **48.** 5.9%   **49.** 3.0   **50.** $7.50

51. $14.58   **52.** $17,997.82   **53.** $10,379.70   **54.** $16,390.91

Percents: Chapter test answers

1. 35%   **2.** $816.\overline{6}\%$ or $816\frac{2}{3}\%$ **3.** 4.7% or $4\frac{7}{10}\%$

4. $0.07\overline{4}$ **5.** $0.000\overline{5}$ **6.** $\dfrac{2}{75}$ **7.** $\dfrac{3}{500}$

8. 71.43%   **9.** 763.64%   **10.** 56.25% or $56\frac{1}{4}\%$

11. 72   **12.** 60%   **13.** $59.21   **14.** 60%

15. $16.65; $28.34   **16.** 850   **17.** $1,781.17   **18.** 30.8%

19. $96; $120   **20.** 75%   **21.** $4,463.40   **22.** $620

23. 4.7%   **24.** $19   **25.** $20,606.02

An Introduction to Algebra: Section 1 answers

1. 2

3. 5

5. $\dfrac{1}{7}$

7. 3.6

9. $4\dfrac{1}{4}$

11. 0.08

13. 6

15. -6

17. 3.7

19. 4.5

21. -5

23. $-\dfrac{7}{9}$

25. 2

27. 3

29. -5

31. -7

33. -6

35. 2

37. 0.3

39. $-3\dfrac{1}{2}$

41. $-a$

43. c

45. 5

47. -3

49. 0.8

51. x

53. $-z$

55. $2\dfrac{1}{2}$

57. 4

59. -3.1

61. -9

63. $\dfrac{9}{5}$

65. -15

67. -7

69. $-2\dfrac{2}{7}$

71. -15

73. 0

75. -18

77. 0

79. $-\dfrac{93}{20}$ or $-4\dfrac{13}{20}$

81. -3

83. -3

85. 7.9

87. $\dfrac{8}{9}$

89. $8\dfrac{3}{8}$

91. $\dfrac{69}{10}$ or $6\dfrac{9}{10}$ or 6.9

93. -11

An Introduction to Algebra: Section 1 answers continued

95. -6 **97.** 13   **99.** $\dfrac{5}{9}$ **101.** -3

103. -7 **105.** -5.9 **107.** -4.9 **109.** $-\dfrac{15}{14}$ or $-1\dfrac{1}{14}$

111. $-\dfrac{31}{20}$ or $-1\dfrac{11}{20}$ **113.** -15 **115.** -15

117. -17.9 **119.** -13.3 **121.** $-10\dfrac{3}{4}$ **123.** $-9\dfrac{1}{6}$

125. 5   **127.** -5 **129.** -4 **131.** 9

133. 2   **135.** 27.6   **137.** -13 **139.** $-\dfrac{73}{36}$ or $-2\dfrac{1}{36}$

141. -45 **143.** -28 **145.** 70.08   **147.** -35.7

149. $-\dfrac{4}{7}$ **151.** $\dfrac{3}{2}$ or $1\dfrac{1}{2}$ **153.** 270   **155.** -24

157. 0   **159.** 21   **161.** 81.27   **163.** -4

165. -2 **167.** -4 **169.** 4   **171.** 4

173. -2.5 **175.** $-3.\overline{3}$ **177.** -5 **179.** 5

181. $-\dfrac{3}{2}$ or $-1\dfrac{1}{2}$ **183.** $\dfrac{45}{98}$ **185.** -9 **187.** -0.75

189. $-\dfrac{1}{2}$ **191.** Undefined   **193.** 12   **195.** 47

An Introduction to Algebra: Section 1 answers continued

197. 100   **199.** 108   **201.** -5.408 **203.** 8

205. 6   **207.** 18   **209.** 14   **211.** -10

213. 100   **215.** 47   **217.** -41 **219.** 5.7

221. -9 **223.** 7   **225.** 5   **227.** 0

229. -2 **231.** $\frac{7}{2}$ or $3\frac{1}{2}$ **233.** $\frac{125}{6}$ or $20\frac{5}{6}$ **235.** $\frac{1}{3}$

237. 2   **239.** $-\frac{1}{3}$ **241.** $\frac{14}{3}$ or $4\frac{2}{3}$ **243.** 14

245. $\frac{32}{43}$ **247.** -3 **249.** -21

An Introduction to Algebra: Section 2 answers

1.   The commutative property of multiplication

3.   The multiplication property of zero

5.   The multiplicative inverse property

7.   The associative property of multiplication

9.   The additive inverse property

11.   The associative property of addition

13.   The commutative property of addition

An Introduction to Algebra: Section 2 answers continued

15. The identity property of addition   **17.** The distributive property

19. The identity property of multiplication   **21.** 0 **23.** $8x$

25. $-10w$ **27.** $2x^2$ **29.** 7 **31.** $6y$

33. $15xy$ **35.** x **37.** -12 **39.** $2.1r$

41. $-4x$ **43.** w **45.** 0.4 **47.** $30p^2$

49. $\dfrac{32}{3}w$ **51.** $-21w$ **53.** $4x$ **55.** $-3x$

57. $-35x^2$ **59.** $42mn$ **61.** $12x+28$ **63.** $0.6x-2.7$

65. $-8y-16$ **67.** $8m+12n$ **69.** $-3a-b$ **71.** $2y+6$

73. $10y+15z-20$ **75.** $-5x+6$ **77.** $21z-56$

79. $45c+54$ **81.** $12x+8y+20$ **83.** $12a-3b-1.5$

85. $5x-3a+4m$ **87.** $-6x^2+12xy$

89. $8x-8y+8z$ **91.** $1.5m+0.5n-0.2$

93. $-15a+20$ **95.** $-6x-7y+3z$

An Introduction to Algebra: Section 3 answers

1. 1st term: x ; variable term; the numerical coefficient is 1

2nd term: $-y$; variable term; the numerical coefficient is -1

3rd term: 6 ; constant term

3. 1st term: $3x^2$; variable term; the numerical coefficient is 3

2nd term: $-\dfrac{2}{3}y$; variable term; the numerical coefficient is $-\dfrac{2}{3}$

3rd term: $8z$; variable term; the numerical coefficient is 8

5. 1st term: a ; variable term; the numerical coefficient is 1

2nd term: -3 ; constant term

7. 1st term: $-0.1a$; variable term; the numerical coefficient is -0.1

2nd term: $5.7b$; variable term; the numerical coefficient is 5.7

3rd term: -25 ; constant term

9. 1st term: $8ab^2$; variable term; the numerical coefficient is 8

2nd term: 40 ; constant term

3rd term: $-6b^2c$; variable term; the numerical coefficient is -6

11. 1st term: 4 ; constant term

2nd term: $-x$; variable term; the numerical coefficient is -1

13. $13x$ **15.** $5x$ **17.** $-5y$ **19.** 0

21. $-3x$ **23.** x **25.** $-a$ **27.** $\dfrac{31x}{20}$ or $\dfrac{31}{20}x$

29. $\dfrac{13y}{63}$ or $\dfrac{13}{63}y$ **31.** $1.3x$ **33.** $-0.9a$

An Introduction to Algebra: Section 3 answers continued

35. $3m+5w$ **37.** $8x-13$ **39.** $12a+6b$ **41.** $-m+4x-3$

43. $21x-15$ **45.** $-6x+2.2y$ **47.** $12x^2-10x$ **49.** $16mn-5$

51. $\dfrac{19}{15}x+\dfrac{8}{15}y$ **53.** 0 **55.** $-5x+48$ **57.** $3m-9$

59. $-x-23$ **61.** $4n-3p$ **63.** 0 **65.** $7a^2-2a-2$

67. $10x^2-6x-4$ **69.** $30.1x-39.9y$ **71.** $\dfrac{32}{3}x-\dfrac{28}{5}y$

73. $8x+11y-11z$ **75.** $11x^2y-7xy^2+3y^2+10$

77. $x^2y-12xy+36y$ **79.** $x^2y+9xy-10y$

An Introduction to Algebra: Section 4 answers

1. $x=7$ **3.** $y=13$ **5.** $x=2.4$ **7.** $a=9$

9. $z=-4$ **11.** $y=-10.2$ **13.** $w=12$ **15.** $n=-4.5$

17. $x=-15$ **19.** $w=-14$ **21.** $y=0$ **23.** $a=-9$

25. $a=-14$ **27.** $y=8$ **29.** $x=21.3$ **31.** $m=-4$

33. $x=\dfrac{3}{2}$ or $x=1\dfrac{1}{2}$ **35.** $w=-\dfrac{1}{2}$ **37.** $x=-\dfrac{5}{18}$

39. $a=-\dfrac{22}{15}$ or $a=-1\dfrac{7}{15}$ **41.** $x=5$ **43.** $y=-3$

An Introduction to Algebra: Section 4 answers continued

45. $a = -\dfrac{25}{6}$ or $a = -4\dfrac{1}{6}$ or $a = -4.1\overline{6}$ **47.** $m = 14$

49. $x = -7$ **51.** $a = 0$ **53.** $m = \dfrac{14}{3}$ or $m = 4\dfrac{2}{3}$ or $m = 4.\overline{6}$

55. $w = -70$ **57.** $y = -\dfrac{5}{18}$ or $y = -0.2\overline{7}$ **59.** $a = 6$

61. $m = \dfrac{1}{30}$ or $m = 0.0\overline{3}$ **63.** $x = 0$ **65.** $w = 0.25$ or $w = \dfrac{1}{4}$

67. $x = 12$ **69.** $z = -\dfrac{70}{3}$ or $z = -23\dfrac{1}{3}$

71. $x = -\dfrac{50}{3}$ or $x = -16\dfrac{2}{3}$ **73.** $a = 30$ **75.** $x = 6$

77. $p = \dfrac{1}{18}$ **79.** $x = 17.5$ or $x = 17\dfrac{1}{2}$ or $x = \dfrac{35}{2}$ **81.** $a = 0$

83. $x = 3$ **85.** $y = -1$ **87.** $x = \dfrac{3}{10}$ **89.** $y = -4$

An Introduction to Algebra: Section 5 answers

1. $x = 2$ **3.** $a = 1$ **5.** $x = -5$ **7.** $z = 7$

9. $x = 3$ **11.** $h = \dfrac{3}{2}$ **13.** $m = \dfrac{3}{2}$ **15.** $y = 0$

17. $n = 1$ **19.** $w = 18$ **21.** $y = -28$ **23.** $x = \dfrac{27}{20}$

An Introduction to Algebra: Section 5 answers continued

25. $w = -5.3$ **27.** $k = \dfrac{7}{6}$ **29.** $w = 4$ **31.** $x = \dfrac{1}{7}$

33. $h = -8$ **35.** $w = -5$ **37.** $w = \dfrac{7}{6}$ **39.** $h = 7$

41. $w = \dfrac{3}{4}$ **43.** $a = 4$ **45.** $x = -\dfrac{4}{3}$ **47.** $x = -\dfrac{3}{2}$

49. $m = -\dfrac{13}{4}$ **51.** $x = \dfrac{1}{3}$ **53.** $a = -7$ **55.** $k = -2.3$

57. $m = -\dfrac{21}{20}$ **59.** $m = 63$ **61.** $x = 2.1$ **63.** $m = -\dfrac{13}{7}$

65. $k = 2$ **67.**   18 minutes   **69.**   264 miles   **71.**   126 therms

73.   410 kilowatt-hours   **75.**   The length is 11 inches

An Introduction to Algebra: Section 6 answers

1.   The mistake is that the constant term 6, should be subtracted from both sides of the equation first. Dividing by 2 first would be okay, but only if every term on both sides of the equation was divided by the 2. The correct solution is $x = 2$.

3.   The mistake is that the coefficient of x, which is 3, needs to be removed by division, not subtraction. $3x - 3$ does not equal x. However, $\dfrac{3x}{3}$ does equal x. The correct solution is $x = \dfrac{10}{3}$.

5. $x = 4$ **7.** $m = -3$ **9.** $w = 3$ **11.** $a = \dfrac{3}{2}$

An Introduction to Algebra: Section 6 answers continued

13. $x = 1$ 15. $m = -\dfrac{7}{2}$ 17. $w = \dfrac{1}{2}$ 19. $a = \dfrac{1}{4}$

21. $x = -\dfrac{5}{3}$ 23. $m = 1$ 25. $w = 7$ 27. $x = 0$

29. $m = -\dfrac{5}{8}$ 31. $w = 1$ 33. $x = 0$ 35. $m = \dfrac{4}{3}$

37. $w = \dfrac{5}{2}$ 39. $k = -\dfrac{1}{3}$ 41. $y = 2$ 43. $m = 1$

45. $a = 3$ 47. $x = -\dfrac{9}{4}$ 49. $w = 2$ 51. $m = \dfrac{5}{2}$

53. $h = 23$ 55. $x = 9$ 57. $w = 3$ 59. $a = \dfrac{7}{9}$

61. $h = \dfrac{5}{7}$ 63. $x = \dfrac{10}{3}$ 65. $x = \dfrac{11}{16}$ 67. $k = 2$

69. $m = 15$ 71. $x = \dfrac{41}{4}$ 73. $x = -\dfrac{1}{4}$ 75. $x = \dfrac{3}{20}$

77. $y = \dfrac{4}{5}$ 79. $a = -12$ 81. $x = 0.5$ 83. $y = 3$

85. $m = 2$ 87. $x = 3.5$ 89. $x = 2.3$

An Introduction to Algebra: Section 7 answers

1. Some possible answers are: x minus seven, seven less than x, x less seven, the difference of x and seven, the difference between x and seven, x decreased by seven, and seven subtracted from x.

An Introduction to Algebra: Section 7 answers continued

3.   Some possible answers are: four plus x, four increased by x, x added to four, the sum of four and x, x more than four, and the total of four and x.

5.   Some possible answers are: two x minus four, four less than two x, two x less four, the difference of two x and four, the difference between two x and four, two x decreased by four, four subtracted from two x, and four less than the product of two and x.

7.   Some possible answers are: two times the difference of x and four, and the product of two and the quantity x minus four.

9.   Some possible answers are: seven minus x, x less than seven, seven less x, the difference of seven and x, the difference between seven and x, seven decreased by x, and x subtracted from seven.

11.   Some possible answers are: one more than the quotient of w and nine, and the sum of w divided by nine and one.

13.   Some possible answers are: three more than four times the difference of two x and five, and three more than the product of four and the difference of twice x and five.

15.   Some possible answers are: four minus the quotient of two x and nine, and the difference of four and the quotient of twice x and nine.

17.   Some possible answers are: six divided into the sum of m and three, and the quantity m plus three, divided by six.

19. $x+6$	**21.** $3-x$	**23.** $2x+7$	**25.** $9x$
27. $\dfrac{x}{2}$ or $x \div 2$	**29.** $x-14$	**31.** $-5-x$	**33.** $6x+80$
35. $4x-3$	**37.** $6x-17$	**39.** $9x+30$	**41.** $4(x-3)$; $4x-12$
43. $\dfrac{x}{2}+\dfrac{x}{4}$; $\dfrac{3x}{4}$		**45.** $5(x+6)$; $5x+30$	

An Introduction to Algebra: Section 7 answers continued

47. $2(8x-3)$; $16x-6$

49. $(x+2)-(x+5)$; -3

51. $4x+7x$; $11x$

53. $x-(-5-x)$; $2x+5$

55. $2x-x$; x

57. $-3(8+x)$; $-3x-24$

59. $4(7-x)+10$; $-4x+38$

61. $(x-17)+2$; $x-15$

63. $3\left(\dfrac{x}{3}\right)$; x

65. $16-(x+14)$; $-x+2$

67. $(x+5)+(x-2)$; $2x+3$

69.   Larger number: $25-n$

71.   John's age: $a-3$

73.   Length of the rectangle: $3W-5$

75.   Smaller number: $48-n$

77.   Total value of nickels: $5n$

79.   Length of the rectangle: $6W+5$

81.   Gwen's age: $a+5$

83.   Width of the rectangle: $\dfrac{1}{2}L-7$

85. $3(26-n)-5$; $-3n+73$

87. $2(a+7)+3$; $2a+17$

89. $3(2W)-4$; $6W-4$

91. $5(d+3)$; $5d+15$

An Introduction to Algebra: Section 8 answers

1. **Step 1:** Find the number.

    Step 2: Call "the number" x.

    Step 3: $4x - 3 = 33$

    Step 4: $x = 9$

    Step 5: The number is 9.

    Step 6: The check is left to you.

3. **Step 1:** Find the number.

    Step 2: Call "the number" x.

    Step 3: $6x + 9 = 33$

    Step 4: $x = 4$

    Step 5: The number is 4.

    Step 6: The check is left to you.

5. **Step 1:** Find the number.

    Step 2: Call "the number" x.

    Step 3: $2(x + 4) = -2$

    Step 4: $x = -5$

    Step 5: The number is -5.

    Step 6: The check is left to you.

7. **Step 1:** Find the number.

    Step 2: Call "the number" x.

    Step 3: $7 - 2x = -13$

    Step 4: $x = 10$

    Step 5: The number is 10.

    Step 6: The check is left to you.

9. **Step 1:** Find the number.

    Step 2: Call "the number" x.

    Step 3: $2x - 3 = 5x - 15$

    Step 4: $x = 4$

    Step 5: The number is 4.

11. **Step 1:** Find the number.

    Step 2: Call "the number" x.

    Step 3: $\frac{1}{3}x + \frac{1}{2}x = \frac{1}{4}x$

    Step 4: $x = 0$

    Step 5: The number is 0.

13. **Step 1:** Find the numbers.

    Step 2: Call "the larger number" x.
    Call "the smaller number" $22 - x$.

    Step 3: $3(22 - x) = 2x - 4$

    Step 4: $x = 14$

    Step 5: The larger number is 14 and the smaller number is 8.

15. **Step 1:** Find the numbers.

    Step 2: Call "the larger number" x.
    Call "the smaller number" $45 - x$.

    Step 3: $2x = 3(45 - x)$

    Step 4: $x = 27$

    Step 5: The larger number is 27 and the smaller number is 18.

An Introduction to Algebra: Section 8 answers continued

17. **Step 1:** Find the numbers.

    Step 2: Call "the larger number" x.
Call "the smaller number" $2 - x$.

    Step 3: $4(2 - x) = -3x$

    Step 4: $x = 8$

    Step 5: The larger number is 8 and the smaller number is -6.

19. **Step 1:** Find the numbers.

    Step 2: Call "the larger number" x.
Call "the smaller number" $\frac{4}{5} - x$.

    Step 3: $6\left(\frac{4}{5} - x\right) = 2x$

    Step 4: $x = \frac{3}{5}$

    Step 5: The larger number is $\frac{3}{5}$ and the smaller number is $\frac{1}{5}$.

21.

	Now	In six years
Jan	$x + 31$	$x + 37$
Isa	x	$x + 6$

    Step 3: $x + 37 + x + 6 = 75$

    Step 4: $x = 16$

    Step 5: Jan is 47 years old and Isa is 16 years old.

23.

	Now	Three years ago
Joe	$2x$	$2x - 3$
Martin	x	$x - 3$

    Step 3: $2x - 3 + x - 3 = 36$

    Step 4: $x = 14$

    Step 5: Joe is 28 years old and Martin is 14 years old.

25.

	Now	In four years
Todd	$x - 5$	$x - 1$
Max	x	$x + 4$

    Step 3: $x - 1 + x + 4 = 45$

    Step 4: $x = 21$

    Step 5: Todd is 16 years old and Max is 21 years old.

27.

	Now	In four years
John	$2x - 3$	$2x + 1$
Mike	x	$x + 4$

    Step 3: $2x + 1 + x + 4 = 35$

    Step 4: $x = 10$

    Step 5: John is 17 years old and Mike is 10 years old.

An Introduction to Algebra: Section 8 answers continued

29.

	Now	In seven years
Pete	$3x$	$3x + 7$
Joel	x	$x + 7$

Step 3: $3x + 7 = 2(x + 7)$

Step 4: $x = 7$

Step 5: Pete is 21 years old and Joel is 7 years old.

31.   **Step 1:** Find the length & the width.

Step 2: Call "the length" $2x$. Call "the width" x.

Step 3: $72 = 2(2x) + 2(x)$

Step 4: $x = 12$

Step 5: The length is 24 inches and the width is 12 inches.

33.   **Step 1:** Find the width.

Step 2: Call "the width" $x - 4$. Call "the length" x.

Step 3: $40 = 2(x) + 2(x - 4)$

Step 4: $x = 12$

Step 5: The width is 8 centimeters.

35.   **Step 1:** Find the length & the width.

Step 2: Call "the length" $3x - 5$. Call "the width" x.

Step 3: $62 = 2(3x - 5) + 2(x)$

Step 4: $x = 9$

Step 5: The length is 22 inches and the width is 9 inches.

37.   **Step 1:** Find the length & the width.

Step 2: Call "the length" $6x + 4$. Call "the width" x.

Step 3: $78 = 2(6x + 4) + 2(x)$

Step 4: $x = 5$

Step 5: The length is 34 feet and the width is 5 feet.

39.

	Number of	Total value of (in cents)
Nickels	$x + 6$	$5(x + 6)$
Quarters	x	$25x$

Step 3: $240 = 5(x + 6) + 25x$

Step 4: $x = 7$

Step 5: Reba has 13 nickels and 7 quarters.

An Introduction to Algebra: Section 8 answers continued

41.

	Number of	Total value of (in cents)
Dimes	$x-8$	$10(x-8)$
Quarters	x	$25x$

Step 3: $305 = 10(x-8)+25x$

Step 4: $x = 11$

Step 5: Harvey has 3 dimes and 11 quarters.

43.

	Number of	Total value of (in cents)
Pennies	$4x+6$	$1(4x+6)$ or $4x+6$
Dimes	x	$10x$

Step 3: $328 = 4x+6+10x$

Step 4: $x = 23$

Step 5: Jim has 98 pennies and 23 dimes.

45.

	Number of	Total value of (in cents)
Nickels	$2x$	$5(2x)$
Dimes	x	$10x$
Quarters	$x-3$	$25(x-3)$

Step 3: $150 = 5(2x)+10x+25(x-3)$

Step 4: $x = 5$

Step 5: Sam has 10 nickels, 5 dimes and 2 quarters.

47.

Step 1: How many miles was the car driven?

Step 2: Call "number of miles" x.

Step 3: $77.88 = 37 + 0.28x$

Step 4: $x = 146$

Step 5: The car was driven 146 miles.

49.

Step 1: How many miles was the car driven?

Step 2: Call "number of miles" x.

Step 3: $130.66 = 2(34)+0.26x$

Step 4: $x = 241$

Step 5: The car was driven 241 miles.

51.

Step 1: How long is the phone call?

Step 2: Call "number of minutes" x.

Step 3: $5.39 = 1.25 + 0.23x$

Step 4: $x = 18$

Step 5: The phone call is 18 minutes long.

53.

Step 1: How much electricity was used that month?

Step 2: Call "number of kilowatt-hours" x.

Step 3: $30.72 = 4.75 + 0.035x$

Step 4: $x = 742$

Step 5: 742 kilowatt-hours of electricity.

An Introduction to Algebra: Chapter review answers

1. $-5\dfrac{3}{4}$ **2.**   4.8   **3.** $\dfrac{10}{21}$ **4.** $\dfrac{44}{7}$ or $6\dfrac{2}{7}$

5. -9 **6.**   12   **7.**   106.8   **8.** $\dfrac{59}{66}$

9.   The commutative property of multiplication

10.   The associative property of multiplication

11.   The additive inverse property

12.   The commutative property of addition

13. -6 **14.** $7w+15$ **15.** $4.8x-2.4$ **16.** y

17. 1st term: a ; variable term; the numerical coefficient is 1

   2nd term: $-m$; variable term; the numerical coefficient is -1

   3rd term: -5 ; constant term

18. 1st term: 30 ; constant term

   2nd term: $-8b^2 d$; variable term; the numerical coefficient is -8

   3rd term: $4ac^2$; variable term; the numerical coefficient is 4

19. $-9.6x+2.2y$ **20.** $\dfrac{1}{15}x+\dfrac{32}{15}y$ **21.** $\dfrac{50}{3}x-\dfrac{38}{5}y$

22. $-x-5y+14z$ **23.** $5x^2 y-xy^2 -3y^2 -18$ **24.** $x^2 y+2xy+20y$

25. $m=0$ **26.** $x=-14$ **27.** $y=19$

An Introduction to Algebra: Chapter review answers continued

28. $a = -1$

29. $n = -12$

30. $x = \dfrac{1}{8}$

31. 22.4

32. $m = \dfrac{10}{27}$

33. $w = 3$

34. $x = 2$

35. $a = 60$

36. $y = -\dfrac{13}{3}$

37. $k = 2.8$

38. $k = \dfrac{5}{12}$

39. 152 miles

40. 228 therms

41. $w = \dfrac{3}{8}$

42. $m = \dfrac{4}{3}$

43. $x = \dfrac{8}{13}$

44. $x = -\dfrac{4}{3}$

45. $x = -\dfrac{29}{4}$

46. $x = \dfrac{45}{2}$

47. $y = 11$

48. $x = 6.5$

49. Four more than the product of six and the difference of five x and seven

50. Three minus the quotient of four times y and seven

51. $x - (-6 - x)$; $2x + 6$

52. $-7(5 + x)$; $-7x - 35$

53. $5(3 - x) + 12$; $-5x + 27$

54. $18 - (x + 12)$; $-x + 6$

55. $4(a + 8) + 6$; $4a + 38$

56. $4(5W) - 3$; $20W - 3$

57. **Step 1:** Find the number.

  Step 2: Call "the number" x.

  Step 3: $5x - 3 = 4x + 6$

  Step 4: $x = 9$

  Step 5: The number is 9.

58. **Step 1:** Find the numbers.

  Step 2: Call "the larger number" x.
  Call "the smaller number" $28 - x$.

  Step 3: $2x = 5(28 - x)$

  Step 4: $x = 20$

  Step 5: The larger number is 20 and
  the smaller number is 8.

An Introduction to Algebra: Chapter review answers continued

59.

	Now	In four years
Ralph	$3x+2$	$3x+6$
Kerry	x	$x+4$

Step 3: $3x+6+x+4=18$

Step 4: $x=2$

Step 5: Ralph is 8 years old and Kerry is 2 years old.

60.

	Now	In six years
Seth	$3x$	$3x+6$
Leroy	x	$x+6$

Step 3: $3x+6=2(x+6)$

Step 4: $x=6$

Step 5: Seth is 18 years old and Leroy is 6 years old.

61.   **Step 1:** Find the width.

Step 2: Call "the width" $x-7$.
Call "the length" x.

Step 3: $38=2(x)+2(x-7)$

Step 4: $x=13$

Step 5: The width is 6 centimeters.

62.   **Step 1:** Find the length & the width.

Step 2: Call "the length" $3x-5$.
Call "the width" x.

Step 3: $54=2(3x-5)+2(x)$

Step 4: $x=8$

Step 5: The length is 19 inches and the width is 8 inches.

63.

	Number of	Total value of (in cents)
Pennies	$3x$	$1(3x)$ or $3x$
Dimes	x	$10x$
Quarters	$x-4$	$25(x-4)$

Step 3: $166=3x+10x+25(x-4)$

Step 4: $x=7$

Step 5: Simon has 21 pennies, 7 dimes and 3 quarters.

64.   **Step 1:** How many miles was the car driven?

Step 2: Call "number of miles" x.

Step 3: $187.13=2(28)+0.31x$

Step 4: $x=423$

Step 5: The car was driven 423 miles.

An Introduction to Algebra: Chapter test answers

1. $-12\frac{7}{8}$ **2.** $19\frac{2}{9}$ or $\frac{173}{9}$ **3.** -8 **4.** $1\frac{14}{59}$ or $\frac{73}{59}$

An Introduction to Algebra: Chapter test answers continued

5.   The multiplicative inverse property

6.   The commutative property of multiplication

7.   8   8. $-1.5y+3$

9. 1st term: $17x^2y$; variable term; the numerical coefficient is 17

   2nd term: -6; constant term

   3rd term: z; variable term; the numerical coefficient is 1

10. $1.3x-8.8y$ 11. $\dfrac{2}{5}x-\dfrac{9}{4}y$ 12. $-4x^2y+8xy-2y+8$

13. $w=0$ 14. $x=1$ 15. $k=\dfrac{20}{21}$

16. $m=18.9$ 17. $p=7$ 18. $x=171$

19. $m=\dfrac{9}{5}$ 20.   268 therms   21. $x=\dfrac{2}{7}$

22. $x=\dfrac{2}{5}$ 23. $x=-\dfrac{21}{5}$ 24. $y=13$

25.   Seven less than the product of negative three and the difference of two y and eight

An Introduction to Algebra: Chapter test answers continued

26. $x-(-12+x)$; 12

27. $5(a-3)+8$; $5a-7$

28.   **Step 1:** Find the numbers.

Step 2: Call "the larger number" x.
Call "the smaller number" $36-x$.

Step 3: $2x=3(36-x)+2$

Step 4: $x=22$

Step 5: The larger number is 22 and
the smaller number is 14.

29.

	Now	Four years ago
Rhonda	$2x+5$	$2x+1$
Jayne	x	$x-4$

Step 3: $2x+1+x-4=18$

Step 4: $x=7$

Step 5: Rhonda is 19 years old and
Jayne is 7 years old.

30.   **Step 1:** Find the length & the width.

Step 2: Call "the length" $3x-7$.

Call "the width" x.

Step 3: $58=2(3x-7)+2(x)$

Step 4: $x=9$

Step 5: The length is 20 inches and
the width is 9 inches.

31.

	Number of	Total value of (in cents)
Pennies	$8x$	$1(8x)$ or $8x$
Nickels	x	$5x$
Quarters	$x-3$	$25(x-3)$

Step 3: $229=8x+5x+25(x-3)$

Step 4: $x=8$

Step 5: Steven has 64 pennies, 8
nickels and 5 quarters.

32.   **Step 1:** How many miles was the
car driven?

Step 2: Call "number of miles" x.

Step 3: $221.09=3(33)+0.29x$

Step 4: $x=421$

Step 5: The car was driven 421 miles.

Formulas & Graphing: Section 1 answers

1. $P = 92 \text{ yd} ;\ A = 435 \text{ yd}^2$

3. $P = (30 + 4\pi) \text{ in.} ;\ P \approx 42.56 \text{ in.}$

$A = (66 + 4\pi) \text{ in.}^2 ;\ A \approx 78.56 \text{ in.}^2$

5. $SA = 36\pi \text{ in.}^2 ;\ SA \approx 113.04 \text{ in.}^2$

$V = 36\pi \text{ in.}^3 ;\ V \approx 113.04 \text{ in.}^3$

7. $SA = 900\pi \text{ m}^2 ;\ SA \approx 2{,}826 \text{ m}^2$

$V = 4{,}500\pi \text{ m}^3 ;\ V \approx 14{,}130 \text{ m}^3$

9. $SA = 240\pi \text{ in.}^2 ;\ SA \approx 753.6 \text{ in.}^2$

$V = 504\pi \text{ in.}^3 ;\ V \approx 1{,}582.56 \text{ in.}^3$

11. $SA = 54\pi \text{ cm}^2 ;\ SA \approx 169.56 \text{ cm}^2$

$V = 54\pi \text{ cm}^3 ;\ V \approx 169.56 \text{ cm}^3$

13.   **a)** $SA = 312\pi \text{ ft}^2 ;\ SA \approx 979.68 \text{ ft}^2$ **b)** $V = 864\pi \text{ ft}^3 ;\ V \approx 2{,}712.96 \text{ ft}^3$

Formulas & Graphing: Section 2 answers

1.   The length is 25 inches.

3.   The length is 39 feet.

5.   The width is 34 meters.

7.   The width is 3.5 yards.

9.   The width is 16 inches.

11.   The width is 3.8 feet.

13.   The length is $5\frac{1}{5}$ meters.

15.   The length is 6 yards.

17. $y = -3$

19. $y = 12$

21. $x = \dfrac{25}{2}$ or $x = 12\frac{1}{2}$ or $x = 12.5$

23. $x = 0$

25. $y = -4$

27. $y = 2$

29. $s = \dfrac{P}{4}$ or $s = \dfrac{1}{4}P$

Formulas & Graphing: Section 2 answers continued

31. $r = \dfrac{d}{t}$ **33.** $r = \dfrac{C}{2\pi}$ **35.** $h = \dfrac{2A}{b}$ **37.** $W = \dfrac{V}{LH}$

39. $h = \dfrac{V}{\pi r^2}$ **41.** $b = P - a - c$

43. $L = \dfrac{P - 2W}{2}$ or $L = \dfrac{P}{2} - W$ **45.** $r^3 = \dfrac{3V}{4\pi}$ **47.** $b = 2s - a - c$

49. $a = \dfrac{F}{m}$ **51.** $x = 5y - 7$ **53.** $x = \dfrac{5y + 7}{3}$ or $x = \dfrac{5}{3}y + \dfrac{7}{3}$

55. $y = 5x + 9$ **57.** $y = 4x - 7$ **59.** $y = -\dfrac{3}{2}x + 6$ **61.** $y = -\dfrac{5}{4}x - 5$

63. $y = \dfrac{2}{5}x - \dfrac{3}{5}$ **65.** $y = -\dfrac{8}{3}x + \dfrac{7}{3}$ **67.** $y = -\dfrac{5}{4}x + 5$

69. $y = \dfrac{8}{3}x - 8$ **71.** $y = \dfrac{5}{3}x + 5$

Formulas & Graphing: Section 3 answers

1. The x-coordinate is positive and the y-coordinate is positive.

3. The x-coordinate is negative and the y-coordinate is negative.

5. Quadrant IV   **7.** Quadrant I   **9.** Between Quadrant I and II

Formulas & Graphing: Section 3 answers continued

11.

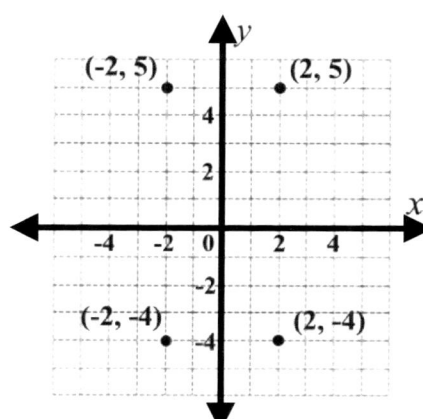

13.

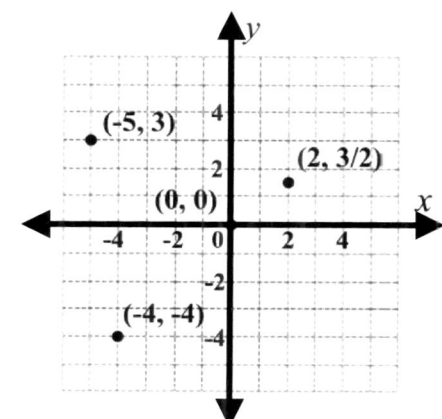

15.

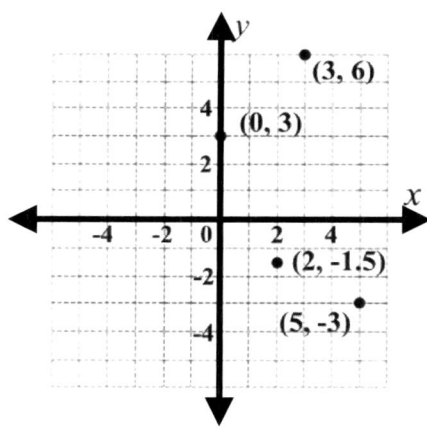

17.

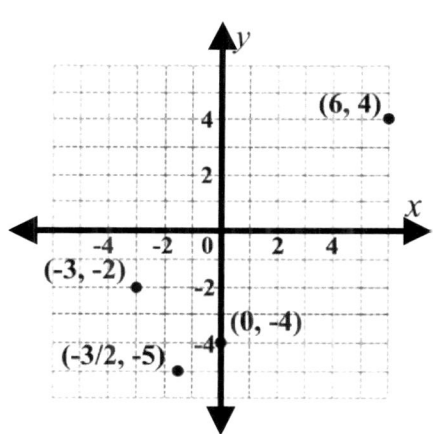

19.

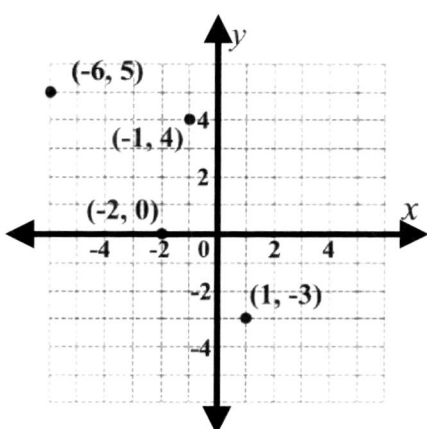

21. $(-2, 5)$

23. $(3, 3)$

25. $(0, 0)$

27. $(2, -2)$

29. $(4, -4)$

Formulas & Graphing: Section 3 answers continued

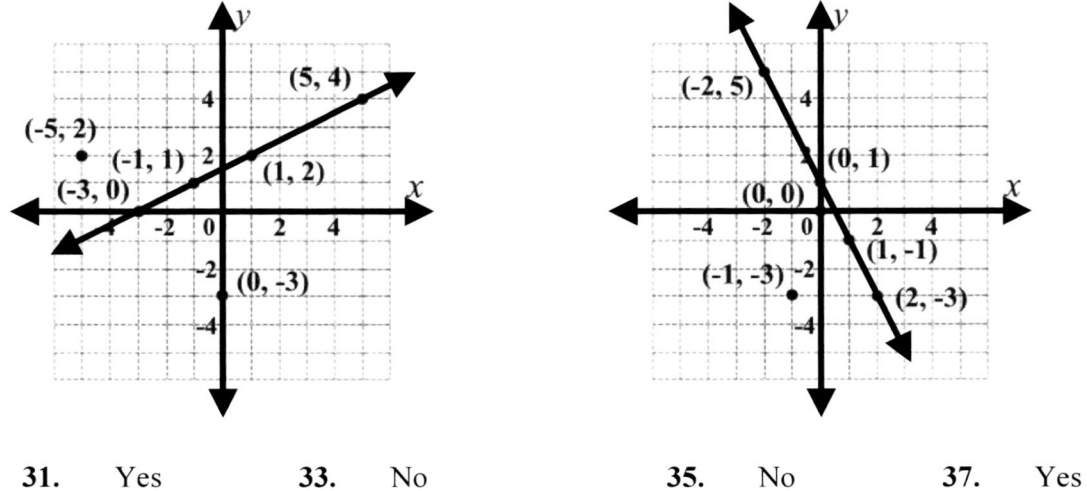

31.   Yes   **33.**   No   **35.**   No   **37.**   Yes

39.

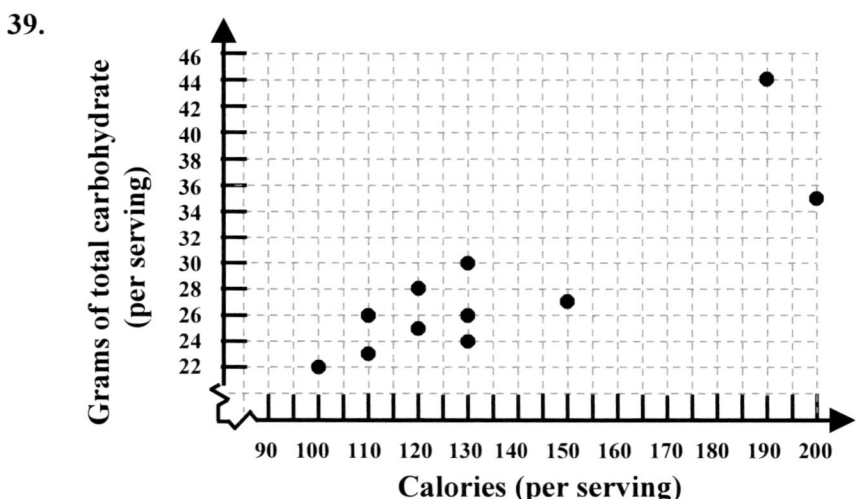

41.

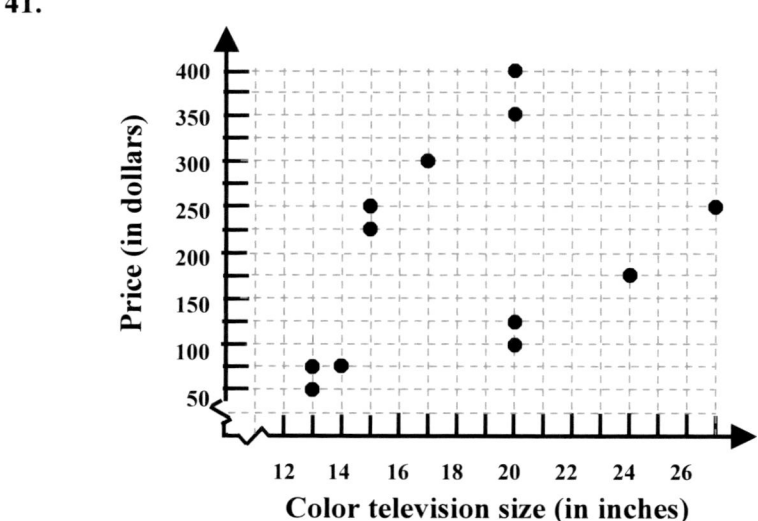

Formulas & Graphing: Section 3 answers continued

43.   **a)**   1983 and 1984   **b)**   1988

Formulas & Graphing: Section 4 answers

1. $(0,12)$, $(-3,24)$, $(5,-8)$ **3.** $(0,5)$, $(3,0)$, $(6,-5)$

5. $(4,7)$, $(3,4)$, $\left(\dfrac{5}{3},0\right)$ **7.** $(-2.2,0.6)$, $(-1.6,0.8)$, $\left(0,\dfrac{4}{3}\right)$

9. $(6,0)$, $(-3,-6)$, $(-6,-8)$ **11.** $(4,7)$, $\left(4,-\dfrac{1}{3}\right)$, $(4,0)$

13. $(0,8)$, $(4,0)$, $(3,2)$

15.

x	y
3	6
-4	-8
-2	-4
4	8

17.

x	y
0	0
$-1/2$	2
-3	12
4	-16

19.

x	y
-2	2
3	-3
-5	5
6	-6

21.

x	y
5	-5
-3	-13
7	-3
14	4

Formulas & Graphing: Section 4 answers continued

23.

x	y
0	-3
4	0
12	6
-4	-6

25.

x	y
-2	-1
$-7/3$	0
$1/2$	$-17/2$
$-11/3$	4

27. $(-2,-1), \left(\dfrac{3}{4}, -\dfrac{37}{4} \right)$

29. $(2,8), (0,0)$

31. $(10,5), (2.5,-1)$

33. $(2,6)$

35. $(4,4)$

Formulas & Graphing: Section 5 answers

1.   No

3.   Yes

5.   Yes

7.   Yes

9.   No

11.   Yes

Formulas & Graphing: Section 5 answers continued

13.
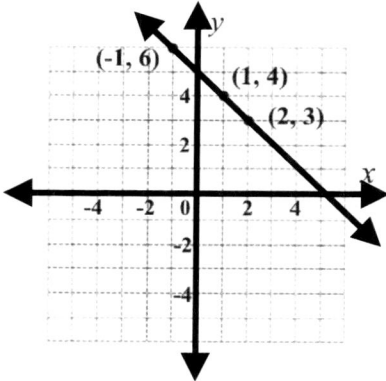

15.
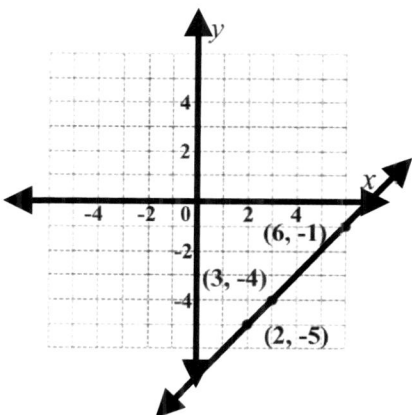

17.
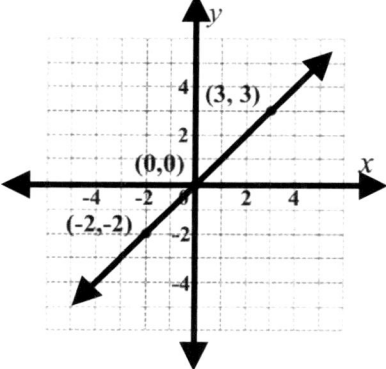

19.
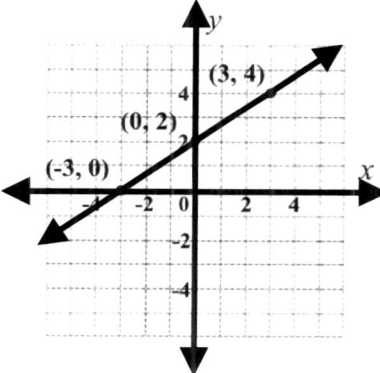

21.
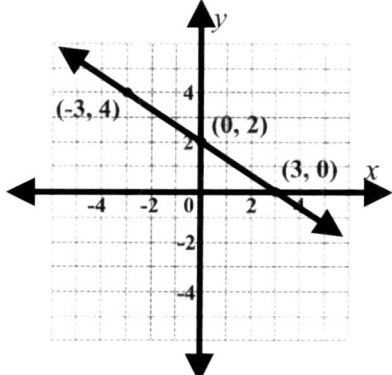

23.
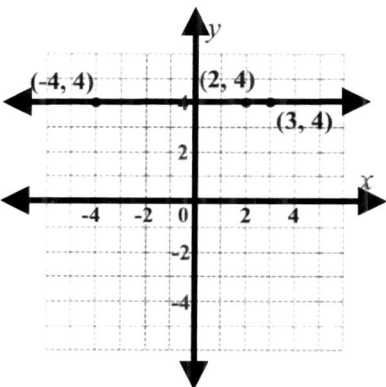

Formulas & Graphing: Section 5 answers continued

25.

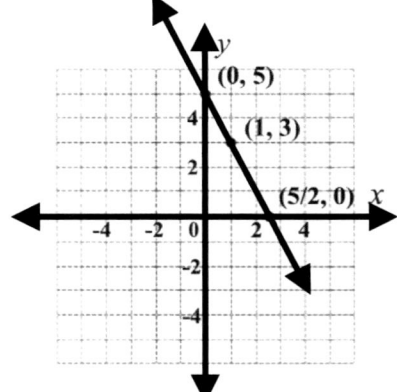

27.

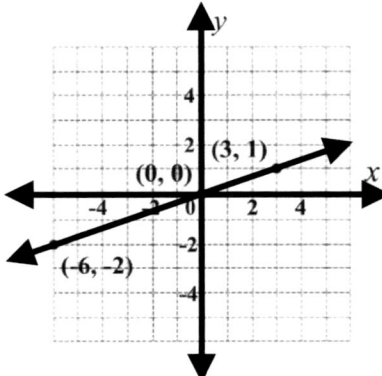

29. a) $y = -\dfrac{3}{5}x + 2$

b) $(-5,5)$, $(0,2)$, $(5,-1)$

c)

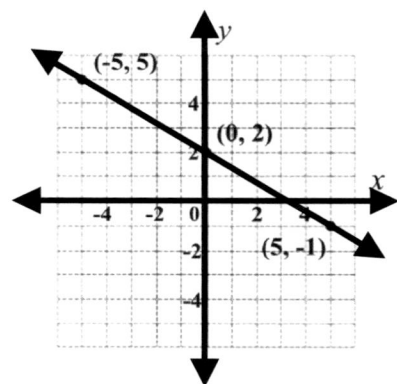

31. a) $y = \dfrac{3}{4}x - 2$

b) $(-4,-5)$, $(0,-2)$, $(4,1)$

c)

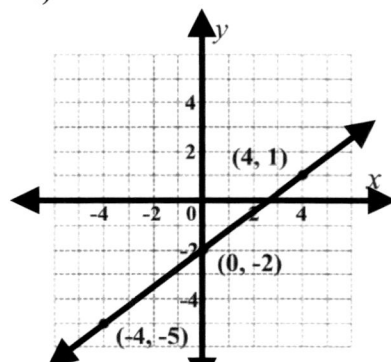

33. a) $y = \dfrac{1}{2}x + 4$

b) $(-2,3)$, $(0,4)$, $(2,5)$

c)

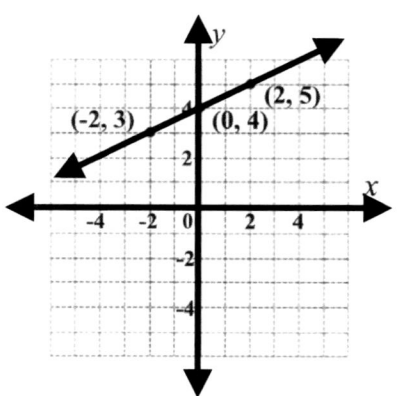

35.

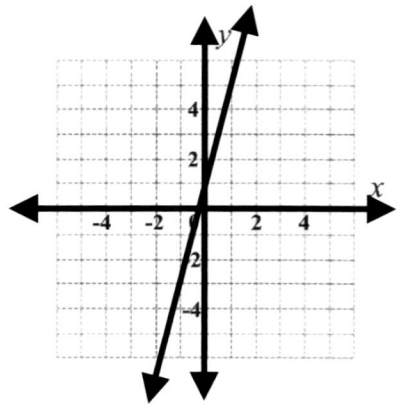

Formulas & Graphing: Section 5 answers continued

37.

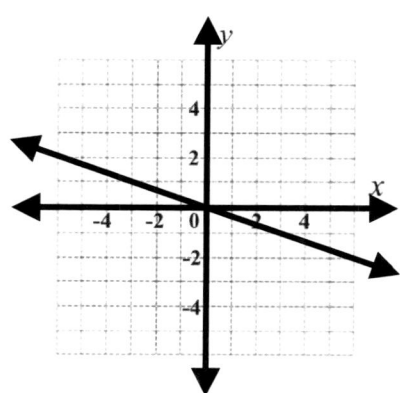

39.

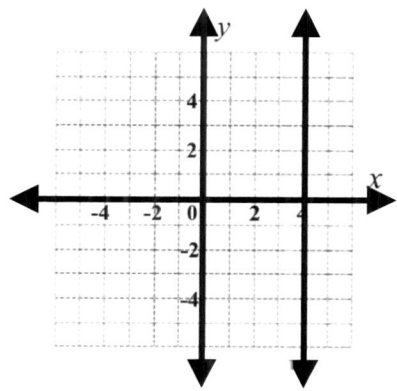

41.

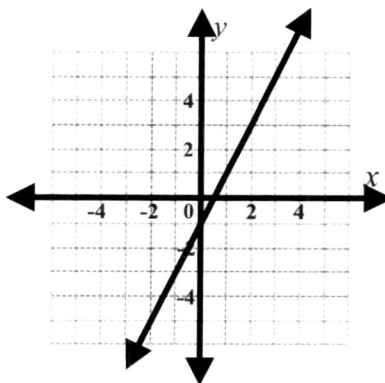

43.

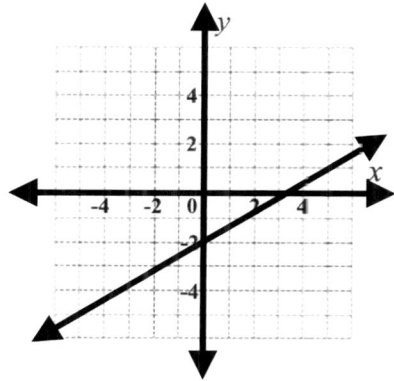

45.

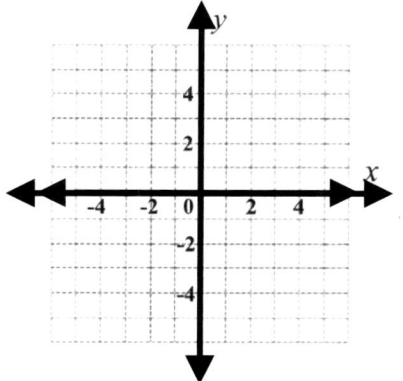

47. y is -2 when x is 0.

49. y is 3 when x is -4.

51. y is -5 when x is 2.

53. x is 2 when y is -1.

55. x is 5 when y is 3.

57. x is 3 when y is 5.

Formulas & Graphing: Chapter review answers

1. $P = (38 + 3\pi)$ in. ; $P \approx 47.42$ in. ; $A = (96 + 4.5\pi)$ in.^{2} ; $A \approx 110.13$ in.^{2}

2. $SA = 36\pi$ ft^2 ; $SA \approx 113.04$ ft^2 ; $V = 36\pi$ ft^3 ; $V \approx 113.04$ ft^3

3. $SA = 112\pi$ in.^{2} ; $SA \approx 351.68$ in.^{2} ; $V = 160\pi$ in.^{3} ; $V \approx 502.4$ in.^{3}

4.   The length is 35 meters.   5.   The width is 8.2 yards.

6.   The width is 13 inches   7.   The length is 10 inches.

8. $x = -5$ when $y = -6$ 9. $y = -1$ when $x = 2$

10. $c = 2s - a - b$ 11. $a = -\dfrac{b}{2x}$

12. $y = -\dfrac{2}{3}x + 4$ 13. $y = -\dfrac{4}{5}x + 4$

14.   Quadrant II   15.   Between Quadrants I and IV

16.   17.

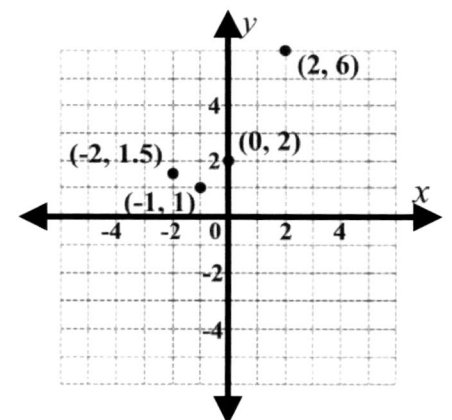

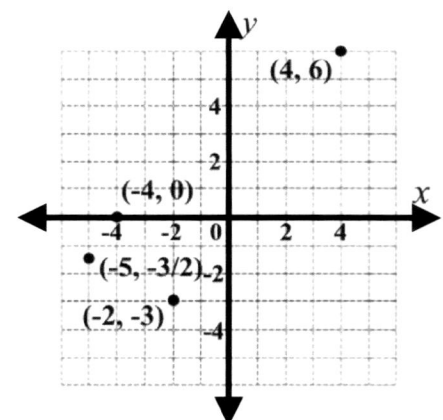

18.   No   19.   Yes

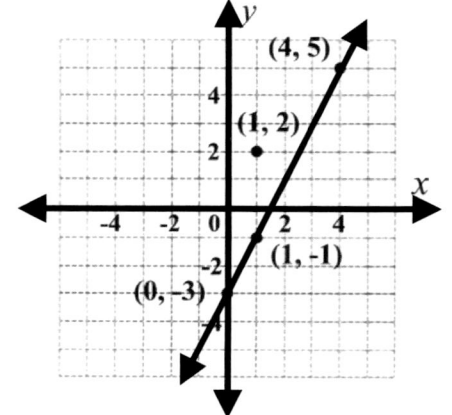

20.   a)   1985

        b)   1987 and 1990

<u>**Formulas & Graphing: Chapter review answers continued**</u>

21.

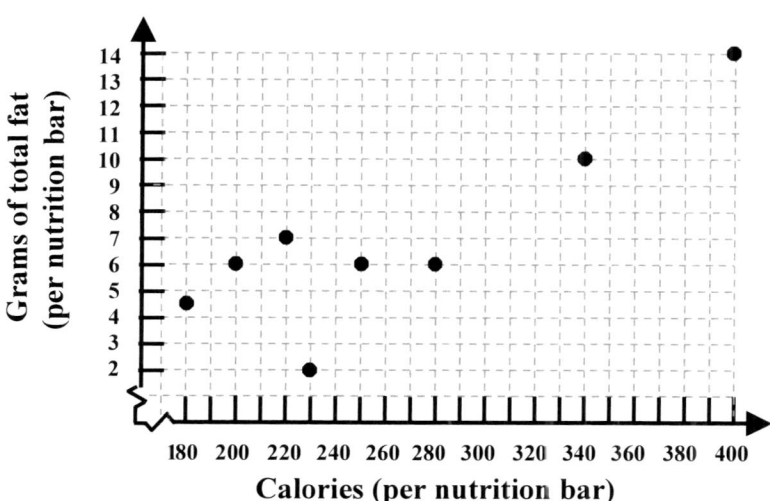

22. $(0,3)$, $(-4,4)$, $(-20,8)$ **23.** $(1.4,-0.8)$, $(-2.6,-12.8)$, $(0,-5)$

24. $(-7,4)$, $\left(-7,\dfrac{2}{5}\right)$, $(-7,0)$

25.

x	y
-3	12.6
-4	16.8
3	-12.6
3.5	-14.7

26.

x	y
-4	4
0	$12/5$
-24	12
21	-6

27.

x	y
0	8
5	-2
4	0
-4	16

28. $(-3,2)$ and $\left(\dfrac{9}{4},-\dfrac{55}{4}\right)$ are solutions.   **29.** $(0,-8)$ is a solution.

30. $(4,1)$ and $\left(\dfrac{7}{3},-\dfrac{2}{3}\right)$ are solutions.   **31.**   Yes, it is linear.

32.   Yes, it is linear.   **33.**   No, it is not linear.

Formulas & Graphing: Chapter review answers continued

34. $(0,-3)$, $(-2,0)$, $(-4,3)$

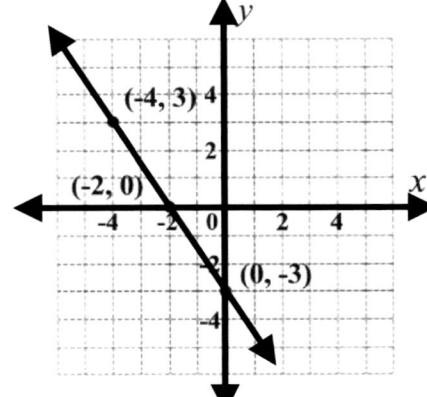

35. $(-3,5)$, $(2,5)$, $(0,5)$

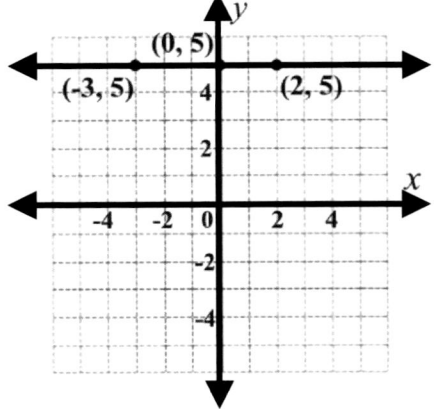

36.

$(0,0)$, $(-4,-1)$, $(2,1/2)$

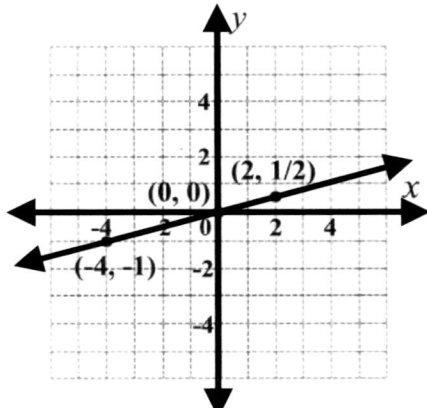

37.   **a)** $y = -\dfrac{3}{4}x + 2$;

b) $(-4,5)$, $(0,2)$, $(4,-1)$

c)

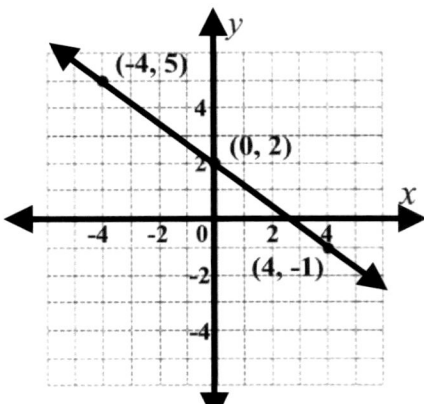

38.   **a)** $y = -\dfrac{1}{3}x + 3$;

b) $(-3,4)$, $(0,3)$, $(3,2)$

c)

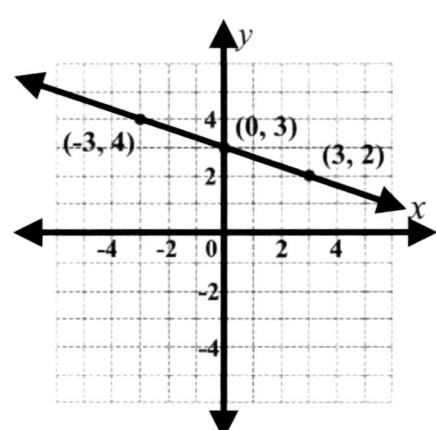

39.

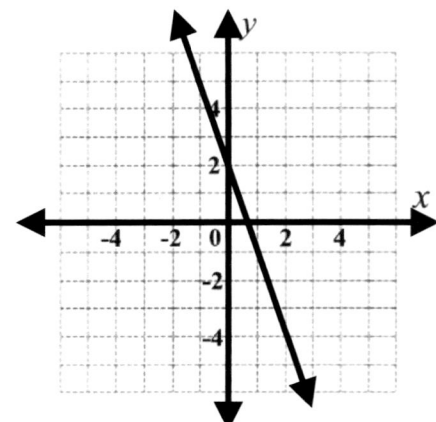

Formulas & Graphing: Chapter review answers continued

40.

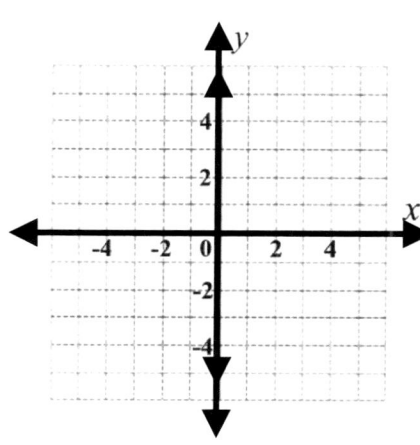

41.

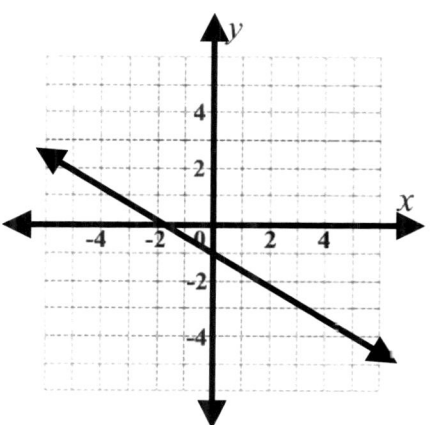

42. y is 4 when x is -5.

43. x is 4 when y is 2.

Formulas & Graphing: Chapter test answers

1. $P = 104$ ft ; $A = 492$ ft^2

2. $SA = 126\pi$ in.^{2} ; $SA \approx 395.64$ in.^{2} ; $V = 162\pi$ in.^{3} ; $V \approx 508.68$ in.^{3}

3.   The width is 12.5 centimeters.

4.   The length is $14\frac{1}{5}$ feet.

5. $y = -\dfrac{19}{3}$ is when $x = \dfrac{2}{3}$

6. $x = \dfrac{y - b}{m}$

7. $y = -\dfrac{7}{3}x + 7$

8.   Quadrant IV

9.

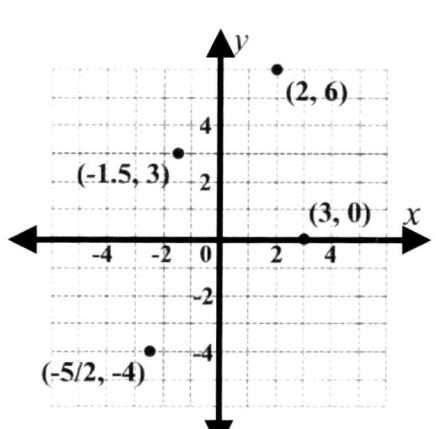

10.   No   **11.**   Yes

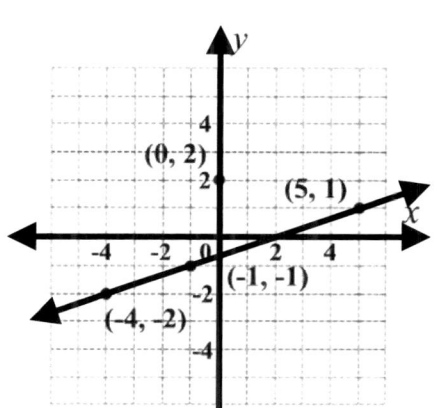

Formulas & Graphing: Chapter test answers continued

12.

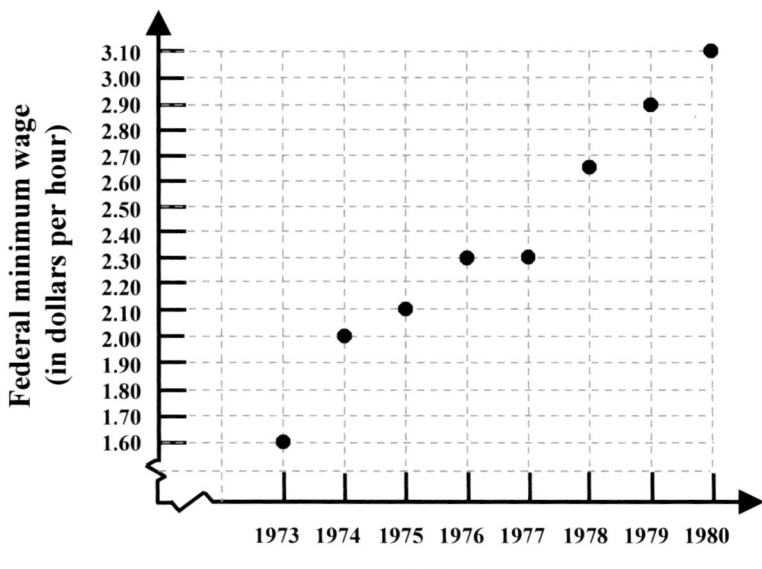

13. $(0,18)$, $(-4,24)$, $(6,9)$

14. $\left(\dfrac{2}{5}, -0.3\right)$, $\left(\dfrac{2}{5}, \dfrac{7}{3}\right)$, $\left(\dfrac{2}{5}, 18\right)$

15.

x	y
-3	-2
-6	-4
9	6
$21/2$	7

16. $(1, -1)$ is a solution.

17. $(3, -2)$ and $(-1, -2)$ are solutions.

Formulas & Graphing: Chapter test answers continued

18.

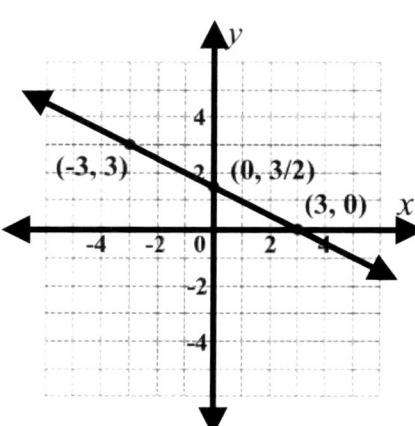

19.   **a)** $y = -\dfrac{3}{2}x - 1$

b) $(-2, 2)$, $(0, -1)$, $(2, -4)$

c)

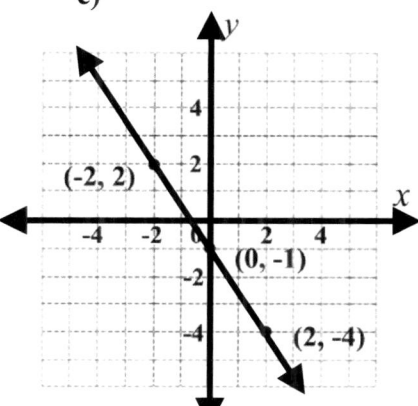

20.

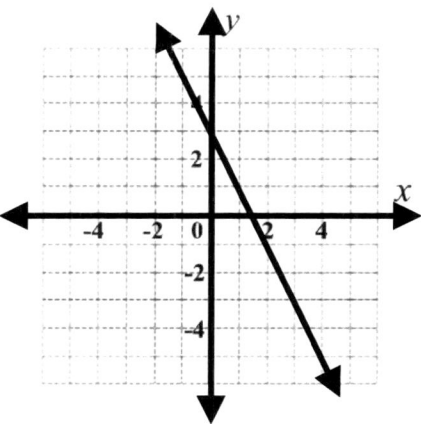

21.

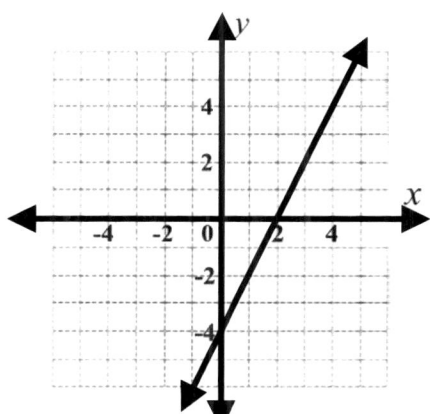

22. x is -2 when y is -3.

Index